# I. L. KANDEL    M.A., Ph.D., Litt.D., LL.D.

Professor Emeritus of Education, Teachers College, Columbia University, Emeritus Professor of American Studies, University of Manchester

# THE NEW ERA IN
# EDUCATION

## A COMPARATIVE STUDY

HOUGHTON MIFFLIN COMPANY

Boston · New York · Chicago · Dallas · Atlanta
San Francisco
The Riverside Press Cambridge

To Anthony and Jonathan
Lisa and David

# Editor's Introduction

In no period in the history of mankind has there been a greater need for people and nations to know and to understand each other than at the present. Individuals and governments express themselves in many ways. One way is through education. It is probably the most important medium of all because of its influential aspects. Education changes behavior. People and nations are as they are because of the educative process.

*The New Era in Education — A Comparative Study,* should contribute to that knowledge and understanding. In it the author, long recognized as an international authority in the field in which he writes and long a distinguished contributor to it, presents logically and clearly the forces that determine the character of education world-wide. The task, an onerous one and difficult without the experience and knowledge of a person of Dr. Kandel's ability and professional competence, so well done, makes the contribution significant indeed. Helpfully, it complements earlier authoritative studies with which the author has been identified. Time and experience have sharpened Dr. Kandel's perspective. An expressed concern to "contribute to an understanding of current trends in education and influences that have produced them" is not only realized but the relationship of these trends and influences to the problems confronting education in its many facets today is brought into sharp focus.

As the title implies, this treatise is more than an authentic and authoritative study of comparative education. In sweep, scope and content it combines history, philosophy, administration, supervision, organization and impact of education world-wide. The student of world affairs as well as the student of education, to whom, of course, the book is primarily addressed, will find it of interest and value. Truly does it describe and analyze today's new era in education and explain why it has come about and the forces that have contributed to it.

Sensitively yet always sympathetically and with understanding does the author treat those phases of education currently receiving much attention — attention which has resulted in a wide range of reaction and criticism today. These issues he presents and discusses forthrightly and in a manner which marks him as a discriminating evaluator. At no time, however, does Dr. Kandel pose as an educational Solomon. His treatment is both logical and reasonable. He raises the problems and suggests the courses available to their solution indicating what the probable results and consequences will be. Throughout the book the climate of the discussion is scholarly and interesting, provocative yet dispassionate and unemotional. Dr. Kandel writes with a knowledge and competence that characterize his pre-eminence in the field. The book is certain to add to the full professional stature which he has already so justly attained.

As a former student of Dr. Kandel's grateful acknowledgment is made of his genuine ability as a teacher, as an able exponent of the need to know and to understand forces that so powerfully impinge upon and affect education and as an exciter of the real and true purpose of education — the satisfaction of intellectual curiosity that the forward and sustaining influence of mankind everywhere may be more freely realized. To all of this *The New Era in Education* contributes admirably.

HEROLD C. HUNT

# Preface

The purpose of the present volume is to contribute to an understanding of current trends in education and influences that have produced them. The trends were already in the making when the author published the volume on Comparative Education in 1933. The crises through which the world has passed since then and the demands for reconstruction to repair the losses caused by World War II as well as the challenge to the ideals of democracy from Communist ideology have intensified the recognition of the important part to be played by education for the fullest development of the individual and the greatest welfare of a nation. But the forces that determine the character of education in any nation have a significance that is of greater importance than the details of its organization and practice. Hence the study of the backgrounds can contribute more to an understanding of an educational system than mere description of it.

The countries selected for study in this book are England, France, Union of Soviet Socialist Republics, and the United States. The study is as much a contribution to the methods of Comparative Education as it is to an understanding of the educational systems of the four countries mentioned. In the last chapter are given the reasons why a larger number of countries has not been included and a general summary of current trends is presented.

With three of the countries — England, France, and the United States — the author is familiar from direct observation and study. For the discussions of the U.S.S.R. the author has had to rely on such literature as is available in English. The details may not always be up to date, but the character of education under a totalitarian regime is, it is hoped, clearly presented to serve as a backdrop, as it were, to the fundamental values of the ideal of democracy and of education under its influence, to which this book is dedicated.

I. L. KANDEL

# CONTENTS

1. **The Content and Method of Comparative Education**       3

An Era of Crisis
Education and Postwar Reconstruction
Scope and Meaning of Comparative Education
Intangible Forces in Education
Foundations of National Systems of Education
Comparative Education and Philosophy of Education
The War of Ideas
Education as an Instrument of National Welfare
Current Issues in Education


2. **The State and Education**       18

Expansion of State Authority
Totalitarianism and Democracy
The Individual and the State
The Purposes of Education
The Totalitarian State
The Democratic State
Contrasting Concepts of the State
Democracy and Freedom
Freedom and Authority
The Challenge to Educate for Democracy
Education as Conditioning
Education as a Socio-political Process

The State and Values
Movements for Educational Reform

### 3. Forces that Determine the Character of an Educational System                                                    45

Education and the Culture Pattern
The Culture Pattern of Conformity
The Culture Pattern of Free Societies
Differences in Culture Patterns
Changing Culture Patterns
The Family and the Home
Emancipation of Children and Youth
The Nursery School
Residual Functions of the School
Democratic Ideals and Educational Reconstruction
Prolongation of Infancy
Technological Changes and Education
Education and Environment
Changing Values
Nationalism and Education
School and Society

### 4. The New Pattern of Educational Reconstruction        65

Totalitarian and Democratic Methods
The Movements for Educational Reform
Planning Reforms During World War II
The Emerging Pattern
Equality of Opportunity as the Ideal

### 5. Equalizing Educational Opportunities                  88

The Problem
Historical Development

Implications of the Principle of Equality
Primary Education
  The Elementary School Tradition
  National Economy and Education
  Vestigial Remains
  Transition from the Old to the New
  The School and Social Services
  Instruction and Class Size
Secondary Education
  Types of Schools and Courses
  The Allocation of Pupils
  Equality and Curriculum
  Education and Social Unity
  A Liberal Education
  One School or Three?

**6. The Administration and Organization of Education** 115

The Modern Educational Systems
Centralization of Administration
Factors Determining the Character of Administration
The Purpose and Function of Administration
Uniformity and Diversity
Centralization and Decentralization
Professional Freedom
Educational Finance
England
  The Background
  The Theory of Administration
  The Inter-war Years
  The Education Act, 1944–The Central Authority
  Local Administration
  Functions of the Local Education Authorities
  Voluntary Schools and Religious Instruction

Development Plans
Auxiliary Services
Educational Finance
Private Schools
The Chief Education Officer
The Educational Highway
France
The French Tradition of Administration
The Central Authority
Regional Administration
Educational Finance
The Educational Career
Private Schools
Union of Soviet Socialist Republics
The Background
Administration of Education
The Educational Career
United States
The American Tradition
Education a Public Concern
Founding the System of Public Education
The Participation of the Public
Leadership in American Education
Federal Government and Education
Maintenance of Standards
The States and Education
Local Administration
Private Schools
Religious Instruction in Public Schools
The Educational Career

**7. The Education of the Child**                              198

Preschool Education
Elementary Education

The New Pedagogy
England
 The New Organization
 Nursery Schools and Classes
 Infant Schools
 Junior School
France
 Reconstruction of the School System
 *Ecoles Maternelles*
 Elementary Education
 Aim and Curriculum
 *Certificat d'Etudes Primaires*
 *Cours Complémentaires*
 Statistics of Elementary Education
Union of Soviet Socialist Republics
 Nurseries and Kindergartens
 Primary Education
United States
 Organization of Elementary Education
 Nursery Schools and Kindergartens
 Elementary School

8. **The Education of the Adolescent**      246

Introduction
England
 Secondary Education for All
 Equality of Opportunity
 Education Act, 1944
 Three Types of Secondary Schools or a Comprehensive
  Type
 Selection Methods
 Secondary Education Under the Education Act, 1944
  The Provision of Secondary Schools
  The Grammar School

Direct Grant Schools
The Private or Independent Schools
The General Certificate of Education
Scholarships
Technical Secondary Schools
Secondary Modern Schools
School Life

France
The French Tradition
*L'Ecole Unique*
Changes in Educational Theory
*Classes Nouvelles*
Plans for Reform
Organization of Education at the Second Level
The Present Situation
Technical Secondary Schools
Guidance

Union of Soviet Socialist Republics
The Unified School
Vocational Education

United States
Secondary Education and Cultural Changes
Articulation with Primary Schools
The Comprehensive High School
Aims of High Schools
Education of the Gifted
Curriculum
Life Adjustment Education
Core Curriculum
The High School Curriculum in Practice
Extracurricular Activities

9. **The Preparation of Teachers**                                322

Introduction

Cultural and Educational Changes and Teacher Preparation

The Beginnings of Reform: Teaching a Profession

Recruitment Standards

Organization of Teacher Preparation

In-service Training

Preparation of Secondary School Teachers

Changing Status of Teachers

England

Proposals for Reform

The McNair Report

The Present System: Area Training Organizations

National Advisory Bodies

Institutions for the Preparation of Teachers

Training College Courses

Preparation of Secondary School Teachers

Assessment for Certification

Salaries and Pensions

In-service Training of Teachers

France

The Tradition

Proposal for Reform

The Present System

Admission Requirements

The Course

Certification

Other Students

Higher Normal Schools

In-service Training

Preparation for Secondary School Teachers

Union of Soviet Socialist Republics

Status of Teachers

The Present System

United States

Current Issues

Institutions for the Preparation of Teachers
Academic or Professional Subjects?
Normal Schools to Teachers Colleges
Administration of Institutions for Preparation of Teachers
Curriculum
In-service Training
Appointment and Status

10. **Problems and Outlook**                                      370

**Index**                                                         379

# THE NEW ERA IN
# EDUCATION

## A

## Comparative

## Study

# 1

# The Content and Method

# of Comparative Education

## An Era of Crisis

The promise of a new era which was envisioned during the years of World War II is far from being realized. The hopes of those years have quickly been succeeded by fear and uncertainty about the future of mankind. Faith in international organizations, which were so ardently promoted and which were to usher in and protect the preservation of peaceful ways among men, gradually declined as a consequence of the tensions produced by the cold war. The second half of the twentieth century opened with grave misgivings but not without hope about the ultimate peaceful settlement of the world to which the United Nations and its various agencies are dedicated. The cold war which exhausts the resources of nations in preparation for a shooting war also diverts the necessary means for the advancement of social welfare and education.

The uncertainty and instability which affect all aspects of social, political, economic, and cultural life throughout the world are reflected in the tempo of educational progress. The critical situation in which the world finds itself is the resultant of an accumulation of forces whose beginnings can be traced back to the gradually extending influence of the development of the sciences upon the material and spiritual values of man. On the one hand, the technological progress that followed in the wake of or accompanied the progressive advancement of scientific theory laid the foundation for and continued to make possible a gradual improvement of human welfare and of the material conditions of life. On the other hand, this progress and faith in the methods of science tended to undermine the acceptance of traditional beliefs, attitudes, customs, and moral standards on the basis of unquestioned authority. Yet it was these beliefs and moral standards that made for social stability, if not for a heightened sense of social responsibility.

That liberalism which had made progress possible gave way to cynicism and scepticism; for the cultivation of reason there was substituted the cult of the irrational, which was in turn used to explain the springs of reason; traditional values were discarded, first merely because they were traditional and then in favor of experimentalism with no other end in view than change for its own sake; and, finally, refusal to accept authority of any kind and in any field of thought or conduct was deliberately cultivated lest it interfere with the free expression of the creative urge within each individual. All these trends were manifested in literature, art, and music, where they were easily recognized. They were marked, only to lead to their own destruction, in areas of politics and government. They existed, although their affinities were not so easily comprehended, in certain philosophical movements and in educational theory and practice.

The outbreak of World War II, if it did not put an end to these trends, at least suspended them for the duration. It was recognized that more was at stake than the cult of individualism, and that the war was a war of ideas and values. It was realized that what was at stake was the preservation of those forms of government that provided conditions for the survival of the ideals of freedom for which man has struggled for centuries. It is not without significance that the advocates of totalitarian forms of government and their dictators, when they wish to rally their people, appeal to them in terms of the ideals of democracy. This has been manifested in all totalitarian states, whether their color has been black, brown, or red. World War II and the cold war that has followed it are a challenge to the genuine democracies to guard and protect their ideals, and the best means to do that is through education.

Far more is involved in the struggle between totalitarianism and democracy than economic forces and imperialist exploitation. The future of democracies is just as much at stake today as it was during the two wars of this century. Today's struggle is to save the democracies from subjugation to the Behemoth of totalitarianism, to liberate human beings from subjection to the monolithic state, and to preserve those moral and spiritual values for which the democratic state exists.

During the war years the fervor for the ideals and meaning of democracy was high. It was during these years that minds turned to the planning of institutions that would eliminate war as a method of settling conflicts between nations, that would make international cooperation the way to world progress, and that would promote the cause of education throughout the world. At the same time plans for the reconstruction of educational systems were widely discussed, particularly with a view to distributing the privileges of education more equally on the basis of individual ability rather than on that of economic or social status.

### Education and Postwar Reconstruction

The promise of this period's enthusiastic recognition of the part that education was to play in the postwar reconstruction of nations has not yet been fulfilled. The sudden relaxation following the tensions and anxieties of war days, the demands of postwar readjustment, and the administrative difficulties in meeting these demands tended on the whole to divert attention from the promised reconstruction of education to meet what were considered to be more urgent and immediate needs. At the same time the economic situation in most countries and the urgency of other needs determined the priorities for which the strained financial resources were to be used; education was not among them.

Nevertheless, from the point of view of the student of education it was clear that a new pattern of educational organization was emerging in different countries. The general outlines of the pattern were everywhere the same, but the completed design would inevitably be inspired by "the color, the shape, and the scent" of all these active forces that make up the culture of each nation.

## Scope and Meaning of Comparative Education

It is at this point that the comparative study of educational institutions of different countries derives its meaning and justification. To study a foreign school system in terms of the character of its buildings — its brick and mortar — or the salary and status of its teachers, or the distribution of its pupils by classes or schools, or even the content and time-schedule of its curricula and the methods of instruction may provide the basic materials for a comparative study but is itself nothing more than descriptive. Yearbooks and other collections of articles on the educational systems of several countries, each written by a different author, may provide the basis for, but would not themselves constitute works on comparative education.

It is not enough, for example, to show that illiteracy was rapidly liquidated in the U.S.S.R. without referring to the political ends that literacy was to serve. The fact of liquidation may be true, but it is far more important to indicate the kind of reading material made available to the newly literate people. When this is done, the contrast is clear; the U.S.S.R. does not have the uncensored and uncontrolled printed materials current in other countries where the primary aim is not to use literacy for purposes of indoctrination in the interests of the monolithic state.

A mere reference to arithmetic, to use another example, and its place in the elementary school curriculum, or of physics in the curriculum of the secondary school, or of history in all schools of Germany under the Nazis would be meaningless without showing the influence of Nazi doctrines of racism and militarism.

But it is not only through a deliberate design to promote political ends that the control of education is affected. A somewhat similar influence may be unconsciously exercised by the action of a nation's culture pattern on the attitudes and modes of thinking of its members. Discussing differences between nations in dealing with the sciences, J. D. Bernal has made the following statement: "More significant are national characters of science and the different relations which exist between science and society in different countries. As has been already said, these intrinsic characters are very complex, but they are to a considerable extent analysable into the resultants of a number of distinguishable causes. To attribute them in a mystical way to the soul of the nation or the blood of the race, as is the position of Fascist ministers of education, is sheer obscurantism and does not help us at all in understanding the various ways in which these different characters can work together for advancing science as a whole." [1]

That professional educators inevitably approach problems which they share with colleagues from other countries in terms of their own cultural conditioning was excellently illustrated when the representatives of several countries came together to discuss the problem of examinations. The inquiry was organized on an international scale by the late Dr. Paul Monroe, then director of the International Institute of Teachers College, Columbia University. The cooperating nations at the first meeting in Eastbourne, 1931, were England, Scotland, France, Germany, Switzerland, and the United States. All the representatives were fully aware of the fact that the problem of examinations presented a serious difficulty in their own educational systems; it was recognized as a common problem. It was only when representative speakers began to explain and define the objectives of education in the light of their respective cultural backgrounds that the differences became manifest. For each definition was redolent of the culture pattern and tradition which gave the national system of education its meaning. The existence of variety within a common framework of unity was recognized and, instead of a common attack on the examinations problem by an international group, it was decided to have the problem investigated in each country by a national committee.

The same phenomenon was noted by Walter M. Kotschnig in his introduction to a collection of essays on the future of universities in different countries. The essays, writes Dr. Kotschnig, "appear to be studies in national psychology rather than essays on the common essence of the universities. Thanks to the services rendered by the translators, the articles, some of which were originally written in French, German, Italian, or Russian offer an extraordinary insight

[1] J. D. Bernal, *The Social Function of Science* (Routledge and Kegan Paul, Ltd., 1939), p. 195. By permission of the publisher.

into the different national modes of thinking. The Italian's eloquence, the German's love for abstract thought, the Frenchman's clarity and precision, the Englishman's sense of the actual are all there. It seems hardly believable that when the authors consented to collaborate in the symposium they all undertook to answer the same question, to follow the same outline." [2]

The same examples illustrate another purpose that the study of comparative education may serve. Educational systems are uniquely national, but the problems that confront them today are very much the same in many other countries. There is no country today where the question of post-elementary or secondary education is not a serious issue. The answers, however, are being determined by political, social, and economic forces as well as by the tradition of education itself. It is unnecessary to cite other current issues, since they will be discussed more fully in the pages that follow. The important fact that stands out is that national systems of education today constitute more than ever experimental laboratories dealing with similar problems, to the solution of which traditional cultural backgrounds and current political and social aims as well as economic forces will contribute more than any universal theory of education. It is with this situation that comparative education is concerned, since it seeks to analyse and compare the forces that make for differences between national systems of education. This can only be done by starting with certain common concepts or problems.

### Intangible Forces in Education

Descriptive analyses of national systems of education are valuable, provided that they are accurate and written with a knowl-

[2] Walter M. Kotschnig, ed., *The University in a Changing World* (London, Oxford University Press, 1932), p. 13. By permission. The influence of the cultural pattern in the study of animal learning was described as follows by Bertrand Russell: "One may say broadly that all the animals that have been carefully observed have behaved so as to confirm the philosophy in which the observer believed before his observations began. Nay, more, they have all displayed the national characteristics of the observer. Animals studied by Americans rush about frantically, with an incredible display of bustle and pep, and at last achieve the desired result by chance. Animals observed by Germans sit still and think and at last evolve the solution out of their inner consciousness." (*Philosophy*, New York, Norton, 1927, p. 30.)

edge of and insight into the forces that give them meaning, and they provide the materials for comparative education without themselves being entitled to be called by that name. Such descriptions are generally limited by a narrow concept of education and deal with its mechanisms and techniques, with administrative and curricular practices, with school organization and types of schools, with time-schedules, and with methods of instruction — in general with the anatomy of education. Such an analysis, though not in itself without interest, fails to contribute to that breadth of approach to the problems of education that is so greatly needed in the present crisis. The student of comparative education must, as Sadler pointed out in a lecture delivered in 1900, "try to find out what is the intangible, impalpable spiritual force which, in the case of any successful system of education, is in reality upholding the school system and accounting for its present efficiency."

What he meant by "the intangible, impalpable spiritual force" that upholds a nation's system of education Sadler defined more fully in another part of the same lecture: "In studying foreign systems of education we should not forget that the things outside the schools matter even more than the things inside the schools, and govern and interpret the things inside. We cannot wander at pleasure among the educational systems of the world, like a child strolling through a garden, and pick off a flower from one bush and some leaves from another, and then expect that if we stick what we have gathered into the soil at home, we shall have a living plant. A national system of education is a living thing, the outcome of forgotten struggles and difficulties and 'of battles long ago.' It has in it some of the secret workings of national life. It reflects, while seeking to remedy, the failings of national character. By instinct it often lays special emphasis on those parts of training which the national character particularly needs. Not less by instinct, it often shrinks from laying stress on points concerning which bitter dissensions have arisen in former periods of national history. But is it not likely that, if we have endeavoured in a sympathetic spirit, to understand the real working of a foreign system of education, we shall in turn find ourselves better able to enter into the spirit and tradition of our own national education, more sensitive to its unwritten ideals, quicker to catch the signs which mark its growing or fading influence, readier to mark the dangers which threaten it and the subtle workings of hurtful change? The practical value of studying in a right spirit and with scholarly accuracy the workings of foreign systems of education is that it will result in our being better fitted to study and understand our own." [3]

Sadler's penetrating analysis of the spirit and method of comparative education, which he so brilliantly applied in the writing and editing of the Special Reports on Educational Subjects, is fully confirmed by the failure of attempts to transfer the educational system of one country to another. This has happened frequently, particularly in the relations between suzerain and colonial peoples or in the well-meant intentions of missionary educators. Just as the teacher in the classroom in order to educate a pupil must learn all that he can about him, so in creating the educational system of a people, it is essential to learn all that can be learned about them. For an educational system reflects the ethos of the people whom it is established to serve. It is the importance of this principle that has introduced a new note into the discussions of the programs of Fundamental Education promoted by UNESCO.

### Foundations of National Systems of Education

It is obvious that a national system of education cannot be established by borrowing a piece from one country, another from another, and so on. Even the educational system of the United States has not yet developed into an articulated and consistent whole so far as its organization is concerned. The American educator would in all probability not admit this, and yet the more serious maladjustments in the organization occur where the different parts borrowed from different foreign systems should be articulated — the elementary school strongly influenced in its origin by the German system, the secondary school a reproduction of the English Latin grammar school, the college originally a transplantation of an English college, and the university idea imported from Germany.

The future student of education will have an oportunity to see how difficult it is to establish a national system of education by "picking off a flower from one bush and some leaves from another"

---

[3] M. E. Sadler, *How Far Can We Learn Anything of Practical Value from the Study of Foreign Systems of Education?* (Guildford, 1900), pp. 11 f.

and expecting the combination to grow as a living plant. This opportunity will be provided when, if ever, a united Germany is again established. At present the four parts of Germany have been exposed to the influence of four different educational systems — the American, the English, the French, and the Russian. The lessons of these systems will not be discarded entirely, but a German system of education as such will have to grow out of German soil from the seeds of German cultural tradition.

In the same way the development of education in Japan will be interesting to observe. Here there was recommended a reconstruction of the Imperial prewar educational system along the lines of the American one with greater participation in its administration by local boards of education, greater freedom for the teachers, extensive educational opportunities on the principle of equality, co-education, and other characteristics of educational organization in the United States. At no point did the reorganization recommended by the United States Education Mission to Japan in 1946 have any relation, direct or indirect, to the Japanese tradition.

The general principle that a national system of education must be inspired by "things outside the schools," and that these things "govern and interpret the things inside" the schools does not mean, however, that a nation cannot incorporate into its own sound ideas found in the educational systems of other countries. The process of cross-fertilization of ideas has always gone on in the history of education, as must be obvious to anyone who has studied the subject. The value of the comparative study of educational systems for broadening the approach to and understanding of one's own system of education — as a contribution, in other words, to a philosophy of education — was emphasized by an American educator who wrote on the subject at the same time as Sadler.

On this subject Dr. Charles H. Thurber wrote: "There are certain problems set for every people that undertake to deal with school organization. There have been various solutions worked out for these problems, chiefly in the nineteenth century, by different nations, each operating in its own historic spirit and environment. The answers obtained may or may not agree, but our view will be widened by seeing more than one solution. Moreover such a study, dealing as it does with fundamental principles, should foster the acquisition of a philosophic attitude toward that wide field of interest covered by the term 'organization of education.' . . . Perhaps, too, we shall see more clearly that education, as a system, is a development, a product of the evolution of society, and that if the form we have seems not quite to fit our highest conceptions, the way to better it is not by bartering what we have for what someone else has, nor by building a lean-to against our present structure. Further study might well be given to the basal problem for each country: how has the existing condition — system or lack of it — been developed out of the cooperation and antagonisms of universal principles and national peculiarities?" [4]

### Comparative Education and Philosophy of Education

The chief contribution, then, of the study of comparative education is that, if properly aproached, it deals "with fundamental principles" and fosters "the acquisition of a philosophic attitude" in analyzing and therefore stimulating a clearer understanding of the problems of education. The study makes the educator "better able to enter into the spirit and tradition" of the educational system of his own nation. These are contributions that cannot be ignored at a time when the characteristic trend in all professional studies is toward intense specialization. Since a nation's education has its roots so deeply embedded in its cultural tradition, is strongly colored by its culture pattern, and at the same time reflects its hopes for the future, those aspects that vitalize the work of the specialist cannot be ignored.

There is another reason for the development and cultivation of a broad philosophic attitude — to counteract a trend to define the ends and explain the processes of education in terms of the contributions of the scientific study of the subject. It cannot be denied that the progress of education can be advanced by the lessons derived from the new science of education through psychology and objective tests and measurements. But, as in the total area of man's quest for knowledge and understanding, there is great

[4] Charles H. Thurber, *The Principles of School Organization. A Comparative Study Chiefly Based on the Systems of the United States, England, Germany and France* (Worcester, Mass., n.d.), p. 6. See also Wilhelm Dilthey, *Über die Möglichkeit einer allgemein-gültigen pädagogischen Wissenchaft* (Berlin, 1888) and Emile Durkheim, *Education et Sociologie* (Paris, 1922).

danger in ignoring the fact that science can furnish only partial answers to this quest. A philosophy of education may use the results that come from the application of scientific techniques, but the scientific study of education is not itself philosophical.

Since the study of comparative education seeks to discover those forces that make the educational system of one nation different from that of another, it is more concerned with "form" than with the details that make up a national system of education. It sets out to find explanations of a particular "form" in the culture pattern and tradition that have shaped the outlook and way of life of a people, in the political theories and ideals that define its political ends, in the relations of the individual to the state and its social and cultural institutions, and in the nature of the state itself. It is this kind of approach that serves as a challenge to examine the roots of the educational system of one's own nation. The comparison helps to bring into sharp focus the similarities and differences between systems of education. At the same time there emerges a certain sensitiveness to common problems and the different ways in which they are solved under different national conditions.

Because a nation seeks through education to mould the character of its citizens and so reflects its aims — political, social, economic, and cultural — a study of its educational system, as here defined, can contribute as richly to an understanding of its aims in general as a direct study of its political policies. Thus, the preparation of the German mind for war was clearly indicated in the changes in education introduced by the Nazis. So, too, the changes in Soviet Russian attitudes to her former allies were manifest in the changes incorporated in the postwar history textbooks. Another example is afforded in a study of the gradual Russification of the textbooks in the schools of the Communist-controlled satellite countries. Nor can the recent attacks on the public schools of the United States and the censorship of some textbooks be dismissed wholly as a revolt against the current philosophy of education.

## The War of Ideas

The importance of the methods of approach suggested here cannot be exaggerated at a time when the most serious conflict in human affairs is between the ideology of totalitarianism and the ideals of democracy. The "cold war" is as much a war of ideas as it is a struggle for power on the one side to dominate the world, on the other to make the world safe for peace. The best method for acquiring an understanding of the meaning of democracy is through the study of the type of social and political organization which is its opposite. This is all the more urgent since spokesmen for totalitarianism in its different forms claim that it is democratic. By studying the contrasts it becomes possible to recognize the dangers that threaten democracy and to provide the best safeguards for its protection and preservation in the minds of children and youth whose continuing task for some time to come must be to defend democracy with full understanding of what it means. For the defense and understanding of democracy cannot be left to be learned from the play of social forces alone. There must be cultivated a loyalty to the ideals of democracy as deep-rooted as that inculcated into the youth of totalitarian regimes for their ideologies.

### Education as an Instrument of National Welfare

Important as the study of the effects of these two contrasting social and political concepts — totalitarianism and democracy — may be on the character and form of education in a country, there are other influences which make for differentiations. Besides the major ideological differences, it is these influences that must be analysed in order to understand fully the major characteristics of an educational system. When the wave of experimentalism in education began there was current the notion that education is autonomous and has its own laws ( *die Eigengesetzlichkeit der Erziehung* ); all that is necessary, according to this notion, is to allow teachers and pupils to come together and proceed as they pleased. Schools along this line were established in Germany during the Weimar regime; they appeared sporadically in England and the United States; they were fostered in the early years of the Communist revolution in Soviet Russia. It is obvious, however, and the history of education offers ample evidence therefor, that an educational system is largely influenced and its character largely determined by factors and forces outside the school. The nature of these factors and forces must be studied to understand the characteristics of an educational system as it is and as it changes.

In the last two centuries education has slowly become an instrument of nationalism and a concern of the state. The concept of nationalism must, therefore, be analysed and the idea of the state must be studied, if their influence on education is to be comprehended. Nationalism as a force in education must be given particular attention at a time when the hopes of men are centered on international understanding and cooperation. The progress and expansion of education as the foundation of social stability and intelligent citizenship have become the concern of the largest sociopolitical unit in every country — the state. At once the question arises as to the degree to which the powers of the state should be used, and to what extent the control of education should be centralized or decentralized. In other words, the issue is whether the state should exercise a monopoly in education or share it with other groups that represent the public. The relations of the individual and organized social and political groups to the state, the control of education in general, the maintenance of standards, the determination of the content and methods of instruction, and the financial support of education are all questions, the answers to which depend upon the prevailing idea of the state.

### Current Issues in Education

It is not only the administrative aspects of an educational system that are affected by these concepts and ideas. They also have an important influence in determining the aims of education. Upon them depends the degree of freedom and authority permitted in a system of education as well as the free flow of ideas and the adaptation to new needs as they arise, whether from the demands of society or from changes in educational theory. Outstanding everywhere today are two issues to the solution of which socioeconomic changes and educational theory have the answer, but the realization of that answer in practice is dependent upon the nature of the controls and their location — whether the determination of educational issues is entirely in the hands of the state or whether the public can express its opinions freely.

The two outstanding issues are the prolongation of school attendance and the provision of equal educational opportunities for all. Neither of these issues is simple and both are dependent upon social readiness and parental cooperation. Both issues involve serious educational implications that involve the organization of various types of schools or one school with different courses, reconsideration of curricula, guidance, and the distribution of pupils in accordance with their abilities and aptitudes. And underlying all these aspects of the outstanding issues are, first, the financial ability of a people to support an extended and differentiated system of schools, and, secondly, the more immediately pressing demands of a rapidly increasing school population which will be felt for at least another decade. Of these aspects the second involves the provision of more school buildings at a time when materials are not yet in full supply and the costs are high, and when the prospects of securing an adequate number of teachers to maintain the present ratio to the number of pupils are not good. They are still less promising if one looks for the provision within a reasonable time of such a supply of teachers as would make possible the reduction of class size to that implicit in contemporary educational theory.

Here perhaps is to be found the most serious obstacle to the advancement of education to the new stage demanded for the defense of democracy and by educational theory. For the present there is everywhere a serious shortage of teachers both in actuality and in prospect. It becomes increasingly obvious that to raise teaching to its appropriate professional level, the remuneration and other rewards must be raised to meet the competition of other occupations, and other standards of preparation must be improved.

Here have been presented some of the problems and issues to be found in all systems of education. A study of these problems and issues and of the ways in which they are, if not solved, at least dealt with will be a contribution to a philosophy of education, to what Dr. Thurber called "a philosophic attitude toward the wide field of interest covered by the term 'organization of education,'" and, to quote Sadler, to make us "better able to enter into the spirit of our own national education." The fact that this is an era of transition when plans for the future development of education are more easily discussed than capable of being carried out renders the study of comparative education all the more valuable as a stimulus to thought. No system of education anywhere, not even in the United States, has reached a stage of equilibrium; all are in a state of becoming and the directions, aims, and forms constitute the materials for the study of comparative education. The promise of new educational reforms of a few years ago has not yet been carried out, but the patterns of these reforms and the issues in education are sufficiently clear and definite to provide the basis for study.

## REFERENCES

Demiashkevich, M. J. "Why Comparative Education." *Peabody Jl. of Education*, Vol. 9, No. 1, July, 1931.

Kandel, I. L. "Comparative Education" in R. M. W. Travers and J. Cohen, *Educating for Democracy*, Ch. XXIII, London, The Macmillan Co., 1939.

———"Comparative Education" in *Rev. of Educational Research*, Vol. VI, No. 4, October, 1936, Ch. III.

——— "National Backgrounds in Education" in National Society of College Teachers of Education, *Yearbook XXV*, 1937, Ch. IX.

# 2

# The State and Education

## Expansion of State Authority

The twentieth century has been marked by the gradual extension of the functions of the state into those areas of human activities which, with the development of democratic institutions, had in the past been left to local groups and community organizations. The line of demarcation which once existed between the functions of the state and the functions of voluntary or corporate organizations within the state was on the way to disappearing. Two World Wars and the reconstruction efforts that followed served to enlarge and expand the authority of the state and to increase the areas of control assumed by the states.

Under such conditions the restrictions imposed on the freedom of the individual and of groups were accepted in the interests of a common cause. Freedom of expression and freedom of thought, if employed to criticize the action of the state, were curbed as was the enjoyment of freedom in many other activities in the affairs of men. In the fervor of loyalty and patriotism demanded for the conduct of the wars criticism tended to be regarded as unpatriotic and disloyal. The same conditions that called for loyalty and patriotism fomented the glorification of one's nation. In the end there resulted an exaggerated form of nationalism despite the contemporary lofty aspirations for the creation of insti-

18

tutions to promote international understanding and international cooperation to insure peace for humanity.

The continuation into two postwar periods of some of the wartime controls and the power of the state to determine priorities — in such matters as the rationing of foods, the distribution of building materials, the administration of the means and methods of communication and travel, and the organization of many other activities which had earlier been normally left to free enterprise — carried over into the so-called peacetimes the wartime curbs on the freedom of individuals and groups. The provision and extension of welfare schemes for young and old, worthy in themselves, only helped to increase dependence on state action.

At the same time other forces were in operation which also helped to subordinate individual thinking to external influences and to encourage conformity. The so-called mass media — the syndicated press, advertising and publicity, books-of-the-month clubs, radio and television, films, and commercialized sport — have limited the areas of choice and restricted intellectual activities to what is for the moment fashionable. As the beneficiaries of the latest gadgets, the results of scientific research and its technical application, there is a tendency on the part of many to rejoice in what they regard as evidences of progress without understanding the operations involved in producing them. Too often there is a failure to realize that advances in material accessories of life do not constitute the whole sphere of what should be man's activities as a rational animal. Further, the use of reason is deprecated ever since complexes have acquired a place in the vocabulary of the man in the street. Since complexes have their origins in some obscure part of the individual, he feels absolved of responsibility for his actions which may be irrational. All these influences have so conditioned the minds of men that, as Gide wrote of the Soviet man, they are in danger of losing even the consciousness of their enslavement.

## Totalitarianism and Democracy

Two wars have been fought within one generation — the first to make the world safe for democracy, the second to save from the

inroads of barbarism freedom in all its meanings for mankind. The
period between the two wars witnessed the emergence of totalitarian forms of government with their various symbols — red, black,
and brown — but each designed to establish a despotism over
the bodies and the minds of men, and each founded on the principle that man is created for the state. This was a complete denial
of the principle that the state exists to serve the interests of man
and to create conditions for the fullest attainment of his dignity
as a man.

World War II brought about the destruction of the black and
brown forms of totalitarianism, but paradoxically strengthened the
red regime which emerged to challenge those democracies that had
fought to preserve the ideals of freedom. The conflict between
the Communist and the democratic regimes — the so-called "cold
war" — has in its turn produced the danger that the methods of
totalitarianism may be resorted to by democracies in order to maintain a united front against communism from within and without.
Paradoxically again, protection against this danger is sometimes
sought at the expense of some of the freedoms that were thought
to have been won. One of the most serious aspects of this danger
is the increase in the police power of the state.

It is here that the gravest threat to democracies is to be found.
For the choice before mankind still is, as it has always been
throughout history, between two alternatives: (1) whether he is
to become a pawn of the state, to think as the state wishes him
to think, to behave as the state orders him to behave, and "to have
no private life except when he is asleep," as a Nazi leader maintained; or (2) whether he is to be educated, in the spirit of freedom and democracy, as a free man — free to think for himself,
free to express his considered opinions, free to order his life as
a free citizen restrained only by a sense of responsibility to his
fellow-citizens as the only check on the enjoyment of his privileges
as a free man.

### The Individual and the State

The relation of the individual to the state of which he is a
member and the concept of the state are not mere academic ques-

tions. They both have today, as they always have had, an important bearing on the kind of education that is provided. There is hardly any aspect in the organization of education and instruction that is not affected by the choice of answers to these questions. Since education is the instrument used by the state to produce either subjects or citizens who will promote its ends, the important question that must be discussed in these critical times is "Where does or where should the control of education lie?" It is, therefore, equally important to consider what is meant by the concept of "the state." It is not without significance that it was in endeavors to answer this question that the earliest and still relevant contributions to the theory of education were produced by Plato and Aristotle.

In the *Republic* Plato wrote that "If by a good education the citizens be made reasonable men, they will readily see through all the questions"; this is fundamental to the stability of the state. In the *Laws* Plato made the Minister of Education of Youth the most important official in the state because "if young men have been and are well brought up, all things go swimmingly" in the state. A system of education determined either by the "guardians" as in the *Republic* or by the Minister of Education as in the *Laws* would guarantee justice, stability, and security in the state.

Aristotle in his *Politics* recognized that the permanence of constitutions or stability of the state can be assured by adapting education to their forms. In his *Ethics* Aristotle stated that "the end of politics is the highest good, and there is nothing that this science takes so much pains with as producing a certain character in the citizens, that is, making them good and able to do fine things."

Both Plato and Aristotle were able to formulate their theories of the state on the basis of precedents as exemplified in the practices of Athens and Sparta. Ideas which were formulated later — like "As is the school, so is the state" and "Whoever controls the youth, controls the future" — have a long tradition behind them. Frederick the Great and Napoleon built the educational systems of Prussia and France on the principle that the control of education should be vested in the hands of the state. And at the beginning of the nineteenth century, when the Prussian educational system was reorganized following the defeat by Napoleon at Jena in 1806,

Von Humboldt enunciated the principle that "What you would put into the state, you must first put into the school." It is significant that every basic political revolution has been followed by a radical change in the content and sometimes the methods of instruction. Adaptations of education to the more gradual political evolution are also marked in democracies.

The contrast between the revolutionary changes and the slow adaptations of education gives the study of contemporary school systems its special significance. In the one case the state seems to enforce its ideology on the individual; in the other the state aims to extend the opportunities for the individual to realize himself and to think for himself. In the one case the state is monolithic and allows no deviations from its ideology; in the other the state is not only different in principle and quality but looks for progress through the exchange of a variety of opinions within a framework of unity. Accordingly it is necessary to understand the political framework in which it is set in order to understand the characteristics of an educational system. As the theme is developed, however, it will also become clear that other forces and influences besides those exercised by the state also play a part in determining the character of an educational system.

## The Purposes of Education

The transmission of the cultural heritage of a group from one generation to another is a universal purpose of education. It is obvious that a common language of discourse and common objects of social allegiance are essentials needed to insure the stability and security of any community irrespective of its size or organization and to provide intelligible means of communication between its members. In addition to the transmission of the cultural heritage there is another purpose that communities set before themselves in establishing and organizing a system of education and that is the training of those who have the ability to interpret, enrich, and adapt that heritage to new needs and to changing conditions as they may arise.

These two major purposes, described by W. E. Hocking as education for reproduction of the type and education for growth beyond the type, are universal. How they are carried out and achieved in practice is determined by a large number of forces, of which the most important since the middle of the eighteenth century has been the political concept and character of the state. For it was in the eighteenth century that Frederick the Great established the pattern by which the state claimed, if not a monopoly, at any rate paramount control of education.

A great volume of literature has been published through the ages on the theory and philosophy of politics and on the meaning of the state. For the purpose of the present study and in the light of political developments in the present century the two outstanding and contrasting concepts of the state are the totalitarian and the democratic. Since the present discussion, which is concerned with the kind of individual — subject or citizen — that the state wishes to produce through education, it is unnecessary to attempt to distinguish between the different types of totalitarian states, since all of them, whether red, black, or brown, have carried out their aims in the same way. So far as the impact of the totalitarian states upon the individual is concerned, the differences between them are relatively unimportant. By contrast, democratic regimes may differ in certain respects; their aims so far as the self-realizing status of the individual is concerned may be the same, but their practices may differ because of their greater flexibility and adaptability.

### The Totalitarian State

The fundamental principle of the totalitarian concept is idealistic, that is, the state is an all-inclusive entity with a life and destiny and soul of its own which exist over and above the wills of the individuals who are its members. The state is an organic whole which embraces and gives meaning to all the activities in which individuals, alone or in groups, may engage. It is only in and through the willing acquiescence in the will of the state that the individual finds the meaning of his existence, and it is only as he subordinates his will to the will of the state that the individual becomes free. Sovereignty is vested in the state and not in the wills or opinions expressed by its members, who have only such protection under a constitution as the state is willing to grant or may withdraw as its own interests may at any time demand. The rights enjoyed by the individual are those conferred on him by the state which demands in return a life of duties not compensated for or balanced by correlative rights. Justice is what the state decides at any particular time to be just and expedient. The individual is free to criticize only the mechanical operation of government and not the ideology upon which it is based. Parliamentary forms may be retained, and the subjects of the state have the right or are even compelled to vote, but the vote is never cast on questions of policy, but for candidates selected by those in power, usually by the members of an inner council of the Party. For the will of the state is expressed and defined by this council and approved by members of the Party, whose head is virtually the dictator of the state. The secret of the influence of those in control in the state is force and the threat of force at any sign of deviation from the direction set by the prevailing ideology.

The impact of the totalitarian state upon the individual is the same, no matter whether the concept upon which it is based stems from Hegel's idealism which conceives of the state as an organism enduring forever, or whether it derives from Marx's dialectical materialism which posits the ultimate withering away of the state. Since the state is an end in itself, the individual exists for the state and his life in all the multiplicity of his activities and relationships is determined by the authority and power of the state. There is no place for group or community organizations of a voluntary kind. The manifold relationships in which the human being engages and cultivates his interests — family, church, work, social clubs, recreational organizations — are all dominated by and must be dedicated to the purposes of the state. The essential principle of life is to accept blindly and to be guided submissively by the orthodoxy and dogma defined by the state. No dissent is permitted; no questioning is allowed; criticisms of the ideological principles, whether explicit or implied, are regarded as "deviations" which may mean expulsion from the Party, imprisonment, exile to forced labor camps, or death.

The nature of the totalitarian state, no matter what its color may be, can best be comprehended if it is looked upon as the negation of all those ideals toward which man has been struggling in his onward progress to democracy. That the great human ideal which man has striven to attain is democracy is confirmed indirectly by the usurpation by totalitarian leaders of the terminology and values of democracy. Universal suffrage, educational opportunities, elections, parliamentary forms, and even freedom are dangled before their deluded subjects as the privileges won by totalitarian revolutions. The enjoyment of these privileges is rigidly confined and controlled, since every individual must be in "the right line" or coordinated with every other individual. Nor is there in fact anything to challenge thought, since the state has a monopolistic control over all mass media of communication, which are used for the sole purpose of indoctrination and propaganda.

The most striking contrast between the totalitarian concept of the state and its opposite — the liberal or democratic — is that the one is based on a metaphysical figment, while the latter rests upon the reality of experience; the one is an abstract idea, the other has a recognizable, concrete form; the one is power supported by force and fear of it, the essence of the other is justice; the one is a police state controlling every aspect of the lives of its subjects in its own interests, the other exercises its authority only to prevent conflicts among and to promote the welfare of its members but with their consent; the one is an end in itself, the other is a means to promote the well-being of each of its members.

## The Democratic State

The democratic state, which stands in contrast to the totalitarian, is an association of individuals, like any other grouping of individuals, organized for the pursuit and conduct of ends common to all and resting upon the consent of its citizens. The policies of the state are determined by the decisions of a majority. The state is not all-inclusive and the multiplicity of interests and relationships among its citizens may be promoted and pursued in a variety of group organizations, provided they do not constitute a threat to other groups or individuals or to the stability of the state.

The democratic state, then, is an agency created and accepted by its constituent members to assume charge of and to promote

such ends as conduce to the welfare of all, and at the same time
to establish and maintain such conditions as will help each individual to realize the best in himself. In tolerating and encouraging
the voluntary organization of active associational groups, the state
realizes that its progress depends upon the cultivation and promotion of a great variety of interests and activities, provided there
is accepted a certain basis of unity that is necessary for stability.

For the essential requirement for the progress of individuals or
of groups is freedom for the exchange and discussion of ideas.
The state exists, therefore, to protect its members in their use and
enjoyment of freedom and in their rights, since both freedom and
rights are essential to the development of the good life and to the
self-realization of a personality. At the same time the individual
as a member of society and of the state must understand that he
owes to both the acceptance and performance of certain duties.

Unlike the totalitarian state which is monolithic and all-inclusive,
the democratic state is pluralistic and encourages variety of opinions and their expression within a framework of unity. While the
subject of the totalitarian state can do nothing but agree to and
accept the dictates of the states, the citizen in a democracy enjoys
the right to disagree within the limits of loyalty to certain accepted
uniformities which provide the common basis of intercourse.

The state thus derives its authority not through fear and force,
but by consent of its members. Consent itself becomes intelligent
because it results from free discussion and free expression of opinions and from voluntary cooperation which help the individual
to understand and to formulate a policy to which he gives or from
which he withdraws or withholds his consent. The democratic
state rests upon the intelligence of its citizens and not upon the
fear of subjects. In general the theory is that opinions freely arrived at are better, even if not correct, than policies imposed by
force, for it gives the citizen a chance to profit by his mistakes.
This was, in fact, stated as a principle by Montesquieu: "Dans
une nation libre, il est très-souvent indifférent que les particuliers
raisonnent bien ou mal; il suffit qu'ils raisonnent; de là sort la
liberté, qui garantit des effets de ces mêmes raisonnements." Still
earlier Massiglio of Padua wrote, "True it is that people at large
are not fit to govern, but they can tell whether they are well or

ill governed, as a man knows whether his shoe fits him or not without being a shoemaker."

To define the democratic state is not easy, for it is not as clear-cut nor as systematically organized as the totalitarian state, which, whether red, black, or brown, had a definite creed. Any attempt to define democracy would omit large areas of activity and life. It is a body of principles, ideals, and values which is constantly expanding in scope and depth of meaning, as the culture of a society changes. This is what Santayana had in mind when he wrote of democracy that "It moves by a series of checks, mutual concessions, and limited satisfactions; it counts on chivalry, sportsmanship, brotherly love, and on that rarest and least lucrative of virtues — fair-mindedness; it is a broad-based, stupid, blind adventure, groping toward an unknown goal."

It is this idea of an adventure always moving forward and becoming enriched in the process that makes any definition of democracy or more specifically of the democratic state so elusive and points the contrast with the clear-cut definitions of the various forms of totalitarianism. This contrast is clearly indicated in a remark of Samuel Butler in *The Way of All Flesh* — "Extremes alone are logical and they are always absurd; the mean alone is practicable and it is always illogical."

Democracy may be a form of government which makes possible the existence within it of a classless or a class-stratified society. But such a concept concerns the political aspect of democracy. More inclusive is the definition of democracy as a way of life, which seeks to combine order and liberty, unity and variety both in government and in the lives of its citizens. The democratic state is founded in freely expressed opinion and majority rule subject to public opinion. Again, in contrast with its opposite, the democratic state protects the individual in his rights under a constitution which only public opinion can in the long run change or amend.

### Contrasting Concepts of the State

A comparison of the two leading forms of the state that are prevalent today reveals two concepts that are diametrically opposed to each other when the relation of the individual to the state is considered. In the totalitarian scheme the individual exists for and is entirely subordinated to the will of the state. In a democracy the true end of the state is sought in the lives of its members as free personalities, for the state exists to make the good life possible for each individual. As Mill wrote in his "Essay on Liberty," "The worth of a state in the long run is the worth of the individuals composing it. . . . A state which dwarfs its men in order that they may be more docile instruments in its hands even for beneficial purposes will find that with small men no great thing can really be accomplished." The worth of the individual grows as he is free to engage freely and intelligently in the multiplicity of varied relationships that enlist his interest and participation in his groups or in his community. Such freedom, however, implies, on the one hand, a sense of responsibility in its use by the individual, and, on the other, the existence of order guaranteed by the protection of law.

The contrast between the two concepts can most clearly be brought out by studying the import of the following quotations. When the Nazis were in power, Goebbels, the propaganda director, said, "Since we National Socialists are convinced that we are right, we cannot tolerate anybody who contends that he is right. For if he too is right, he must be a National Socialist, or if he is not a National Socialist, then he is simply not right." And this conformity was insisted upon in a May Day Speech (1937) delivered by Hitler against the Church for criticizing aspects of the regime in power: "We shall simply walk over any groups who go against us. They must either bow to us or be broken. There can be only one authority. That applies to the Churches too." No better expressions of the essence of totalitarianism can be found than this emphasis on both conformity (*Gleichschaltung*) and silent acquiescence (*Verschwiegenheit*). These quotations, of course, present only the negative side of totalitarian control ("Thou shalt not . . ."); the positive side of moulding the mind through propaganda and indoctrination — later called "brain-washing" — was carried on in the educational systems.

Other illustrations could be cited from Fascist statements, and it is only necessary to refer to the title of the office created in the Department of Education of Japan in 1935, first as the Bureau of Student Control and later as the Bureau of Thought Supervision to prevent students from "harboring dangerous thoughts." These regimes have disappeared, but the Communist form not only continues in Soviet Russia but is now extended and imposed upon the ten satellite states that border on Russia and upon China. What was true of Soviet Russia, as described in 1937 by André Gide, can now be found in China and in Russia's satellite states.

Writing of the cultural conditions in Soviet Russia in *Return from the U.S.S.R.*, Gide said, "In the U.S.S.R. everybody knows beforehand, once and for all, that on any and every subject there can be only one opinion. And in fact everybody's mind has been so moulded and this conformism become to such a degree easy, natural and imperceptible, that I do not think any hypocrisy enters into it. . . . Every morning the *Pravda* teaches them just what they should know and think and believe. And he who strays from the path had better look out! So that every time you talk to one Russian you feel as if you were talking to them all." With only one source of information the individual begins to believe without question everything that he is permitted to read, and, his mind "loses even the consciousness of its enslavement." [1]

More recently Michael T. Florinsky wrote: "The betterment of the economic and cultural standards of the masses is the paramount aim of socialism and communism. In the U.S.S.R. the Communist Party and the State control and direct not only social security, public health and the schools but also all manifestations of spiritual and cultural life. . . . No censorship is needed in the U.S.S.R. because only Communist papers are permitted to appear. After one has glanced at the insipid and ponderous pages of *Pravda* or *Izvestia* it would be a waste of time to read the other 8,000 papers; they all say the same thing." [2]

If it is objected that this quotation comes from a critical opponent of Soviet Communism, the fact of censorship and dictatorship is corroborated by another writer who, while not a supporter

[1] André Gide, *Return from the U.S.S.R.* (New York, Alfred A. Knopf, Inc., 1937), p. 27. By permission of the publisher.

[2] Michael T. Florinsky, *Towards an Understanding of the U.S.S.R.* (New York, The Macmillan Co., 1951), pp. 181 and 189. By permission of the publisher.

of the ideology, seeks to present a friendly view of Soviet Russia. Corliss Lamont writes: "According to Marxist theory, when the Soviet political dictatorship fades away, the dictatorial controls over Soviet culture will also disappear. This is a consummation most earnestly to be desired. For otherwise the art, literature and science of the U.S.S.R. will in the long run find themselves at a dead end, with originality, fresh ideas and that questioning of authority and basic assumptions so necessary to progress all stifled in a dreary mediocrity of official doctrine and prescribed taste." [3]

When the Constitution was adopted in 1936 it was claimed that the U.S.S.R. had become a leading example of genuine democracy. In the same year Stalin said in an address to the Eighth Congress of the Soviets, "I must admit that the draft of the new Constitution actually leaves in force the regime of the dictatorship of the working class as well as preserves unchanged the present leading position of the Communist Party." But even the dictatorship of the working class was a myth, for control remained in the hands of the small minority that constitutes the Party and is enforced through a hierarchy, the army, and the security police. All activities are conducted and policy determined "in conformity with the interests of the working people," who are themselves never consulted except to cast an affirmative vote, if desired.

The relations between the individual and the state in the U.S.S.R. are succinctly summarized in the following statement: "The long and principal aim of the State guides the Soviet citizen through his daily routine, regulates the conditions under which he lives and works, measures out his 'living space,' confers upon him decorations and honorary titles if he is diligent and docile, or, with the assistance of the ubiquitous police and of an elastic and comprehensive penal code, chastises him if he is recalcitrant, unappreciative, in-

---

[3] Corliss Lamont, *Soviet Civilization* (New York, Philosophical Library, 1952), p. 226. By permission of the author. *The Country of the Blind* by George S. Counts and Nucia Lodge (Boston, Houghton Mifflin Co., 1949) seems to indicate that "the dead end" in intellectual matters has already been reached. How the control was imposed in the field of literature is clearly illustrated in the detailed study, *"The Proletarian Episode in Russian Literature, 1928–1932,"* by Edward J. Brown (New York, Columbia University Press, 1953). In view of Stalin's statement that "Culture is the weapon of the class struggle," dictatorial control need cause no surprise.

efficient, or, perhaps, unable to keep pace with the speed-up of industrialization. Intellectual pursuits, the press, the arts and science are rigidly controlled by an omnipotent bureaucracy whose chief qualification is unfaltering adherence to the 'party line.'"[4]

The Communist Party control over culture and intellectual pursuits has been introduced into all the satellite countries. One example of the effects of this control — in Hungary — will suffice. After discussing the stifling repression in the arts and education and the saturation of every art form with Communist ideology in order to make it serve as a Communist weapon, William Juhasz in a chapter on "Science, Scholarship, and the Arts" in Hungary reaches the following conclusion: "Perhaps the least successful branches of education from the Communist viewpoint are those dealing with science and the arts. This is an inherent weakness that stems from the imposition of the police state mentality on the artist, the scientist, and the scholar, starting with his training, and which makes his full and complete development by western standards almost impossible."[5]

### Democracy and Freedom

The emphasis in the democratic state is on the free exchange of ideas and the function of the state is not to impose its views upon the individual but to create conditions that will enable him to develop what is best in him. The state, in other words, exists for the individual and depends upon his judgment intelligently formulated. Thus Stanley Baldwin in an Empire Day Address (1937) stated that "The British Constitution has grown to what it is through the work of men like you and me — just ordinary people who have adapted the government of the country in order to meet the environment of the age in which they lived, and they have always preserved sufficient flexibility to make that adaptation to be accomplished."

Two years later President Franklin Delano Roosevelt, on the occasion of a Jefferson Day address, said that "He (Jefferson) believed

[4] Florinsky, *op. cit.*, p. 17.
[5] William Juhasz, *Blueprint for a Red Generation* (New York, Mid-European Studies Center, 1952), p. 65.

as we do that the average opinion of mankind is in the long run superior to the dictates of the self-chosen. . . . It may be that the conflict between the two forms of philosophy will continue for centuries to come, but we in the United States are more than ever satisfied with the republican form of government based on regularly recurring opportunities to our citizens to choose their leaders for themselves."

There is implicit in the last two statements the notion that the freedom of the individual involves the acceptance of a certain responsibility in the use of that freedom; that while the government is made by the votes of individuals, they must use their opportunities intelligently. There is a further idea implicit in the statements: while the state refrains from coercion, a certain amount of common purposes, a certain degree of consensus must exist among the members of a community or state by which their freedom is to some extent limited, but without which they could not exercise the privilege of freedom. Those limits are set by the state in the interests of all by the enactment of laws, which represent the will of the public and ensure a measure of stability in which action by individuals or groups may take place. There must exist some guarantee of order and permanence, created by law or accepted by custom, within which the gradual adaptation to changing environmental or cultural conditions may be proposed, discussed, and achieved by individuals or groups in the exercise of their freedom of thought, freedom of discussion and expression, and freedom to initiate action. But in the exercise of that freedom there must also be a sense of direction, a sense of what under given circumstances is possible. That sense of direction is implied in the existence of order or authority in the community or the state. For freedom has meaning only in a social setting. On the other hand, order or authority may be synonymous with coercion or force.

### Freedom and Authority

Order or authority and freedom are facets of the same environment. The one implies stability or permanence, the other makes growth or adjustment to new needs possible. At the Harvard Tercentenary Conference of Arts and Sciences John Dewey, in an address on "Authority and Resistance to Social Change," said: "In effect, authority stands for stability of social organization by means of which direction and support are given to individuals, while individual freedom stands for the forces by which change is intentionally brought about. The issue that requires constant attention is the intimate and organic union of the two things: of authority and freedom, of stability and change. The idea of attaining a solution by separation instead of by union misleads and thwarts endeavor whenever it is acted upon. The widespread adoption of this false and misleading idea is a strong contributing factor in the present state of world confusion." [6]

The same idea was tersely expressed by C. Delisle Burns in one sentence: "Thus, as liberty is the principle of change, so order is the principles of permanence; and civilized life demands both." [7]

Freedom can have no meaning except in a social environment and authority rather than restraint is its guarantee. The misinterpretation of freedom and authority continues and totalitarian apologists tend to perpetuate the misinterpretation in order to deprive freedom of its values and to justify authoritarianism carried into all aspects of life. But the recognition of freedom and authority as complementary to each other is at least as old as Plato, who wrote in the *Laws* that "It may fairly be said that the end of government (and of law) is to promote liberty, so far as governmental coercion prevents worse coercion by private individuals." The same idea was expressed more tersely by Aristotle when he wrote that "Men should not think it slavery to live according to the rule of the Constitution; for it is their salvation."

It is here that the supreme difference between totalitarian and democratic states lies. In the former there is order, but order secured by force or fear of force with little opportunity for the individual to exercise judgment or to express an opinion on policy except to endorse policies of those in power. He knows exactly where he is, but whither he is tending only the self-chosen leaders

[6] *School and Society,* October 10, 1936, pp. 437 ff. The address was reprinted under the title, "Science and the Future of Society," in *Intelligence in the Modern World: John Dewey's Philosophy,* edited by J. Ratner, pp. 343 ff. (New York, The Modern Library, 1939).

[7] C. Delisle Burns, *Political Ideals* (London, Oxford University Press, 1930), p. 52.

know, and the line of progress may not be straight and may be determined by opportunism.

No better summary of the place and function of the democratic state can be cited than the following passage written by the late Jan Christiaan Smuts: "The end of government is not merely good government but the education of people in good government, its self-education in running its own affairs. . . . Liberty as a form of political government is a difficult experiment. . . . But it is at any rate less dangerous than its alternatives and under modern conditions it is probably the only system that promises to endure. The consent of the governed is the only secure and lasting basis of government, and liberty is the condition of consent. Only free men can consent to their form of government. Where there is no freedom and no consent there must be a basis of force. . . . Bolshevism and Fascism, which are the current alternatives to democratic liberty may be defended as a way out of intolerable situations, but they are temporary expedients, often tried and discarded before, and they will be discarded again after present trials. The only philosophy which holds the field is that which recognizes the fundamental ideals of human life in human government and of these the greatest is liberty. No educational system can be established on the negation of liberty, even if it comes with the temporary gift of good government." [8]

### The Challenge to Educate for Democracy

Because the concept of democracy is difficult to define the ideal has been taken for granted as something natural in the hopes and aspirations of men. A statement on *Democracy and Education in the Present Crisis* [9] referred to this weakness in the following terms: "We have taken democracy for granted — have failed to realize that its perpetuation and development require from each generation an even deeper search for fuller understanding and for more inclusive application of its principles, as well as struggle, vigilance,

[8] Jan C. Smuts, *Africa and Some World Problems* (London, Oxford University Press, 1930), pp. 175 f. By permission of the publisher. Had he written three years later, the author would of course have included National Socialism with Bolshevism and Fascism.

[9] Prepared by the Faculty of Teachers College, Columbia University, 1940.

and sacrifice. We have not defined clearly and fully the meaning and implications of democracy for all areas of our life, especially under the profoundly changed conditions of today. As a result, our national ideals and aims lack clarity and definiteness."

In the same year, Professor Fred (later Sir Fred) Clarke wrote of the situation in England: "It is the weakness of a lack of critical self-awareness, opposing as it does a formidable obstacle both to intelligent readjustment at home and to sympathetic understanding abroad. Continuance of such a weakness in the conditions amid which we now have to maintain ourselves might well prove fatal." [10]

In so far as the ideal of democracy has been given practical implementation it has been more in administration and organization of education than in the content of instruction. Except through courses in history, where the rise of free and democratic institutions may have been discussed, little was actually done in the schools to develop an understanding of the meaning of democracy. This was due partly to the fact that in the English-speaking countries at any rate more reliance has been placed on the performance of everyday activities and relations than upon direct inculcation to develop the democratic way of life. And this was in fact the consequence of a misplaced fear of indoctrination.

In the face of the challenge, first, of World War I, fought to make the world safe for democracy, second, of Bolshevism, Fascism, and National Socialism, and then of World War II, which threatened at one time the complete destruction of existing democracies, it was realized that something more direct and explicit must be done to make citizens more intelligent about the meaning and significance of democracy for the future of mankind. In order to develop a critical awareness about the democratic ideal and its opposites, it was seen that it must be brought to the forefront of intelligence rather than be allowed to become a part of conduct through the accident of practical activities.

The responsibility of education for the defense of democracy was grasped in the United States in 1940, even before the country was attacked. In a statement on "Education and the Defense of Ameri-

---

[10] Fred Clarke, *Education and Social Change, An English Interpretation* (London, The Sheldon Press, and New York, The Macmillan Co., 1940), pp. 7 f. By permission of the publisher.

can Democracy," prepared and issued by the Educational Policies Commission of the National Education Association in July, 1940, the first requirement in the moral defense of democracy is declared to be the achievement by the American people of "a clear understanding of the nature of democracy and of the goals to which this democracy aspires."

The importance of this task is explained in the following passage: "Education can help to clarify the nature and goals of democracy. It can portray the American dream of a nation with liberty, justice, and opportunity for all in the broad sweep of history from the time of the nation's founders. It can promote understanding of the civil liberties and the political institutions through which the democratic ideal finds expression. It can focus the searchlight of free and constructive enquiry on those economic and social problems which, if allowed to remain unsolved, threaten to disintegrate democracy from within. It can confirm that faith in the worth and improvability of the individual which is the basic tenet of democracy. It can provide opportunities to *live* democracy, in the school and the home, in the workshop and the market place. Slogans, rituals, and appeals to emotion are not enough. Knowledge, reflection, and the master teacher, experience, are essential to moral defense." [11]

### Education as Conditioning

A totalitarian state has a far simpler task since the primary aims of its educational system are direct indoctrination and moulding the individual to a particular pattern — clear-cut, definite and determined by those in power. Education is, as Stalin is reported to have said to H. G. Wells, "a weapon in the hands of the State," and it is used to condition the individual so that he willingly acquiesces in and submits to the dictates of those in authority.[12] This is accomplished by withholding all access to information that is considered to lead to questioning. In contrast to the limitation of society's concern for education in a democracy to the formal work of the

[11] Educational Policies Commission, *Education and the Defense of American Democracy* (Washington, D.C., 1940), p. 12. By permission of the Secretary of the Commission.

[12] See Raymond A. Bauer, *The New Man in Soviet Psychology*. (Cambridge, Harvard University Press, 1952).

school, the totalitarian state neglects no opportunity that can be effective in the conditioning process, so that all experiences that can in any way have a formative influence on the individual are under control. Uniforms, slogans, rituals, fanatical worship of the leader, organizations for children, youth, and adults, work and leisure, military service, and welfare schemes are all parts of the process of conditioning.

There is no break in gauge in the totalitarian state between formal schooling and influences outside the school, and all the influences that affect the mind and emotions stem from the same source and are directed to the same end. During and after World War II a good example was afforded of the way in which the minds can be manipulated to suit the policy of those in power. At the opening of the war Russians had been directed to be friendly to the German Nazis. After Hitler invaded Russia, the direction was reversed in favor of the Allies. Since the end of the war another campaign has been successful in inculcating hatred of the former allies as imperialists and bourgeois, and this has been accomplished by falsifying textbooks within a few years of each other.

Unity and comformity are the tests of loyalty to the totalitarian state, which has absorbed within itself all these associations that make a community — the family, the church, trade unions, cultural associations, and so on. Departure from the imposed conformity is regarded as a deviation from the "Right Line," and exposes the individual to punishment. A democracy, on the other hand, is characterized by variety within a framework of unity, because it is believed that through variety of interests the life of the individual is enriched, while at the same time the opportunities for progress are increased through the free interaction of individuals stimulated by diverse interests.

Since truth stands revealed either in the statement of its ideology or in the mind of its leader, a totalitarian state cannot tolerate search for it by its subjects. The leader may redefine and re-interpret the original gospel, until similarity between the new and the old is found with difficulty, as in Stalin's interpretation of Lenin's ideology; the leader alone may determine the road to be followed at a particular time. That freedom of religious discussion, advocated by Milton in his *Areopagitica* and applicable to freedom to discuss all that arises in human affairs could not be tolerated in a totalitarian regime, for the very reasons that Milton put forward to justify freedom: "Where there is much desire to learn, there of necessity will be much arguing, much writing, many opinions; for opinion in good men is but knowledge in the making. Under these fantastic terrors of sect and schism, we wrong the earnest and zealous thirst after knowledge and understanding which God hath stirred up in this city. What some lament of, we rather should rejoice at, should rather praise this pious forwardness among men, to reassume the ill-deputed care of their religion into their own hands again. A little generous prudence, a little forbearance of one another, and some grace of charity might win all these diligencies to join and unite into one general and brotherly search after truth."

### Education as a Socio-political Process

It should be obvious that the kind of educational system and the character of the education given in it is strongly affected by the political nature of the state that they are created to serve. Everything that has been said or cited in the present chapter is evidence of this. Nevertheless, there has been a tendency to argue that education should be autonomous, that teachers should not be mere tools in the hands of the state or servants of the dominant class, and that there should be no external restraints placed between pupils and their teachers. In 1949 the president of the London Teachers' Association said that "We do not want education for industry, education for citizenship, or even education for the benefit of an international state. We want education for children so that they can live a full life and offer useful service to others." The statement ends on somewhat of a paradox which negates everything that preceded it. This statement is hardly representative of English professional views, although it describes the principle on which a very small number of private schools were based. It does, however, echo a philosophy current for a time under the Weimar Republic when some German educators put forward a theory of *Die Eigengesetzlichkeit der Erziehung* (the autonomy of education). The idea was based on the theory that growth is its own justification and pupils must be allowed to grow without interference from parents, church, or any political organization — local or national. From another point of view the idea of the autonomy of education also advocated the de-politicization of education (*Die Entpolitisierung der Erziehung*), for which there was more justification at a time when education had become the football of all political parties.

The German educators, including some of the leading advocates of educational autonomy, soon discovered that education is a concern of the state, when the National Socialists came into power. Soviet Russia, soon after the Revolution of 1917, undertook a wholesale experiment with the child-centered schools, but that was largely because politically reliable teachers were not available. The experiment was abandoned in 1932 partly for political reasons, partly because the standards of attainment of the pupils were found to be unsatisfactory. The school cannot, in fact, be independent of its environment, in which political life plays an important role. The provision of education and its maintenance has increasingly become a concern of the larger political entity, the state. The character of that education is a reflection of the political theory that the state reflects.

The concern of the state for education within its borders does not spring merely from a desire to maintain its stability or to produce a body of literate citizens. The political theory upon which a state is founded is not concerned with the facts and structure of government and its operation alone, but represents also values and objects of allegiance that men hold in order to maintain and support the state and government. Plato in his *Republic* attempted to draw a picture of the *just* state and Aristotle dealt with *Politics* and *Ethics* as two aspects of the same problem. Separated for a long time, these two phases are again being brought together in so far as the discussion of political theory and of politics is directed to a consideration of the good life. For men are affected in their choices not only by the immediate conditions and forms in a given situation but also by inherited values and long established ideals. Such ideals are embodied in the American Constitution and the Bill of Rights or in the concepts of freedom and more recently of equality in Britain and France. By contrast it may be pointed out that where totalitarian dictatorships of a leader or party have been established, their acceptance was tolerated by peoples long inured to a tradition of authoritarian control.

Political theories, then, are more than theories of government.

They are theories of social life which determine the relations of men to one another and to groups. In a totalitarian state these relations are dominated and controlled by the interests of the state and by the ideology in which it is founded. In a democratic state these relations gradually expand in range, scope, variety, and values. In the present critical state of the world, however, the gradually expanding scope of government even in the democratic state is a serious challenge to these relationships, calling again for intelligent vigilance for the protection of liberty. Viewed from this point of view the importance of education cannot be exaggerated.

### The State and Values

The nature of the state thus determines the status and the kind of individuals who are its members and in turn influences the character of the education by which they are formed. But the individual is not only a member of the state; he associates with other individuals and forms groups that expand in variety of aims, activities, and interests. The individual, in other words, is a creature of all the varied components that make up the culture of the state. But the culture itself, in its nature, form, and creation, is also influenced by the character of the state and in turn exercises an impact on education. This connection of the state and its culture also has some bearing on progress, which may under cne form of state be controlled by those in power and under another form be the result of free adaptation to changing circumstances.

From whatever angle the nature of the state is discussed, it leads inevitably to some evaluation, some assessment of values and ends of political life and to a consideration of the ways in which education is directed to their attainment. Accordingly education under any circumstances is a means for the development of the individual and the cultivation of human personality in conformity with the nature of the state.

From this major premise a number of questions emerge, of which the following may be cited as examples:

What should be the function of governmental agencies in education?

Should the control of education be centralized or decentralized?
What is the purpose of education and who should define it?
To whom do the schools belong?
What are the relations between the state and cultural institutions within it?
What are the influences of the culture pattern on education?
What are the relations of the individual to the group, the community, society, the state and of these to education?
How do the concepts of totalitarianism and democracy influence the character of education, its administration and organization, and its content and methods of instruction?
What is the status of teachers?

Von Humboldt's statement that "What you would put into the state, you must first put into the school," and another educational maxim, "Whoever controls the youth of a country, controls its future," have been amply illustrated in the past three decades. Every revolution — in Germany from a monarchy to a republic, then to the Nazi state, and in the postwar years to a republic; in Italy from a monarchy with parliamentary government to Fascism, and then to a republic; in Russia from the Tsarist regime to the Soviet Republics — has been followed by a change in the educational system to bring it into conformity with the principles of the revolution. But it does not always need a revolution to produce a change, more or less radical, in a system of education. Adaptation to changing circumstances may demand such changes.

## Movements for Educational Reforms

Both the First and Second World Wars challenged those countries that were involved to examine their educational system and to inquire into their effectiveness. Since both wars were entered by the Allied countries to preserve the freedom of democracy, the challenge led to examining whether the educational systems were genuinely democratic. The provision of equality of educational opportunities now began to be recognized as a primary requisite of a democratic system of education. Even before World War I was brought to an end there was initiated a movement for the

*école unique* or common school system in France and for "secondary education for all" in England. In Germany a corresponding
movement for the *Einheitsschule* was started in 1918. In the United
States in the same period the doors of the high schools were opened
wider by proposals to adapt the curriculum to the needs of adolescent boys and girls, and there was a marked increase in enrollment of students in liberal arts colleges.

Radical changes in political, social, and cultural institutions can
be brought about by a stroke of the pen, once the leaders of a
totalitarian revolution have successfully established themselves in
power. In education there is one reservation, however, to this
statement: an interval must elapse before a body of reliable and
trustworthy teachers can be prepared. This was particularly true
in Soviet Russia, which tolerated many kinds of experiments in the
schools and opened the doors of higher educational institutions to
all who wished to enter without insisting on standards of attainment until 1932 when the Central Committee of the Communist
Party set up controls and standards. In Germany the National Socialists put an end to the movement for the *Einheitsschule* which
was again revived after World War II.

The tempo of social reforms in democracies, however, is much
slower. Since reforms of this kind depend upon the support of
public opinion, that opinion must be educated. The process of
educating that amorphous and varied group called the public is
long drawn out. Thus the movements for the *école unique* in
France and for "secondary education for all" in England were implemented in instalments without, however, producing a complete
reorganization of the educational systems before World War II
broke out. The years of the war were devoted to planning that
reorganization and an impressive literature on needed reforms in
education was published in Great Britain, the British Dominions,
and France.

In view of the subject of this chapter it is significant to point out
the difference in methods of bringing about reform under a dictatorship and in a democracy. In the former the reform is made at the
will of those in authority and, even where Constitutional provisions
exist, they may be set aside by decree and the Constitution later
amended to legalize a decree that was unconstitutional when issued. This was done in the U.S.S.R. when fees were introduced in

1940 for all forms of higher education in violation of the provision of Article 121 of the Constitution (1936) making all education free. In a democracy the process of reform is much longer because it cannot be enacted without consultation between all political parties, voluntary agencies, and the government in power. This will be discussed in detail in a later chapter.

It was inevitable in order to keep the contrasting concepts of the state clear and to emphasize the differences in their impact on the individual and on social and cultural institutions, that other influences that affect the character of education should be kept in the background to be discussed in the following chapter. The whole issue of the relation of the state to education assumes a new importance not only because of the challenge of totalitarianism to democratic ideals but also within democracies because of the extension of the control and authority of the state in so many different directions. It is incumbent upon all who are concerned with the preservation and protection of freedom of the mind in particular to safeguard it against the encroachments of what has been called "the new despotism," that is, control of bureaucracies. There must be a clear and definite line of demarcation between those aspects of an educational system that the state through a bureaucracy may control in the interests of efficiency and uniformity of action and those that organization, mechanization, and dictatorial prescription would in the end destroy. In a democracy there is a clear and definite answer to the question, "To whom do the schools belong?" The answer should be that the state is only a partner in an enterprise in which all cultural groups within it are concerned and involved, and in the determination of which they should, therefore, have a voice.

One of the fundamental problems of education today is how to reconcile the aim of developing the intelligent, freedom-loving individual with the general trend toward the positive state, how to cultivate in the individual a sense of responsibility for the enjoyment and protection of his own freedom at a time when the state appears to be undertaking large schemes for the welfare of all. The issue may be phrased in another way — how can planning by a central governing body be reconciled with the preservation of freedom? To some extent such planning involves restrictions on freedom, even though it is directed to ensuring "freedom from want, disease, ignorance, squalor, and idleness," to use the words of Sir William Beveridge. This raises still another question. The main-spring of the idea of social and economic planning is the desire to provide equality of opportunity for the improvement of standards of living. How can the ideals of equality and freedom be imple-mented without ultimately destroying both? This is not an aca-demic position. The Communist state promised equality in all things and in accepting it the members of the state surrendered their freedom; in the end they were deluded even in their hopes of gaining equality. The lessons of totalitarianism impinge on all aspects that give point and meaning to the ideals of democracy. Totalitarian revolutions have shown how easily liberty may be lost and what must be done to preserve it. They have shown also that their concept of equality has no solid foundation in fact and that stratification in the sense of differentials in rewards for different kinds of services ultimately emerges. In the light of that develop-ment there is also imposed upon democracies the responsibility of defining clearly the meaning of equality of opportunity and in par-ticular in education.

## REFERENCES

Ewing, A. C. *The Individual, the State, and World Government.* New York, 1947.

Kandel, I. L. *Conflicting Theories of Education.* New York, The Mac-millan Co., 1938.

——— *Comparative Education,* Ch. III. Boston, Houghton Mifflin Co., 1933.

Kohn, Hans. *Revolutions and Dictatorships.* Cambridge, Harvard Uni-versity Press, 1939.

Laski, Harold J. *A Grammar of Politics.* New Haven, Yale University Press, 1934.

MacIver, R. M. *The Modern State.* London, Oxford University Press, 1928.

Mayer, J. P., ed. *Political Thought, The European Tradition.* New York, Viking Press, 1939.

Smith, W. O. Lester. *To Whom Do Schools Belong?* Oxford, Basil Blackwell, 1949.

Wilson, F. G. *The Elements of Modern Politics.* New York, McGraw-Hill Book Co., 1936.

# 3

# Forces that Determine the Character of an Educational System

## Education and the Culture Pattern

The study of comparative education is not concerned primarily with analyzing how an educational system is organized or how it is administered in different parts of the world. It seeks rather to discover why in each nation or society or group it is organized and administered as it is. It devotes attention first to the foundations of education, and only in the second place does it undertake to analyze the details of the system of education that is being studied. It deals, therefore, with all those forces that determine the character of an educational system, since the dynamics and strategy of education come first and give meaning to the tactics of educational organization and administration.

It has already been pointed out that from the political point of view education cannot be autonomous; it is equally true that it cannot escape the influences of the culture pattern in which it functions and proceed without regard to the particular environment which it is organized to serve. Philosophers and theorists may discuss the aims of education in universal terms; they may define the ideals that educators should strive to achieve; but education does not proceed in a vacuum. An educational system is exposed to a great variety of forces within the culture pattern that determine its character and define the problems that the schools must face. Educational systems, then, differ with the differences in the culture patterns in which they are set.

More clearly than any other approach to the subject the study of comparative education, continuing the study of the history of education and bringing that history down to the present, unfolds the intimate relations that must exist between education and the culture pattern of the group that it serves. It is, in fact, impossible to understand any educational system and the differences between systems without going behind them to discover the influences that help to shape them. Educational systems, therefore, are relative to their cultural environments. Not only do national systems differ from each other, but within a democracy which encourages decentralization local systems may also differ from each other in certain respects.

## The Culture Pattern of Conformity

In the preceding chapter the relation between the state and education was discussed. The state, however, is only one of the many and varied forces that determine the character of an educational system. Under totalitarian regimes educational systems are similiar to each other in aims and control, whether the regimes are red, black, or brown. The essence of totalitarianism is that all influences which might affect the lives of a people are either suppressed or subjected to the same type of control. The dominant characteristic of thinking and behaving is conformity with the will of the individual or party in power. The state enters into the home, into religious affairs, into economic activities, into creative activities, and into all manner of personal relations. In the U.S.S.R., Fascist Italy, and Nazi Germany literature, the arts, and even the sciences were (and in the U.S.S.R. still are) under the control of cultural bureaus or of "academies" which have the same dictatorial authority. Under the domination of totalitarian ideologies the individual, as a Nazi leader declared, "has no private life, except when he is asleep."

Totalitarianism, it is claimed by its theorists, knows no compromises. Nevertheless changes in basic principles are made as those in power decide and as circumstances may demand, but there is no place for the free play of circumstances upon the action of men.

## The Culture Pattern of Free Societies

By contrast, the essence of the democratic state — even where administrative control may be authoritarian and bureaucratic over certain activities — is freedom for the exchange of ideas and sufficient flexibility to permit adaptation to changing conditions in the environment. In other words, what makes up the culture pattern of a people is not under the control of a political power, but exists and is modifiable as environmental conditions create a ferment of new ideas and new modes of behavior and thought. The culture pattern of a people includes all those ideas, ideals, and institutions that make the life of a society a reality; it includes the language, arts, skills, beliefs, values, mores and manners, economic and political institutions, and institutions for the preservation and promotion of intellectual and spiritual values. In the preservation and transmission of these institutions and values many agencies may play their part — the home, the church, the school, the club and the gang, the shop and the factory, institutions concerned with creative activities, and the agencies of government, national and local.

## Differences in Culture Patterns

People who live differently think differently, wrote Laski. Hence the culture pattern of different nations differs, even though the form of government and the poltical ideals may be the same in all. The reasons for the differences are difficult to estimate, but the tempo of change and adaptation of the pattern to changing environmental conditions can be explained. The strength of traditions may play an important part in retarding the processes of change. A well-entrenched class organization may make for conservatism. Differences in the processes of adaptation may be caused by the nature of a people's economy — whether it is agricultural or industrial, rural or urban. The pattern may vary again in the same social entity because of modes of communication and transportation. It may be too early yet to evaluate the results, but it may be expected that the spread of the use of mass media may help to reduce diversity within a culture pattern. The degree to which invention, that is, the discovery of new ways of doing things or of new ideas, is encouraged and the progressive development of technology is accepted, exercises an influence on the shape and character of the culture pattern.

It is the differences in the culture pattern of a people that makes them "typical" — a typical Frenchman, a typical Englishman, a typical American, and so on. Unfortunately the types become stereotypes and continue to be such long after changes in them have occurred. The result is a tendency to look for differences rather than similarities in character. Nevertheless the differences may form the basis for the choice of a particular kind of personality to be produced through the educational system of a nation. For the first objective of education everywhere is to induct the young into membership of their group, community or nation by transmitting to them their social heritage or that part of the culture pattern that will enable them to live in association wih their fellow-citizens, and to have a feeling of belongingness. The education of those who will have the ability and insight to change the culture pattern is a later development.

Since the "type" is the resultant of living under the impact of a particular culture pattern, it is axiomatic that the individual is the creature of his cultural environment. It would, however, be erroneous to deduce from this that one can characterize as of one type all the members of a whole nation, for within any one nation the individual is the creature of the particular experiences that he may have enjoyed within the common framework of the culture. In other words, within a total pattern there may be sub-cultures which produce differences within the same national group and so tend either to create or perpetuate class-stratification until new conditions arise that bring about new realignments.

Thus, in discussing the movement to increase educational opportunities in France, Henri Laugier pointed out that there were some groups which were so class-conscious that they would not believe that the opportunities were also intended for their children. In

England the phrase, "It ain't for the likes of us," which applies as much to educational opportunities as to other aspects if social living, is the result of class consciousness which it will take long to eradicate; or, when the opportunities are made available, special prestige value may be attached to the type of school hitherto considered beyond the reach of certain classes. Even in the United States the choice of courses in high schools — academic, general, or vocational — as well as participation in extra-curricular activities is not infrequently determined by social status.[1]

## Changing Culture Patterns

The world is today passing through an era of transition. Changes are taking place in the cultural environment, bringing with them new orientations in education. New types of schools are proposed or have already been established. Changes are under way in the curriculum and courses of study and in methods of instruction. To claim that these changes are due wholly to the efforts of educators would be inaccurate. It would rather be more correct to say that the changes arise from the necessity of meeting new social needs, with which the educator must be familiar if he is to bring his professional insight to bear on the task assigned to him. This becomes obvious as one examines movements for the reorganization of educational systems throughout the history of education down to the present. The one principle that emerges is that educational systems develop and expand to take care of the residual functions of society. As non-school agencies for education, whether formal or

[1] Laugier's statement in the *Educational Yearbook, 1944,* of the International Institute of Teachers College, Columbia University, pp. 136 f., was as follows: "So many generations in France have lived in this atmosphere of theoretical equality and actual inequality that the situation has in practice met with fairly general acceptance, induced by the normally pleasant conditions of French life. Of course the immediate victims are hardly conscious of it or do not suffer from it in any way. It does not occur to the son of a worker or agricultural laborer that he might become the governor of a colony, director of a university, an ambassador, an admiral, or an inspector of finance. He may know that such positions exist, but for him they exist in a higher world which is not open to him."
For the American situation see: W. Lloyd Warner, R. J. Havighurst, and M. B. Loeb, *Who Shall Be Educated?* (New York, Harper & Bros., 1944); A. B. Hollingshead, *Elmtown's Youth* (New York, John Wiley & Sons, 1949).

informal, fail to perform their tasks, they are gradually transferred to the school, if society considers such tasks valuable or important for its own welfare.[2]

## The Family and the Home

One of the profoundest changes in the culture pattern of the twentieth century has been the change in the character of the family and the home. This has resulted in part from the emancipation of women and their entrance in increasing numbers into wage-earning careers. It has been due also to a certain relaxation of sanctions, religious and social. The size of the family has become smaller, partly because of the movement for planned parenthood and dissemination of knowledge of methods of birth control, and partly because of the expense and a desire to give the smaller number of children a better start in life. Where living in apartments and high rents are common, they have exercised a profound effect both upon family relations and upon the character of the home.

The home itself has in large measure ceased to be the center of family life which is in competition with commercialized entertainment both in and outside the home. Further, many of the activities which occupied the time of a housewife have been displaced by the advent of prepared commodities.

The family, once the cradle or nursery of social training in habits, manners, discipline, religion, ideas, and ideals, no longer performs this function to the same degree as in the past. The home has also ceased to be a center for recreational and leisure activities. Motion pictures, radio, television, and comics have lures that tax the educational and disciplinary ability of parents.

## Emancipation of Children and Youth

To all these aspects of change in the culture pattern must be added another that tends to be overlooked — the emancipation of children and youth. Almost from its beginning this century was referred to as the "Century of the Child." To some extent the emancipation was brought about by the new psychological approach, to

[2] See the reasons given for the reforms proposed by the Langevin Commission, Chapter 4, pp. 83 f.

which there was later added the psychoanalytical. To a certain degree the emancipation was a revolt against the harshness of nineteenth-century discipline both in the home and in the school. There has also taken place a certain relaxation in the authoritarian status not only of parents but of all adults in relation to children. The new methods introduced in schools — the shift from subject matter to the child, from mass to individual instruction, and the encouragement of critical thinking — have also contributed to the child's emancipation. Finally, the absence in two wars of fathers and older brothers while children were growing up as well as the years of tension that followed them have created problems for both school and society. All the changes in the culture pattern, restricted as they are to one aspect only, have made demands upon systems of education. The new demands have in turn affected the change of emphasis in education from imparting knowledge to the development of personality, an aim which cannot be achieved in the large classes suitable for mass instruction. The type of school buildings and classrooms which are replacing the antiquated buildings of the past reflect changes in the social status of children and youth.

## The Nursery School

One of the recent claimants for inclusion in educational systems is the nursery school. France has had maternal schools for very young children for a century and a half. They have existed for a century in Italy. In England children under five years of age, when compulsory attendance begins, were for a long time admitted to infants schools in England. But the institutions that these pre-school children attended were not regarded as essential parts of the educational systems. The modern nursery school, however, which is spreading slowly from its country of origin, England, was at first a product of changing social conditions; it was only later that the educational justification for the provision of the nursery school was supplied. Its creation was due to a number of influences — the changing character of the home, urban congestion and inadequate housing, the entrance of mothers into wage-earning occupations, and, equally important, the desire of the state and of society to give all children an opportunity for a better start in life.

The nursery school, which was first established to care for the children of working mothers in a slum area, became an object of national interest when war was taking its toll of men and the birth rate was falling and the problem of manpower arose. The movement had the support of psychoanalysts who claimed that many of the complexes of adulthood could be prevented by care in the early years of life. It also had the support of physicians and educators who stressed the importance of early surroundings for the physical and mental growth of the child.

In the United States a different set of circumstances contributed to the creation of private — and expensive — nursery schools. The career mother, the small apartment, the lack of playmates, and a little knowledge of psychology and psychoanalysis have all been responsible. In the U.S.S.R. another reason exists for the provision of schools for very young children; their purpose is to loosen family bonds as early as possible and to begin the process of conditioning the child so that he will be malleable material for those in power.

### Residual Functions of the School

It is difficult to estimate the effect of the change in the character of the home and the family on primary education. It is significant, however, that manual training and household arts activities were introduced into the primary schools of many countries as opportunities for engaging in them in the home declined. In view of the time devoted by children and youth to the radio, television, motion pictures and comics, there is a growing feeling that the schools at an early stage undertake the task of developing standards of taste and discrimination in relation to these activities. Whether the more general use of motion pictures, radio, and television as aids to teaching will be able to overcome the competition outside the school is an open question. But, in general, changes in the primary school for children from six to eleven years of age have been influenced more by improved knowledge of the learning process, of individual differences, and of the meaning of interest than by external cultural changes. Better school buildings, brighter classrooms, smaller classes, adequate equipment and supplies are and will increasingly be the results of the recognition of the importance of the environment for healthy mental and emotional growth. Parents and public cannot be ignored, however. The public must be prepared through understanding to accept increasing expenditure for education. And parents must be brought into cooperation with the school and be helped to understand the departures from the traditions under which they were educated. The recent attacks on the public schools in the United States were due, but only in part, to the objection of some parents to certain innovations in curriculum content and methods of instruction.

### Democratic Ideals and Educational Reconstruction

The most crucial educational problem in most countries at the present time concerns the reorganization of the educational system at the postprimary level. The characteristic form of educational organization everywhere except in the United States has been the dual system — elementary education for the masses and secondary education for the few. In some countries opportunities were provided for pupils to continue their schooling beyond the elementary stage but not in secondary schools proper. This division of educational provisions followed the lines of class stratification, partly because only the wealthy could afford to pay the fees, partly because of a notion that brains and class went together and that occasionally an able boy or girl could be found in the working classes to whom a scholarship could be awarded. Nor can "the prolongation of infancy" which a complete course of secondary education required, together with the cost of maintaining children for the longer period and the loss of wages that they might earn, be left out of consideration as a factor in the class discrimination.

Attention began to be given during World War I to the problem of postprimary education as part of the movement for the complete reorganization of the educational system. The movement was part of a general movement for a broader interpretation of the concept of democracy. The central ideal of democracy, it was felt in both world wars, is the recognition of the worth and dignity of the individual as a human being and as a potential worker and citizen. It was also realized as early as World War I that a great deal of talent was allowed to go to waste because of lack of educational opportunities. In the name of democracy a demand began to be made in World War I and was continued through World War II for a common school system with primary education and some form of postprimary or secondary education for all.

On the general principle of providing equality of educational opportunities for all and to keep young persons in school as long as possible it is not difficult to secure general consensus. The difficulties arise when the principle has to be implemented in the form of an organization of schools. Hitherto the traditional secondary school has been selective; the new organization should provide for the equable distribution of secondary education opportunities according to abilities. Leaving out for the present the professional problems of discovering abilities and creating differentiated types of secondary education, a more serious problem is involved in educating public opinion to accept the new types of secondary education as of equal standing with the traditional academic type. The traditional academic secondary school curriculum has come to be associated in the minds of the public with status and has acquired a prestige even among those sections of the public that are not familiar with its content. The new types of secondary schools that are proposed are looked upon as inferior substitutes for the academic type.

Other difficulties in implementing the ideal of equal opportunities arise from a certain class consciousness. Those classes which because of social position or wealth have in the past sent their children to academic secondary school, even though they did not have the ability to profit intellectually from the course, feel a certain shock to their pride if it is suggested that some other type of secondary school would be more appropriate. The working classes, which have grown accustomed to look upon the academic secondary schools as a means of entering the white-collar or black-coat class and escaping from manual labor, also resent it if their children are assigned to a new type of secondary school or course.

One way out of these difficulties is advocated by political groups which seem to be more interested in equalitarianism than in educational standards; it is the proposal that all types of secondary education be provided in the same school, the multilateral or comprehensive secondary school. The suggestion will be examined critically later. It is mentioned here as an example of a force that must be taken into account in developing an educational system.

## Prolongation of Infancy

There is general agreement, however, on one point: the period of compulsory school attendance must be extended. This "prolongation of infancy" has been forced on the attention of educators by changes in the political and economic milieu. Politically the prolongation is advocated in order to provide a broader and richer preparation for the future citizen as a worker, a citizen, and a human being. The social, economic, and political problems of today are becoming more complex than they were in a more stable century and demand longer education, an education that should be continued beyond the compulsory period through life. The general extension of the period of education, whether up to the age of compulsory attendance or voluntarily beyond, inevitably imposes a financial burden on many families. This situation gives rise to the question of public responsibility to meet the cost of the families by increasing the number of scholarships or of maintenance grants.

The prolongation of compulsory school attendance is facilitated by another change in the culture pattern — the increased mechanization of industry through the advances of technology. The results, while generally beneficial to society as a whole, have produced a situation in which adolescent youth are unemployable in any occupation that has the promise of a career. Keeping youth in school longer provides the opportunity for vocational guidance, which the schools have had to take over from parents and their friends, and for vocational preparation which was formerly acquired through apprenticeship. Hence one of the serious issues outside the United States is the establishment of technical schools at the secondary level and the determination of the relation of such schools to the various types of industry.

Another objective of the prolongation of education, whether compulsory or after formal schooling has been completed, is preparation for the proper use of leisure. The progress of technology and the mechanization of industry have made increased production and shorter hours of labor possible. Educational institutions, whether

at the compulsory stage or later, have assumed the task of providing the kind of preparation that would meet the needs of youth
and adults for leisure-time activities. This function of education is
acquiring new importance since another set of products of technology compete for the leisure time both of youth and of adults.
The advent of motion pictures, radio, television, and phonographs
has introduced a wide range of activities for leisure hours that have
displaced the family and the home as the natural setting for such
activities.

The task imposed upon educators and teachers is to develop standards of criticism and taste which in the long run may lead to an
improvement in the quality of the visual and aural programs available. At the same time there is some danger that reading may be
displaced by these new devices. To avert this danger is an obligation which schools must undertake. For purposes of the present
discussion it is important to note that here is an example of what
Sir Michael Sadler meant when he wrote that "the things outside
the schools matter even more than the things inside the schools, and
govern and interpret the things inside." He might have added also
that it is the function of all concerned with education to be aware
of "the things outside the schools," for they are the forces that
determine the character of education.

## Technological Changes and Education

The technological changes that have been proceeding with increasing tempo since the opening of the twentieth century have
had a more far-reaching effect in changing the population distribution in many countries. With the spread of industrialization the
same process is continuing in countries whose economies were predominantly agricultural with a small number of craft industries.
There has been a shift of population from the rural to the newly
developing and in some cases fast-growing urban centres. This shift
has been made possible by the extensive mechanization of industries
with mass production of products distributed by improved means
of transportation and communication. At the same time, although
the rural population has declined relatively to the rise of the urban,
agricultural production has increased also through mechanization
and scientific methods.

The shift of population has brought in its train a number of problems. The exodus from the agricultural areas has directed increased attention to rural education and its improvement both in organization of schools and in appropriate content of instruction. An important contribution to the improvement of rural education has been the emergence of the consolidated school, made possible by the improvement of roads and means of transportation and communication. The growth of urban areas has, from one point of view, reduced some difficulties by making larger and more varied types of schools possible but it threatens to bring with it a loss of interest on the part of the public and demands new methods for keeping that interest alive. Interest in a single school can be maintained without difficulty by the creation of a parents' association, but to secure and hold the interest of the public at large, which is responsible for the support of a whole system of schools, is a more difficult matter; administration of such a system is a problem in itself in those countries in which education is provided through a partnership between central and local authorities.

### Education and Environment

Nor can the immediate cultural backgrounds of the pupils — their health, their nourishment, their educational environment at home — be left out of consideration. And as those experiences that influence the development of attitudes, ideas, modes of behavior, and speech radiate outward from the home, the culture pattern of the neighborhood from which pupils are drawn cannot be disregarded. To educate a pupil, it is essential that those who undertake the process should have all the information about him that can be obtained. This applies not only to instruction but also to problems of discipline. If the school, as Sir Michael Sadler once defined its task, is to give children and youth new things to love and admire, teachers should know the extent to which they have to supplement what pupils already acquire in their immediate backgrounds and the degree to which they are likely to find resistance on account of such backgrounds.

Within a general unifying culture pattern with its common objects of allegiance, understanding, and communication there exist differences that arise from class standards, occupational influences, religious affiliations, and local traditions expressed in speech, dress, food habits, as well as in ideas and ideals. The importance of awareness about the differences within a common culture pattern was perhaps disregarded when the dual system of education consisted of one type of school devoted to the development of literacy among the masses and another type for a selected minority to be educated as potential leaders. With the movement for common school systems intended to implement the ideal of equality of educational opportunity, the common ends must be reached by recognizing both individual and group or class differences. For to equalize educational opportunities more is needed than access to secondary schools and beyond without payment of fees; it demands careful consideration of all the conditions in the culture pattern of the milieu from which the pupils are drawn and which may prove to be obstacles to the fullest enjoyment of the privileges of educational opportunities. Even in the United States, with its long tradition of equality of educational opportunities, obstacles to the broadest realization of them have been found not so much in economic conditions, which can be overcome, but in differences in the culture pattern of different neighborhoods,.

### Changing Values

The rapid changes that have taken place, particularly since the opening of the century, have tended to undermine faith as an important force that makes for social stability. In those countries which have adopted secular systems of public schools the "Godless" schools are charged with responsibility for the decline of religious faith. Nevertheless, the same decline has taken place in those countries in which religious instruction is imparted as a regular subject of the curriculum. What is not recognized is that decline in faith is part of the same change of attitude that has taken place toward authority and discipline of any kind. Established controls, whether external or internal, have been weakened with "the revolt of the masses," as Ortega y Gasset describes the trend of recent decades.

With the lessening influence of the traditional agencies that contributed to the religious education of children and youth there is a marked movement to charge the schools with responsibility for such education. The most difficult phase in the enactment of the Education Act, 1944, in England arose both when the status of denominational schools was discussed and when it was proposed to introduce some general form of religious instruction in the publicly provided schools. In France the demand for aid for denominational schools became a serious political issue. In the United States the question of religious instruction in public schools has been more widely discussed in the past decade than at any other time since the opening of the present century.

That an important educational influence is in danger of being lost is generally recognized, as may be gathered from the suggestion put forward by practically all contributors to a volume of articles devoted to a consideration of plans and for the postwar reconstruction in the allied nations.[3] The need that was recognized as the most urgent was a re-emphasis on moral and spiritual values, either through direct religious instruction or in any other way that would be permissible in those school systems in which religious instruction is excluded from the curriculum. In the English reconstruction the first method has been followed, and religious instruction on the basis of "Agreed Syllabuses" and the opening of the schools with a corporate act of worship constitutes part of the regular program of county or publicly maintained schools, while denominational religious instruction is given in the various types of nonprovided schools of the educational system. In the United States, where religious instruction in public schools has been prohibited by state constitutions or by court decisions, the Educational Policies Commission of the National Education Association has given a lead by the publication of a pamphlet on *Moral and Spiritual Values in Public Schools* (Washington, D.C., 1951). Other methods for meeting the need have been adopted in different parts of the country, such as week-day religious schools and released time which permitted children to leave school before its close to attend religious classes of their own denomination.

There is, of course, another aspect of this problem when it becomes a political issue, as it has done from time to time in England, or in the United States over the question of federal aid for educa-

[3] *Educational Yearbook, 1944,* of the International Institute of Teachers College, Columbia University (New York, 1944).

tion, or in the postwar years in France when direct aid to denominational schools granted by the Vichy Government was abandoned and the support of such schools became crucial.

## Nationalism and Education

Long before organized systems of education were established, the family or the group to which it belonged recognized a culture pattern or social heritage that it considered not only desirable but essential to transmit to the younger generation as a necessary condition of membership or belongingness and of the stability and survival of both the group and the family. With the rise of the nation-state, systems of formal education began to be established primarily to preserve its culture and to promote its own national ends. In terms of the subject discussed in this chapter, nationalism came to represent everything connoted by the term "culture pattern" of a particular group that considered itself a nation. Nationalism became one of the strongest forces in determining the character of an educational system. The dominant aim in education came to be the development of a sense of loyalty to the nation, represented by a monarch, the state, or the total community embraced in it.

What constitutes a nation has been widely discussed and a variety of criteria have been put forward to define it. The notion that the essential basis of national consciousness springs from a common racial origin — the keystone of National Socialist ideology — was never accepted by historians or anthropologists familiar with the migrations and intermingling of peoples of different stocks. With the rise and spread of the ideal of freedom of religious worship and of religious tolerance the principle adopted in the sixteenth century that whoever rules a land can determine its religion ( *cujus regio, ejus religio* ) has also been recognized as untenable.

The view that a common language is a criterion of a nation has no foundation in reality. There are peoples of different nations that speak the same language ( English-speaking and Spanish-speaking ). There are also many nations whose members are bilingual or multilingual (Belgium, Canada, Switzerland, South Africa). At the same time national revivals have sought to develop national self-consciousness by reviving the language of the group as the current means of communication and intercourse (Celtic in Eire and Hebrew in Israel), while a virtually new language was created on the basis of an older one for the same purpose (Afrikaans in South Africa). The U.S.S.R., however, professed to develop a union of peoples retaining their own languages; but these national groups have no right of self-determination and each is subjected to the ideological control of the Communist leaders in Moscow. The same process is developing in the satellite countries of the U.S.S.R., where the number of translations of Russian books and the study of the Russian language are proceeding at a rapid pace. The importance of a common language as a common basis of discourse cannot be exaggerated, but it is not the only means for disseminating through the schools common objects of social allegiance.

That self-consciousness or sense of belongingness or like-mindedness grows as people live together on a common territory, develop common interests, have a common history, accumulate the same traditions, and share the same ideas, ideals, and modes of thinking and behavior. Having all these things in common they also accept a common government which gives expression to their ideals and aspirations and protects their interests. Nationalism is, then, a spiritual quality based on corporate life, self-consciousness and self-respect which arise from a community of culture.

Since community of culture or a common culture pattern is essential as the quality that gives meaning to a nation, it is obvious that it must play an important part in determining the character of an educational system. It is for this reason that centralized control of education has for a long time been characteristic of most national systems of education. For, by prescribing what teachers must teach and how they shall teach, uniformity and conformity, loyalty and patriotism are expected to be promoted.

There is, however, a failure in this method to note that to control the culture of a people means stagnation and inertia, as was exemplified in Nazi Germany and Fascist Italy, and as is illustrated today in the U.S.S.R. Progress can be secured not through conformity and uniformity, but only through the free exchange of ideas and adaptations to changing conditions in the environment. The culture pattern of a people is made up of a number of patterns that express the ideas and attitudes of the various social groups that make it up. Patriotism and loyalty to one's nation are not diminished but are rather enriched as children and youth manifest these qualities at the levels of their own group experiences and acquire those ideals and moral standards that accompany their expanding experiences as they grow into adulthood and enter upon their responsibilities as citizens. A sense of unity is not only desirable; it is essential in the interests of communication and of common action. But equally important is that variety of ways of responding to the environment which makes a pluralistic nation without disturbing its essential unity. Certainly as a guide for educational activities what is needed is variety set in a framework of national unity.

There is, however, another aspect of the concept of nationalism that demands consideration in the present crisis in world affairs. In the cult of nationalism the tendency has generally been to emphasize national interest, national security, national superiority, and through the teaching of history, geography to some extent, patriotic poetry and songs to develop a kind of self-centered feeling against other nations. The problem today is whether that feeling of nationalism can be compatible with a sense of internationalism. The concept of nationalism as the expression of a people's culture provides the opportunity to solve this problem. There are few nations in the world today which have not profited from conscious or unconscious borrowings from cultural contributions from all parts of the world. National cultures have grown by the process of cross-fertilization which is still going on and at a faster rate than ever before because the world has been made smaller through modern means of communication.

There must then be taken into consideration another force which has been growing since World War I — the realization of a certain interdependence of the nations of the world and the need for international understanding and cooperation. This force may have its effects upon education in different ways — revision of the content of history and geography courses, increased attention to the study of foreign languages, and the development of interest in the culture of nations hitherto ignored. It was to promote these ends that the United Nations Educational, Scientific, and Cultural Organization (UNESCO) was established, as is clearly stated in Article I of Unesco's Constitution on "Purposes and Functions":

"The purpose of the Organization is to contribute to peace and security by promoting collaboration among the nations through education, science and culture in order to further universal respect for justice, for the rule of law and for the human rights and fundamental freedoms which are affirmed for the people of the world, without distinction of race, sex, language or religion by the Charter of the United Nations.

"To realize this purpose the Organization will: (a) collaborate in the work of advancing the mutual knowledge and understanding of peoples, through all means of mass communication and to that end recommend such international agreements as may be necessary to promote the free flow of ideas by word and image."

### School and Society

Since education is a social process, differences between educational systems can best be understood by considering what is meant by the phrase "school and society." More is implicit in this phrase than the idea that the function of the school is to prepare its pupils for membership in a particular society. It means more than the notion that the school is itself a society with a corporate life of its own. To the degree that the school is created by the state or the nation or society to carry out certain objectives and since the educative process is not limited to the few hours spent by a pupil in school, it is important that those responsible for the work of the school understand that "the things outside the schools matter even more than the things inside the schools, and govern and interpret the things inside." These words were written long before sociology became a subject of study and long before the concept of the culture pattern was formulated. It must be remembered that when Sadler wrote these words he was seeking to provide a guide for the study and understanding of the school systems of foreign nations.

### REFERENCES

American Association of School Administrators. *Expanding Role of Education.* Washington, D.C., 1948.

Benedict, Ruth. *Patterns of Culture*. Boston, Houghton Mifflin Co., 1934.

Clarke, Fred. *Education and Social Change*. London, Sheldon Press, and New York, The Macmillan Co., 1940.

Cook, Floyd A., and Elaine F. Cook. *A Social Approach to Education*. New York, McGraw-Hill Book Co., 1950.

Counts, G. S. *Education and American Civilization*. New York, Teachers College, Columbia University, 1952.

Dobinson, C. H., ed. *Education in a Changing World*. Oxford, 1951.

Durkheim, Emile. *Education et Sociologie*. Paris, Felix Alcan, 1922.

Kandel, I. L. *Conflicting Theories of Education*. New York, The Macmillan Co., 1938.

———— ed. *Educational Yearbook, 1929*, of the International Institute of Teachers College, Columbia University. New York, 1929.

———— "The End of An Era." *Educational Yearbook*, Teachers College, Columbia University, 1941.

Lowndes, G. A. N. *The Silent Social Revolution*. London, Oxford University Press, 1937.

Mead, Margaret. *The School in American Culture*. Cambridge, Harvard University Press, 1951.

Moore, Clyde B., and William E. Cole. *Sociology and Educational Practice*. Boston, Houghton Mifflin Co., 1952.

National Society of College Teachers of Education, "The Use of Background in the Interpretation of Educational Issues." *Yearbook* No. XXV, Chicago, 1937.

Ottaway, A. K. *Education and Society*. London, Routledge and Kegan Paul Ltd., 1953.

# 4

# The New Pattern of
# Educational Reconstruction

## Totalitarian and Democratic Methods

Nothing points the contrast between the operation of totalitarian and democratic forms of government as strikingly as the procedure by which social changes and reforms are introduced. The totalitarian authorities bring about changes by fiat, by dictation, without consulting those who may be affected by them. Even if the change violates the Constitution, the Constitution can be subsequently amended to sanction the change. This was done in 1947, seven years after fees for higher education had been introduced throughout the U.S.S.R., although the Constitution of 1936 guaranteed free education at all levels.

The democratic process is much slower, because the government in power at any time recognizes that the consent of all concerned must be secured for the adoption of any important change or reform. The administration of government itself is an educative process and the public mind must be brought into a condition of readiness to weigh the merits of government action. This process has long been recognized in the American tradition and it is the essence of British government. In both countries there is always resistance to bureaucratic control of the kind that is found in other countries where laws may be modified or new legislation adopted by decrees. But even here there is a difference between an authoritarian and a totalitarian government in the fact that bureaucratic action in the former may be discussed by the people's representatives. The progress of democracies depends in fact not only on the right of the individual to express his considered opinions but also on the educative influence of pressure groups. When agencies of criticism disappear or are inactive, the political health of a community suffers. The totalitarian state tolerates neither criticism nor pressure groups.

It is not without interest in view of the challenge of totalitarianism or even of the extension of the powers of the state in democracies to recall that the earliest arguments in favor of public education in the United States were based very largely on the desire to promote "the idea of self-direction and self-government" upon which, as Richard Price put it in the early years of the Republic, liberty depends. Thus George Washington in his Farewell Address urged the promotion of "institutions for the general diffusion of knowledge." For, as he argued, "in proportion as the structure of government gives force to public opinion, it is essential that public opinion be enlightened."

The same principle was basic to Thomas Jefferson's plea for education. He argued that "The functions of every government have propensities to command at will the liberty and property of their constituents. There is no safe deposit for these but with the people themselves; nor can they be safe with them without information." The purpose of general education, as Jefferson wrote on another occasion, is accordingly "to enable every man to judge for himself what will secure or endanger his freedom." Enunciated in the early years of the Republic, this argument for public education became rooted in the American tradition.[1]

In England, on the other hand, it was fear of state control that for so long delayed the creation of a publicly provided system of education. While Jefferson saw in education the best protection of the citizen against the encroachment of government on his liberty, John

[1] U.S. Office of Education, Bulletin, 1940, No. 10, *Expressions on Education by Builders of American Democracy* (Washington, D.C., 1941). By permission of the Acting Chief, Reports and Technical Services.

Stuart Mill feared that the state, if it controlled education, would exercise a despotism over the mind and then over the body of the individual.

## The Movements for Educational Reform

The tradition of public enlightenment as the basis of social and political progress was in effective operation in the planning of the postwar reconstruction of education in a number of countries. Leadership in promoting plans for educational reform came in most cases from individuals and voluntary groups rather than the government itself.[2] It must be remembered, however, that plans for educational reform were not inspired by the recognition of postwar needs alone. Rather it would be more correct to say that such plans were the culmination of movements which anteceded World War II by many years, but that the conditions of the war gave a new impetus for their speedier realization.

In England, for example, the "Silent Social Revolution," as G. A. N. Lowndes described it,[3] had been going on in education since the beginning of the century. The revolution gained a little impetus in 1918 with the passing of the Education Act, 1918 — the Fisher Act — which raised the age of compulsory school attendance to fourteen without any exemptions, extended the system of provision of meals and health care for children in school, proposed compulsory part-time education to eighteen, and opened the way for extending educational opportunities. It was at this time that "secondary education for all" — the English analogue for the *école unique* in France — began to be urged.

This proposal stimulated an evaluation of the whole system of education in England. In 1924 the Consultative Committee of the Board of Education, under the chairmanship of Sir Henry Hadow, undertook an investigation into the problem of the education of the adolescent in schools other than the traditional secondary schools. The function of the Consultative Committee was to collect evidence

[2] In the same way leadership in promoting the movement for education for national defense in the United States came from voluntary organizations. See I. L. Kandel, *The Impact of the War upon Education in the United States* (Chapel Hill, University of North Carolina Press, 1948), Chapter II.

[3] *The Silent Social Revolution* (London, Oxford University Press, 1937).

on the subject of its inquiry from all possible sources, lay and professional, on the basis of which it formulated its reports. The report on the *Education of the Adolescent* which was published in 1926 recommended a reorganization of the school system with a break at the age of eleven plus and the distribution of the pupils according to their abilities into selective and non-selective senior schools. Such schools were established by the local education authorities without further legislation, so that an increasing number of pupils began to have the benefit of some form of postprimary education other than the traditional secondary.

This inquiry was followed by one on *The Primary School* (1931) and another on *Infant and Nursery Schools* (1933). In 1934 the Consultative Committee began to investigate secondary and technical schools and in 1938 published its report *Secondary Education with Special Reference to Grammar Schools and Technical High Schools,* generally known as the Spens Report (Sir Will Spens having succeeded Sir Henry Hadow as chairman of the Committee).

In 1936 the compulsory school attendance age was raised to fifteen; the law was to have gone into effect in 1939 but the threat of war prevented its enforcement. In the interwar years the foundations for another change which was to be effected later were laid in the report (1925) of a Departmental Committee of the Board of Education on the preparation of teachers for elementary schools. The planning of the curricula of teacher training institutions was placed in the hands of regional committees which cooperated under a Central Advisory Committee.

The movement for the reorganization of the educational system of France began in the First World War. It was during the war that *Les Compagnons de l'Université Nouvelle* (The Advocates of the New Educational System) put forward the proposal for the *école unique,* the common school system. The proposal would abolish special educational privileges based on class stratification, would provide the same primary school education for all boys and girls, and would extend opportunities for postprimary education so that every French child would receive the education best suited to his abilities. The proposal was widely publicized and adopted by a number of lay organizations. It was put into effect, however, only in installments. The curriculum of the fee-charging *classes préparatoires* to the *lycées* which gave the children of the well-to-do an advantage so far as admission was concerned over pupils from the public elementary schools was made the same for all pupils in 1925. Fees for secondary education were abolished in 1931. Efforts were made to reduce the overload (*surmenage*) of school and homework on pupils in secondary schools. In 1936 the age of compulsory school attendance was raised from thirteen to fourteen. At the same time two innovations were introduced in secondary schools. The first was an experiment with activity methods (*classes d'orientation*) to help the increasing number of pupils to select the course most suited to their abilities. The outbreak of World War II and especially the advent of the Vichy Government not only put an end to any reform movements, but indicated clearly what a program of reaction would mean for France.

An examination of the history of education in other democracies would show the same trends. The tempo may be slower in those countries in which the control of education is centralized through an accident of history rather than for political reasons. In New Zealand and Australia, for example, there was an awakening, slow but certain, before World War II. The adequacy of the centralized system of administration began to be discussed and in some of the Australian states and in New Zealand some decentralization, particularly in matters of curriculum-making, was permitted and the rigidity of inspection was gradually reduced. At the same time the increasing number of pupils able to remain in school beyond the compulsory age limit virtually compelled a reconsideration of the system of educational organization and particularly of the character of secondary education. In both New Zealand and Australia the creation of the Councils for Educational Research, with support originally from the Carnegie Corporation of New York, made invaluable contributions to the study of education and to educational thought, which was supported by the recently created faculties of education in some of the universities.

The design for educational reorganization in those nations of the world that have already made a good start was indicated in a series of articles on "Postwar Educational Reconstruction" prepared by representatives of sixteen countries and published in 1944.[4] There

[4] I. L. Kandel, ed., *Educational Yearbook, 1944* of the International Institute of Teachers College, Columbia University (New York, Bureau of Publications, Teachers College, Columbia University, 1944).

are certain aspects of educational reform on which all writers are agreed. This agreement can be traced to the universal dissatisfaction with the traditional dual system of education — the elementary schools for the masses and the secondary schools for the select minority. Hence the major proposals for reorganization are inspired by the desire to provide equality of educational opportunity. This at once raises the crucial problem of the meaning and scope of secondary education and particularly the types of courses to be offered and whether they should be offered in one or several schools. There appears to be general dissatisfaction with the traditional secondary school for two reasons: the first is the overburdening of pupils on account of both the curricular content and the homework; and the second arises from what is regarded as an overemphasis on the academic and intellectual and too little attention to the practical. Another aspect of the dissatisfaction with another type of secondary school comes from the fear lest in the technical and vocational courses the general or cultural education of the pupils will be neglected. So far as aims are concerned those who contributed to the symposium are agreed that more attention should be devoted to spiritual values and religious and moral instruction and to promoting faith in democratic institutions with a proper sense of balance between freedom and authority. The difficulties lie in providing equality of educational opportunities. It is recognized that to implement the ideal larger units of administration must be established. In order to enable the individual pupil to profit from such opportunities there must be created systems of educational guidance. But even when these needs have been met, there remains the difficulty of persuading parents of the parity of different types of secondary schools or courses, since the traditional academic course with the privileges to which it led — either entrance to the universities or preferred white-collar jobs — has acquired a prestige which seems to be everywhere unshakeable. There has thus developed a common language of discourse in education. Other factors and forces, however, determine the rate and tempo at which new ideas can be implemented in practice. The method by which attention can be focussed on them was illustrated in several countries during the war.

## Planning Reforms During World War II

The plans for the reorganization of education in England were not the work of the government or of its ministries or of any one political party. All parties and all voluntary organization, lay and professional, readily accepted the following statement which appeared in a pamphlet issued by the Subcommittee on Education of the Central Committee on Post-War Reconstruction of the Conservative and Unionist Party Organization: "Of all the State's activities education is the basic activity, because it conditions the future character of the entire community. Since it is essentially a long-term activity, nothing but the direst necessity should be allowed to hamper or interrupt it."

Education in England has always made its greatest progress in times of social or political crises. The dislocation of education resulting from the outbreak of war concentrated attention on the children and their schooling. Evacuation of children and schools may have been feats to be admired, but the mingling of children from different socio-economic levels and localities, urban and rural, reminded many that England still consisted of the two nations that Disraeli had deplored about a century earlier. It was realized that the health of the children must be safeguarded and that education for national well-being must be taken seriously.

Here a remarkable number of voluntary organizations took the initiative and were soon supported officially. Pamphlets on educational reconstruction were published by the Conservative, Liberal, and Labour Parties. The Cooperative Union, the Trades Union Congress, and the Workers' Educational Association put forward suggestions for reform. The Board of Education circulated a "Green Book" among those whose advice was desired; some idea of the Board's recommendations were made public in summaries. The National Union of Teachers published its own "Green Book" under the title "A Report of Proposals by the Executive of the National Union of Teachers Adopted by the Conference, Easter 1942," and the Association of Directors and Secretaries of Education issued an Orange Book, "Education, a Plan for the Future." These are only a few of the many publications that appeared on the subject of educational reform.

The common threat that ran through all the recommendations was the desire to eliminate those inequalities in educational opportunities that arise from the economic conditions of parents and the accidents of residence. The principles which it was sought to establish were the substitution of a unified and articulated system of education for the traditional dual system and the creation of a system based on equality of educational opportunities.

According to the recommendations the blueprint for the reorganized system provided for nursery schools for children between three and five, compulsory school attendance from five to fifteen (later sixteen), and compulsory part-time education from fifteen to eighteen. Primary education would continue from the age of seven to the age of eleven. Postprimary education would consist of three types of schools: modern schools (eleven plus to fifteen plus); grammar schools (eleven plus to sixteen or eighteen); and technical and commercial schools (eleven plus to fifteen or sixteen). To solve the troublesome and difficult problem of finding the appropriate type of school for each pupil and avoiding too premature a choice it was suggested that the curricula of all three types of secondary schools remain the same for two years in order to facilitate the transfer of pupils, if necessary. The need of larger units of administration was recognized as well as a revision of the financial arrangements between the Board of Education and the local authorities. Despite war conditions there could be no excuse for public apathy about education when the government indicated in a White Paper, *Educational Reconstruction* (1943), the general principles on which legislation would proceed.

Plans for the postwar reconstruction of French education began to be drafted and discussed while the French government was still in Algiers. The defects of the prewar system were fully recognized. Of these the chief stemmed, as in England, from the traditional dual system and manifested itself in the absence of a thorough articulation of the different levels — primary, secondary, vocational, and higher. The consequence was that the public and parents tended to look upon the system as a series of discrete divisions rather than as a continuous whole. As Henri Laugier pointed out,[5] there were still families that felt that they were not entitled to the privilege of secondary education for their children despite the

[5] In *Educational Yearbook, 1944*, pp. 136 f.

abolition of fees in 1931. The curricula and courses of study were criticized as too overcrowded, while the tyranny of examinations was deplored. At the same time it was felt that pressure to cover the extensive content and to prepare for the examinations resulted in a lowering of standards of the *baccalauréat* and encouraging cramming. Many students who succeeded in passing the *baccalauréat* were in fact not ready to undertake university studies.

The needed reforms of French education were outlined by M. René Capitant, Commissioner for National Education, in an address delivered at the opening convention of the University of Algiers on December 18, 1943. He emphasized the provision of greater equality of educational opportunity for all in the interests of social justice and the principle of recognizing the dignity of the human being. The reconstruction of France must be based on the principles of liberty and equality. In the interests of society "there is, in truth, no better investment of funds than that devoted to the instruction and education of children." The provision of equal opportunities for education would require the creation of a common school system leading the child from one level to the next without social distinctions and with general and vocational education for each according to his ability. Such a system must provide several branches of education in accordance with the individual differences and the needs of the pupils. The common school system must not neglect the provision of an appropriate education of an élite selected not by the accident of social status but by choice from among the ablest in all social classes. But education must not be too theoretical and exclusively intellectual nor, on the other hand, should vocational education be too narrow. The common task for all branches of education would be to develop a sense of national community and human brotherhood. To secure this end, M. Capitant cited a proposal that the school should be organized as a miniature university, in which all pupils, irrespective of the courses taken, would rub shoulders with each other in their recreational and leisure periods.

In January, 1944, M. Capitant appointed a *Commission pour la Réforme de l'Enseignement*, which, in view of the political situation, did not present a systematic plan for reconstruction but outlined in general the issues involved and the direction that such reconstruction should follow. The Commission amplified and underlined the needs that had been defined by M. Capitant earlier. The important point to note, however, is the fact that the Commission presented the views not of its members alone but of professional experts and lay representatives whose opinions were secured by sub-committees. Proposals of other groups were examined and the reforms in England and elsewhere were studied. The Commission discussed the extension of the age of compulsory full-time and part-time education, new methods of instruction, a common primary school followed by three types of secondary schools (classical, modern, and technical), exploratory or guidance classes, greater flexibility and balance in the secondary school curriculum, and higher standards for entrance to the universities.[6] The importance of the planning in Algiers lies more in the method of canvassing public opinion as widely as was possible under the circumstances. This activity could not be as extensive as it was in England during the same period, but the principle underlying it was the same — reforms in education or in any other sphere of public welfare depend upon the consent of all concerned.

Soon after the liberation of France a new commission was appointed (*Commission Ministérielle d'Etude*) under the chairmanship of M. Paul Langevin to draft a report on needed reforms in education. In 1946 the Commission published its report, *La Réforme de l'Enseignement,* which was the result not only of the Commission's own deliberations but also of the work of four sub-committees which secured the help and advice of specialists, representatives of various organizations, and of leaders in French culture. While the report received far wider attention and publicity than the report of the Algiers Commission, its recommendations paralleled those of the earlier report and amplified other aspects. The root principle of the Langevin report was that of justice. Reform along this line — that is, of providing equality of educational opportunity — had become urgent because the existing system was not coordinated and articulated. Reorganization had become necessary to meet the new needs.

"The educational structure," says the Commission, "should be

6 The address of M. Capitant and the report of the Commission were published in a special issue of the *Bulletin Officiel du Ministère de l'Education Nationale,* November 16, 1944.

adapted to the social structure. The educational structure has not been seriously modified for half a century. On the other hand, the social structure has undergone a rapid evolution and fundamental changes. Mechanization, the use of new sources of energy, the development of means of transportation and communication, industrial concentration, the increase of production, the entrance of women into economic life, the spread of elementary education have profoundly changed the conditions of life and social organization. The rapidity and extent of economic progress, which in 1880 made the diffusion of elementary education necessary among the working masses, today poses the problem of recruiting an ever-increasing number of personnel as managers and technicians. The middle class, hereditarily called to hold positions of direction and responsibility, will not be able in the future to do so alone. The new needs of modern economy impose the necessity of a reorganization of our educational system, which in its present form is no longer suited to the social and economic conditions."

The educational system should accordingly be designed to meet new conditions, should be more closely identified with life, and should educate the future citizen with an objective and scientific knowledge of economic and social facts and with critical judgment for a life of liberty and responsibility. At a time of social and economic reconstruction every child should have the opportunity for the fullest physical, intellectual, aesthetic, and moral development. There should be an open road for all according to their abilities through a system of education that is unified and coordinated. The Langevin report continued to be the basis for the gradual reform of the French system of education.

The same principle was implied by the New Zealand Minister of Education in October, 1944, at a conference of representatives of about sixty bodies to discuss postwar developments in education. The Minister declared that "It is becoming increasingly evident, not only in New Zealand but throughout the British Commonwealth, that after the war there must be a great expansion in the scope of education, particularly to cater for those below and beyond the present limit of compulsory education. It is equally evident that genuine advances in education, although they may be fostered by a Government, cannot simply radiate from a central authority. The great bulk of the people must not only understand what is afoot, but must also take an active part in working out the kind of educational system they want for themselves and their children."

The fear of regimentation which is characteristic of both authoritarian and totalitarian regimes is ever-present in the minds of the American public where education is concerned. In a paper on "The Public Schools in American Democracy," the late Lee M. Thurston, State Superintendent of Public Instruction in Michigan and U.S. Commissioner of Education shortly before his death, said "We Americans do not want our schools run from above. We insist on running them from below. . . . The American citizen doesn't like government very well, and he doesn't trust government very much. He trusts distant government least of all when it comes to education. There may be some European official who sits at the summit of government and decides vital educational questions, like how much tax money will be used to pay the teachers, and whether a new schoolhouse will be built, and what is to be taught in it, and who is going to school there, and what books he is going to study. Not so in America, where matters of deadly importance like these are settled in our towns and villages and cities by representatives of the people usually chosen directly by the people." [7]

Finally, the following statement contained in the address by M. Capitant, discussed earlier in this chapter, is an excellent summary of the contrast between totalitarian and democratic methods of government and administration: "We have come to realize in recent years the formidable danger inherent in the subjection of the individual to the state. We have seen the state — in Germany, in Italy, in Spain, in France — assume control of all the means of education and public expression, take possession of minds and bodies, train the young as they will and for their use, reduce all men to be less than slaves, machines for thinking and acting according to the whims conveyed to them through the press, through radio broadcasts or through surges of fear. France knows that such a system means the destruction of humanity. It is entirely opposed to such barbarism. . . . This is why she wants her institutions to protect human liberty."

[7] A paper presented to Educational Policies Consultants and National Education Association Delegates, Detroit, Michigan, July 2, 1952.

## The Emerging Pattern

The pattern of educational reconstruction emerged clearly during the war years. As has already been pointed out, the pattern is the culmination in several countries of movements that had been going on since World War I but given special emphasis because of the threat of totalitarianism to democratic institutions. There was developed during the war years a profounder recognition of the importance of education for national well-being and for the preservation of democratic ideals and institutions and of the task of giving real meaning to these ideals by breaking down class barriers and providing equality of opportunity for all boys and girls. The keynote of the approach to education in the discussion of plans for the future can be realized from the following statements:

"In the youth of the nation we have our greatest national asset. Even on a basis of mere expediency we cannot afford not to develop this asset to the greatest advantage." (England, Board of Education, *Educational Reconstruction*, 1943.)

"The greatest wealth of New Zealand or any country is in its children. But like minerals hidden in the earth, till it is developed that wealth is only potential. To develop that wealth thoroughly requires education in its broadest, richest, and fullest measure." (Educational Reconstruction Policy of the New Zealand Educational Institute, *National Education*, September, 1943, p. 208.)

"I believe with you that if anywhere in this country a child lacks opportunity for home life, for health protection, for education, for moral and spiritual development, the strength of the Nation and its ability to cherish and advance the principles of democracy are thereby weakened." (President Franklin Delano Roosevelt, *School Life*, March, 1940, p. 187.)

"One of the major problems confronting the American people is that of further conserving and developing our human resources through education." (*Proposals for Public Education in Postwar America*, National Education Association, 1944.)

"My general thesis is that if we are serious about the need of planning a better world after the war — and if we are not we may as well resign ourselves to the prospect of intolerable lives — the first thing to start thinking about is education. . . . A democracy is a system of society in which a large majority of citizens are not only qualified in mind and body to play a significant part in the common business of the community, but actually have opportunities of doing so. . . . Education is the process by means of which boys and girls do or do not become citizens so qualified." (J. D. G. Medley in *Education for Democracy,* the first of a series of pamphlets on "The Future of Education" published by the Australian Council for Educational Research, Melbourne, 1943.)

M. Capitant's statement, already quoted, that there is "no better investment of funds than that devoted to the instruction and education of children" was the theme of a report *Education — An Investment in People,* published by the Committee on Education of the United States Chamber of Commerce in 1945 and amply illustrated with statistics to prove the relation between economic well-being and education.

The new recognition of the value and importance of education for national well-being and particularly for the preservation of democracies through the appropriate training of its citizens inspired at the same time a restatement of the aims of education as well as a reconstruction of its organization. The publication that had the most far-reaching influence not only in England but in the Dominions and other countries was the Board of Education's White Paper, *Educational Reconstruction.* The White Paper, which will prove to be an outstanding contribution not only to educational literature but also to the politics of education, was presented to Parliament in July, 1943, by the President of the Board of Education, R. A. Butler. Introduced by a citation from Disraeli, "Upon the education of the people of this country the fate of this country depends," the White Paper states the basic principle of reconstruction in the first paragraph as follows:

"The Government's purpose in putting forward the reforms described in this Paper is to secure for children a happier childhood and a better start in life; to ensure a fuller measure of education and opportunity for young people and to provide means for all of developing the various talents with which they are endowed and so enriching the inheritance of the country whose citizens they are. The new educational opportunities must not, therefore, be of a single pattern. It is just as important to achieve diversity as it is to ensure equality of educational opportunity. But such diversity must not impair the social unity within the educational system which will open the way to a more closely knit society and give us strength to face the tasks ahead. The war has revealed afresh the resources and character of the British people — an enduring possession that will survive the material losses inevitable in the present struggle.

"In the youth of the nation we have our greatest national asset. Even on a basis of mere expediency, we cannot afford not to develop this asset to the greatest advantage. It is the object of the present proposals to strengthen and inspire the younger generation. For it is as true to-day, as when it was first said, that 'the bulwarks of a city are its men.'"

The same emphasis on the fullest and richest development of the future citizen is found in the statement of aims in another of the pamphlets issued by the Australian Council for Educational Research, *A Plan for Australia* (1943), which reads as follows: "The school has failed, no matter what academic levels of attainment are attained, unless the final product of the school is an individual with a zeal for further knowledge, with a passion for truth-seeking, with some idea of how and where to look for truth, with a cooperative attitude towards his fellow-creatures, with a willingness to express himself and assume measures of responsibility, with the development of capacity for appreciation of the beautiful, and finally with some knowledge of how to lead a healthy life and to conduct his practical affairs."

The New Zealand Educational Institute, the largest teachers' organization in the Dominion, in discussions of the reconstruction of education which appeared in its journal, *National Education,* in 1943, defined the aims of education in the following terms: "In a well-functioning democracy, the will of the people should decide the pattern of their lives, a pattern which must be ever changing and ever approaching, however slowly, the ultimate ideal; within the framework of such a pattern it is surely the function of edu-

cation to evolve, from its present pattern and method, a system
which will in the future guarantee each child greater happiness,
greater opportunity to develop to the fullest extent his natural
talents, and greater ability to take his place as a citizen fully
equipped, physically, mentally, and morally, to enjoy and enhance
the rich inheritance so dearly bought for him by those who have
gone before, appreciating as he does both the privileges and the
responsibilities of such an inheritance."

The first chapter of a comprehensive report on the needs and
suggestions for the improvement of education published by the
Survey Commission of the Canada and Newfoundland Education
Association in 1943, closes with the statement that "along with
more generous budgets must come a keen and intelligent interest
in the effect of education on personality, a lively public concern
about the purposes of public education and a general conviction
that an efficient school leads to a better community, because it
will eventually consist of responsible, enterprising, and cooperative
citizens."

Similar statements could be quoted from the *Report on Educational Reform,* issued by the Federal Council of Teachers in Northern Ireland, and from the report on *Educational Reconstruction,*
issued by the Educational Institute of Scotland. A general summary of most of the statements on aims of education is implicit
in the following definition of the General Purpose of "The Program to be Provided" which appeared in the pamphlet of the
National Education Association *Proposals for Public Education in
Postwar America.* That General Purpose is "To provide for every
child, youth, and adult attending a public school, college, or
university the kind and amount of education which (a) will cause
him to live most happily and usefully according to the principles
of American democracy and (b) lead him to contribute all he can
to the development and preservation of a peaceful, cooperative,
and equitable world order."

## Equality of Opportunity as the Ideal

In studying these aims it should be noted that there is no mention of the claims of the state but rather a universal recognition

in the democracies concerned that the strength of the nation-state depends upon the character and intelligence of its citizens. Hence the emphasis upon the education of the individual as a human being responsible for his "self-direction and self-guidance" rather than upon education for submissive acceptance of the will of the state. The corollary of such statements of aims was the proposal to substitute for the traditional dual systems a system based upon the ideal of equality of educational opportunity.

The universal support for this ideal was a frank admission that so far as the organization of education was concerned the traditional dual system was far from being democratic. That tradition was based on the acceptance of class stratification and the differentiation of schools for the children of the masses and for the children whose parents were able to pay tuition fees or who were able to win scholarships to enter secondary schools. There were few countries outside the United States where more than 10 per cent of the adolescents were enrolled in any type of postprimary school. It was generally recognized that in order to implement the ideal of equality of educational opportunity a number of difficult problems would arise. It must be remembered, however, that the ideal and the practical issues involved had been discussed in many countries since World War I.

It was generally agreed that the differentiation between primary and postprimary education must take place at the age of eleven or twelve. More difficult was the question of types of postprimary schools to be provided. As long as the traditional secondary school was selective and its curriculum was academic, the enrollments could be kept down by admitting pupils capable of profiting by such a curriculum. The adoption of the principle of equality of educational opportunity, however, meant the provision of secondary education for all. The academic curriculum was not considered suitable for all boys and girls with a wider range of individual differences of ability and a greater diversity of educational and occupational needs. The solution of the problem that was widely accepted was to provide three major types of postprimary or secondary schools — the academic, the modern or general, and the technical.

The acceptance of the solution of the problem of types of postprimary schools raised still another question, which turned out to have more serious social and political implications. That question was how to devise a satisfactory method for distributing pupils into the types of schools best suited to their abilities. It was felt that examinations were unreliable as indicators of future development and that to determine at about the age of twelve the type of school that a boy or girl should enter was to decide their future careers prematurely. Two possible solutions were proposed: one was that the curriculum of all types of schools should be the same for the first two years of the courses, so that pupils could be transferred from one type to another better suited to their abilities; the other solution was to adopt the American practice and create comprehensive high schools, in which all types of courses would be offered.

So far as the pattern of education in the future was concerned there was unanimous agreement in all the plans for reconstruction. The implications of the ideal and the problems involved in implementing it in practice were not fully realized until the time for reorganizing some of the educational systems arrived. These and a number of other aspects of the question will be discussed in a later chapter. Whatever form the future organization will take — three secondary schools or one — the important point to be emphasized is that the undemocratic character of the dual system of education was recognized during World War II and that the ideal of providing equality of educational opportunity has been generally accepted and with it the realization that systems of education must be reorganized. Such reorganization would help all boys and girls to develop their abilities to the fullest and would in the end contribute to the progress of the nation of which they are citizens.

It is not inappropriate to summarize the position on the principle of equality of educational opportunity by quotations from two reports. They are as follows: "We believe that, in the best interests of the community as a whole, educational facilities should be provided to enable every individual to develop his or her capabilities to the greatest possible extent.

"Primary and secondary education should prepare the child to lead a useful life in the service of the community, and to carry out the tasks for which his natural talents best fit him; at the same

rate had not been anticipated so that the reduced number of class-rooms had to accommodate an increased number of pupils. These difficulties were further intensified by the shortage of teachers. Nevertheless, these difficulties will be overcome and the pattern that emerged during the war years will be the basis of the development of education in the second half of the present century. Even though it is not likely to come within the range of practical politics in many countries for some time, the important stage that has been reached is that the principle of equality of opportunity has been endorsed in so many plans for educational reconstruction. The principle has also been confirmed on an international basis — in 1946 by the International Conference on Public Instruction, convened by the International Bureau of Education in Geneva, and in 1948 in the United Nations Declaration of Human Rights and the subsequent Draft Conventions. It has also been included in the Constitution of the United Nations Educational, Scientific and Cultural Organization (UNESCO), which became effective on November 4, 1946.

The International Conference on Public Instruction, held in Geneva in 1946, adopted the following recommendations to be submitted to Ministries of Public Instruction of the member states of the International Bureau of Education:

"(1) Admission should depend, as it already does in many countries, more on the pupils' previous activity and on the teachers' reports than on the result of an examination bearing on knowledge or techniques acquired;

(2) In countries where secondary education is in principle compulsory, the distribution of pupils between the different types of teaching should be decided largely in the light of the systematic investigation of their aptitudes rather than primarily from the pupils' own preferences or those of their parents;

(3) A continuous system of guidance, particularly during the first few years of secondary education, should offer the pupil frequent possibilities of trial, choice and passage from one type of school to another;

(4) Such a system of guidance should be accompanied by a detailed examination of aptitudes, an examination conducted by

means of psychologically controlled observation and investigation directed more towards the study of mental processes than on the mere recording of correct results;

(5) The greatest importance should be attached to the granting of substantial financial aid to gifted but needy children; not merely by granting them free tuition, scholarships or monetary grants, but also by recouping the parents for the loss of possible wages earned by the children, by helping towards the cost of board and lodging, and by providing for these pupils access to sources of information and cultural enrichment not available in their ordinary environment;

(6) In cases where pupils are already in paid employment, facilities should be granted to them to follow courses, permitting them to complete their secondary education." [8]

The Draft Covenants on Human Rights include the following provisions on education in Article 13 of the section on Economic, Social and Cultural Rights:

"1. The State Parties to the Covenant recognize the right of everyone to education and recognize that education shall encourage the full development of human personality, the strengthening of respect for human rights and fundamental freedoms and the suppression of all incitement to racial and other hatred. . . .

2. It is understood

(a) That primary education shall be free and available free to all.

(b) That secondary education in its different forms, including technical and professional secondary education, shall be generally available and shall be made progressively free."

Finally, the creation of UNESCO was the consequence of the belief of the States members "in full and equal opportunities for education for all" as well as in promoting international cooperation for peace — accordingly, the Constitution of the United Nations Educational, Scientific and Cultural Organization (UNESCO) includes the following about its purposes and functions (Article I):

---

[8] International Bureau of Education, *Equality of Opportunity for Secondary Education* (Geneva, 1946), p. 47. By permission of P. Rossello, Directeur Adjoint.

"(b) Give fresh impulse to popular education and to the spread of culture by collaborating with Members, at their request, in the development of educational activities;

by instituting collaboration among the nations to advance the ideal of equality of opportunity without regard to race, sex, or any distinction, economic or social;

by suggesting educational methods best suited to prepare the children of the world for the responsibilities of freedom."

A few countries are already on the way to putting into practice the principle of equality of educational opportunity as one upon which the educational system of the United States has been based from the beginning of the Republic in theory and in practice progressively for the past century. But apart from the obstacles in the way that have already been mentioned, it must again be reiterated that the tempo of educational change is slow. It must be recalled that the principle of universal elementary education which was enunciated in the eighteenth century has not yet been firmly established in many parts of the world. Furthermore, the full implications of the principle have not yet been fully comprehended. Before the principle is established, even in those countries where it has already been accepted, there may be a long period of experimentation in the efforts to define the implications.

## REFERENCES

Gal, Roger. *La Réforme de l'Enseignement et les Classes Nouvelles.* Paris, 1946.

Kandel, I. L. *Education in an Era of Transition.* London, Evans Brothers, 1948.

——— ed. "Post-War Educational Reconstruction in the United Nations" *Educational Yearbook 1944,* of the International Institute of Teachers College, Columbia University. New York, 1944.

Lauwerys, J. A. and N. Hans, eds. *The Year Book of Education 1952.* London, Evans Brothers, 1952.

# 5

# Equalizing
## Educational Opportunities

### The Problem

The provision of equality of educational opportunities has been universally accepted as a basic principle of organization. The implications involved in this principle have, however, not been given full consideration. Discussions of the practical realization of the principle have concentrated more on the provision of secondary education for all and on the question whether such education should be provided in one school — the comprehensive or multilateral — or in three or more separate schools. The principle is more far-reaching than the issue of postprimary education. If the premises upon which it is based are examined, it becomes clear that genuine equality of educational opportunities must be considered at every level of education, from the preschool to the university.

The ideal of providing equality of opportunities for education became a problem of practical politics as the ideals of the emancipation of the individual and of freedom for the individual as an active member of his community were generally accepted. The acceptance of these ideas was gradual and the opposition of those already in enjoyment of the privileges of full membership in society had to be overcome. There was thoughout the nineteenth century a fear, which in some countries has not entirely disappeared, that increased educational opportunities would deprive a nation's economy of its labor supply and that the more educated the common man became the more he would become, as Bacon had already remarked three centuries earlier, *materia rerum novarum* ("material for subversive ideas").

## Historical Development

Proposals for the provision of equality of educational opportunities did not become general until the latter part of the eighteenth century. The Enlightenment with its emphasis on reason and the free play of individual thought together with the influence of natural laws and of the theory of man's unlimited perfectibility combined to merge the ideas on education with the social and political ideas of the times. The philosophy of natural rights included the right of the individual to the fullest development of his abilities through education. One of the earliest definitions of this right was the succinct statement of Rolland d'Erceville: *"Chacun doit être à portée de recevoir l'éducation qui lui est propre"* (1760), a principle cited on the title page of the report of the Consultative Committee of the English Board of Education on *Secondary Education* (1938). Talleyrand, Condorcet, and other leaders of French thought were ardent advocates of the ideal of extending educational opportunities to all in accordance with their abilities.[1]

The creation of an educational system based on the principle of equality of opportunities was even more widely discussed in the United States before the end of the eighteenth century.[2] It was generally implied that poverty should not be a bar to educational opportunities, provided the poor boy had the ability to profit by the only type of secondary education then offered, the classical. It was not long, however, before it was found necessary to offer

[1] See F. de la Fontainerie, *French Liberalism and Education in the Eighteenth Century* (New York, 1932).

[2] See A. O. Hansen, *Liberalism and American Education. Education in the Eighteenth Century* (New York, 1926).

new types of secondary school courses to meet the different abilities of the pupils. Although the ideal of equality of educational opportunities was accepted early in the United States, its realization and interpretation have been gradual.

In other countries any proposal in the nineteenth century based on the principle of equality would have been premature. In the first half of that century few countries except Prussia had yet even seriously considered the establishment of systems of compulsory elementary education. In so far as any effort to equalize the educational provisions for those able to pay fees for secondary education was concerned, internal reforms in content and methods and new types of secondary schools were introduced. The type of school that continued for a long time to enjoy prestige was that which offered the traditional classical curricula and prepared for entrance to the universities, until this monopoly was broken at the end of the nineteenth century by accepting graduates of modern types of secondary courses for admission to the universities.

The normal practice in most countries was to accept the fact of the existence of "two nations" and to build the educational system on that fact with one type of education for the privileged class of society and with another for the masses. The gradual development of industries stimulated a demand for workers with more than elementary education. This demand was met not by increasing opportunities for secondary education but by extending elementary education by the creation of *écoles primaires supérieures* in France, *Mittelschulen* in Germany, and higher grade schools in England. The division of classes was still further marked by the existence of fee-paying primary schools which gave special preparation for entrance to secondary schools (*Vorschulen* in Germany, *classes préparatoires* in France, and preparatory schools in England). There was in the acceptance of this situation an assumption that ability for intellectual activities and leadership in national affairs was to be found only in the upper classes; occasionally a small number of poor boys of ability would be selected from the masses and awarded scholarships to proceed from the elementary to a secondary school.

The dual system had two consequences. The first was that access to positions of social, political, and economic influence — to the directive classes — was in the vast majority of cases open to a limited group only. The second consequence was the psychological effect upon the minds of certain social strata, so clearly described in the statement by M. Henri Laugier (p. 49), that they refused to believe that the new educational opportunities created in France in 1931 were open to them. In this study, *Social Progress and Educational Waste* (London, 1926), Kenneth Lindsay pointed out that in some underprivileged areas in England fewer pupils were candidates for the scholarship examinations than in better neighborhoods, that even when they were successful parents refused to accept the opportunities for their children, and that in any case fewer scholarship awards were won in such areas.

In both France and England it was clear that the opportunity for education beyond the level of elementary schools depended upon the accident of residence as well as on family circumstances, which were as much psychological as economic. This condition may be contrasted with the American attitude described by the authors of *Middletown:* "If education is sometimes taken for granted by the business class, it is no exaggeration to say that it evokes the fervor of a religion, a means of salvation, among a large section of the population." [3]

Because of the existence of the psychological attitude described in England and France, and side by side with it fear on the part of those already in enjoyment of educational privileges, of a reduction of the supply of "manual workers, artisans, agricultural laborers," and of increased competition for directive positions, proposals for the reconstruction of the educational systems were either ignored or implemented in instalments. And even when partial reforms were introduced, as, for example, the conversion of the last years of the elementary school into "senior schools" following the recommendations of the report on the *Education of the Adolescent* (1926), they continued to constitute part of the elementary education system. In France the proposals were put into effect piecemeal with an attempt in the early twenties to reduce such variety of opportunities as existed in the secondary school by making Latin and Greek compulsory for all pupils. The attempt failed and the foundations of the dual system were slowly undermined,

[3] Robert S. and Helen M. Lynd, *Middletown* (New York, 1929), p. 187.

by abolishing the special status of the *classes préparatoires,* by abolishing fees for secondary education, and by introducing guidance classes to help pupils select the curriculum best suited to their abilities.

## Implications of the Principle of Equality

While the proposals to reorganize systems of education completely so as to give reality to the ideal of equality of educational opportunities were nowhere carried out, they were kept constantly in the foreground. World War II gave a new impetus to those who supported the proposals. The general tenor of the plans for reconstruction was discussed in the preceding chapter, but not what is involved in putting the proposals into practice. The basic problem which is arousing serious controversy is to discover methods of allocating pupils on completing the common primary education to the type of postprimary school or course best suited to their abilities and aptitudes. This is not only a technical but a social problem on account of the prestige so long enjoyed by the traditional academic secondary education. There is, as a result of this prestige, a tendency on the part of parents to look upon any other type of secondary education as an inferior substitute. In view of these facts the organization of an educational system, if it is to do justice to each pupil according to his abilities and aptitudes, must make provision for a system of guidance. The function of a guidance system is to help in placing each pupil in the school or course best suited to him and to provide adequate evidence to parents of the soundness of whatever advice is indicated by the techniques employed.

The problem was clearly recognized in 1920 by Sir Graham Balfour as the central task of the educational administrator, which he described as follows: "To enable the right pupils to receive the right education from the right teachers, at a cost within the means of the state, under conditions which will enable the pupils best to profit by their training." In 1937 the French Minister of Education, M. Jean Zay, in explaining to the Chamber of Deputies the motives for issuing the decree for the creation of guidance classes (*classes d'orientation*) in a few secondary schools, said: "This has always impressed itself upon the attention of educators — to place the individual who is appropriate in the position appropriate to him is not only a condition of well-being for the individual and guarantee of stability for society. It is also demanded by social justice."

The reconstruction of an educational system so as "to make a ladder from the gutter to the university along which any child may climb," as Huxley proposed, and the abolition of fees do not in fact remove all the barriers to educational opportunities. This has long been recognized in England and Scotland, as, for example, by the provision of meals for necessitous children and later to other children whose parents could pay for them, and by medical inspection and treatment, both of which reach all boys and girls in school up to the age of eighteen; in addition, books and clothing may be supplied to those who need them. The importance of the health of the school child and of the relations between educational progress and social background was in fact noted in some of the proposals for educational reconstruction.

The report of the Scottish Educational Institute on Educational Reconstruction included the broadest and most significant discussion of the vital relationship between educational opportunities and health and social background. The discussion paid attention to housing, malnutrition, want, insecurity, unemployment, and the decline of spiritual influences and their effects upon the child and its educational progress. The statement runs as follows: "The question of the 'Health of the School Child' must not be limited to considerations of bodily welfare, but must be taken to include mental, moral, and spiritual health. . . . The more completely one views the child the more it must be realised how important is the social background — how important the environment provided by the community no less than the home. All efforts toward educational reconstruction are doomed to frustration unless accompanied by reform of the social conditions under which many children live. Too long have teachers, doctors, and psychologists labored to heal damaged bodies, to restore warped minds, and to undo bad habits *after* children came to school, when the seeds of disease, mental illness, or juvenile delinquency have already been sown. . . . A great deal is heard these days about equality of educational opportunity, but merely to open the doors of all schools to all pupils will not in itself provide equality. That will depend upon the social background."

Another important contribution toward the provision of genuine equality of opportunities is the provision of compensation to parents for the loss of wages if their children continued in school. This compensation may take the form of maintenance grants or *bourses d'entretien*. Much may also be done to equalize conditions in the provision of recreational facilities, and extracurricular activities, the cost of which has been described as "hidden tuition costs" in American high schools which either deprive poorer pupils of their opportunities or else impose a burden on their families. Perhaps more consideration should also be given to providing in each school quiet places for study and for the preparation of homework which is often rendered difficult when family conditions are such that a quiet corner is not available at home.

In the current movement more is involved than providing easier access to educational opportunities by the abolition of fees. Equality of conditions can never be attained, as has already been demonstrated in the Communist-dominated country, since individuals differ in physical and intellectual capacity and in social and cultural backgrounds. Nevertheless it is now generally accepted that, so far as society can achieve it, more attention should be devoted to ensuring a healthy start for children, providing for all an environment that will promote healthy growth — physically, intellectually, and socially — and facilitating continued education, as far as talent and ability justify it, by the provision both of maintenance grants and suitable conditions for study. But even with these provisions other aspects of the problem of equalizing educational opportunities within the schools must be considered.

## PRIMARY EDUCATION

### The Elementary School Tradition

The gradual development of systems of compulsory elementary education in a little more than a century is rightly considered to be a great step in the progress of education. Certain traditions have, however, grown up around elementary education which must be eliminated if equality of educational opportunity is to be provided. In most countries of the world elementary education has meant a type of education rather than a stage in what should be a continuous process. Except in the United States the elementary school has been looked upon as an institution for the children of the "lower" or "poorer" or "working" classes. The task of the elementary school was to impart the elements of an education and frequently the pupils acquired little else than the tools of learning with content that had little meaning for them. The elementary school was not regarded as a stage in which the foundations were to be laid for further education and continuous development — aesthetic, physical, moral, and intellectual — of the pupils. Attendance in a public elementary school implied not only that the pupils belonged to a certain social class but that for the large majority education would be completed on leaving the elementary school, since the chances of transfer to a secondary school were minimal, even for the very able.

There was in fact no articulation or "end-on" connection between the elementary and secondary school. Each type of school constituted a separate system differing in almost every element that makes up a school organization — buildings and playgrounds, size of classes, textbooks and equipment, methods of instruction, preparation and status of teachers, and public esteem. With rare exceptions elementary and secondary schools were intended to cater to pupils coming from different social classes and environments, physical and cultural, and differed also in both educational and social aims. There prevailed an assumption that pupils in elementary schools went as far as their abilities permitted and that intellectual ability was confined to the upper classes except for an occasional boy or girl who might be discovered in the elementary school to have outstanding ability and be awarded a scholarship to a secondary school.

### National Economy and Education

Changes not so much in the status of elementary schools as in their aims, content, and methods of instruction were introduced more rapidly in countries with an industrial than in those with an agricultural economy. Industrialization, which led to the factory system and large-scale manufacture, promoted the growth of urban centres. The rise of labor unions developed an interest on the part of workers in their own status and in the education of their children. The political emancipation of the working classes as well as the needs of industry for better educated workers and foremen contributed to an improvement of elementary education and the provision of higher elementary schools.

The situation in countries with an agricultural economy or even in the rural areas of countries with an industrial economy was improved, but far more slowly. While in industrialized countries urbanization made it possible to establish large school buildings easily accessible to large numbers of pupils and facilitating their appropriate classification, in the agricultural countries sparsity of population and distances, lack of good means of communication and transportation as well as inadequately prepared teachers retarded the extension of school opportunities of any kind over a large part of the world or limited the opportunities to elementary education only. To the retarding influences other difficulties can be added, such as the common practice of using the labor of young children, the absence of public support or even resistance from public opinion, and in most cases the failure to adapt the curriculum to the environment with which the pupils are familiar. Under these conditions there can be no equality of educational opportunity for rural children as compared with urban. To some extent the differences may be compensated for by the creation of consolidated schools, but even these must wait on improvement of roads and means of transportation and especially change in public attitude.

The enactment of laws for compulsory school attendance has been widespread throughout the world. Nevertheless laws may be on the statute books but their enforcement may be neglected, as may be gathered from the study of statistics of illiteracy in many parts of the world. Laws are frequently passed before schools are made available or before there is accommodation in existing schools. Attendance may not be adequately enforced or may be unsatisfactory because of bad weather, distances, or ill health.

What has happened in many countries which enacted compulsory education laws relatively recently may to some extent be witnessed in the more advanced countries as a result of the unanticipated increase in the birth rate following World War II. Under such conditions children in over-large classes often taught by inadequately prepared or overburdened teachers are deprived of their right to equality of educational opportunity.

## Vestigial Remains

The history of the elementary school has left certain vestiges that militate against the realization of the ideal of equality of educational opportunities unless removed. It is no depreciation of the contribution made to public welfare and progress by elementary education in the past century to examine these vestiges. Of these the first, which has already been mentioned, is the survival of the idea that elementary school is a type rather than a stage in the education of children and youth. The derogatory reference in France to *l'esprit primaire* succinctly expresses the qualitative difference between elementary and secondary education — the former loading the minds of pupils with a small quantum of information, the latter training them to deal with ideas. To this must be added the social distinction between the two. The implication of both the qualitative and the social distinction is that the elementary school pupils are trained to become adjusted to their environment, while the pupils in the secondary schools are trained as the potential leaders.

A further consequence of these differences is the survival of the notion that young children can be instructed in large classes, while the secondary school pupils, needing more individual attention, can only be taught in small classes. This notion is based on unsound psychological premises and on the traditional practice of providing elementary education at as cheap a price as possible. Because the size of classes was large in the elementary schools the character both of methods of instruction and of discipline differed from those in the secondary schools. It need cause no surprise that the few pupils who were successful in securing scholarships to transfer to secondary schools found it difficult for some time to adjust themselves to the new methods of instruction and of study.

Further, partly because of the prevailing theory of elementary education and the content of instruction, and partly for financial reasons, a difference was maintained in the preparation, remuneration, and status of elementary and secondary school teachers. That difference was carried still further and influenced the preparation of each group in the notion that an elementary school teacher should know how to teach and a secondary school teacher should have a mastery of what to teach. Thus the distinctions which derived from the dual system of education were carried into the teaching profession and affected the esteem in which each group was held by the public.

Finally, the narrow concept of the purpose of elementary education left its mark on the work of the elementary school in most countries. The emphasis was placed upon intellectual or mental training; the training of the emotions, except by indirection, was almost completely neglected. Intellectual training was justified in the belief that knowledge is power and that the mind trained in acquiring knowledge of any kind would be able to cope with new situations. Physical training, like mental training, was narrow, rigid, and formal, while aesthetic training was generally limited to learning a few songs and memorizing a few poems without necessarily understanding what they meant.

In general the permanent stamp left on elementary education everywhere has been that the primary task is to disseminate literacy, an aim whose survival is illustrated by the movements in the so-called backward countries to liquidate illiteracy. This is based on the assumption that a people able to read would become intelligent citizens and workers. The inadequacy of this assumption and the need of a broader approach to elementary education from the social and economic points of view have been demonstrated by UNESCO's support for the theory of "fundamental education." [4]

The value and importance of literacy as an essential aim of sound

---

[4] See UNESCO publications: *Fundamental Education: Common Ground for All Peoples* (1947); *Fundamental Education: A Description and Programme* (1949) and *Quarterly Bulletin of Fundamental Education* (1949–    ).

education cannot be denied. In any consideration of the obstacles in the way of realizing the ideal of equality of educational opportunities the failure to raise the standards of taste and the interests through the dissemination of literacy cannot be disregarded. Sir Richard Livingstone stressed the importance of taking account of this failure in the first paragraph of his book, *The Future of Education*. To this should be added the fact that to teach people to read without training them in critical ability to analyse what is read is to place a formidable weapon in the hands of propagandists. This has happened in the U.S.S.R., which have pointed with pride to the rapid liquidation of illiteracy, while the use made of the newly acquired literacy for propaganda purposes is never mentioned. But the utilization of literacy as an instrument of propaganda outside totalitarian regimes is not unknown. The failure to raise standards of taste and to create new interests resulted from an emphasis on the mechanics of reading instead of an intelligent and critical reading of content, which would have the double effect of helping to raise standards and to protect against propaganda.

### Transition from the Old to the New

At the beginning of the present century a transformation of the elementary school began. But change from the old to the new is always slow in education, partly because parents prefer that their children should have the same education as they have had, and partly because teachers tend to get set in routine practices. The change was brought about in the main by the new developments in psychology and child study. There resulted a realization that the child is not a miniature adult but has interests appropriate to each stage of growth and that the development of each individual is continuous and does not proceed from one distinct stage to another. Two consequences followed: first, the approach was shifted from the adult point of view to one that took into account the interests of the child in a particular environment; and, secondly, education was recognized to be a continuous process, differing only as the abilities of each individual vary. Both consequences have an important bearing on the realization of the ideal of equality of educational opportunities. They help to undermine the notion of organizing an educational system on the basis of types instead of stages, and they stress the importance of adapting an educational program to the abilities and aptitudes of each pupil as an essential aspect of equalizing opportunities for education. From the point of view of organization elementary education could no longer be regarded as a type of education intended for the masses; instead it was given its rightful place as the *primary* stage in a continuous process. This was recognized in England, for example, when the Consultative Committee followed up its enquiry into *Primary Education* (1931) with one on *Infants and Nursery Schools* (1933).[5] In France M. Jean Zay as Minister of National Education was responsible, shortly before the outbreak of World War II, for an important change of terminology — *l'enseignement élémentaire* became *l'enseignement du premier degré*. The names of divisions in the Ministry in charge of each stage changed correspondingly. The changes in terminology in England and France represent installments resulting from the movement for "secondary education for all" in one country and for *l'école unique* in the other. The stage was set for the reconstruction of the educational systems to give effect to the ideal of equality of educational opportunities.

### The School and Social Services

More is involved, however, in this movement than facilitating access from primary school to some form of secondary education. A system of education must provide such services as will enable pupils to derive the greatest benefit which they are capable to receive from their attendance at school. Pupils who come to school hungry or suffering from malnutrition, or who are inadequately clothed, cannot profit from membership in the school, either socially or scholastically. Pupils who are in poor health, or whose hearing and vision are not normal, are handicapped in their scholastic progress. The objection to the extension of the services of the school

---

[5] The full implication of this does not appear to have been noticed, for in 1937 the *Handbook of Suggestions for the Consideration of Teachers and Others Concerned in the Work of Public Elementary Schools,* the older terminology is retained.

beyond its traditional function and that the feeding, clothing, and care of the health of children should be left to the home is as valid as the objection that their education should be left to the parents. Since a close relationship has been found between physical condition and school progress, it is obviously a waste of public funds to maintain schools for a purpose whose achievement is rendered impossible by conditions beyond the control of the schools. The social services provided in a school system have their place because they contribute to equalizing educational opportunities.

The attention devoted to the education of young children of preschool age has been stimulated as much by the aim of providing equality of opportunity by giving all children a healthy start in life as by educational considerations. The nomenclature "nursery school," more than the French equivalent *l'école maternelle,* conveys the idea that its function is to provide for the young child of the underprivileged classes the same kind of environment as that enjoyed by the children of the privileged in their nurseries at home. Not only does the nursery school represent the recognition of the importance of a good environment in a program for equalizing opportunities, but it serves as an excellent medium for enlisting the interest and cooperation of the home and for educating mothers in the care of young children.

## Instruction and Class Size

Reference has already been made to the relationship between size of class and methods of instruction as well as discipline. The large class with more than thirty pupils is likely to encourage mass instruction to the neglect of individual differences. The shift which has taken place in the last few decades from the subject to the child can have meaning only in the opportunity given the teacher to become acquainted with the aptitudes and abilities of each child and to adapt methods of instruction accordingly. To educate the whole child or to promote the fullest development of personality is impossible without a thorough understanding of the child. From this point of view the shift from the subject to the child must be considered as an element in the realization of equality of opportunity.

The provision of equality of educational opportunities cannot accordingly be limited to providing secondary education for all. The whole system of education must be inspired by the ideal. So far as the primary school is concerned a broader concept of its aims than imparting a fixed quantity of knowledge is essential. Greater attention should be given to the abilities and interests of each pupil as a person as well as to his whole development — emotional, physical, and moral — no less than intellectual. The pupil must be an active participant in the learning process rather than a passive recipient of the content presented by the teacher. Active participation implies that the pupil understands the meaning of what he is studying.

The task of the teacher has changed at the same time and makes greater demands upon him than the traditional practices. With the gradual abandonment of the connotation of elementary education as a class institution and its recognition as a stage in a continuous process, it follows that the status of primary teachers must be improved both in general and in professional preparation. Since the teacher must know his pupils as individuals and since content must be related to the environment in its broadest sense, the traditional type of training must be abandoned in favor of genuine professional preparation. To raise the standards of the preparation of primary school teachers would be a necessary corollary to the change in the status of the primary school as the first stage in a continuous process of education. While this change in status is an important aspect in the reconstruction of educational systems on the principle of equality of educational opportunities, it should be clear from the discussion up to this point that within the primary schools there may still remain some barriers to be removed before equality of opportunity for every pupil is realized.

## SECONDARY EDUCATION

### Types of Schools and Courses

The most crucial problem in the movement to equalize educational opportunities arises from the difficulties of determining the nature of education at the secondary or postprimary level. The age of compulsory school attendance has already been raised in many countries. There is general agreement that primary education should continue to the age of eleven or twelve, and that it should be followed by some form of secondary education. It is at this point that the most serious difficulties arise on account of the traditional concept of secondary education which persists in the minds of parents, the public in general, and many members of the teaching profession.

Since special privileges have been associated with the completion, in whole or in part, of the secondary school curriculum, the connotation of the term "secondary education" came to be limited to a particular curriculum — the academic. The certificates or diplomas awarded at the end of the secondary school course acquired an exaggerated value, because those obtaining them were entitled to be admitted to universities or other institutions of higher education or to some special grades of employment in public or private services. Schools that prepared pupils for the certificate or diploma examinations were preferred by parents to other schools whose curriculum might be better suited to the abilities and aptitudes of their children. Other types of secondary education than the academic were considered by parents and public alike as inferior substitutes. This attitude, which has been referred to as "inverted snobbery," has militated against diversification of education for pupils of the age range in secondary schools.[6]

The overemphasis on certificates and privileges, which reflects social and economic ambition rather than educational principles, has complicated the problem of diversification most seriously. Equality of educational opportunities has come to be confused with identity of opportunities, as though all pupils could be expected to profit equally from the same type of education. Social equalitarianism seriously affects proposals to provide some form of secondary education adapted to the ages, abilities, and aptitudes of the pupils. The arguments against diversification of courses or schools vary. It is argued, for example, that the traditional dual system of education with one type for the masses and another for a selected minority prevented the development of common understanding between

[6] I. L. Kandel, "Inverted Snobbery and the Problem of Secondary Education in New Zealand," *Studies in Education* (Wellington, 1937), No. 2.

different social classes. It is objected in another argument that it is too early at the age of eleven or twelve to determine the abilities and aptitudes of pupils and to assign them to a course by which their future careers would be determined. In order to equalize educational opportunities it is accordingly proposed that all boys and girls on completing the primary school course continue their educational careers in a common (comprehensive or multilateral) secondary school, where all would follow a common course up to a certain point after which they could begin their specialization according to their abilities and aptitudes. The model cited for this plan is the American comprehensive high school without taking into account the fact that the difficulties of assigning pupils to the courses best suited to them have not been overcome. Nor are the criticisms considered that the American high school caters to the average to the neglect of those pupils who are above or below the average.

The task of reorganizing school systems "to enable the right pupil to receive the right education from the right teacher" or "to place the individual who is appropriate in the position appropriate to him" [7] is not an easy one. That the education of all potential citizens and members of society who will be called upon to participate in certain common duties and who will enjoy common rights should be directed to this end is obvious. At the same time, however, different types of courses should be provided to meet the requirements of individual differences of abilities among the pupils. The issue, then, is whether the provision of differentiated courses is likely to be more effective in one school or in separate schools dedicated to a specific function. This does not mean that strict and rigid differentiation or specialization must begin at the age of transfer to the secondary school at about the age of twelve. At this age only a rough estimate of the special abilities of pupils is possible and then not on the basis of a single examination but of a cumulative record card continued through the primary school years, and objective and intelligence tests.

## The Allocation of Pupils

The technical problem of discovering differences in abilities be-

[7] See pages 92f.

tween those who can profit from an academic course — linguistic-literary or mathematical-scientific — or from some more modern or practical course is admittedly not simple. Errors may be made in allocating pupils to courses best adapted to their abilities, but they may be corrected by adequate provision for the transfer of pupils to the course appropriate for them, when necessary. Such errors may occur even in the single comprehensive high school, as American experience has shown. The traditional practice permitted pupils to discover through failure that they did not have the requisite ability for a course that they chose. Probably a large number of parents would still prefer to follow this trial-and-error principle. A program of providing equality of educational opportunities cannot be carried out in this principle of *caveat alumnus*. The fundamental principle that should be followed, if equality of opportunities means the provision of the right education for the right pupil under the right teacher, is to discover what a pupil can do and help him to do it.

The heart of the modern problem is to be found in the development of adequate systems of guidance and of appropriate techniques for conducting it successfully. More important perhaps and more difficult than putting the fundamental principle and a system of guidance into practice is the task of convincing parents of the soundness of any professional advice that may be offered them about the education of their children. In France, for example, the question of how the results of the experimental guidance classes, introduced by M. Jean Zay shortly before World War II, might be used in advising parents almost became a political issue. Parents insisted that they alone had the right to determine the kind of education that their children should have.

One important aspect of the whole problem of providing equality of educational opportunities is sometimes overlooked. A system of guidance may serve not only to assist pupils to take the course best suited to their abilities and aptitudes but also to help parents to understand the opportunities for careers for their children. The social and cultural values of education cannot be ignored, nor can vocational ambitions be left out of consideration. The provision of secondary education for all cannot be altogether divorced from a consideration of the absorptive capacity of a nation's economy. This aspect of the problem was discussed as early as the sixteenth century by Richard Mulcaster in his *Positions* (1581), and in the next century by Bacon in his *Advice to the King Touching Mr. Sutton's Estate,* and by Cardinal Richelieu in his *Testament Politique* (1640). Lost sight of for nearly three centuries, the problem began to claim attention in a number of European countries because of the number of unemployed university graduates.[8] This aspect has not been fully taken into account in discussions of secondary education. Overproduction whether for professions or for occupations can become as serious a menace to national stability and morale as overproduction in industry and agriculture. It is consequently of vital importance for the welfare of both society and the individual to bear in mind the opportunities for employment open to young men and women who have completed their secondary or university education. The guidance of youth is accordingly concerned with the general education appropriate to their abilities and with the vocational preparation best suited to their aptitudes and interests.

## Equality and Curriculum

The chief difficulty in expanding the opportunities for secondary education lies in the notion, already mentioned, that such education is for the improvement of social status and leads to protected or guaranteed careers with security of tenure and security in old age. Secondary education was traditionally associated not only with certain occupations but with the study of certain subjects which in turn were regarded as preparatory to white-collar or black-coat jobs. As a consequence the idea of differentiated types of secondary schools with curricula different from the traditional is rejected as offering inferior substitutes. Objective evidence is available, but is rarely published, that would indicate the number of pupils who leave the academic secondary school at the earliest possible opportunity without completing even the first stage of the courses, and of others who continue to the end and fail in the final examinations. French educational literature contains frequent references to *non-valeurs,* while the statistics of the *baccalauréat* ex-

[8] See Walter M. Kotschnig, *Unemployment in the Learned Professions* (New York, 1937).

aminations indicate not only a large number of failures but also of repeaters. The statistics of the results of the school and higher school certificate examinations in England also reveal a large percentage of pupils for whom the traditional curricula were unsuitable. It was evidence of this kind (retardation, elimination, and mortality) that directed attention to the need of greater variety and flexibility in the provision of curricula in the American high school in the first decade of the present century.

The provision of equality of educational opportunities means that the differences in the abilities and aptitudes of the pupils must be considered and that different types of courses should be offered to meet these. The first task is to discover what a pupil can do and help him to do it. This does not mean, of course, that the pupil should be allowed to do what he wants but that whatever abilities he reveals should be developed as far as possible. At the same time, however, education is a social process, provided and maintained by society to ensure certain common ends. Beyond that it must be remembered that, besides being a citizen of a particular nation, each individual is also a human being — heir not only to a particular culture, but also to the culture of humanity. In the present era of uncertainty and unrest, when the world is again menaced by the resurgence of a narrow spirit of nationalism, the last point needs special emphasis. The history of human culture has been the history of cross-fertilization with national cultures profiting from each other's contributions.

### Education and Social Unity

The provision of equality of educational opportunities requires the adaptation of the secondary school courses to individual differences of abilities. From the social point of view, however, it is equally important to impart a foundation of common understanding to all. The promotion of social unity in so far as it can be achieved by a common curriculum should not be neglected and differentiation or specialization should be introduced gradually. A common curriculum, however, does not mean an identical or uniform curriculum for all, but the study of the same general areas that will contribute toward a common language of discourse but with content and methods of instruction adapted to the abilities of the pupils.

The common basis of the content should be determined by the fact that the individual is not only a worker but also a citizen, the member of a family, participant in a great variety of organizations, exposed to the appeal of a great variety of interests, and a human being. With the rapid mechanization of most occupations the amount of training to be provided can be given in a very short time. To this should be added the gradual reduction of the hours of labor, leaving a large amount of leisure time to be usefully employed. The duty of the school at all levels is not merely to build an education on the basis of the pupils' interests but to start with these interests and to make them over into interests that are likely to be enduring. The task can, of course, never be completed during the school days of any individual, but a foundation can be laid upon which a program of adult education can later be built.

### A Liberal Education

The common element in all types of courses, whether offered in one school or in more, should be the imparting of a liberal education. Like the term "secondary education," the term "liberal education" acquired a particular connotation, associated in part with the knowledge of certain subjects and in part with a social class or with social status. Liberal education is generally contrasted with practical or vocational education, a contrast which goes as far back as Aristotle and which was later re-enforced, when the subjects that were assumed to be the essential marks of a liberal education were required for entrance into the white-collar or black-coat occupations as well as into the liberal professions.

It is increasingly recognized, however, that a liberal education does not necessarily mean the knowledge of certain subjects, but rather certain habits of mind, certain attitudes, a certain sense of responsibility, and breadth of interests — personal and social. The contrast between academic and practical education can no longer be maintained, for the academic fails if it is not practical in the sense of informing character and conduct and of stimulating living interests, while the practical becomes merely a training in mechanical skills unless some ideas and some appreciation of ends and means and concepts of social relevance emerge from the training. Academic education is frequently criticized as bookish, but it is not academic education that is at fault so much as the fact that what is taught in its name is not related to living interests and is not given meaning in terms of the contemporary world of the learners.

Hitherto the differential of the traditional secondary school curriculum was the study of foreign languages, ancient or modern. When secondary school opportunities are made universal, the question arises whether all pupils should learn foreign languages or whether they can profit by studying them. If the essence of a liberal education is the cultivation of living interests common to all in order that all shall share in the common cultural heritage and so develop some common understanding, an entirely different approach must be made.

It is clear that all pupils should acquire an adequate mastery of their own language — ability to express themselves clearly, ability to read with understanding, and ability to appreciate their literature. They should have an understanding of the world in which they live — its history and geography and some of the economic, social, and political issues of their day. Increasingly the world in which the present generation is growing up demands that all pupils acquire an understanding of their physical environment, of the influence of science and technology on the life of man, and of those aspects of science that affect daily living. Similarly, a knowledge of some mathematics and its uses in the everyday conduct of affairs is coming to be regarded as an essential equipment of an educated person. Physical education has acquired a new position of importance both because of its value for physical well-being and because of the close interplay between health and physical well-being, on the one hand, and scholastic progress on the other. Finally, the educative as well as the social value of music and the arts and crafts has at last been accepted and the subjects are recognized as essential aspects of life and of a liberal education, and not merely as useful pastimes for the intelligent use of leisure.

A concept of liberal education is here suggested which can be made the common foundation of secondary education for all. There would, of course, still have to be some differentiations in content and methods of instruction in accordance with the abilities of the pupils, but at least all will be given access to a share in the common heritage. The traditional concept of a liberal education in terms primarily of the study of foreign languages is thus abandoned. Such study would undoubtedly have its place but not in the common core of the education imparted to all.

It is not out of place in this connection to cite the following definition of a liberal education: "A liberal education then can only be conceived of, as it has always been, as an education that emancipates and liberalizes men. A truly liberal education implies, then, an understanding of the world in which one lives, cultivation of breadth of interests, training in ability to educate one's self, development of capacity for judgment, acquisition of standards of right and wrong, stimulation to a readiness to work and co-operate with others, and initiation into the art of living. It does not set up artificial barriers between education for work and education for leisure. And, finally, a liberal approach to education will refuse to tolerate any longer that distinction which goes back to Aristotle between an education for the masses and an education for the classes. If it is truly liberal such an education will be looked upon as one continuous whole inspired throughout by the spirit of liberty and the ideals of democracy which recognizes the equality of all individuals before God and before man, allowing only for differences of capacity, but seeking to give to each a share in the common purposes of life, moral and religious, material and spiritual, in accordance with his capacities." [9]

## One School or Three?

The last few words of this quotation — "in accordance with his capacities" — constitute the core of the problem of creating a system of education to carry out the ideal of equality of opportunities. They imply not *selection* but rather the *distribution* of pupils to types of schools or courses in the light of what can be discovered about their abilities and aptitudes. They also raise the question of the type of organization of secondary or postprimary schools ap-

[9] *Report of the Committee Appointed to Enquire into the System of Secondary Education in Jamaica*, p. 15. The writer served as chairman of the Committee in 1943.

propriate to the different types of abilities among the pupils. The issue, put simply, is whether to have one school for all, like the comprehensive high school in the United States or the omnibus school in Scotland or the multilateral school proposed in England, which offers a variety of types of courses in the same institution, or whether to have several types of courses in separate institutions each offering a specific type of course — academic, general, or technical.

The advocates of one school for all adolescent pupils argue that attendance in the same institution would break down class distinctions of the kind that were perpetuated by the existence of separate types of schools. It is claimed further that, if all types of courses — academic, general, technical or any other that may be offered — are available in the same school, they would enjoy equal repute and help to destroy the privileged status enjoyed by the traditional academic course; all courses and teachers would enjoy parity of esteem. A third argument is that the transfer of pupils from the course not suited to their abilities to one more appropriate would be facilitated and the number of failures and maladjustments would be reduced, particularly since the allocation of pupils to appropriate courses in the same school would be simplified. Finally, it is especially emphasized that the organization of secondary education with a single school is more democratic, does not raise distinctions as to status, and can more successfully contribute than separate schools to the development of common social understanding. In particular, class and intellectual distinction, it is said, would be eliminated, if all children of all social classes and of every level of intelligence capable of profiting from secondary education attended the same school. The last argument follows from the objection that the traditional organization of separate schools, of which one enjoyed a greater social esteem than the others, catered to an élite and that such an élite is selected either because of the ability of parents to pay the fees and bear the cost of prolonged maintenance of their children while in school, or because of intellectual ability which enables pupils from the less privileged classes to gain scholarships.

This objection is not new in the discussions of the ideal of equality of educational opportunities. It was met most cogently in a forceful speech by Edouard Herriot in a debate on education in the French Chamber of Deputies in 1931, when he stressed the need of an élite in a democracy in the following words: "Not only do we believe that aristocracies of mind are needed, but we say definitely that no regime needs these aristocracies of mind more than a republic. The more a country is inspired by the spirit of liberty, the more there must be encouraged the training not only of intelligence but of character, capable later to order, dominate, and even at certain times give directions to others. What we desire is that this search for élites be carried on by natural selections and not by selection by chance . . . I am convinced that we are defending the interests of the nation which has too great a need of all the forces not to permit the children of the humblest origin to attain to full knowledge, to general culture not by the chance of a scholarship but by normal system of selection. Democracy is not the regime which reduces all men to the same level and to the lowest level; it is a regime which allows every child to rise without ever encountering any obstacles to the point where his labor and ambition will lead him." [10]

The arguments in favor of the comprehensive secondary school are inspired by social and political motives or are doctrinaire assumptions based on unverified information about the American high schools. The failure of these high schools to achieve any of the results that are claimed from the single school whether in promoting common understanding between different social groups or in providing a preparation for an élite is ignored. There is no reference to the studies that show how strongly the activities of the high schools are affected by the social origins of the pupils. [11] Finally, the influences that determine social, political, and economic attitudes after school days are over are omitted from consideration. Whether the effects of subsequent social stratification can be offset by educating all the children of all classes in the same school is doubtful, but that the attempt would be made at a sacrifice of the right education for the right pupil is indicated by the American experience. On this Dr. James Bryant Conant, formerly President

[10] Translated from the quotation of the address in H. Ducos, *Pourquoi l'Ecole Unique?* (Paris, 1932), pp. 40 f.
[11] See page 49 for reference to such studies.

of Harvard University, wrote as follows: "For there is no doubt that the use of our public schools consciously or unconsciously to keep our society 'democratic' and fluid presents us with an educational dilemma. The more we try to employ the instrument of universal education to offset these forces of social stratification inherent in family life, the more we jeopardize the training of certain types of individuals. In particular, we tend to overlook the especially gifted youth. We neither find him early enough, nor guide him properly, nor educate him adequately in our high schools." Accordingly he suggested the need of an organization to "take some dramatic action to demonstrate a vigorous interest in the gifted boy or girl." [12]

There has, in fact, been a belated recognition in the United States that the comprehensive high school is "too fast for the slow and too slow for the fast," that it caters to the average, and that the needs of the gifted and dull pupils are not being met. It must be noted, however, that the process of selection is much longer in the United States than elsewhere. There is a screening of high school graduates for admission to the four-year college, and a further screening of college graduates who wish to undertake graduate studies.

Whatever organization — with a single school or with several schools — may be adopted, an important advance is promised in the acceptance of the ideal of equality of educational opportunities. The provision of secondary education for all will require further research to discover techniques for the discovery of the abilities and aptitudes of the pupils at the point of transfer from the primary to the secondary schools. The purpose of such techniques is not to *select* pupils but to *distribute* them to the type of education best suited to their abilities.

Before turning to an account of the present situation in secondary education in the countries discussed in this book one other difficulty in realizing the ideal of equality of educational opportunities needs to be mentioned. The barriers to such equality in rural areas have been discussed in relation to primary education. A possible solution that was then suggested would be the consolidation

[12] James Bryant Conant, *Education in a Divided World* (Cambridge, Harvard University Press, 1949), pp. 64 and 228 f. By permission of the publisher.

of small schools. The provision of secondary education may be met in this way, but in view of the expense it becomes clear that the areas of administration must be larger than they have been in the past, wherever local authorities participate in the provision of education. The development of larger areas of administration at present under way in England and in the United States is to be explained by the recognition that the resources of larger areas must be pooled, if opportunities for education are to be expanded.

## REFERENCES

Ducos, H. *Pourquoi l'Ecole Unique?* Paris, 1932.

James, Eric. *An Essay on the Content of Education.* London, George G. Harrap & Co. Ltd., 1949.

———— *Education and Leadership.* London, George G. Harrap & Co. Ltd., 1951.

Kandel, I. L. *Conflicting Theories of Education.* New York, The Macmillan Co., 1938.

———— ed. "Expansion of Secondary Education," *Educational Yearbook, 1930,* of the International Institute of Teachers College, Columbia University. New York, 1930.

National Education Association, Educational Policies Commission. *Education of the Gifted.* Washington, D.C., 1950.

# 6

# The Administration and Organization of Education

## The Modern Educational Systems

The conduct of a modern system of education has become one of the largest public enterprises undertaken by the governments, both central and local, of most countries. The functions of administration have changed considerably since the days when an educational system was concerned only with elementary schools for the masses and secondary schools for a select minority. Then the task consisted mainly of management through prescribed courses of study and textbooks, through the inspection of schools to see that the regulations prescribed were faithfully observed, and through the conduct of examinations. The reorganization of educational systems which began to be discussed during and after World War I and which has now reached the stage of realization in practice is dependent upon the promotion and continued maintenance of the interest and support of all concerned with education as an instrument for securing the welfare of the individual and the progress of society.

Proposals for the reorganization include increased provision for the education of very young, preschool children, and for the extension of school attendance from the primary school to postprimary schools of different types. Changes are taking place in the aims and process of education and instruction and therefore in the preparation of teachers. Increased facilities for the physical and social welfare of pupils and the utilization of a manifold variety of informal agencies for education are needed. And since education is considered to be a lifelong process, provisions for the education of out-of-school youth and adults must be extended. Finally, the formulation of educational policy can no longer be dependent on determining how much and what kind of knowledge and information should be imparted in the elementary and secondary schools. The nature of the individual as a growing personality and the complexity of modern society must both be taken into account in formulating policy, the major premise of which is the provision of equality of opportunities.

The general outlines of educational reconstruction have been widely discussed, as already indicated in Chapter 4, and in some countries the plans are being put into effect gradually as the present economic situation and other conditions permit. The methods of administration vary, however, although the general framework for reorganization may be the same. The reasons for this variation are obvious, since the character of administration is determined by the political nature and aims of the state. Under a totalitarian regime the purpose of educational administration is to mold the individual to a particular pattern, politically and culturallly; the end to be attained is uncritical conformity. For this purpose even progressive methods of instruction can be used; activity programs and methods were used in Fascist Italy, Nazi Germany, and in the early years following the revolution in Soviet Russia. Propaganda and indoctrination take the place of education. In order to carry out the ideological purposes set for education, administration is centralized and control is kept entirely in the hands of the authorities. So little opportunity is there for criticism that important changes in editions of textbooks published within a short period of each other are accepted without comment, as was the case when the changes were made in Soviet history textbooks to reflect the changed attitude of the Soviet leaders to their World War II allies.

## Centralization of Administration

Centralization of control with little or no participation on the part of others concerned in the education of children and youth may in some countries have been continued to the present because of entrenched traditional practices. Thus in the nineteenth century in countries in which the population was sparse and widely distributed, with inadequate means of communication and without systems of local government, schools would not have been available had they not been provided by the central authority. The origin of centralized systems of New Zealand, of the states of Australia, and of the Latin-American countries can be explained in this way. Unfortunately centralized control tends to become bureaucratic and a bureaucracy may become so entrenched as to oppose proposals for greater flexibility in administration. In France centralized control is characteristic of the administration of all public affairs because it is thought that they can be best conducted by experts and specialists; in education there is an added reason for centralized control — to maintain political stability and promote cultural unity. Under conditions of centralization education is conducted by regulations, prescriptions, and inspection, through prescribed courses of study and methods of instruction, detailed definitions, and examinations. Such centralization is efficient only in the sense that the end of uniformity is secured, but there is little progress. This is well illustrated by the fact that the course of study for elementary schools remained virtually unchanged in France from 1887 to 1923, and the edition of 1923 did not suggest any radical changes. One of the most serious weaknesses of the type of centralization here discussed is that when new ideas are finally accepted the machinery to put them into practice is not available and the teachers must undergo a period of preparation before changes can be introduced. The radically new theories of education adopted in Germany under the Weimar Republic almost resulted in chaos when put into practice by teachers accustomed to carrying out prescribed regulations. The fate of the *classes nouvelles* in France may in part be due as much to the ineptitude of some teachers as to the opposition of teachers accustomed to the traditional methods.

The current trends in educational theory cannot be carried out successfully under a centralized system of administration. Instead of molding the individual to a preconceived political pattern or of placing the emphasis on securing cultural uniformity, modern educational theory, inspired by the ideal concept of the individual in a democracy and influenced by the contributions from psychology, seeks to promote the fullest and richest development of each individual, according to his capacities, as a responsible member of society. Efficiency and uniformity are just as important in the administration of an educational system inspired by this aim as in centralized regimes or in the administration of an industrial or commercial concern or of some other forms of government affairs. But efficiency and uniformity in the administration of a modern system of education must be directed to creating those conditions under which the educative process can best be carried out.

The principles of scientific management developed in business and industry can be applied only to a slight degree in the administration of education. The success of business and industry depends upon the production and distribution of products that are uniform in size and quality. Education, however, is devoted to dealing with human beings, and, while it is concerned with standards, it cannot be either successful or efficient if its aims are designed to securing a standardized product. The whole trend in education today is opposed to mass instruction and in favor of individualized instruction, so that a system of administration which ignores the fact that those engaged in the educative process, whether as teachers or as pupils, are individuals with personalities to be developed and encouraged, must result in formalism and stagnation. The fact that there has been a shift of emphasis from the subject to the child demands the introduction of a new spirit into administrative practices. But besides the teachers and pupils, administration must concern itself with the various persons and groups that have an interest and stake in education — parents, the churches, industry, the community, and the nation.

The ends of education that are to be promoted must have the intelligent support, at any rate, of a majority of all concerned in their successful attainment both because of their interest in the welfare of their community and nation and as taxpayers. Such a

principle is of far greater importance and significance than mechanical devices in determining the character of administration in
a democracy. To concentrate on the machinery of administration
rather than on the purposes that it should be designed to promote
is to court the danger of exposure to what a British administrator
has described as "the occupational disease of self-importance," only
too often exemplified in the conduct of officials of a centralized
system of governmental administration.

### Factors Determining the Character of Administration

The character of educational administration is thus determined
in general by two factors — the theory of the state and the theory
of education that is prevalent. The totalitarian, or even the authoritarian, state tends to have a highly centralized system of administration and provides little or no opportunity to the public or
to local governmental bodies or to professional groups to participate in the determination of policy. The democratic state, on the
other hand, recognizes that a central governmental body cannot
claim omniscience and is not restricted by the obscurantism of
bureaucrats with vested interests in maintaining the *status quo.*
Accordingly the rights of local groups or communities to determine
their own affairs with a minimum of interference are recognized
and a partnership in ideas as well as in finances is entered into between the central and local authorities to which a certain amount
of responsibility is delegated.

The principles upon which such partnership is based are, first, an
assumption that some uniformities must be established, such as the
range of compulsory school attendance, healthy school environments, qualifications and salaries of teachers, and some common
content in the curriculum; and, second, the view that environmental
conditions — natural, economic, social, and cultural — may differ
sufficiently to justify local adaptations rather than the adoption of
a uniform national pattern. Under the totalitarian and authoritarian
systems every aspect of the educative process is prescribed and
controlled; the democratic system is content to set up minimum requirements that must be met and to leave the rest to the initiative
of the teaching profession and local authorities. An administrative

system based on such principles is itself educative for all those who participate in it. A system that encourages local and group participation, as Woodrow Wilson once wrote of English and American law, "not only presupposes intelligence and independence of spirit on the part of the individual: such a system elicits intelligence and creates independence of spirit."

The totalitarian regime is posited on the theory that the state is responsible for defining the culture pattern in all its ramifications; the authoritarian system is inspired by faith in the cultural heritage which it wishes to preserve and to transmit; the democratic system realizes that that culture pattern is neither fixed nor subject to simple definition and that it develops and changes through the free intercourse of men, through the impact of mind upon mind, and through the adaptation of man to his changing environment. The culture pattern is not something static, but, while it contains values that a group wishes to perpetuate because they are accepted as essential to its stability, yet becomes modified by external conditions or by man's own reinterpretation. To this process free exchange of ideas and intelligent initiative can contribute.

### The Purpose and Function of Administration

In a totalitarian system the purpose and function of the administration of education are clear. They are to provide a type of education through which there would be inculcated submissive acceptance of the ideology of the party in power without question and to conform to the particular social pattern insisted upon by the state for its own ends. The starting and terminal points are the state. In the democratic system of education the starting point is the individual and administration is directed to the establishment of those conditions that will make possible his fullest development as a human being, as a worker, and as an intelligent citizen. The welfare of the state, it is considered, rests upon the intelligence of its citizens.

Fundamentally, then, the function of educational administration in a democracy is to bring pupils and teachers together under such conditions as will most successfully promote the ends of education. Or, to quote again in a different context the definitions of the English and French administrators, that function is, according to Sir Graham Balfour, "to enable the right pupils to receive the right education from the right teachers, at a cost within the means of the state, under conditions which will enable the pupils best to profit by their training." The French parallel, which was enunciated nearly twenty years later by M. Jean Zay, Minister of National Education, and has already been cited earlier, was as follows: "This has always impressed itself upon the attention of education: to place the individual who is appropriate in the position appropriate to him is not only a condition of well-being for the individual and a guarantee of stability for society. It is demanded by social justice." [1]

Simple as these two statements of the function of educational administration appear to be, there is scarcely a word in them that does not require further interpretation. What is "the right pupil" or "the appropriate" position for the individual? What is "the right education" or "the appropriate" education for the individual? What is the meaning of "the right teacher"? And how can the "cost within the means of the state" be determined?

The fundamental question is, to use the title of a book by W. Lester Smith, *To Whom Do Schools Belong?* This question is easily and clearly answered in the totalitarian or bureaucratic system of administration, under which all aspects of education are determined and prescribed by a central authority, even though in some cases it does not bear the whole cost of education. In a democracy, however, education is not the concern of the state alone, for if the phrase, "school and society," is to have a real meaning, the administration of education must enlist the intelligent support and active interest of all the members of the state or community — parents, the public in general, professional associations, organizations created for civic, recreational, and economic purposes, religious groups, and so on. Such groups and organizations,

---

[1] Sir Graham Balfour, *Educational Administration* (London, The Clarendon Press, 1921), p. 38. M. Zay during his term of office was responsible for the change of terminology (*Direction de l'Enseignement du premier Degré* and *Direction de l'Enseignement du second Degré*) which brought primary and secondary education into line with each other. He was also responsible for the experiment with guidance classes (*classes d'orientation*) which later were broadened into the *classes nouvelles*.

either directly or through their representatives, can play an important role in discussing and contributing to the formulation of a national policy and, within its framework, of local policy.

Control must, of course, be concentrated in the hands of a body which will determine and have executed the details of the national policy as best adapted to local conditions. The major principle underlying such an arrangement is that rigidity of policy must be avoided and sufficient scope be permitted for such flexibility and variations as local conditions may require. The conduct of educational administration is based on a partnership between central and local authorities with opportunities for consultation and settlement of conflicts. Under the local authorities the participation of the public, of the teachers, and of voluntary organizations must be encouraged. The function of administration is to ensure that pupils and teachers are brought together under conditions that make possible the successful conduct of instruction and education. One of these conditions is the understanding and interest of the public.

Where the administration of education is under the control of a central authority the curricula, the courses of study, the methods of instruction, the standards of achievement, and the details of classroom management are prescribed in detail, sometimes with, but generally without, consultation with representatives of the teaching profession. The training of teachers is determined accordingly with an emphasis on routine methods. The control of education is by means of rules, regulations, and inspection in which the machinery of administration assumes greater importance than the encouragement of initiative and intelligence on the part of those charged with the actual conduct of a school or the work in a classroom.

### Uniformity and Diversity

The right education of pupils cannot be defined except in general terms. The actual process of education and instruction should be determined by knowledge and understanding of the abilities of each pupil in a given environment. Soundly conceived, education cannot be reduced to mechanical routine, for it is something that results from the impact of the personalities of teachers and pupils upon each other. Hence variety within a common framework, which should be a characteristic of education in a democracy, is more important than the uniformity and standardization achieved under centralized control. The educational machine may be made to run smoothly and uniformly under a bureaucratic administration, but efficiency of this kind is secured by the development of routine methods and too often by an emphasis on only one of the several ends to which education should be directed; initiative on the part of the teacher is discouraged and adaptations to cultural changes take place only when the central authority takes the initiative. The example of the longevity of the curriculum and course of study prescribed for elementary schools in France, which has already been mentioned, has a parallel in Prussian education where the elementary school course of study continued relatively unchanged from 1872 to 1919.

In so far as it has certain advantages, a centralized system of administration succeeds in maintaining a uniform level of standards; it equalizes opportunities for elementary education by providing every child, irrespective of place of residence, with a teacher qualified to carry out the course of study as prescribed. Its weaknesses, however, derive in the main from its failure to respond to the principles of education as currently defined. It discourages experimentation and puts a premium on the faithful execution in the classroom of the rules and regulations officially prescribed for the educative process.

The solution, however, does not lie in abandoning central in favor of local authorities or decentralized administrative areas. Even in the United States some of the difficulties in providing equality of educational opportunities in some states is due to failure to pool the resources of the whole nation to distribute the cost of education more equably. Education, as has been frequently pointed out, is an instrument for the development of intelligent citizens; the state or nation has an important stake in seeing to it that other provision and aims of education are adequately met. But even if education were not as broad-based as this, the equable distribution of opportunities requires the pooling of resources of the larger area to overcome the maldistribution of wealth owing to variations in economic conditions locally.

While the education of the children and youth of a nation should be the concern of the whole nation, if an alert public interest in education is to be encouraged, that can only be done by enlisting that interest in the schools of a local community, beginning with the parents and radiating out to reach the public in general. Another reason that justifies decentralization is that experimentation can be encouraged within the framework of the common national policy. In such experimentation lie the possibilities for leadership to emerge and for progress through emulation between different schools and different localities. From this point of view what is desirable in a system of administration is variety set in a national framework. The same principle can be applied to the schools under one local authority, so that each school has the opportunity to adapt its program to the needs of the pupils in their environment without, however, losing sight of common objectives.

### Centralization and Decentralization

From this discussion there emerges the issue of the relationships between central and local authorities for the administration of education. It is obvious, from the frequent references that have already been made to a national or common framework, that the function of a central authority should be to define general policy after consultation with local authorities, professional associations, and voluntary organizations of citizens interested in education in general or in some special phases of it. On the basis of such consultations new laws and regulations should be based. In a national framework of policy there should be defined common standards for compulsory school attendance and its enforcement, the length of school year, standards for school buildings and size of classes, the various types of schools to be provided, and the qualifications and remuneration of teachers. Provision should be made for adequate systems of inspection and supervision, for submission of reports, for the principles of financial aid in order to maintain at least a satisfactory minimum of standards.

Because of the position that it occupies, a central authority can amass a wealth of information about the progress of education under its supervision. So equipped it can exercise leadership and give guidance and advice without encroaching upon the freedom of local authorities. The central authority should encourage investigation and research and stimulate official and other publicly recognized agencies to appraise and critically evaluate various aspects of the educational systems and to offer constructive suggestions for improvement, if found necessary or desirable. In addition to the dissemination of information and the publication of reports on the progress of education at home, reports should from time to time be published on such progress in other countries.

### Professional Freedom

Up to this point no mention has been made of curricula, courses of study, methods of instruction, and standards of achievement, that is, the *interna* or the work that should proceed in the classrooms between teachers and pupils. The functions of the central authority should be limited to defining those conditions under which the process of education can best be carried on and to see to it that equality of educational opportunities which a democratic system of education should provide is made available under all local authorities. Such conditions may be described as the *externa* or the fabric of an educational system. A completely centralized system of administration goes beyond defining the requirements of the *externa* and prescribes also the details of education and instruction by somewhat rigidly prescribed courses of study and methods of teaching, and by inspection and examinations. Such a system makes for uniformity and discourages the spirit of initiative and intelligent adaptation to local environments and to the capacities and needs of the pupils.

The current trends in educational theory require greater freedom for the teachers, but freedom defined and determined by their professional preparation. If teachers are to be free to adapt their work to the capacities and needs of their pupils in their environment, they should be free from detailed prescriptions as to what to teach and how to teach, except for the guidance of outlines or suggestions which provide a common foundation issued by the central or local authorities or both. The fear lest such freedom might be abused is mitigated by the professional preparation of teachers, by suggestions or outlines, by cooperation and consultation with colleagues in the preparation of courses of study and articulating one class with the next, by public opinion and by the views of parents, by in-service courses and discussions, and by the advice of inspectors.

Inspection no longer carries the connotation of inquisitorial control to see that prescribed regulations are faithfully carried out and to ensure uniformity and standardization. The wide range of experience enjoyed by inspectors helps to make them agents of cross-fertilization of ideas garnered during the course of their duties.

Only through extending the opportunities for participation in the administration of education concerned with defining policies to all individuals and groups already mentioned is it possible to avoid that danger which John Stuart Mill feared so strongly from a state-controlled system of education and which has been exemplified in the modern totalitarian state. In his essay *On Liberty* Mill wrote nearly a century ago that "A general state education is merely a contrivance for moulding people to be exactly like one another, and as the mould in which it casts them is that which pleases the predominant power in the government . . . it establishes a despotism over the mind, leading by natural tendency to one over the body."

## Educational Finance

Circumstances rather than theory are bringing the danger which Mill feared nearer in countries where there exists a general line of demarcation between the functions of the central and local authorities with reference to the *externa* and the *interna*. With an expanding program for the provision of educational opportunities, the financing of education is becoming a serious problem. Rising standards for the preparation and therefore the remuneration of teachers, the increasing cost of buildings and equipment, and the provision of special services in some systems — these are part of the problem. Its seriousness is further aggravated by the increasing cost of central governments, partly because of the expansion of services and the increased burden of national debts. There has accordingly arisen serious competition between central and local authorities for revenues from taxation. Where the administration of education has been centralized the problem does not arise, although even here the central authority has been obliged to increase its appropriations to local governments for the cost of school buildings for which they have in the past been responsible. Where, however, the cost of education was equally divided before World War II between central and local authorities, the changing economic situation and the shift in revenues has tended to place a larger share of the burden on the central authority, even after areas of administration have been enlarged. It is this shifting of the burden that has aroused fear in some quarters lest it may lead to more dictation and control of the *interna*.

Should such an extension of control take place, more would be lost than freedom to develop educational systems in accordance with the needs of local environments and the capacities of the pupils. It would mean, as it has meant where local school committees have no voice in determining policy, that the public would lose that sense of responsibility for and interest in the progress of education. It may be paradoxical but it is nevertheless a fact that the most heated controversies about the cost of education do have an educative value for those responsible for providing the resources, that is, the taxpayers. It is not an accident that with the expanding range of systems of education and consequently of the budgets to finance them a stimulus has been provided both in England and the United States for the publication of handbooks on local education, the organization of educational days and weeks, and the formation of parents' and other associations. It has been realized that to maintain the interest of the public in education various devices must be employed. Such publicity is not needed in those countries in which both the *externa* and the *interna* of education and its financial support are entirely in the hands of the central government.

The advantages in terms of a sound theory of education lie, however, with decentralized administration. What is lost through the absence of uniformity is more than compensated for by the vigor and vitality which come from a sense of responsibility and freedom to experiment. The official of a centralized system tends to become a bureaucrat; the administrator of a local authority must be an educational statesman and leader of both the public and the teachers in his area.

The problem that is emerging out of the question of financing education was admirably discussed in the following paragraph of an address by Sir John Maud, who until last year was Permanent Secretary of the Ministry of Education for England and Wales: "Finally, there is a challenge which is presented with particular directness to all people like myself who profess to be educational administrators, but it is one that affects the whole of education. Can administrators remain uncorrupted by increasing power? Nearly £350 million will be handled by public administrators of education this year, as servants of the central or of the local authorities. Every pound of that sum will be compulsorily contributed by all the citizens — contributed (as someone has said) either in sorrow as taxes or in anger as rates. We administrators have therefore good reason to remember that we serve the public that foots the bill and do our best to make sure that the public gets full value for its money. But if we are to serve the public as we should, our chief concern must be to serve the teachers and all who do the work of education — and in particular to remember for ourselves, and persuade our public masters to believe, that the more free educators are, and feel themselves to be, the better they will educate (and the better value the public will therefore get for its money). The more that education becomes dependent on public money, the more public money that is spent on education, the more necessary the educational administrator becomes, the stronger grows the temptation for him to think he is more important than he is, and the greater his obligation to remind himself that he is not his own master — or the master of anyone else.

"If I may for the first time this afternoon now speak not only for myself but for my colleagues in the Ministry of Education, I swear that as best we may we will resist the occupational disease of self-importance. The chief end of education, I believe, is individual personality, and the chief means to that end is the teacher. And so, as the service that civil servants like myself owe the public is to promote education. I declare myself unreservedly a servant of the teacher — sometimes a disobedient humble servant, but never his master." [2]

The educational systems selected for discussion and description in the rest of this chapter represent different types of administra-

2 Sir John Maud, "1851–1951: A Century of British Education," *Journal of the Royal Society of Arts,* June 15, 1951, p. 570. Quoted by permission.

tion. Of these the first is expanding its program for a national democratic system of education; the second illustrates the system of administration under bureaucratic control; the third is today the outstanding example of education under a totalitarian regime; and the fourth has long been the unique representative of a nation's faith in education and its provision and administration of the principles of democratic policy.

## ENGLAND [3]

### The Background

The educational facilities provided for the children and youth of England have not in the past constituted a national system as that term is generally understood. Nor was a system ever planned until the deliberations that led to the passing of the Education Act of 1944. Education was provided and administered in several systems which had grown up more or less fortuitously and independently without being closely articulated or coordinated. There existed, on the one hand, a system of publicly maintained elementary schools created in 1870 and of secondary schools established under the Education Act of 1902, but the two types of schools were not articulated except that early in the century free (later special) places provided opportunities for able boys and girls to find their way, by success in a competitive examination, from the elementary to the secondary schools at the age of eleven plus. This was, of course, a survival of the traditional system with one type of school for the masses and another for a minority of the pupils.

But the English system of elementary education was "dual" in another sense. It included "provided" schools, that is, schools wholly maintained by the public authorities and permitted to give undenominational religious instruction only, and "non-provided" or denominational schools supported out of public funds and giving

[3] The educational system of Wales is also administered by the Ministry of Education, as it was formerly by the Board of Education, but with a Welsh Department in Cardiff to expedite most of the educational administration affecting Wales and Monmouthshire.

religious instruction of the denominational group which established and in part supported them.

Side by side with these schools — publicly maintained elementary and secondary schools — there was a system of "Public Schools" and a large number of other private or independent schools which charged fees, which might under certain conditions receive grants from the central government and be inspected by it, and others which might on request be inspected without receiving any grants.

The organization of education continued to bear the marks of the "two nations" — the privileged and the unprivileged — described by Disraeli, while the elementary schools from the social point of view could not shake off the connotation of their origin in 1870 as schools for the education of children of the laboring classes. Nevertheless the elementary schools overcame the handicaps of their origin largely because they were released from the incubus of external examinations in 1895, and as a result of the slow but certain improvement in the preparation of their teachers, and the progressively enlightened suggestions from the Board of Education and the guidance of its inspectors.

Elementary education was established in 1870 to provide literate workers for the rapidly expanding industrial development of the country and at the same time to prepare them to play their part as citizens when the right to vote was gradually extended to them. The development of industry was increasingly stimulated by the application of technological science which required workers with more than elementary education. The need was met in the last decades of the nineteenth century by the creation of higher elementary or higher grade schools which provided a more advanced program of instruction than the elementary schools and by the establishment of technical day and evening schools. When secondary schools began to be provided at public expense under the Education Act of 1902, nothing was done to integrate the different types and levels of schools into a single articulated system.

The failure to develop a national system of education, when the opportunity arose at the beginning of the present century, was not accidental. It was due not only to a general distrust of planning which might result ultimately in rigidity and prove to be an obstacle to adaptation to changing circumstances. It was the result also of a traditional fear lest a national plan might mean control by a central authority which might ultimately lead to extension of the powers of the state. Mill's argument against a state system of education (see p. 67) was widely shared even though it retarded the development of education long after it had already begun to be organized in other countries. The principles of administration that were slowly developed to govern the relations between the central and local authorities reflected this fear. They were based on the general theory that public affairs are the concern of all the public and of the state or local governments alone. There emerged, as a result, a system that not only encouraged but required general discussion by all concerned in any measure of state or local administration both in and out of Parliament and between the relevant central and local authorities involved.

The importance attached to these relationships and to participation was amply illustrated in the discussions that preceded the enactment of the Education Act in 1944 (see p. 126). The central and local authorities have cooperated on the principle of partnership, even when the former increased its share of the burden of educational expenditures. Matters in dispute between the central and local authorities were first discussed by representatives of both bodies and submitted to Parliament only if a settlement could not be reached.

### The Theory of Administration

The contribution of English practice to a sound theory of administration in a democracy is so important that a few statements may pertinently be cited to illustrate it. In 1927 the President of the Board of Education, Lord Eustace Percy at that time, received a request from a patriotic organization that the systematic teaching of patriotism should be made a compulsory part of the curricula of schools. The President refused on the following grounds: "If governments, whether local or central, began to prescribe to the teacher a certain method of teaching, or even attempt to influence him in such matters, we run the risk of all those evils that we have seen in various forms, both in the Prussia of the past and in the Russia of today."

The same principle was restated a few years later by Mr. H. Ramsbotham (now Lord Soulbury) when he was Parliamentary Secretary to the Board of Education: "It was because he attached so much importance to the development of the individual that he was apprehensive of any extension of state control. There were people, particularly in other countries, who held that the individual existed, and should exist, for the sake of the State. He was not one of them, and he was thankful to say that neither the theory nor the practice of education in our country was founded on such a philosophy. Our whole plan of decentralization, the relation of partnership between the Board of Education and the local authorities, the weight that was given to the views of the latter, the encouragement that was offered to local sentiment, the policy of constant consultation, and the great reluctance of the Board to apply coercion were all part and parcel of a general desire to foster the spirit of individualism, originality, and experiment. . . . If we want uniformity, standardization, general docility, and dullness we should find either oligarchy or autocracy a means to the end. But we must be prepared to risk the loss of self-discipline, independence, and individuality. Living in any society involved a certain surrender of freedom. Parents were compelled to send their children to school because most of them preferred civilized beings to savages, and if society was, as Schopenhauer says, 'like a collection of hedgehogs drawn together for the sake of warmth,' we should always need to rely on education to blunt the edges of each other's prickles. So there must be considerable restraint placed upon the development and exercise of individuality. But our methods of restraining it were not those of the ant-heap or the bee-hive. The desire and the ability to experiment, even at the risk of making mistakes, were an essential part of educational liberty." [4]

On the eve of the outbreak of World War II another Parliamentary Secretary to the Board of Education, Mr. Chuter Ede, when requested to issue a circular urging local education authorities to re-

[4] *The Times Educational Supplement,* London, March 10, 1934.

quire teachers to give instruction on the virtues of freedom, rejected the request with the statement that "It is essentially a teacher's problem and teachers can be in no doubt as to the importance which the Board attach to it." In answer to another request that a recent anthology on freedom be recommended for use in schools Mr. Ede replied that "It is not the practice of the Board to recommend particular textbooks — that is part of the freedom that we are allowing local education authorities."

The local education authorities in turn also refrain from prescribing the content and methods of instruction in schools under their charge. To quote from Lady Simon's *How the Manchester Education Committee Works* (1934): "There is also remarkable unanimity amongst them with regard to the freedom for the teaching body. Questions of curricula are never discussed by the Education Committee, and any tendency to do so . . . is quickly discouraged. . . . The content of Education, what it is and what it ought to be, is just as technical a subject as methods of teaching and the proper balancing of the curriculum. . . . If governing bodies as such began to consider these questions it would mean the end of that freedom for the teachers that is just as essential for the teacher in the elementary school as for the professor in the University."

There was thus established as the basis of educational administration the principle of freedom which not only made possible but actually encouraged flexibility and adaptation to local conditions. The Education Act of 1918 (the Fisher Act), which represented an important advance in the organization and provision of education, placed the responsibility for the advance on the local education authorities. These were required to conduct surveys of their needs and to draft schemes for the comprehensive and progressive development of education in their areas. The schemes were submitted to the Board of Education for approval but the Board had only the power to offer suggestions and advice and could not reject a scheme. If after consultation between the Board and a local authority's representative, an agreement could not be reached, the matter could be referred to Parliament, which as the representive of the public was the final court of appeal.

## The Inter-war Years

The Act of 1918 did not empower all local education authorities to provide secondary education and the dual system of elementary and secondary education thus survived. Some authorities, known as Part III [5] authorities, were permitted to provide only elementary schools in their areas. The weakness of the system which failed to provide some form of secondary education for all was recognized. In 1926 the Consultative Committee with Sir Henry Hadow as chairman recommended in its report on *The Education of the Adolescent* the organization of the last three years of the elementary school for pupils eleven to fourteen years of age as "senior schools" which would offer a type of junior secondary education but would still operate under the regulations for elementary schools. Other aspects of education were investigated by the Consultative Committee and reports were issued on primary schools, on nursery and infants' schools, and on secondary education. In 1936 the age limit for compulsory school attendance was raised to fifteen, the provision of the Act to come into effect in 1939; war conditions, however, prevented its enforcement.

The period between the two wars was in a sense a period of preparation for consolidating the variegated patchwork of educational facilities into a unified national scheme. The outbreak of the war hastened the movement for reconstruction. The weaknesses of the system or lack of system were recognized. How much still remained to be done was revealed when schools were evacuated and different strata of society discovered how the others lived. The continued existence of the "two nations" was forced upon the attention of all concerned with the evacuation. The difficulties in securing adequately trained manpower for the war industries brought to the forefront the unsatisfactory provision of technical education, while the low level of the interests of the members of the Allied Forces could also be interpreted in part as a reflection on the quality of education generally.

[5] They were so called because legislation concerning such areas was dealt with in Part III of the Education Act of 1902.

## The Education Act, 1944 — The Central Authority

The movement for postwar reconstruction of education in order to meet the needs of the nation as a whole gained momentum. The widespread interest in the movement has been described in a previous chapter (see pp. 78 ff). The two guiding principles upon which reconstruction was to be based were, first, the words of Disraeli quoted at the head of the Board of Education's pamphlet on *Educational Reconstruction* (1943), "Upon the education of the people of this country the fate of this country depends." The second principle was contained in the statement in the first paragraph of the pamphlet that "In the youth of the nation we have our greating the annual grant.

Whatever the weaknesses of the administrative organization before the passage of the Education Act in 1944, there had been established the principle that the conduct of education must be built up on a partnership of all concerned in it — the central and the local authorities, the public and voluntary agencies as well as the teachers and their professional associations. What was needed, however, in view of the different sizes of the administrative areas, the uneven distribution of wealth, and the varied kinds of economy in different parts of the country was stronger and more direct leadership than could be exercised by the Board of Education. The President of the Board was charged with "the superintendence of matters relating to education in England and Wales." Accordingly the Board could act by means of suggestions, advice, and consultations except on matters where statutory powers could be enforced or pressure be exercised on local education authorities by withholding the annual grant.

The most important change in the relations between the central and local authorities was made in the first section of the Education Act of 1944. The Board became the Ministry of Education under a Minister who is normally a member of the Cabinet of the Government. As contrasted with the power of the President of the Board the Minister was charged with the duty "to promote the education of the people of England and Wales and the progressive development of institutions devoted to that purpose, and to secure the effective execution by local authorities, under his control and direction, of the national policy for providing a varied and comprehensive educational service in every area."

Anticipating, no doubt, the protests that might be aroused by the words of this section "under his control and direction," the President of the Board in an Explanatory Memorandum to the Education Bill (1943), wrote, "The change will not involve any diminution in the responsibility of local education authorities, to whom wider opportunities will be afforded than ever before. What is involved is a recognition that the public system of education, though administered locally is the nation's concern, the full benefits of which should be equally available to all alike, wherever their homes may be."

In view of the tradition that has been built up, it is not likely that any Minister of his staff will exercise too rigidly the power to "control and direct" in any aspect of education except the *externa*. There is always open the ventilation in Parliament of serious conflicts between a central and local authority; on some issues definite provision is made in the Education Act for appeals to Parliament. The determining factor will be the local implementation of "the national policy." The approval of the Minister must be obtained for a number of activities in which local education authorities have in the past been relatively free. The Act imposed more duties upon the local education authorities with the definite aim of improving the educational opportunities and the well-being of children and youth. At the same time the Act gave the Minister more powers to approve or withhold approval on such matters as agreements between local education authorities and "managers" of voluntary schools or between such authorities and "divisional executives" to be described later. The Minister must be consulted on and may prohibit the appointment of a "chief education officer" proposed by a local education authority. He may prevent the "unreasonable" exercise of functions by a local education authority on managers or governors of a school, a power which gives the Minister full authority to define "unreasonable." The Act provides for the registration, under an administrative officer of the ministry as "Registrar," of private or independent schools after inspection; proprietors of such schools will, when this provision of the Act becomes effective, have the right to appeal to the Independent Schools Tribunal against adverse refusal to register them. The general expectation is that most of these powers "will remain in the background and continue to be used sparingly and only as occasion may demand." (Report of the Ministry of Education Sub-committee of the Local Government Manpower Committee, July 1951, p. 4).

The enlarged scope of the provisions of the Act of 1944 is indicated by the growing size of the staff of the Ministry of Education which is one of the largest of all the Ministries. The Minister, who is normally a member of the Cabinet is assisted in Parliament by a Parliamentary Secretary, who is a member of Parliament and of the Government in power. The Ministry consists of permanent civil servants, with a Permanent Secretary at the head, who are responsible for all aspects of administration. In the areas of the local education authorities the work is in the hands of Her Majesty's Inspectors (H.M.I.'s) who inspect and report on the efficiency of schools, and who advise teachers individually or in groups when attending short courses. The inspectors serve as liason officers between the Ministry and local education authorities and other bodies concerned with educational policy.

The following statement in the Report of the Ministry of Education Sub-Committee of the Local Government Manpower Committee (July 1951, p. 6) is a succinct summary of the duties of the Minister: "While the Minister should have a general oversight of the field of education, we think that he has six duties from which the points at which it is necessary for him to exercise control should be derived: (1) He must be satisfied that educational facilities and auxiliary services are provided in sufficient quantity and variety. (2) He must be satisfied that educational establishments and auxiliary services are well managed, equipped, staffed and maintained. (3) He must ensure the proper freedom of parents, teachers and other third parties. (4) He must be satisfied of the qualifications of teachers and medical officers to the extent necessary to safeguard their and the children's interests. (5) He must control the fees charged and awards and allowances made to the extent necessary to safeguard the interests of local education and other school authorities, parents and students. (6) He must control the provision of educational premises."

The Consultative Committee created in 1899, when the Board of Education was established, to advise the Board on matters referred to it was replaced by the provision in the Education Act, 1944, for the creation of two Central Advisory Councils, one for England and the other for Wales and Monmouthshire. The Councils are expected to advise the Minister not only on questions that he may refer to them but also on such matters of the theory and practice of education as they think fit; they cannot consider questions of educational administration. The members are appointed by the Minister for a term of years determined by him.

There are in addition several *ad hoc* Committees which may be called upon by the Minister for advice and which issue reports periodically on their activities. These Councils, set up by the Minister, are Secondary School Examinations Council, the National Council on Education for Industry and Commerce, and the National Council on the Training and Supply of Teachers. The Councils, whose members are appointed on the nominations of relevant bodies in the country "focus opinion not only at the national but also at the regional level, and they form part of a comprehensive system of advisory bodies covering the whole country." The Ministry is also represented on some independent bodies like the National Foundation for Educational Research, the National Foundation for Visual Aids, and the Central Bureau for Educational Visits and Exchanges, to which financial support is given.

## Local Administration

Responsibility for the local administration of education rests with the councils of the counties and county boroughs (a city with not less than 50,000 population); they are the local education authorities (L.E.A.'s). The councils are elected for the administration of the affairs and the provision of necessary services in their areas. No member is elected to the council because of special interest in education. After the council has been formed, its members are assigned to a variety of committees of which the education committee is one established for the efficient discharge of the council's functions with respect to education. Every education committee is now required to include as co-opted members persons of experience in education and acquainted with the educational conditions of the area concerned. The majority of the members of an education committee must be members of the local authority's elected council. These committees are no longer required, as they were formerly, to have one or more women members unless they happen to be among those by election. The committees commonly create a number of sub-committees to expedite the consideration of the various aspects of the educational system including selection of teachers and finance the control of which for an area rests, however, with the whole council.

The most important change in the administrative provisions of the Education Act of 1944 was the abolition of what were known under the Education Act of 1902 as Part III authorities, that is, local education authorities in areas assumed to be too small or too poor to provide more than elementary education. Their size was determined by the census figures of 1900, but since that time some Part III authorities have grown or fallen in size of population. Further because of the movement of industries new aggregations of population have emerged. Before 1944 there were 315 local education authorities. On the abolition of Part III authorities the number was reduced to 146 by entrusting the local administration of education to the councils of sixty-two counties and eighty-three county boroughs and one joint education board for a city and contiguous part of a county. The enlargement of areas of administration, strongly resisted by the Part III authorities, was inevitable in order to make possible for all boys and girls the extension of opportunities for primary, secondary, and other education by pooling the resources of the larger area. It may yet be found that even with this important change some areas may still be unable to provide the educational facilities proposed in the Act and that regional areas may have to be created as already suggested some thirty years ago by Lord Haldane.

The Part III authorities may have been too small to provide an adequate system of education; some may even have been inefficient. Nevertheless they appear to have enlisted public interest which was in danger of being lost with their abolition. To keep that interest alive and to enable officials to act with knowledge of local circumstances provision was made in Section 6 and Part III of the First Schedule to the Education Act for the delegation to "divisional executives," or districts within a county, of the functions, mainly with respect to primary and secondary education, under schemes prepared by the local education authority of the council and approved by the Minister. The divisional administration, provided under the Schemes, is entrusted to an *ad hoc* body of from twenty to thirty members representing the local councils concerned and the county local education authority, and co-opted members. "The object of these provisions is to secure that while, within the framework of national policy, the education service in county areas shall be administered under the general control and supervision of the local education authority, it shall not lose the inspiration to be derived from more immediate local interest and local initiative." [6]

"Excepted districts" represent another method of conserving local interests in education. Boroughs and urban districts with a prewar population of not less than 60,000 or with not less than 7,000 pupils on the rolls of the elementary schools may request authorization to become "excepted districts" with their local councils serving as divisional executives. Both the excepted districts and the divisional executives generally have charge of primary and secondary education, but do not have the power to borrow money or to levy rates (i.e., local taxes). Control of expenditures and responsibility for formulating policy remain under the control of the local education authorities of the counties in which they are located.

In order to encourage closer and more personal interest in each school the Act requires that for every county or voluntary primary school an "instrument of management" be drawn up providing for the constitution of a body of managers. For every county secondary school an "instrument of government" must be drawn up to provide for the constitution of a body of governors. Both instruments must be approved by the Minister of Education. The bodies of managers

[6] Ministry of Education, *Circular No. 5*, September 15, 1944, "Local Administration of Education, Schemes of Divisional Administration," p. 3. This and all other quotations from official English publications are cited by permission of the Controller of Her Britannic Majesty's Stationery Office.

and of governors include members appointed by the local education authority.

## Functions of the Local Education Authorities

Responsibility for organizing the system of public education is placed upon the local education authorities. The traditional dual system of education with elementary schools for the masses and secondary schools for a minority is replaced by an articulated system which is defined as follows in the Act: "The statutory system of public education shall be organized in three progressive stages to be known as primary education, secondary education, and further education; and it shall be the duty of the local education authority of every area, so far as their powers extend, to contribute towards the spiritual, moral, mental, and physical development of the community by securing that efficient education throughout these stages shall be available to meet the needs of the population of their area."

It is accordingly the duty of local authorities to provide primary and secondary schools "sufficient in number, character, and equipment to afford for all pupils opportunities for education offering such variety of instruction and training as may be desirable in view of their different ages, abilities, and aptitudes and of the different periods for which they may be expected to remain at school, including practical instruction and training appropriate to their respective needs." Nursery classes in the primary schools or separate nursery schools must be established unless a case can be made out that such provision would be inexpedient. Provision must be made for the education in special schools or otherwise "for pupils who suffer from any disability of mind or body." An innovation is the permission to provide boarding accommodations, either in boarding schools or in hostels "for pupils for whom education as boarders is considered by their parents or by the authority to be desirable." The innovation means that local authorities may establish their own boarding schools or hostels or pay the fees for pupils who may be admitted to a private or a "Public" school.

A local education authority has the power to establish primary and secondary schools and to maintain such schools whether established by them or otherwise, and, with the approval of the Minister, to assist any such school not maintained by them. Schools established and maintained by local education authority are known as "county" schools; schools not so established, are known as "voluntary'" schools. The peculiarly English dual system of provided and non-provided, now county and voluntary schools, has been retained, but with some changes in the relations of the voluntary or denominational schools to the local education authority in respect to financial support and religious instruction.

### Voluntary Schools and Religious Instruction

The Act provides for three types of voluntary schools as follows: (1) Controlled schools are denominational schools whose managers are unable to pay half the cost of alterations necessary to bring the schools up to standard or half the cost in the future of repairs to the schools and playgrounds. The local education authorities assume the cost of alterations, repairs, and maintenance charges, but may appoint two-thirds of the managers and the teachers, except that one-fifth of the teachers must be "reserved teachers." Religious instruction in such schools is given according to an "agreed syllabus," but for two periods a week reserved teachers may give denominational instruction, if desired by the parents.

(2) Aided schools are denominational schools whose managers are able to meet half the cost of alterations and repairs; the other half is paid by the local education authorities who appoint only one-third of the managers. The managers appoint the teachers and control the denominational instruction with the reservation that at the request of parents instruction in an agreed syllabus may be arranged.

(3) Special Agreement Schools are schools of denominational bodies to which capital grants of 50 to 75 per cent were made for buildings under the Act of 1936 in expectation of raising the age of compulsory attendance to fifteen.

The provisions for religious instruction in the county schools are defined in the Act. Such instruction is given according to an agreed syllabus, but teachers are not compelled to give such instruction nor pupils to receive it, if their parents wish to withdraw them from it. An agreed syllabus of religious instruction is one prepared at conferences convened by the local education authorities at which teachers' associations, religious denominations, and the local authorities are represented. A further provision of the Act is that the school day in every county and voluntary school should begin with collective worship. The act of worship must "not be distinctive of any particular religious denomination" nor should an agreed syllabus "include any catechism or formulary which is distinctive of any particular religious denomination." Religious instruction, which before the Act had to be given at the beginning or end of a school session, may now be given at any time of the school day.

### Development Plans

For the purpose of organizing their systems of primary and secondary education, local education authorities are required to make a survey of the needs of their areas and to draft a development plan. In surveying their needs they must take into account the existing county and voluntary schools, state the number of new schools to be proposed, the alterations to be made to bring existing schools up to standard and the arrangements to be provided for boarding schools, if considered expedient, for special schools, and for the transportation of pupils to schools. The report must also include schools not maintained but assisted by the authorities. Before a development plan is submitted to the Minister, all bodies concerned with education — denominational bodies, governors of secondary schools, teacher training colleges — must be consulted.

The Minister, after receiving a development plan, may make such alterations in it as he considers necessary after consultation. When the plan is approved, the Minister makes a local education order for the area concerned with respect to primary and secondary education. The order then acquires the authority of a statute. A local education authority aggrieved by the order or any amendment of it may lay the order before Parliament and either House may annul it within forty days.

There is also imposed on local education authorities the duty to provide facilities for further education for "(a) full-time and part-time education for persons over compulsory school age; and (b) leisure-time education, in such organized cultural training and recreative activities as are suited to their requirements, for any persons over compulsory school age who are able and willing to profit by the facilities provided for that purpose."

The Act provides for the establishment under this section of "county colleges in which young persons who have completed full-time education will have to attend up to the age of eighteen for one whole day or two half-days a week for forty-four weeks or for a session of eight weeks or two sessions of four weeks." Such part-time continuation schools would give "physical, practical, and vocational training as will enable them to develop their various aptitudes and capacities and will prepare them for the responsibilities of citizenship." The date for establishing county colleges and enforcing attendance has not yet been announced.

Nevertheless, local education authorities are required to submit schemes for further education, which are expected to include, in addition to county colleges when required to be established, evening and day schools for technical, commercial and art education, and for general cultural education and for the education of adults either directly or in cooperation with other bodies.

## Auxiliary Services

No country has recognized as clearly as England the importance of provisions for the health and physical welfare of the child as essential concomitants of a sound education. The arrangements for the medical inspection of elementary school pupils were instituted in 1907; treatment was added later. The Education Act of 1944 makes it a duty of local authorities to provide for the medical inspection and treatment of all children in their schools. The responsibility for this service is shared by the Minister of Education and the Minister of Health, the school and other medical services being linked by the chief medical officer of both Ministries. The system of school medical service is closely associated now with the national health scheme, so that parents can now be advised where to send their children in need of treatment. Further, parents may be required to submit children for medical inspection and may be liable to a fine in the absence of a valid excuse. Three inspections of children are required — on entering the primary school, on leaving the primary school, and on leaving school at the compulsory age limit. The health scheme also includes dental service with full and part-time dentists.

Since 1906 under the Provision of Meals Acts meals could be provided for necessitous and undernourished children in the elementary schools. The service was expanded during the war and proved so valuable that the Act has made it the duty of local education authorities to provide milk, meals, and other refreshment at schools maintained by them. Parents are charged at a price not to exceed the cost of the food, but it is expected that, as soon as a national service can be established, meals will be free. The central authority bears almost the full cost. The chief difficulty has been to arrange for suitable accommodations (canteens) for the meals and for the supervision of the children during meal tmes. The first difficulty can only be solved by new buildings; the latter must be determined by the effect upon the work of teachers who undertake such supervision. Local education authorities may also provide boots and clothing when a child is "unable by reason of the inadequacy of his clothing to take full advantage of the education provided," but parents may be required to pay for this service according to an income scale.

Because of their recognized value for education local authorities have the duty to secure that primary, secondary, and further education "include adequate facilities for recreation and social and physical training." They may accordingly, with the approval of the Minister, maintain and manage "camps, holiday classes, playing fields, play centres, and other places (including playgrounds and swimming baths not appropriated to any school or college)." They may also defray or contribute toward the expense of organized games, expeditions and other activities for persons in primary, secondary, and further education. Community centers may be established as part of the program to promote social and physical training of the community; although these are not specifically mentioned in the Act, it is generally understood that they are covered by provisions of the Physical Training and Recreation Act, 1937.

Equally important are the organizations for Youth Service in which the Ministry, local education authorities, and voluntary bodies cooperate. The Youth Service is an outgrowth of the Juvenile Organizations Committee, created during World War I and transferred to the Board of Education in 1919. The Committee's function was to encourage the formation of local committees to promote the development of the social and recreational interests of young persons not attending full-time education. The work flourished for some years but declined owing to economic conditions. In 1939 the Government set up a National Youth Committee to look after the Youth Service (social and recreational) for young persons from fourteen to twenty. The Board of Education (later the Ministry), local education authorities, and voluntary organizations cooperate in this service. The majority of the local education authorities have local youth service committees and have appointed youth service officers to supervise the execution of local policy. Direct grants are made by the Ministry to voluntary organizations and local education authorities are reimbursed for expenditure on account of youth service. The most serious difficulties that handicap the operation of youth service are a shortage of buildings and of youth leaders. The latter shortage is met by grants to persons who attend one-year courses offered by several universities. In 1951 the National Advisory Council on the Training and Supply of Teachers published a report on *The Recruitment and Training of Youth Leaders and Community Centre Workers*, which dealt with the selection, training, and remuneration of youth leaders. In 1942 the National Youth Committee was replaced by the Youth Advisory Council which considers and reports on problems referred to it by the central authority.

### Educational Finance

The financing of education in England, as in many other countries, shows a tendency to increase not only relatively to prewar expenditures but absolutely. The increased number of children to be educated, the rising salaries of teachers, and the provision of secondary education for all make this absolute rise in the cost of education inevitable, and does not include the capital expenditures for buildings and equipment. In England the financing of education is based upon a partnership between the central authority and the local educational authorities. The cost was shared almost equally until 1944 when the government's share was increased by 5 per cent. Despite this shift the local education authorities were faced with increasing difficulties. The fluctuating economic situation, the cost of buildings and equipment, and the general cost of maintenance and of teachers' salaries rose, while the methods of levying rates (local taxes) based on property valuation still needed revision.

The situation was simply stated in the *Report of the Ministry of Education* for 1950 (p. 32): [7] "The growth of the public education service inevitably bears heavily upon both central and local funds. . . . The lack of resilience of the rates as a source of revenue might suggest 'bigger and better' Exchequer grants as a ready solution to the local problem. Such a solution should, however, be looked upon with a critical eye by all those who have at heart the preservation and development of the principle of responsible local government which has been evolved in this country during the last hundred years and which underlies the present partnership in the administration of the public education system. For it is the very essence of partnership that each partner should make a reasonable and proper contribution, financial and other, to the furtherance of the common objective; otherwise the relationship risks degeneration into one of principal and agent, paymaster and payee."

In 1948 a new formula for sharing the financial burden was introduced in the Local Government Act. The aim of the formula was to relate the grant of the Exchequer to the number of children in an area and the area's capacity to pay for their education. The grant under the formula consists of the payment of 120 shillings per unit of average enrollment in the schools maintained or assisted by a local education authority, *plus* 60 per cent of the authority's net recognizable expenditure for educational purposes, *less* the product of a 30-pence rate in the area. The last provision is intended to help the poorer areas. The formula does not include the grants made separately for school milk and school meals, and for training colleges. The grant for school medical services is made by the Minister of Health.

As a result the Ministry of Education, which secures its funds by

[7] This report presents an account of "Education, 1900–1950."

appropriations from Parliament, will bear about 64 per cent of the educational burden, the grants being paid to the local education authorities by the Exchequer. The increasing share of the burden borne by the central authority is viewed with alarm lest it may lead to dictation. The statement quoted earlier provides ample evidence that the Minister has no intention of changing the relationship between his department and the local education authorities. That the problem of financing education is serious, however, is indicated by the fact that the percentage of local revenues from rates required to be spent for educational purposes has risen in recent years from about 25 per cent to 33 per cent.

### Private Schools

There is in England an extensive supply of private or independent schools ranging from nursery schools and kindergartens to the famous "Public Schools." These schools are not under the control of the central or the local education authorities, except that schools providing education for children of compulsory school age could, if desired, be inspected for efficiency in teaching the elementary school subjects. Independent schools may request the Ministry of Education to inspect them and many of the most distinguished independent schools have been so inspected. No such school may, however, receive a grant unless it is a secondary school and provides free places up to 25 per cent of its enrollment and is inspected regularly. Such schools, privately founded and not run for private profit, are known as "direct grant" schools. Since one of the requirements of eligibility for a free place is that a pupil must have spent at least two years in an elementary school, the direct grant schools are closely linked to the publicly maintained schools.

In 1932 a Department Committee submitted a report on *Private Schools and Other Schools Not in Receipt of Grants From Public Funds*. The Committee recommended that such schools should be inspected both as to instruction and premises, and the proprietors of private schools should be required to register their schools with the local education authority of their area and request inspection either by the central or the local education authority. A school not complying with the minimum requirements could be refused registration and closed with the proprietor having a right to appeal.

These recommendations were not put into effect. The Education Act of 1944 requires the Minister to appoint a Registrar of independent schools and to keep a register of such schools open to public inspection. Applications for registration may be made by the proprietor of any independent school. If an application should be denied, an appeal against the decision could be made to the Independent Schools Tribunal to be set up under the Act. The Act has, however, not yet come into effect but nearly 4,000 independent schools have at their own request been inspected and, if satisfactory, will be recognized as efficient. It is expected that registration will become compulsory in 1957. If parents choose to pay fees for the education of their children, they have the right to select whatever school they wish without any guarantee as to its standing or quality such as might be provided by registration.

Local education authorities may, as pointed out earlier, establish their own boarding schools or hostels, especially for pupils living in rural areas, or, where circumstances warrant it, may pay the fees in whole or in part of pupils from the primary schools of their areas to continue their education in an independent boarding school. There was for a time in the Ministry a Committtee on Boarding Education which maintained a list of places put at its disposal by the independent schools. The local education authorities are now in direct contact with such schools and the Committee serves only in an advisory capacity.

### The Chief Education Officer

The local education authorities are now required as a duty to appoint a fit person to be its chief education officer. Vacant positions are normally advertised, applications scrutinized, and a short list of suitable candidates is drawn up. Until the Education Act of 1944 the local education authority had full right to make the final selection. Under the Act, however, the final appointment can be made only after consultation with the Minister of Education. He must be furnished with particulars as to the previous experience and qualifications of candidates and may prohibit an appointment, if, in his opinion, the candidate is not a fit person. The same procedure must be followed by a local government in appointing such officers as the medical officer of health, the highway engineer, or the chief constable of a police authority. There is no indication in the Act as to the meaning of "a fit person" to become the chief education officer nor have the qualifications for the position even been defined. In the United States there are nation-wide facilities for the preparation of school administrators; in England no such facilities exist. The usual course for a person who expects to make the administration of education his career is to acquire the necessary qualifications, after a university education and perhaps some years of teaching, in the office of an education committee.

The organization even of a local education system has become so vast an enterprise that it requires wise guidance and leadership. The chief officer of education is responsible for the business side of administration — finance, buildings and equipment, auxiliary services and so on — and he must be an educational leader both of the lay public and of the teaching body under him. The success of such an officer depends in the main on his ability to influence and educate the members of his education committee and its sub-committees. There have, in fact, been instances where the chairman of such a committee has earned a wider reputation nationally than the chief education officer. It is significant perhaps that there is developing a preference for the title "chief education officer" rather than "director of education," which until recently was more common. Like other government officials the school administrator and his staff of local inspectors, organizers, welfare officers, and others are expected to influence those with whom he must deal by suggestions and advice rather than by "directions."

### The Educational Highway

The educational career of the English children and youth now proceeds on a broad highway rather than up a ladder. The route is not as direct as in the United States but it has ceased to be as complicated as it was before the 1944 Education Act. Two serious obstacles have been removed; place of residence and economic circumstances of the parents no longer stand in the way of child's progress "from the gutter to the university." At the age of two and until the age of five a child may attend a nursery class or nursery school. Compulsory school attendance begins at the age of five and, since April 1, 1947, continues to fifteen. The Act provides that the age limit may be raised to sixteen by Order in Council. The child need not attend a publicly maintained school, since the law only makes it "the duty of the parent of every child of compulsory school age to cause him to receive efficient full-time education suitable to his age, ability, and aptitude, either by regular attendance at school or otherwise." Accordingly parents have a choice between sending a child to a private school at their own expense or to a county school, that is, a publicly maintained school. In the former case parents have the responsibility of proving that a child is being efficiently educated. Failure to send a child to school at all is, of course, a legal offense punishable by fine or ultimately imprisonment.

There is no longer any provision for the payment of maintenance grants to children in secondary schools. In schools that are maintained at public expense fees have been abolished and any hardships that might be imposed on parents by the raising of the school age to fifteen (or later to sixteen) are mitigated by the provision of meals and milk as well as shoes and clothing as part of the auxiliary services, and by the family allowance scheme created in 1945. Under the Family Allowance Act which went into effect in August, 1946, allowances of eight shillings (originally five shillings) per week for each child other than the first are now paid to the parents while such child is of school age or up to August 1st following the sixteenth birthday if the child is undergoing a course of full-time education or is an apprentice.

At the age of five the child enters upon his primary education, which is given in the first two years (five to seven) in the "infants school" and continued in the "junior school" (seven to eleven). At this point there survives a serious difficulty for which a solution has not yet been found. The years from eleven to fifteen are to be devoted to some form of free secondary education, given in three types of schools — grammar or academic, modern or general, and technical. The type to which a boy or girl will be advanced de-

pends on his previous school record and an examination to discover his ability and aptitude. [8] The burning issues in England
almost since the Education Act was passed centers on the question whether abilities and aptitudes can be tested at the age of
eleven, and on the kind of organization to be provided for secondary education — three types of schools, multilateral schools, or
comprehensive schools. These issues will be discussed in a later
chapter.

On completing the four remaining years of compulsory schooling
a boy or girl may continue for two or three years more until ready
to enter a university. Access to university education has been considerably facilitated by the expanding provision of state and local
scholarships. Many may at about the age of fifteen become ap-
prentices or trainees in an office and prepare to enter, by taking
appropriate examinations, any one of a growing number of professional careers that do not require university preparation.

When the Act is fully in force young persons will be required to
attend "county colleges" or continuation schools for one full day or
two half-days each week for forty weeks in each year or for one
continuous period of eight weeks or two continuous periods of four
weeks each, up to the age of eighteen. The county colleges will
form part of the schemes for "Further Education" which local authorities are required to provide and include an extensive range of
day and evening schools and institutes for various types of vocational training and for general or leisure-time education. Adult
education is provided by local education authorities, the universities, and a number of voluntary organizations of which the best
known is the Workers' Education Association. Residential colleges
offering courses lasting a week end or several weeks are spreading
rapidly. Nor can the contribution to the education of children
through the school broadcasting system and of adults through the
general radio program be omitted in a consideration of opportunities for informed education.

This system is at present in process of being organized. How
long it will be before the principles on which the Education Act of
1944 is based will be fully realized in practice depends upon the

[8] A boy or girl may, of course, continue to a private fee-paying school if
parents so desire.

economic situation. For the present the three chief obstacles to the full reconstruction of the educational system are due to the unanticipated increase in the birth rate during and since the war which swells the enrollment in the schools each year and will continue to swell until about 1960. There is consequently a shortage of school buildings and classrooms; about half the children in elementary schools are still in oversize classes without any likelihood that the norm planned in 1950 — thirty pupils per class in primary schools and twenty-five in secondary schools — can be established for many years. There is also a shortage of teachers not only as a result of the increased enrollment, but also because the number of recruits is falling. Equally difficult to deal with is the fact that the distribution of pupils varies from locality to locality, because of a movement to urban areas. It may take several decades before the Act can be implemented in its entirety.[9]

## FRANCE

### The French Tradition of Administration

For more than a century and a half the administration of governmental affairs in France has been centralized. Although France has accepted centralization as the most efficient method of administration, it is important to note that the principle was confirmed by periodic recurrences of crises. The purpose of centralization in the administration of education differed, however, from that in totalitarian regimes. Centralization of control was not directed to the subordination of the individual in mind and body to the will of the state, nor was it intended, except under Napoleon, to indoctrinate the citizen with a particular political ideology. The primary purpose of centralization has been to develop a sense of national unity and solidarity in the face of threats to the country's stability from within and from without. National solidarity, however, does not mean, as it does in totalitarian states, the complete and unquestioned subordination of the individual.

Through education on different levels the aim has been directed

---

[9] See P.E.P., "Schools Under Pressure: I. The Shortage of Teachers, and II. Buildings and Costs," *Planning*, Vol. XIX, No. 359, December 21, 1953.

to develop a sense of loyalty and patriotism through an intelligent understanding of that cultural heritage of the nation which is common to all without conflicting with the local and regional traditions. The matrix from which the content of the curriculum is derived for both elementary and secondary schools is *culture générale*. As the late M. Bouglé explained in 1931, "If you now ask me to tell you what we understand by general culture and why we defend it, I would, in answer to the second question, answer that we defend it because we are a nation of individualists and because we wish to be a democratic nation. We are, therefore, compelled to impart a minimum of general culture, even to the humblest citizen, simply because they are citizens." [10] At the elementary level the aim that has persisted was enunciated in 1887 by Octave Gréard: "The object of elementary education is not to include in the different subjects that are treated everything that it is possible to know, but to learn in each of them those things of which we cannot be ignorant."

The secondary school curriculum has in the same way been dominated by the emphasis on *culture générale* not only as a body of knowledge to be mastered by the educated person and particularly by the élite of the nation but as a method of intellectual training, *culture d'esprit*. No better contrast between the French authoritarian scheme in the content of education and that of totalitarian regimes can be mentioned than the ends sought in the training of the élite — critical ability, clarity of thought and expression, and refinement of taste and appreciation.

Undoubtedly the French system of administration has been bureaucratic but not for political purposes so much as because it is a logical scheme for maintaining a certain uniformity and unity in education under the leadership of trained and experienced experts. And yet the state does not claim a monopoly of education; the existence of private schools is not prohibited provided that they are not conducted by religious associations and that they meet some minimum standards. There is also a certain clear-cut orderliness in a centralized system that is not found where local committees are permitted and encouraged to exercise some initiative in their

[10] *Conference on Examinations,* held at Eastbourne, England, May 1931 (New York, 1931), p. 46.

educational planning. The bureaucracy, however, does not function completely without consulting, if not public, at any rate professional opinion. At every level of organization the government officials have the cooperation of councils or consultative bodies which represent different levels of the teaching profession, and for elementary education the public in general.

The educational system of France, like that of other nations, will undoubtedly be reconstructed before long. It is significant, however, in studying the major proposal for reform, that of the Langevin Commission, and other discussions of educational reconstruction which are based on the latest educational theories, with their emphasis on the individual, individual growth, guidance, activity methods of instruction, and adaptation of the curriculum to the environment, that no suggestion is made that the system of administration would also have to be changed. The centralized system secures uniformity; the proposed reform calls for greater flexibility and initiative and greater variety and diversity within a national framework. In such a reform there would be little room for prescribed courses of study and textbooks or even for examinations conducted by a central authority.

Thus, instead of the traditional approach to education, whether in the elementary or in the secondary schools, the project for the reform of education, now known as the Langevin Report, submitted to the Ministry of National Education, starts from a different premise but without losing sight of the traditional aims. "The structure of education must in fact be adapted to the social structure. In the last half century the educational structure has not been profoundly modified. The social structure, on the other hand, has undergone a rapid evolution and fundamental changes. Mechanization, the use of new sources of energy, the development of new means of transportation and distribution, concentration of industry, increasing productivity, the striking entrance of women into economic life, the spread of elementary education have profoundly modified the conditions of life and the social organization. The rapidity and the extent of economic progress, which in 1880 made the diffusion of elementary education necessary among the working masses, to-day present the problem of recruiting an ever more numerous personnel of managers and technicians. The middle class called by heredity to fill the places of leadership and responsibility will no longer be able by itself to suffice for this. The new needs of modern economy make it necessary to reconstruct the educational system, which, as it stands, is no longer adapted to the economic and social conditions.

"This lack of adaptation of education to the present state of society has as a visible sign the absence of inadequacy of contacts between school at all levels and life. Elementary, secondary, and higher studies are too often on the margin of reality. The school seems to be a closed environment impenetrable to experiences of the world. The divorce between school education and life is accentuated by the permanence of the educational institutions in the midst of a society in a state of rapid evolution. This divorce deprives instruction of its educative character. A reform is urgent which will remedy this deficiency of the school in the education of the producer and the citizen and will enable it to give everybody a civic, social, and humane training."

This definition of the relations of education to the culture pattern is new in the discussions of educational theory in France, although the experiments started shortly before World War II with guidance classes leading to the *classes nouvelles* and the use of activity methods pointed in a new direction to which a centralized system of administration could not lead.

Nor was the organization of the educational system immune from criticism. Like most national educational organizations the various types and levels of schools had grown up without a plan by the addition of new types, which, although needed, were not articulated with the existing schools. Not only was there an absence of integration; there was a considerable amount of overlapping. French education was marked not only by the traditional dual system of elementary schools for the masses and secondary schools for a minority, but there developed since 1910 a third strand with the rapidly growing system of technical education. The active movement for educational reform began during World War I when *Les Compagnons de l'Université Nouvelle* launched their proposal for *l'école unique* or a common school system with primary and secondary education articulated and variety of courses at the secondary level, and organized on the principle of providing equality of educational opportunity for all.

Some progress was made but considerably more was needed. The distinction was abolished about 1925 between elementary education as given in the public primary schools and in the fee-paying preparatory classes attached to the *lycées* which gave an advantage to the children of the privileged for admission to the secondary schools. Fees in the secondary schools began to be abolished in the thirties. In 1936 the age of compulsory school attendance was raised to fourteen. The approval in 1937 through the efforts of M. Jean Zay, then Minister of National Education, of an experiment with guidance classes (*classes d'orientation*) was more significant than appears on the surface. The experiment meant a shift of emphasis, not too marked but nevertheless significant in the light of the French tradition, from the subject to the pupil. This experiment was followed by another after World War II with *classes nouvelles* or activity methods in which the Commission on Reform, appointed in 1943 by M. René Capitant when the government was in Algiers, already showed a great deal of interest. Both experiments meant an important innovation in two respects — the acceptance of the results of modern psychology and a greater interest in the pupil as an individual. These changes could, in fact, not be carried out without allowing teachers in each school and in each classroom greater freedom and initiative in adapting the educational program and methods of instruction to the capacities of each pupil and without taking the environmental conditions into account.

It is, therefore, all the more striking that in the proposals for reconstruction which in many respects are more radical than others put forward in other countries, no suggestion has been made for more relaxation of centralized control. The only suggestion of the Langevin Commission on this point was a change in the function of inspection. The Constitution adopted in 1946 continues the existence of councils of departments and communes elected by universal suffrage but the Council of Ministers is empowered to designate delegates to the local councils to coordinate national and local interests. The Constitution, Article XXV, makes the following provision for education: "The widest possible culture must be offered to all without other limitation than the aptitudes of each one. Every child has the right to instruction and education in the respect of liberty. Organization of public education at every stage is the duty of the State. This education must be free and made accessible to all by material aid to those who without it would not be able to pursue their studies."

## The Central Authority

The administration of all cultural activities of France — art, letters, science, adult education, and physical education — is under the control of the Ministry of National Education. At the head of the Ministry is a Minister who is a member of the cabinet. The Minister is assisted by staff members who are appointed by him and constitute his personal cabinet. He usually has associated with him a Secretary and Under Secretary of State, each with specially delegated responsibility as, for example, for technical education or division of sports and youth. Since the Minister, like all other members of the French government, is subject to the winds of politics, his tenure of office and the tenure of his cabinet staff is very short. Here may be found another reason for centralization in the hands of a permanent staff of officials. The Ministry is divided into a number of divisions, each under a director assisted by a professional staff. These divisions are: general administration (personnel, budget, accounting, etc.), school buildings, and *Centre National de Documentation Pédagogique* or *Musée Pédagogique;* education (primary, secondary, technical, and higher); cultural relations with other countries; and *le Centre National de la Recherche Scientifique.* Each division is again divided into bureaus, each of which has its special area of competence.

The Minister is responsible to Parliament for the conduct of national education, prepares and presents the budget, supervises the execution of the laws, and has the power to draft decrees which, when signed by the President, have legal validity. He nominates for appointment by the President the important officials of the educational service — directors of divisions, inspectors-general, and rectors and inspectors of academies. The inspectors-general are specialists in different levels and subjects of education and periodical visits to and report on schools. It is their function to plan and suggest needed changes in curricula and methods of instruction. The Minister with the advice of his staff prescribes the curricula, courses of study, methods of instruction for all schools and the examination requirements for examinations and scholarship awards.

A number of agencies which serve in an advisory capacity have for a long time been associated with the Ministry. The most important of these is the Higher Council of National Education (*Conseil Supérieur de l'Education Nationale*) which consists of *ex officio* members, of members appointed by the Minister from the ranks of higher officials and university professors, and of elected members — eighty in all. The Council serves as the highest disciplinary court for members of the profession. Together with Educational Councils (*Conseils d'Enseignement*), constituted in the same way as the Higher Council but concerned in the case of each with one particular level of education, the Higher Council serves as a channel for consultation by the Minister on all plans for the reform of education, courses of study, examinations, the regulations for institutions and personnel, and the approval of textbooks. There are in addition professional committees and committees on administration attached to the Ministry and each division, consisting of equal numbers of members appointed by the Minister and of elected members. The joint professional committees (*Comités Techniques paritaires*) advise on new educational regulations and on regulations for personnel, the joint committees on administration (*Commissions Administratives paritaires*) advise on nominations, transfers, promotions, and penalties for personnel.

### Regional Administration

The administrative organization of the central authority is reproduced on a smaller scale in the various types of regional administration divisions — the seventeen academies, the ninety-seven departments, and the communes. The head of each academy is the *Recteur*, who is at once the head of the university in the academy, the representative of the Ministry, and the administrator technically of all education in his area, but generally concerned directly only with secondary and higher education. Since the war the *Recteur* has the assistance of an inspector-general of primary education, a chief inspector for youth and sport, and one or more chief inspectors of technical education. A number of councils are available for advice. They include the University Council (*Conseil de l'Université*) and academic councils (*Conseils Académiques*) for each level of education. As in the Ministry joint professional and administrative committees have been added to advise the *Recteur*.

The administration of education in each department is entrusted to an academy inspector who represents the *Recteur* of his academy and the Minister of National Education. He has charge of primary education in the department and has under him a number of primary school inspectors of Youth and Sport. His advisory body is the *Conseil Départemental*, which consists of members elected by popular vote. Here again is repeated the organization introduced in the Ministry of joint professional and administration committees to advise this inspector. The departmental council is of interest in the hierarchy of centralized administration as the first body which includes representatives directly elected by the people, by men and women teachers, and by private school managers. It is responsible in the main for primary education and more particularly for the preparation, appointment, and promotion of primary school teachers. Since the war an important change has taken place in this respect. The prefect, formerly responsible for all aspects of administration, including primary education and the first appointment of teachers, has been replaced by the academy inspector. The departments are responsible for the building and maintenance of normal schools, and the approval of plans for school buildings to be constructed by the communes.

The departmental council appoints one or more delegates for each canton (one of about 3000 in the country) for three-year terms. The responsibility of the cantonal delegates is to exercise general oversight over the elementary schools in their area, to advise on the closing of schools or the need of new ones; they may visit schools and report on them to the primary inspector, and they may be members of the departmental *conseil de l'enseignement* of the examining committee for the elementary school certificate, of the school library committee, and the departmental committee to supervise vacation centers and foster children; and they are expected to assist in promoting social services in the schools.

By the time the communes are reached very little is left for them to administer in education. They are required to provide buildings for primary schools; they may, if permitted by the Ministry of National Education, provide and maintain buildings for secondary schools (*collèges*), keep the school census, and encourage school attendance. In these activities the chief responsibility rests with the elected mayor, who is assisted by the *conseil municipal* (town council). Beyond these functions the only participation left to the localities is to provide the special services, like school canteens and clothing for necessitous children. Social services are provided locally by such organizations as the *comité de patronage* or committee of ladies appointed by the academy inspectors to look after the welfare of maternal and other schools and to raise funds for the benefit of the pupils; the *caisses des écoles* are funds established in all communities under the supervision of a board to be used to facilitate the school attendance of poor pupils. Parents' associations have been established in many schools but have been more successful in secondary than in primary schools.

The Social Security system, established by an act of 1942 and amended several times since then, provides allowances to families with at least two children to support. The system provides for the prenatal care of mothers and postnatal care of mothers and children, and pays family allowances where there are two or more children. The allowances for children are contingent on their satisfactory attendance at school during the years of compulsory attendance and may be continued to seventeen if they are apprenticed or to twenty if studying. The regulations for the payment of allowances for children are issued by the Ministers of Labor and Social Security, Finance, Agriculture, Education, and Population. The system adopted for demographic reasons has been a useful instrument for the improvement of school attendance and for the relief of families from any economic handicaps they may incur as a result.

Since 1945 a School Health Service has been in existence under the supervision of the Ministry of Health. Pupils in both public and private schools are examined periodically and their parents are informed of the medical findings. The teachers also have the advantage of health examinations under this service which is conducted by specialized doctors and nurses working from established medical centers.

### Educational Finance

The cost of education is borne mainly by the State since it assumes as ordinary expenditure the payment of all salaries and supplements for such special positions as those of principals, the maintenance of students in normal schools, and aid to necessitous communes. The departments are responsible for the maintenance and repair of normal school buildings, the provision and maintenance of an office for the inspectors in charge of departmental education, and the maintenance of students not living in the normal school dormitories. The communes pay the indemnities for rent for teachers, the wages of maternal school assistants, the cost of teachers' lodgings and repairs, light and heat of the schools, and the supply of school materials and equipment. The cost of the health service established in 1945 under the Ministry of National Education is divided between the three authorities — 50 per cent is borne by the state and 25 per cent each by the departments and communes.

### The Educational Career

The educational career of the French child does not yet follow the broad highway of educational opportunity proposed by the Algiers Commission in 1943 or the Langevin Commission in 1947. France, like England, has been so considerably handicapped that any reform plan, even one far less radical than that of the Langevin Commission, would be impossible for many years to achieve. There is a shortage of school buildings, and materials and manpower to build new schools are inadequate. This shortage is aggravated by a shortage of teachers, whose numbers were reduced by war casualties and by smaller entries into the profession, and an increase in the number of children to be educated. A few reforms have been introduced. The school age raised to fourteen in 1936 has been continued with a special curriculum in the last year of the last two classes of the elementary school. The higher elementary school has been given the name of *collège moderne* and is now a school at the second level ( *du second degré* ). Fees for secondary education, reintroduced by the Vichy government among many other reactionary steps, have been abolished. The standards of teacher preparation have been raised with somewhat higher standards of admission. On the other hand, access to the Universities has been made more difficult by the introduction after the *baccalauréat,* which was formerly required for admission, of a preparatory year (*l'année propédeutique*) at the close of which there is an examination to determine whether students should be permitted to continue university studies.

At present a child's educational career may begin at the age of two if a maternal school (*école maternelle*) is available where he lives. Compulsory school attendance begins at the age of six and continues to the age of fourteen. At the age of six the pupil enters the primary school (*école primaire élémentaire*) and may remain there until he leaves at the age of fourteen as do the majority of children. They then enter some occupation which permits them to take a wide choice of vocational courses. At the age of eleven some may continue their education in a continuation course (*cours complémentaire*) which provides a shortened form of the course of the *collège moderne.* The more able pupils have the choice at the age of eleven of entering an academic secondary school (*lycée* or *collège*) or a modern secondary school (*collège moderne*), both of which constitute *l'enseignement du second degré.* A technical secondary school (*collège technique*) has been added at this level very recently. The academic secondary school course is seven years in length, divided into two cycles, of which the first four years offer general courses, and the second is more specialized with a final year of specialization in philosophy and letters or philosophy and science, or mathematics. The *collège moderne* offers a general course of four years and in an increasing number is extending its course to seven years. Pupils who intend to leave school at fifteen or sixteen may take an examination at the end of the fourth year and, if successful, receive a *brevet d'études du premier cycle du second degré.* At the end of the sixth year pupils may take the first part of a *baccalauréat,* and the second part at the end of the seventh year.

The Langevin Commission, which was appointed in 1944 and submitted its report to the Minister of National Education in 1947, recommended a complete reorganization of the educational system to meet the new social, economic, and cultural conditions of France and to provide equality of educational opportunities for all. They proposed the extension of compulsory school attendance from six to eighteen, the period to be divided into three cycles. From three to seven, children would attend the maternal schools. From seven to eleven they would attend the primary school which would constitute the first cycle. The second cycle would continue from eleven to fifteen and would be devoted to discovering the abilities and aptitudes of the pupils (*cycle d'orientation*). The years from fifteen to eighteen would constitute the third cycle for specialization (*cycle de détermination*) either in a full-time or part-time school. The Commission also recommended some changes at the university level and the integration of *les Grandes Ecoles* with the universities. The Commission, recognizing the existence of obstacles to the reconstruction of the educational system, suggested as an immediate step the raising of the age of compulsory school attendance to fifteen. There is lacking, however, any suggestion of the probable cost of putting the complete reform into effect.

### Private Schools

The state does not exercise a monopoly in education and private schools may be established at all levels, including higher. The state only reserves the right to set up certain standards for private education (*l'enseignement libre*), primarily to ensure that the character of the education given is not contrary to the Constitution and secondly to see that the sanitary conditions are satisfactory. Otherwise the only requirements are that the principal and teachers in technical, primary, and continuation schools have the necessary certificates of competence, and that in the secondary schools the principal has at least the *baccalauréat* and five years of service in a public or private school. Except for these conditions the schools are free in matters of curriculum and methods. This freedom is limited, however, by the necessity of preparing for examinations conducted under state auspices for the award of recognized certificates.

Individuals or associations, provided that they are not religious congregations, may establish schools, after careful inquiry by local and state authorities on the basis of which permission from the Minister of National Education may be granted. The restoration after World War I of Alsace and Lorraine, where a majority of the schools were denominational, compelled the government to assist them financially. The Vichy Government gave financial assistance to all denominational schools. The postwar government was consequently faced with a serious difficulty in withholding aid. Political agitation resulted in 1951 in the enactment of a law creating a special fund from which payments are made to heads of families having children in elementary schools. The allocation amounts to 1000 francs per child per term of school. In the case of children attending public schools, the grants are paid over to departmental school funds to be used for general elementary school purposes. The allocations for children attending private schools are paid to the parents' associations of the schools.

In 1952–53 the private elementary schools, mostly denominational, had an enrollment of 965,671 pupils (403,358 boys and 562,313 girls) as compared with 4,699,919 pupils (2,445,832 boys and 2,254,087 girls) in public elementary schools. At the secondary level, including preparatory classes and post-*baccalauréat* classes, there were 359,316 pupils (167,988 boys and 191,328 girls) in private schools as compared with an enrollment of 483,052 pupils (254,753 boys and 228,299 girls) in public secondary schools.

## UNION OF SOVIET SOCIALIST REPUBLICS

### The Background

Education in the Union of Soviet Socialist Republic (U.S.S.R.) was given the priority in the revolutionary ideology that it has always received in modern totalitarian revolutions. A complete change not only in the economic foundations but also in the world outlook or ideology upon which the country was to be rebuilt made the emphasis on education inevitable. For it is the essence of scientific materialism as well as of dialectical materialism that traditional culture patterns — superstitions, beliefs, religion as "the opiate of the people" — must be eliminated. The emphasis on education was based partly on the Marxist principle that all cultures reflect their economic environment, and on Lenin's practical opinion that "You cannot build a Communist state with an illiterate people."

Hence the first task to which the leaders of the Communist Revolution turned their attention was the liquidation of illiteracy. For this there were several reasons, all of them political and pragmatic. The Revolution had succeeded and maintained itself by coercive violence and force. Ultimately, however, persuasion was to take their place. A people had to be made literate in order to be more susceptible to and approachable by whatever those in power permitted to be printed and circulated. As Stalin later defined the process, "education is a weapon whose effect depends on who wields it." The idea of education as a weapon appears to be a favorite analogy, for the authors of a Russian treatise on *Pedagogy,* quoted by Counts and Lodge wrote: "Education in the U.S.S.R. is a weapon for strengthening the Soviet state and the building of a classless society." [11]

The weapon is definitely loaded with content for propaganda and indoctrination rather than for the development of an independent and enlightened mind. That content is entirely inspired by the doctrines of Marx, Lenin, and Stalin. What was perhaps inevitable in the early years of the Revolution has become the normal practice, although more than one generation has by this time been exposed to the propaganda machine and knows only that much of past and contemporary history as the authorities permit. Trained to accept everything without question and believing everything when it is repeated frequently, acceptance is rationalized as a patriotic duty. For the task set before every Communist in the U.S.S.R. is to contribute to the plan "to overtake and surpass in the shortest possible historical period the most advanced capitalistic countries and thus to insure the victory of socialism in its historic competition with the system of capitalism." That readiness for quiescent and submissive acceptance is further strengthened by what is claimed to be its result — the victory in the "Great Patriotic War" won wholly by the efforts of the people of his country.

[11] George S. Counts and Nucia P. Lodge, *I Want to be Like Stalin* (New York, The John Day Co., 1947), p. 14. By permission of the publisher.

It was perhaps only in these ways that "new minds, new men" could be formed.

Education has continued to be a loaded weapon. Having consolidated the gains over men's minds since 1917 by force, purges, and persuasion, the authorities are using the weapon to win new victories over the environment by extensive training for Communist loyalty and for devotion to work as a duty and an honor. According to the Constitution of 1936, Article 12, "In the U.S.S.R. work is a duty and a matter of honor for every able-bodied citizen, in accordance with the principle: 'He who does not work, neither shall he eat.' The principle applied in the U.S.S.R. is that of socialism: 'From each according to his ability, to each according to his work.' "

Among the many expectations which were aroused in the interests of propaganda was the slogan that in time, when socialism was fully in operation, the state would wither away. There is less talk today than there used to be about this, just as there is less talk about the class struggle now that the hostile exploiters and enemies of the proletariat of the workers and peasants have been removed. Neither slogan would have the support of the large armed forces maintained by the state or of the horde of bureaucrats, both new constituting new social classes.

To read the Constitution or Fundamental Law adopted in 1936 is to run the risk of being trapped into believing the Communist claim that it is the most democratic constitution in history. Universal suffrage is extended to all men and women over eighteen years of age regardless of race, nationality, or educational attainment. A bill of rights guarantees the rights to leisure, to maintenance in old age or in case of loss of capacity to work and sickness, to education, to special care of women, and to equality of all irrespective of nationality or race "in all spheres of economic, state, cultural, social, and political life." The law guarantees freedom of speech, of the press, of assembly and holding of mass meetings, and of street processions and demonstrations. Article 126 guarantees the right to unite in public organization; these include the Communist Party in which "the most active and politically most conscious citizens in the ranks of the working class and other sections of the working people unite." The Party is stated in this article to be "the vanguard of the working people in their struggle to strengthen and develop the socialist system and is the leading core of all organizations of the working people, both public and state."

The position of the Communist Party, whose membership consists of only about 3 per cent of the population, was admitted by Stalin. In an address to the Eighth Congress of the Soviets on November 28, 1936, Stalin said, "I must admit that the draft of the new Constitution leaves in force the regime of the dictatorship of the working class as well as preserves unchanged the present leading position of the Communist Party." [12] It is the Communist Party that approves the list of candidates to be "freely" elected to the various representative organs from the All Union Supreme Soviet to the local Soviets of Working People's Deputies. The Party determines policy, guides the proletariat "dictators," and directs the work of the Soviet and other agencies of government as well as of all organizations of workers and peasants — trade unions, cooperatives, cultural groups, and youth organizations. The Party has also played an important role in determining educational policy, particularly in putting a stop to so-called progressive education in 1931 and insisting on a return to more traditional organization of the school program. The successes in the sphere of public education have been achieved, according to Professor Y. N. Medinsky, "thanks to the great attention paid to the education of the peoples of the U.S.S.R. by the Communist Party, the Soviet Government and by J. V. Stalin personally." [13]

To understand the background, however, the following description of present conditions in the U.S.S.R., already quoted earlier, must be borne in mind: "The long and powerful arm of the State guides the Soviet citizen through his daily routine, regulates the conditions under which he lives and works, measures out his 'living space,' confers upon him decorations and honorary titles if he is diligent and docile, or, with the assistance of the ubiquitous police and of an elastic and comprehensive penal code, chastises

[12] Quoted by Michael T. Florinsky, *Towards an Understanding of the U.S.S.R.* (New York, The Macmillan Co., 1951), p. 69.
[13] Y. N. Medinsky, *Public Education in the U.S.S.R.* (Moscow, Foreign Language Publishing House, 1951), p. 34.

him if he is recalcitrant, unappreciative, inefficient, or, perhaps unable to keep pace with the speed-up of industrialization. Intellectual pursuits, the press, the schools, the arts, and science are rigidly controlled by an omnipotent bureaucracy whose chief qualification is unfaltering adherence to the 'party line.'" [14]

The Constitution of 1936, Article 121, guaranteed the right to education to all citizens at all levels, including higher education, without fees and with "state stipends for the overwhelming majority of students in the universities and colleges." In 1940 fees were introduced at the university level and in the last three years of ten-year secondary schools. The reasons for this were the heavy burden of defense expenditures and the improved economic status of the workers. The introduction of fees also helped to keep the number of students down to correspond with the probable number of appointments available for highly trained personnel. Fees were introduced in 1940 but the Constitution was not amended until 1947 to read as follows: "Citizens of the U.S.S.R. have the right to education. This right is guaranteed by universal, compulsory elementary education, by free seven-year education; by a system of state stipends to outstanding students in higher schools; by the conducting of instruction in the schools in the native language; by the organization in factories, state farms, machine-tractor stations, and collective farms of free vocational, technical, and agronomical training for the workers."

In 1943 coeducation, adopted in 1917 to mark the equality of the sexes, was abolished in schools in the cities and later in other schools on the basis of the discovery that the educational and psychological needs of girls differed from those of boys. Actually the changes in the curriculum of girls' schools emphasized training in home economics and child care; women would in future help to repair the terrific losses in the war. Another important change of attitude was the banning of "pedology," or the more recent developments of modern educational psychology, especially tests and measurements, described as bourgeois pseudo-science. The main reason, however, was that its findings were inconsistent with the Marxist point of view on heredity and environment and on nature and nurture, which assigned the predominant influence to

[14] Florinsky, *op. cit.*, p. 17.

environment or nurture in molding intelligence and shaping character.

The characteristic innovation in education during the early years of Soviet organization was the emphasis on polytechnic education. Starting with "socially useful labor," polytechnization gradually inducted the pupils into the foundations of vocational education. A conflict arose about 1930 among educators on the value of polytechnic education; some interpreted it as activity education, others as actual industrial or agricultural education. By 1930 it was decided to abandon polytechnization in favor of general education with especial emphasis on the study of those sciences necessary for the pursuit of technical education. Polytechnic instruction survived but was directed to the development of an understanding of the organization and importance of industry and agriculture in the economic life of the nation.

The change in favor of general education was justified by citing both Lenin and Stalin. Lenin's injunction was that "You can become a Communist only when you enrich your mind with a knowledge of all the treasures of mankind." [15] In 1938 Stalin in an address to students said that "To build, one must possess knowledge, one must study persistently, patiently." In 1949 Stalin was quoted in an educational journal as saying that "The level of culture — education of the whole population, workers and peasants — must be raised in order to build our society." [16]

### Administration of Education

To the task of organization and administration of the educational system a large number of agencies, governmental and nongovernmental, are devoted, although in the Soviet State it is something of a paradox to distinguish between the two types of agencies. Everything that is of an educational or cultural character is under the control of government or of the Communist Party. The Constitution, Article 14 which defines the activities within the jurisdiction of the Union of Soviet Socialist Republics includes "(r) Es-

[15] Medinsky, *op. cit.*, p. 12.
[16] Elizabeth Moos, *The Educational System of the Soviet Union* (New York, National Council of American-Soviet Friendship, 1950), p. 7.

tablishment of the basic principles in the sphere of education and public health." In practice the control and administration of all education except higher education and some types of secondary schools are left to the government of each Republic. For higher education there is a Ministry (formerly known as the People's Commissariat of Culture) with a Minister in charge.

All other types of general education — primary and secondary schools, schools for adults, schools for young industrial and agricultural workers, children's homes, special schools, and out-of-school establishments for leisure, recreational, or cultural activities — are administered by a Minister and his department in each Republic. Other forms of education and training, such as labor reserve schools, teacher training institutions, schools for nurses and medical aids, are under special relevant Ministries.

Locally the supervision of education is entrusted to committees appointed by the executive committees of the Soviets of Working People's Deputies. These are elected in territories, regions, districts, cities, and rural localities to direct among other activities "local economic and cultural organization and development and draw up the local budgets" (Constitution, Article 97). These committees appoint the teachers in the schools under their supervision and prepare the budgets. Each school has its own council which includes teachers, the school physician, representatives of the Communist Party, trade unions and Komsomols. The council and teachers may formulate and submit suggestions bearing on the work of a school, but the principal is not required to accept them. In general the administration of education is governed by Lenin's principle of "centralized supervision and decentralized activity," a principle that restricts the initiative of local committees and teachers. In practice control is exercised from the relevant central authority down to each institution.

Although there does not exist a central authority for the administration of all education throughout the U.S.S.R., uniformity is secured, first through the supervision and definition of policy by the Communist Party, and secondly by the acceptance of the policies and practices of the Russian Soviet Federative Socialist Republic (R.S.E.S.R.) as a model, such adaptations of the model as may be required by the local environment may be made in accordance with Lenin's principle that culture should be "national in form and socialist in content." The aims of education are the same throughout the U.S.S.R. What was hailed as a great political achievement of the Revolution, the autonomy of national universities, simply means that in education their own languages may be used but for the one purpose only — "to educate fighters for the workers' cause and builders of the socialist state." At the same time the study of Russian has been pushed in the Republics as also in the satellite states. The authors of *Pedagogy,* B. P. Yesipov and N. K. Goncharov, are quoted as claiming that "compulsory uniformity of program is one of the most valuable conditions for the improvement of school work in our country." [17]

The support of the schools is provided by the central U.S.S.R. government on the basis of budgets drawn up by each Republic and its localities. The revenues are derived from the state enterprises, direct and indirect taxes on individuals and on cooperative farms. Some support for special activities is derived from trade unions and agricultural organizations.

## The Educational Career

The Soviet educational system is founded on the principle of equality of opportunity according to ability and aptitude. It is widely ramified and includes not only the formal organization of schools, but a wide range of provisions for informal or leisure education and activities. Both formal and informal institutions are inspired by the same ideological aims. The mass media of communication are under the control of the Communist Party and "are oriented toward a single goal. They serve as instruments through which the party and government *mobilize* the mind and will; they must see to it that what ought to be done *is* done, what should be thought and felt *is* thought and felt." A large amount of space is devoted to educational and cultural material but "they are justified to the extent to which they facilitate the prime task of more effective party rule of the nation. There is no such thing as art for art's sake in the Soviet Union." [18] There is no break in gauge between education and life.

[17] Counts and Lodge, *op. cit.,* p. 19.
[18] Alex Inkeles, *Public Opinion in Soviet Russia: a Study in Mass Persuasion* (Cambridge, Harvard University Press, 1952), pp. 317 and 318.

The young Soviet infant up to the age of three may be left in the care of a nursery and at three may enter a kindergarten or playground, if one is available. Compulsory education begins at the age of seven and continues to the age of fourteen. In the rural areas, however, only a four-year elementary school has been available until recently, when the seven-year school began to be established more generally. In the cities the seven-year school or incomplete middle school is the common school with a ten-year school or complete middle school in the larger cities. The first four years constitute the primary school, the rest are devoted to general secondary education. There is a promotion examination at the end of the fourth year and leaving examinations at the end of the seventh and tenth years. The ablest students proceed to some form of higher education which is predominantly professional. Secondary vocational schools for technicians which prepare teachers, nurses, librarians, dental technicians, medical aids, and specialists in various arts are available to students who complete the first seven year course. For out-of-school hours there is an extensive provision of clubs for leisure and recreational activities, libraries, theatres, parlors, and centres for literary and scientific circles. The Young Pioneers (ten to fifteen years of age) and the Komsomols or Young Communist League (fifteen to nineteen) play an important role in providing these activities as well as serving to disseminate political education and to prepare for later membership in the Communist Party.

Side by side with the schools for general education is the organization for vocational training. There are schools for young industrial and agricultural workers and adult workers who need further training while spending part of the day in some occupation. There is a program for the labor reserve to train adolescents (boys fourteen to nineteen and girls fifteen to eighteen) in trade, railway, or factory training schools for periods of varying duration at the end of which the worker must serve for four years at jobs to which they are assigned by the Ministry of Labor Reserves. In factories there are also schools for "upgrading" trained skilled workers.

Finally, provision is made for adult education at all levels of formal education and informal activities of a recreational or cultural character. In addition to the schools cultural establishments, clubs, centers, and Palaces of Culture are provided under the supervision of a Committee for Cultural Educational Establishments.

## UNITED STATES

### The American Tradition

The principles upon which the organization and administration of education should be based were already well defined in the United States at the beginning of the nineteenth century. Of these the first was a strong faith in education and the ideal of equality of educational opportunities in contrast to the "aristocratic" or class organization which had been brought over from Europe. The second principle arose from the widespread opinion that the studies provided by the Latin grammar schools and liberal arts colleges were themselves "aristoractic" or "monarchical" and helped to perpetuate class distinction. The third principle was that new types of studies must be introduced to meet the conditions of new times and a new government. Since the resources of this new environment were still to be explored, developed, and exploited, the new studies, it was held, must include these sciences and other subjects which would promote the progressive improvement of the economic life of the nation.

The young Republic thus started with a strong faith in education and in equality of opportunities. But it was in the conquest of the frontier that the ideals and character of the American were formed. The pioneering conditions of the frontier demanded resourcefulness and self-reliance on the part of the individual, and provided opportunities for every individual to make the most of himself. At the same time these conditions, before local governments were established, called for readiness and ability to cooperate for the common good, for teamwork, and for neighborly cooperation. The same conditions, however, were responsible also for the development of certain attitudes of mind which have not altogether disappeared — wastefulness of resources, which were regarded as unlimited, contempt for the expert and theorist, an emphasis on the rights rather than the duties of the individual, and an emphasis on freedom rather than on responsibility. The exploitation of the unlimited resources of the country developed in the American a restless, nervous energy, and a buoyancy of spirit and optimism which have always disposed him to look for bigger and better things, for change and innovations. The contrast between the old and new outlook has been well stated by Carl Russell Fish in *The Rise of the Common Man:* "Whereas Washington devoted his attention to bringing his garden to an exquisite perfection, the men of the thirties and forties sought novelty rather than perfection," a feature of American life already noted in the eighteen-thirties by de Tocqueville.

The conditions of frontier life were responsible for another characteristic — the emphasis on the practical and on immediate returns, an emphasis which, on the one hand, tended to look with suspicion on theory, and, on the other, developed the belief that only those ideals are worth while that can be made to work.

All the forces that have been mentioned contributed to produce that impatience and restlessness which broke down conservatism and the worship of tradition and precedent, and resulted in a readiness to experiment and in a national mentality that differentiates the American from the Englishman.

The development of the frontier in the United States provided extensive opportunities for all and made the emergence of the common man possible without the stratification characteristic of European countries. Severe and ruthless as the economic exploitation may have been in the industrial development of the United States, socio-economic stratification did not become marked. There exists a social mobility which is taken for granted and to that mobility educational opportunities have made an important contribution.

### Education a Public Concern

The idea of publicly provided and maintained schools, already adopted in some of the colonies, was accepted as a definite principle as soon as the Republic was established. Until state governments were organized the only schools available in many places were private. Nor was there any thought of creating a nationally maintained and controlled system of education. It was understood that the failure to refer to education in the Constitution implied that its provision was left to each state. Congress did, however, look to the future, and in 1785 and 1787 set aside sections of land in each township of states already formed or to be formed as the population moved westward. The motive for the provision of land as the financial basis for establishing school systems was clearly defined in the sentence "Religion, morality, and knowledge being necessary to good government and the happiness of mankind, schools and the means of education shall be forever encouraged."

The views of American statesmen on the importance of education have always expressed the nation's aims. They can be traced through from the statement by George Washington in his Farewell Address until the last decade in the bulletin by the U.S. Office of Education, "Expressions on Education by Builders of American Democracy." President Franklin Delano Roosevelt's letter to the president of the National Education Association (1935) presents a concise summary of these expressions: "Education must light the path for social change. The social and economic problems confronting us are growing in complexity. The more complex and difficult these problems become, the more essential it is to provide broad and complete education; that kind of education that will equip us as a nation to decide these problems for the best interest of all concerned. Our ultimate security, to a large extent, is based upon the individual's character, information, skill, and attitude — and the responsibility rests squarely upon those who direct education in America. It is your duty, no less than mine, to look beyond the narrow confines of the schoolroom; to see that education provides understanding, strength, and security for those institutions we have treasured since we first established ourselves as a nation and shall continue everlastingly to cherish."

### Founding the System of Public Education

Although the general outlines of an educational system which would provide equality of educational opportunities and a curriculum better adapted to the new form of government and the new environment had been discussed before 1800, some time was to elapse before the plans could be put into effect. There were still some, like Thomas Jefferson, who favored the provision of some education for all but who continued to be wedded to a selective system for the best minds. The Jacksonian era which marked the rise of the common man definitely marked the period of transition when the foundations were laid for the common school.

By 1830 the general principles of an educational system for all were clearly established, but there were many difficulties in the way of realizing them in practice. Central administrative agencies or state boards of education had to be established; teachers had to be trained; the conflicting interests of different religious denominations had to be settled; the people had to be reconciled to the payment of taxes for the support of education. The leadership was assumed by public-spirited leaders and organizations; of the leaders the names best known abroad were those of Horace Mann and Henry Barnard, but there were many others who in the decade from 1830 to 1840 laid the foundations for a public, tax-supported, and secular system of education in each state. The first concern was the establishment of elementary schools; public secondary or high schools followed slowly and it was not until 1874, after the court decision in the Kalamazoo Case, that the provision of free secondary education as part of the common school system was recognized as legal. Free state universities had begun to be established in the first quarter of the nineteenth century, and the country, as the population began to move westward, was provided with a large number of denominational colleges.

Thus the United States had a start of a century as compared with other countries, and the pattern of a common system of public education was already envisaged. The pattern was not fully attained, however, without serious difficulties, which the late Professor Cubberley referred to as battles — for taxation, for compulsory attendance laws, and for secular schools.[19] Nor is the pattern yet fully realized so far as the universal provision of equality of educational opportunities is concerned. It is characteristic of that restlessness and desire for constant adaptation to changing condi-

[19] See Elwood P. Cubberley, *Public Education in the United States* (Boston, Houghton Mifflin Co., 1919), pp. 118 ff.

tions, to which reference has been made earlier, that the pattern is constantly being revised, while the fundamental ideals remain the same.

The American system emerging out of plans discussed before 1800 grew slowly until there has been developed a unitary system from the kindergarten to the university. Modifications have been made in order to promote better articulation between the different levels of education. The idea of the common school, which at first included only the eight years of elementary education, was gradually extended to twelve years. More recently it has been proposed to extend it still further to fourteen years. Ten years before England recognized the importance of educating the masters by passing the Education Act of 1870 for the education of children of the working classes, the public school of the United States had already been defined by the Secretary of the Massachusetts Board of Education as "a school established by the public — supported chiefly or entirely by the public, controlled by the public, and accessible to the public upon terms of equality without special charge for tuition."

### The Participation of the Public

The participation of the American public in its educational concerns is real and has its advantages as well as its disadvantages. The United States has succeeded in developing a classless system of education, which will be strengthened if plans go through to provide financial assistance to pupils in schools and students in colleges and universities who are not able to take full advantage of the opportunities now available. Parents are not, however, prevented from sending their children to private schools, but only about 12 per cent of the pupils are enrolled in private elementary and secondary schools, the largest number in Roman Catholic schools. The number of schools maintained by other denominations is very small. Of the other private schools some are boarding or day schools, charging high fees, while others are experimental schools which also charge fees. But the American, when he thinks of education below the college level, thinks only of public schools.

The American educator and the public in the main understand

fully the implications of the phrase in the English Board of Education's White Paper on *Educational Reconstruction* that "In the youth of the nation we have our greatest national asset." The White Paper defines those aims of education which American education seeks to achieve. The American since the early days of the Republic has always recognized the importance of this idea, which he may define in different terms. According to a publication, "Proposals for Public Education in Postwar America," issued by the National Education Association in 1944, the General Purposes of Education were defined in these words: "To provide for every child, youth, and adult attending a public school, college or university the kind and amount of education which (a) will cause him to live happily and usefully according to the principles of American democracy, and (b) lead him to contribute all he can to the development and preservation of a peaceful, co-operative, and equitable world order."

The American has discovered that "Education Brings Dividends" in individual happiness and national welfare, both materially and spiritually. Because the provision and progress of education is not dependent upon a central national or even state authority, but mainly upon each locality, special attention is devoted to enlisting public support and interest. There is on the whole far greater participation in education by the public in the United States than elsewhere. That participation may sometimes be carried too far when the public interferes in matters which it is not qualified to judge, particularly in smaller communities. One of the most important functions of a superintendent of schools is to promote the right kind of publicity to keep the public informed on educational matters in its area, and at the same time to educate it since it is, to use an Americanism, the ultimate consumer and paymaster. In this activity he has enlisted the press which has found that education is news. But many other devices are employed to keep the cause of education before the public — through parent-teachers associations, service clubs, local and national organizations, and associations definitely organized to keep a watchful eye on the schools. One effective method recently introduced is the publication of annual reports, attractively printed and illustrated. Such reports may be open to criticism for presenting only the best features of a school system. The criticism may be valid, but the public is presented with pictures of the kinds of schools that should be available for children and young people.

## Leadership in American Education

Leadership in the development of the theory and practice of education is provided by a great variety of professional institutions and organizations. Among these are the teachers colleges and schools of education of the leading universities of the country, and the experimental or demonstration schools attached to these or privately established as "progressive schools." An important influence has been exercised by the numerous professional associations of administrators, of elementary school and secondary school principals, many of which are grouped together under the National Education Association, the National Society for the Study of Education, the National Society of College Teachers of Education, the John Dewey Society, and the associations concerned with the teaching of different subjects. The investigations or surveys of local or state systems of education or special aspects of these systems played an important part in promoting improvement or reorganization. Such surveys, which began to be made in 1911, were conducted by experts from university departments of education, or appointed by educational foundations. Their reports were generally published and widely studied.

To these unofficial professional sources of leadership must be added the influence that followed the gradual improvement of the standards for the preparation of teachers and the creation of expert administrative and research staffs in state departments of education and local boards of education.

In the formulation of policy there is widespread cooperation between administrative authorities and teachers, professional organizations, institutions for the study of education, lay organizations, and the public in general. Since the schools are considered to belong to the public, the public occasionally tends to disregard the line that should distinguish the formulation of public policy in general and the formulation of policy in matters that should properly be assigned to the expert. The attack launched against the public schools by individuals or groups of individuals since the end of World War II were too often concerned with matters of content of the curriculum and methods of instruction. Nevertheless, there is a constant ferment in education which has no parallel in any other country. What Sir Joshua Fitch wrote in 1901 of American education is still applicable: "Hence America may be regarded as a laboratory in which educational experiments are being tried out on a great scale, under conditions exceptionally favorable to the encouragement of inventiveness and fresh enthusiasm, and to the discovery of new methods and new truths."

It is this ferment from one end of the country to the other that has produced an American system of education without the intervention of a national agency for the administration of education. The mobility of the population helped to disseminate the same idea of a public system of education and the same common aims; the mobility of administrators and of teachers contributed to the same end, as did the opportunities for the study of education in university departments which acquired the status of national centers, attended during the regular academic sessions or during the summer by teachers from different parts of the country; the professional organizations with their national and local meetings and the nation-wide distribution and use of school textbooks have all played their parts in developing a national system of education with such differences as may be produced by state or local conditions of environment, population, and economy.

### Federal Government and Education

Three levels of government are involved in the administration of education in the United States — the federal, state, and local governments. Although the amount of funds devoted to educational purposes by the federal and state governments is increasing, the major responsibility for the maintenance and supervision of education is delegated to local authorities, mainly because they acquired a vested interest in their schools before the states were administratively organized or had created agencies for the supervision of education in their areas. Further, the principle has been widely accepted that the success of an educational system depends upon enlisting the support and interest of the local public.

The Federal Government, while it appropriates considerable

funds distributed for educational purposes through a large number of its departments, does not control any aspects of the system of public education except through grants for special purposes, such as vocational education. Indirectly the Office of Education exercises some influence through its publication, research, and the conduct of surveys when requested. Created originally in 1867 as the Department of Education, the agency has undergone frequent changes of title and of assignment as a division of different government departments. Transferred in 1939 to the Federal Security Agency from the Department of the Interior with which it had been associated for seventy years, the Office of Education became in 1952 a division of a new Department of Health, Education, and Welfare under a Secretary with a membership in the President's Cabinet. The Office under the Commissioner of Education, appointed by the President, subject to approval by the Senate, is primarily an agency for the collection of statistics on the progress of education throughout the country, for the publication of reports and information, for engaging in research and conducting investigations, and for promoting conferences on educational issues of national interest. It administers the funds for land-grant colleges, established under the Morrill Act in 1862 and with funds increased under subsequent Acts, and the funds for vocational education initiated in 1917 under the Smith-Hughes Act and expanded since then. During the depression of the thirties the Office was charged with the responsibility for administering some emergency measures, such as the Civilian Conservation Camps (C.C.C.) and National Youth Administration (N.Y.A.) grants. During and since World War II it has administered a program of school assistance for federally affected areas, that is, areas in which federal activities have created special educational problems that could not be met by the local authority.

Of the other federal departments or agencies that are concerned with education the most important are the Children's Bureau and the Department of Agriculture. The Children's Bureau, established in 1912, after being under the Department of Commerce and Labor and in 1946 placed under the Federal Security Agency, is now a division of the Department of Health, Education, and Welfare; it investigates and publishes reports on all matters that concern the care and welfare of children, and "the welfare and hygiene of maternity and infancy." The Department of Agriculture is responsible for the administration of funds for and the supervision of agricultural experiment stations, agricultural extension service initiated under the Smith-Lever Act, 1914, and since the depression years a school lunch program. The school lunch program was revised and strengthened in 1946 by the National School Lunch Act under which funds and food can be distributed to the schools. The purpose of the Act was "to safeguard the health and well-being of the nation's children and to encourage the domestic consumption of nutritious agricultural commodities and other foods, by assisting the states, through grants-in-aid and other means, in providing an adequate supply of foods and other facilities for the establishment, maintenance, operation and expansion of non-profit school lunch programs." [20]

Despite the worthy purpose of the school lunch program a number of localities have refused to accept the funds provided for it through fear of federal control. This fear has long stood in the way of all measures proposed in Congress to provide federal aid for education. The movement for federal aid for education began in 1917 and has been continued ever since with an accumulation of evidence that, if equality of educational opportunities is to become a reality throughout the country, federal aid must be provided. Apart from inequalities in many states between urban and rural areas, there are striking inequalities from state to state in the character of school buildings, in the qualifications and remuneration of teachers, in the amount of money available, and, therefore, in the per capita cost of education for each pupil, and in the length of school year. These facts have always been known and were made available in the reports and surveys of the Office of Education as well as in the publications of the National Education Association and other organizations. A flood of light was thrown on the educational inequalities and deficiencies by the census of 1940 and by the findings of the Selective Service during World War II. A large number of American citizens were found to be illiterate; a large

---

[20] For detailed accounts of federal activities in education see Office of Education, Federal Security Agency, Bulletin 1952, No. 12, *Federal Funds for Education 1950–51 and 1951–52* (Washington, D.C., 1952).

number were functionally illiterate; and a large number of men were rejected for physical deficiencies.[21]

These conditions have arisen not through indifference or neglect but as a result of the unequal distribution of taxable wealth, for which the Federal Government has more recently become the most serious competitor. Further, the poorer states have the larger number of children to educate. It has been proved a number of times in trustworthy studies that the poorer states put forth greater effort to secure the little that they can provide for educational purposes than the richer states.

In a study published by the National Education Association, it was shown that the number of children per 1000 of the population was 226 for the country as a whole, but 296 in South Carolina, 193 in New York State, and 178 in California. The per capita income ranged from $960 in Nevada to $105 in Mississippi, resulting in an income of $5,140 per child to be educated in Nevada and only $690 in Mississippi. The median cost per classroom unit (that is, teachers' salaries, textbooks, equipment, and current expenses for maintenance) was $1,600 with a sum of $6,000 spent for about 20,000 children in more favored areas and less than $100 in the most underprivileged areas. The school buildings ranged from one-room shacks with one teacher to spacious buildings with the most up-to-date equipment, small classes, and well-qualified and (at that time) well-paid teachers.

Bills for federal aid for education have repeatedly been introduced in Congress and have invariably failed to be enacted on the ground that control would follow the appropriation of federal grants to the states and that the Federal Government would encroach on states' rights. Opposition has also come from Roman Catholics chiefly on the ground that all private and denominational schools have always been excluded from the benefits of any proposal of federal aid. Despite all efforts that have been made to allay the fear of control, the efforts to secure federal aid have failed, nor are they likely to succeed for some time because of retrenchment of government expenditure.

The last notable bill for federal aid, the "Educational Finance

[21] See I. L. Kandel, *The Impact of the War Upon American Education* (Chapel Hill, University of North Carolina Press, 1948), pp. 41 ff.

Act," was introduced in 1949 by the late Senator Robert A. Taft, long an opponent of federal aid. Senator Taft sought by the provision in this act to allay fear of control and invasion of states' rights and at the same time to appease the opposition from private denominational schools. The bill forbade any agency or official in the Federal Government "to exercise any direction, supervision, or control over, or to prescribe any requirements with respect to any school or any State educational institution or agency," and prohibited any federal agency from seeking "to prescribe any requirements with respect to the administration, the personnel, the curriculum, the instruction, the method of instruction, or materials of instruction." Denominational and private schools were not excluded from the operation of the proposal, but it was left to the States in such cases to use the grants as they pleased.

For the present there is no further discussion of federal aid although the need is growing greater. The most serious problems faced at present arise from the increasing shortage of teachers due not only to better opportunities outside the profession but also to a serious reduction for some time past of the number of young people entering institutions for the preparation of teachers. The shortage of teachers is having the double consequence that too many persons are employed on emergency certificates with a low minimum of qualifications, and increase in the size of classes due in turn to the increased birthrate in the postwar years and the shortage of new buildings and classrooms. With the present economic conditions and the competition for the taxable wealth of the country in which the federal, state, and local governments are engaged, it is at present difficult to anticipate how the problem of educational finances will be met.

## Maintenance of Standards

One of the arguments in favor of centralized agency for the control of education is that the maintenance of standards is thereby facilitated and uniformity secured. In the United States different methods of maintaining standards have been developed mainly through professional organizations, on the one hand, and the use of achievement tests, on the other. New York State is the only state which conducts examinations (the Regents' Examinations). On a national scale examinations, upon the results of which high school graduates are admitted to liberal arts colleges, are conducted by the College Entrance Examinations Board, established in 1900 to save the Eastern colleges from the confusion of a multiplicity of entrance examinations. The Educational Testing Service in Princeton, with which the College Entrance Examinations Board is now associated, conducts a variety of objective tests examinations all over the country. In the Middle West and in the West generally the accrediting system has been adopted to regulate the relations between high schools and colleges. Originating at the University of Michigan in 1871, the system of accrediting was adopted by many universities until finally regional organizations were created to serve a number of institutions. Among these are the Association of Colleges and Secondary Schools of the Middle States and Maryland, the New England Association of Colleges and Secondary Schools, the Northwest Association of Secondary and Higher Schools, and the North Central Association. The standards that are administered are in the main quantitative and are concerned with the adequacy of buildings, equipment, laboratory and library, and the number and qualifications of teachers. No system has yet been devised, although it has been considered, for standardizing on the basis of quality of instruction.

### The States and Education

The Tenth Amendment (1791) to the Constitution left to the states powers not specifically assigned to the Federal Government. Accordingly each state has assumed responsibility for the provision and administration of education on the principle that the education of all children of the state are its concern. Local control had, however, preceded the organization of state governments. The state on assuming responsibility for education within its area limited its activities through most of the nineteenth century to supervising the operation of laws enacted by the state legislature, collecting data, and issuing reports on the status of education. With the expansion of the scope of education and the need to equalize educational opportunities the functions of the state were enlarged to define policy and to furnish leadership in education. Accordingly the functions of the states in the administration of education have expanded in the present century, particularly since the states have been compelled to bear an increasing percentage of the cost of education. Except for the administration of state institutions of higher education or for special education, for which separate boards are designated, the actual administration and operation of school systems are left to the local areas — rural districts, towns, cities, or counties.

The power of the states to intervene in educational matters is defined in their constitutions and the general requirements are laid down in laws enacted by the state legislatures. The supervision of the operation of the laws and of education in general is in all but six states entrusted to a state board of education. The boards are variously constituted. In nine states (Colorado, Florida, Kentucky, Mississippi, Missouri, Nevada, North Carolina, Oregon, and Texas) the boards consist of state officials (generally the governor, the treasurer, the secretary, the attorney-general, the auditor, and the superintendent of public instruction). State officials *ex officio,* school officials, and laymen, appointed or elected, make up the boards in twenty-two states (Alabama, Arizona, Arkansas, Connecticut, Georgia, Idaho, Indiana, Kansas, Louisiana, Michigan, Montana, New Hampshire, New Mexico, North Dakota, Oklahoma, Pennsylvania, Rhode Island, South Carolina, Tennessee, Virginia, Washington, and Wyoming). Nine state boards consist of members elected by the legislatures or appointed by the governor (California, Delaware, Iowa, Maryland, Massachusetts, Minnesota, New Jersey, New York, and Vermont). All the boards have the same title (State Board of Education) except in Massachusetts (Advisory Board of Education), in New York (Board of Regents of the University of the State of New York), in North Dakota (State Board of Administration), and in Pennsylvania (State Council of Education). The most usual number of members on a board is seven and the term of office is generally six years.

The functions of the boards are to establish minimum standards so that each child has the benefit of a foundation program of education, to define the qualifications of teachers, to prescribe the length of school year, to ensure suitable standards for school buildings, to supervise the program of education in general, and to provide financial support. Some state boards select textbooks for state adoption; some prescribe the curriculum, which in many instances is also prescribed by the state legislatures, especially the teaching of history and citizenship, and physical and health education.

The actual administration is entrusted to a state superintendent of public education or commissioner of education. The practice is developing of using the title "chief state school officer." The methods of appointment have not yet changed however. In most states the superintendent is elected by popular vote; in some he is appointed by the governor of the state; in others he is appointed by the state board. The qualifications for the office of chief state school officer are gradually being raised, but in general they are higher in those states in which the candidates do not have to take the risk of election on a political partisan ticket. The chief state school officer is responsible to the people through the state board of education and has charge of a department of education whose functions are now becoming widely ramified into every aspect of education, including research. He is the responsible leader and adviser on educational matters in his state. He supervises the enforcement of laws and regulations, and the execution of state policies, certificates teachers, supervises the preparation of courses of study, and is responsible for the collection of statistical returns and the preparation and publication of reports. The functions of the state department of education have been defined as follows: "The state department of education, consisting of the chief state school officer and his staff should be organized as a state service agency, to provide professional leadership in developing a sound education program consistent with the policies of the state board of education." [22]

Despite the expansion of the functions of the state authority for education, the principle of leaving as much initiative as possible with the local authority is safeguarded. The control of the curriculum and courses of study and the selection of textbooks by the state legislature or board of education are open to criticism. In

[22] National Council of Chief State School Officers, *Our System of Education: A Statement of Some Desirable Policies, Programs and Administrative Relationships in Education* (Washington, D.C., 1950), p. 20. By permission of the Council's Secretary.

general, however, local authorities enjoy a great deal of independence despite the fact that the states are assuming an increasing portion of cost of education. In the past twenty years the percentage of the educational expenditures borne by the states has more than doubled, while that of the local authorities has dropped by about one-third. According to the latest report the cost of education was distributed as follows: Federal 2.9 per cent, states 39.8 per cent, counties 6.1 per cent, local bodies 51.2 per cent, as compared with the following distribution in 1929–30: Federal .4 per cent, states 16.9 per cent, counties 10.4 per cent, local bodies 72.3 per cent. In the apportionment of funds to local areas the states are increasingly adopting the principle of equalizing educational programs and of matching the funds to need and effort of the localities. The states are assuming the responsibility of guaranteeing "that every child shall have at least an adequate foundation opportunity, including all essential facilities and services." A foundation program is designed "to provide every child an opportunity for at least an elementary and secondary education of high quality wherever he may live." [23]

## Local Administration

The immediate control of education — the provision and maintenance of schools and their administration — is largely delegated by the states to the local units, of which there are some 90,000, a number that is being constantly reduced by consolidating areas of administration. The chief areas of administration are districts, towns and townships, counties, and cities. The current movement to ensure better education and equality is in the direction of larger areas of administration.

The administrative unit that is most generally characteristic of the United States is the district which originated in New England and spread through the Middle West, North-Central, and Northwestern states. Successful in the past in stimulating and holding public interest and affection, the district school has proved to be an obstacle to the fulfilment of the American ideal of equality of opportunity. The development of improved means of communica-

[23] *Ibid.*, pp. 25 f.

tion and of transportation has made it possible to absorb the district system in larger units of administration which consolidated schools in better buildings and with better qualified teachers and administrative officials than the districts could afford.

The districts were absorbed into towns in New England and townships in some of the North-Central states. These units have not been found satisfactory for educational purposes. In the North-Central states the township system co-exists with the district which maintains the elementary school, while the township provides the high school.

In the Southern states the most common form of administrative unit is the county although local areas may retain their autonomy within the county. While large enough to maintain satisfactory systems of schools, the counties are weak on the administrative side, since the boards of education and the superintendents are generally elected; the qualifications of these superintendents are too frequently not adequate for the kind of leadership demanded of an administrator of education today.

The characteristic features of American administration and the American school system have been developed in the cities which enjoy a considerable degree of autonomy in education subject to minimum requirements prescribed by state laws and state boards of education. The cities have until recently had adequate resources for the development of school systems with competent teachers and professional supervisors and administrators. They have succeeded to some degree in taking education out of politics by securing boards of education either elected or appointed and independent of other agencies for local government. In some cases the boards have also obtained fiscal independence so that they can levy their own taxes without control of the local financial authority.

The tendency is to keep the number of members of boards of education small — five to nine members. The chief function of a board of education is to establish broad policies of education, responsive to needs of the local community. The functions that such policies should promote have been defined as follows: "Within its legal authority, the local administrative unit should exercise all functions necessary for the satisfactory operation of schools, among which are to select and employ properly qualified teachers and administrative staff, to determine the nature and scope of the curricula, to locate, construct and equip functional school buildings, to provide certain special services such as school lunches, transportation, and health and recreation services, and to prepare the budget and exercise fiscal functions necessary to carry out the program." [24]

In the formulation of policies and in reaching decisions on the increasing number of issues that arise in a modern system of education a board of education must have the services of a competent school superintendent. This position has become one of crucial importance as the programs of education have expanded. It is, on the whole, the city school superintendent who determines the character and place of education in the American scene. The last thirty years have seen the gradual development of professional training of administrators. This training has been carried one stage further by the Project to Improve the Professional Preparation of School Executives which is being carried out in a number of centers throughout the country under a five-year grant made by the W. K. Kellogg Foundation in 1950.

The range of activities for which the school superintendent is responsible includes supervision not only of those aspects that might be described as the business side of administration, but also of the strictly educational aspects. These include curricular revision, the preparation of courses of study, the classification of pupils, the construction of objective tests, the keeping of records and reports, vocational guidance, special classes and psychological clinics, and the preparation of the budget. In most of these activities the superintendent must rely on a staff of specialists qualified in each area, and increasingly upon the participation of the teachers. The tendency to bureaucratic control is gradually disappearing for two reasons. The first is the gradual improvement in the qualifications of teachers which makes it possible to encourage initiative in accordance with their professional preparation and responsibility. The second is the realization that one of the major functions of an administrator is to educate those whose support is of primary importance for the successful conduct of a school system — the public and the teacher. Publicity and the promotion of sound public relations are of paramount value. Hence the importance of educa-

[24] *Ibid.*, p. 14.

tion in the news, of parent-teacher organizations, or of public education associations. An interesting development in this connection has been the formation in 1949 of the National Citizens Commission for the Public Schools, in which Roy Larsen, president of Time, Inc., is the moving spirit and president. The Commission was formed at a time when the schools were under attack, partly because of increasing costs, and partly on educational grounds. The purpose of the organization is to promote the interest of laymen in education and bring them into closer touch with the schools and the administrative organization. It was also in a sense an attempt to meet the growing size of school systems and a consequent removal from the immediate concern of the public. The Commission promoted the establishment of lay advisory committees of which there are now about 6,000 in the country. The functions of these committees is to promote public opinion and support their board of education and administration when such crucial issues as raising money or constructing new school buildings or any other matter that merits public attention and backing. The Commission and lay advisory committees conduct meetings and conferences and disseminate publications prepared by the Commission to familiarize the public with their school systems.

City school systems are supported by local taxes and state grants and are encountering the same difficulties as other local areas in raising money to meet the increasing costs of education. The taxes are levied mainly on land and buildings, a method which was adopted when these were the main forms of wealth. With the rise of the wealthy industrialized cities the method is beginning to be considered obsolescent and proposals are made to substitute a tax on income. The problem is serious and the increasing share borne by the states is likely to prove only a temporary palliative.

## Private Schools

There are in general no restrictions on the establishment of private schools. A law enacted in Oregon in 1922, which required all children between the ages of eight and sixteen to attend public schools, was declared unconstitutional in 1925. The Supreme Court held that "It is not seriously debatable that the parental right to guide one's child intellectually and religiously is a most substantial part of the liberty and freedom of the parents." At the same time the Court affirmed the right of the State "to regulate all schools, to inspect, supervise and examine them, their teachers and pupils, to require that all children of proper age attend some school, that teachers shall be of good character and patriotic disposition, that certain studies plainly essential to good citizenship must be taught, and that nothing be taught which is manifestly inimical to the public welfare."

The decision and opinion in the Oregon case represents the situation throughout the country. The right of parents to send their children to schools of their own choice is confirmed. The American, however, when he thinks of education thinks only of publicly maintained schools. Private schools, whether denominational or not, do not receive aid from public funds, although in a number of states free textbooks are furnished to parochial schools and in seventeen states parochial school pupils are transported to their schools at public expense. Of all the pupils enrolled in elementary and secondary schools nearly 12 per cent attend private schools, the majority of which are provided and maintained by Roman Catholics. Other private or "independent" schools are either experimental, progressive schools or college preparatory schools and all charge fees.

The opposition to giving financial aid to denominational schools is based on the same principle as opposition to religious instruction in public schools — that the American public school has developed in the past century as a secular, nonsectarian common school for the education of all the children of all the people. The opposition to both aid and religious instruction is founded on the constitutional principle of separation of Church and State. Factually there would be other difficulties because of the existence in the country of more than two hundred and fifty different religious sects, each of which might conceivably establish its own schools and claim financial aid from public funds, or insist on the teaching of its own tenets of religious instruction.

### Religious Instruction in Public Schools

The issue of religious instruction in public schools has been widely discussed in the last decade but without any solution being reached. The released-time program for religious education which spread from its place of origin in Gary, Indiana, in 1914 and has been adopted in more than two thousand communities, still supplies the only, even though unsatisfactory, solution. Under this program pupils are released from school for a number of hours each week to receive religious instruction in institutions of their own denomination but not on public school premises.

On the issue of religious instruction in the public schools and as part of the regular curriculum two important reports have been published representing two different points of view. One report was the result of deliberations of The Committee on Religion and Education of the American Council on Education, *The Relation of Religion to Public Education: the Basic Principles* (1947). The Committee's thesis is that "unless the schools are content to leave one of the major areas of life unexplored, the specifically religious beliefs and aspirations of human beings must have attention." Hence if religious education "does not impel students toward the achievement of a faith and to that end create a sensitive awareness of the religious resources upon which men have learned to rely, it is less than education ought to be."

The second report, *Moral and Spiritual Values in the Public Schools* (1951), was prepared by the Educational Policies Commission of the National Education Association. The Commission rejects the idea of "a common core of religious belief" and in this agrees with leaders in the field of religious education. While the public schools cannot give direct religious instruction, they can "teach objectively *about* religion without advocating or teaching any religious creed," and so develop in the students respect for "the rich religious traditions of all humanity."

### The Educational Career

The road from the kindergarten, which is not provided in all systems, to the university, is straighter in the United States than in any other country. Compulsory school attendance begins at the age of six or seven, and in some states eight, although by custom most children start on their educational career at the age of six, and continue to fourteen, fifteen, sixteen, seventeen, or even eighteen. The pupil spends eight years in the elementary school and continues to the high school for four years in some systems, or he may spend six years in the primary school and six years in the high school or divide the time into three years in the junior and three years in the senior high school. There are no roadblocks in the form of entrance examinations, and the twelve years of elementary and secondary education are regarded as a unit. Except in a few larger cities which have separate specialized schools, all forms of secondary education are provided in the comprehensive high schools which in the majority are coeducational. The choice of courses is made with the advice of a counselor or guidance teacher. Upon graduation from high school after studying certain prescribed subjects the student passes on to the liberal arts college without an entrance examination except for admission to a number of private colleges. Another choice upon graduation is to enter a junior college, public or private, which offers the first two years of a liberal arts college course or a technical vocational course for two years. Upon graduation from college there is open graduate study leading to the master's degree or the Ph.D. degree.

As distinguished from systems like those of England or France very few scholarships or maintenance grants are provided. On the other hand, there are no school fees, and in the tax-supported colleges and universities the fees are minimal. In lieu of scholarship aid or maintenance grants the American student in high school and in college may "work his way through" without any loss in status. Fellowships are available in larger numbers for graduate and postgraduate study. The need of providing financial aid for able students to continue from high school to college and beyond is beginning to be recognized. The need has impressed itself upon the attention of educators by the fact that many able high school graduates do not continue their education for financial reasons. That there must be an appreciable sacrifice of ability was strikingly demonstrated after World War II by the large number of able young men and women whose college and university education was made possible under the G.I. Bill of Rights and who without this benefit would not have been able to continue their education.

## REFERENCES

### General

Kandel, I. L. *Comparative Education.* Boston, Houghton Mifflin Co., 1933.
——— *Types of Administration.* Melbourne University Press, 1938.
——— *The Impact of the War Upon American Education,* Ch. I. Chapel Hill, University of North Carolina Press, 1948.

### England

Alexander, W. P. *The Education Act: A Parents' Guide.* London, Phoenix House, 1946.
——— *Education in England.* London, Newnes Educational Publishing Co., 1954.
Beatty, D. J., P. S. Taylor, and Evan T. Davis. *The New Law of Education.* London, Butterworth & Co., 1944.
Dent, H. C. *The Education Act,* 1944. London, University of London Press, 1944.
——— *Growth in English Education, 1946–1952.* London, Routledge and Kegan Paul Ltd., 1954.
Ministry of Education, *A Guide to the Educational System of England and Wales.* London, H.M.S.O., 1945.
Smith, W. O. Lester. *To Whom Do Schools Belong?* Oxford, Basil Blackwell, 1949.
Wells, M. M. and P. S. Taylor. *The New Law of Education,* 4th edn. London, Butterworth & Co., 1954.

### France

*Avenirs,* 60.61 February-March, 1954.
Centre National de Documentation Pédagogique. *L'Organisation de l'Enseignement en France.* Paris, 1951.
Debiesse, J. *Compulsory Education in France.* UNESCO Studies in Compulsory Education II. Paris, 1951.
Glatigny, M. *Histoire de l'Enseignement en France.* Paris, 1949.
Soleil, J. *Le Livre des Instituteurs.* Paris, 1949.

### U.S.S.R.

Medinsky, Y. N. *Publication in the U.S.S.R.* Moscow, 1951.
Moos, Elizabeth. *The Educational System of the Soviet Union.* New York, National Council of American-Soviet Friendship, 1950.

## United States

Allen, H. P. *The Federal Government and Education*. New York, Mc-Graw-Hill Book Co., 1950.

American Association of School Administrators. *School Boards in Action*. Washington, D.C., 1946.

————— *Public Relations for America's Schools*. Washington, D.C., 1950.

————— *The American School Superintendency*. Washington, D.C., 1952.

Chase, Francis S., and E. L. Morphet. *The Forty-Eight School Systems*. Chicago Council of State Government, 1952.

Moehlman, A. B. *School Administration*. Boston, Houghton Mifflin Co., 1950.

Mort, P. R. *Principles of School Administration*. New York, McGraw-Hill Book Co., 1946.

National Education Association, Educational Policies Commission. *The Structure and Administration of Schools in American Democracy*. Washington, D.C., 1938.

————— *Federal-State Relations in Education*. Washington, D.C., 1948.

Remmlein, M. K. *The Law of Public School Administration*. New York, McGraw-Hill Book Co., 1953.

# 7

# The Education

# of the Child

Nothing better illustrates the change from the nineteenth to the twentieth century than the change in the attitude to the child, which justified the title of Ellen Key's book, as *The Century of the Child* (1909). Beginning with the work of Preyer (*Die Seele des Kindes*, 1882), attention was directed to the psychological study of the child's physical and mental development which grew in volume in the early years of this century in Germany, Switzerland, and the United States with repercussions in other countries as well. The studies, based on observation and experiment, produced profound changes in three respects — the nature of growth, the development of interests, and the learning process. The results tended, but very slowly, to displace the traditional psychological approach with its emphasis or faculties, discipline and transfer. The emphasis shifted from memorization, drill, and rote-learning, in which the child was assumed to be a passive recipient, to activities, spontaneous interests, the study of the environment, and creativity.

The emphasis, in other words, shifted in teaching from the subject to the child, as was stated in the last edition of the *Suggestions to Teachers,* issued before World War II by the English Board of Education. But long before that publication appeared, the new psychology of the child had already been put into practice in private experimental schools in a number of countries, and in many of the public school systems in the Weimar Republic of Germany and the United States.

## Preschool Education

It was soon recognized that the educative process begins before the child enters school under laws of compulsory attendance. A sound physical and mental development, it was realized, depends on a good environment not only in the home but also in the immediate neighborhood. At the age of five or six children may already have become "damaged goods." Since not all homes are able to provide the right kind of environment for the growth of children, it was soon realized that the responsibility for the preschool education of young children must be undertaken by some agency, public or private, to supplement or advise on their care in the home.

Provision had already been made chiefly through philanthropy for the care of very young children in day nurseries or crèches, but these were child-care institutions rather than educational institutions under trained and qualified teachers. The kindergartens which were private or public admitted children of a slightly more advanced age and were founded on a different theory from that on which nursery schools were advocated.

To the psychological bases, which stimulated interest in the development of young children, a number of other arguments were put forward in support of bringing them under professional supervision. The movement for equalizing opportunities included provision for very young children of the underprivileged classes who were to be given as sound a physical and mental start in life as those of the privileged classes. It was not an accident that the term "nursery school" was adopted and accepted in all English-speaking countries, since it endeavored to provide for the young underprivileged child what was provided for the privileged in a good nursery — a cheerful environment, fresh air, rest periods, and good meals. The nursery school could give more; under trained personnel group and individual activities and play could be encouraged, the development of interests could be stimulated, and a sense of cooperation and companionship could be stimulated.

It is not one of the less important arguments in support of the nursery school idea that it provides companionship and thus social training to children who cannot find it in the modern home of small families. The dwindling size of families furnishes another reason for the provision of the nursery school; it can serve as a means of human conservation. It not only trains in social habits but it can develop personal habits of cleanliness, regularity, and diet. Since parents, especially mothers, are likely to be frequently in and out of the school, the teachers can guide and advise them on the care of their children. Further, such schools generally take a particular interest in the health of their charges to avoid risk of infections and provide for daily inspections and periodical medical inspection, so that information can be transmitted to the home.

The changing social situation provides a series of additional arguments for the school care of young children. Whether it is the changing standard or the high cost of living or the emancipation of women in this country, more women are engaged in work which takes them from the home for many hours in the day. It was, of course, for children of women who worked because they had to that the day nursery or crèche was originally established. Today the nursery school answers the need of women who work because they wish to. The school is not a simple solution to the serious problem of the career mother, nor can it be claimed that the school can fulfill the function of a good home. It can, however, serve as a stabilizing function in the emotional development of the child and so supplement the influence of the home, and in the connotation of the French term, *écoles maternelles,* for schools for young children.

It is from this point of view that the early school care of children is advocated, because the early years are regarded as crucial in their emotional development. Whether the argument on this ground is valid or not, it is undoubtedly a fact that everywhere a happy childhood is regarded as a factor that is most important in a child's development. This is all the more urgent in view of the tensions that prevail everywhere. Nor can the factor of urbanization be neglected; play spaces become scarcer and are in any case of little educative value without supervision, and the streets are everywhere becoming more and more hazardous because of modern traffic. The nursery school has come to stay; that it is not yet firmly established as a part of the public school systems is indicated by the facts that in the interests of economy it appeared for a while that they would be suspended in England, and that in the United States, except as a war measure, they have not been incorporated into many systems.

The nursery school serves as a link between the home and school and is not infrequently grouped with the beginning classes of the primary school, like the kindergarten-primary grades in American public school systems. This combination has had the effect of extending to the early years of the compulsory school the methods of the nursery school and of postponing the more formal instruction of the school subjects. Except in the United States the nursery school or *école maternelle* has taken the place of the kindergarten, which may admit children from nursery schools at the age of four.

### Elementary Education

More important perhaps than the earlier start that is being made in the education of the child is the change in the status of elementary education, both in social status and in educational theory. In the nineteenth century and in the early years of the present century elementary education was looked upon as a type rather than a stage of education. Except in the United States it was administered separately from other branches of education, its teachers were trained differently from other teachers for other schools, and the content was directed to imparting skill in the three R's and the rudiments of general subjects. The methods of instruction emphasized the mastery of subjects, a mastery tested mainly by ability to repeat what was taught. The individual was lost in the mass and lack of ability was attributed to laziness. The elementary school did not lead on, when completed, to other full-time education except with more advanced elementary studies to a teacher training institution. Elementary education was definitely regarded as the education of a class, predominantly the working class, whose members were to be taught their place in society.

The change in the status of elementary education was brought about by a number of factors which stimulated the movement for the provision of the equality of educational opportunities. The changing status of workers to which the growing power and influence of labor unions contributed in no small measure produced a realization among their leaders of the importance of education. The changing character of industry as a result of technological advances led to a demand for better educated and better trained personnel. At the same time the gradual reduction of the hours of labor left a great deal of leisure for the use of which the individual needed preparation. More important than these influences, which were gradual, was World War I which required the same sacrifices from all social classes, advanced further a realization of the meaning of democracy, and directed attention to the importance of a common education for all in the interests of mutual understanding and solidarity. The idea of a common foundation in the education of the children of all classes which had been woven into the American tradition was ignored in the educational organization of other countries until after World War I. The concept was well expressed by Stanley Baldwin in his "Message on a New Step in Education" (1929),[1] in which he stated that "One of the strongest bonds of union between men is a common education. England has been the poorer that in her national system of schooling she has not in the past fostered this fellowship of the mind. The classification of our schools has been on the lines of social rather than educational distinction. . . . The great new fabric is already taking shape: the outworn elementary structure is at last being superseded."

A few years earlier Leon Brunschvicg compared a desirable educational organization to a tree, when he wrote that "It was important that all the children of France should be considered alike as living plants, whose spontaneous growth will be assured by the same methods; only the trunk will be allowed to grow up to a certain height before the branches are permitted to shoot out with-

[1] See I. L. Kandel, ed., *Educational Yearbook, 1928,* of the International Institute of Teachers College, Columbia University (New York, 1922), p. 39.

out the opposition of any artificial obstacle to the expansion of their being, whose innate powers will raise each up to the level designed for it." [2]

The political and social forces were not the only ones that brought about a change in the status and character of elementary education. So far as organization was concerned the effect of these forces was ultimately to produce a change in nomenclature and status. The connotation of "elementary education" was recognized to be detrimental to the idea of a common school, which should be a stage in education rather than a type. The change in terminology which would incorporate the early years of education into a national system without distinction of class and leading on to other opportunities for education did not take place until many years had elapsed.

### The New Pedagogy

The other forces were due to the changes in the psychology and philosophy of education. From the psychological side the place of the child as an individual with a personality of his own was stressed and with it the importance of giving due attention to individual differences of ability. Education as a development of personality meant that it could not be limited to intellectual training only but must contribute to the development of the whole child — intellectually, emotionally, and physically. The individual is an active being who learns by experience, but since not all experiences are educative or conducive to developing a socialized personality, the function of the school is to present the individual with experiences which are socially useful and valuable. But a further function of the school is to guide the pupil and help him to select the right kind of experiences which will promote the growth of his personality and at the same time make him a useful member of society. In learning through socially desirable experiences the pupil's activity must be engaged. The pupil learns as he is interested in his activities; this does not mean that the pupil is free to follow his own interests without regard to ultimate ends. Since the pupil is immature, these ends must be in the mind of the teacher in selecting the desirable experiences which enlist the

[2] L. Brunschvicg, *Un Ministère de l'Education Nationale* (Paris, 1922), p. 79.

active participation of the pupil. In other words, the pupil becomes interested and participates to the extent that he sees meanings in the experiences that constitute the curriculum. Where these experiences are to be found is at the start in the immediate environment. From them new interests emerge and the pupil can learn by vicarious experiences.

The revolt against the tradition of elementary education was twofold: it was directed both against the curriculum and against the methods of instruction. On the curriculum side the criticism has been that the content did not arise from nor was related to the pupils' experiences. It consisted, it was alleged, of a quantum of knowledge, facts, and information which it was thought might at some time be found useful or, if not, would at least train the minds of the pupils. The methods, it was charged, relied too much on passive learning through drill, repetition, and memorization often without understanding what was learned. Since classes were large and individual differences were not considered, the dosage of knowledge was the same for all and strict discipline helped to maintain the attention required by the methods used.

What took place, however, as a consequence of this revolt, was a swing of the educational pendulum from one extreme to the other. Because the tradition emphasized the acquisition of knowledge and facts, they were discarded as an unnecessary burden on the mind. Because the curriculum was organized in terms of subjects, the shift of emphasis from subjects to the child was assumed to mean that there must be freedom for the child to follow his own interests and choose his own experiences; the value of the social heritage was minimized and logical organization of a curriculum was discarded in favor of the psychological. Nevertheless, as was pointed out by Dewey, the immediate needs, interests, and experiences of the child can only serve as a start; facts and ideas must be organized in the process of education. Because pupils were expected to be passive imbibers of lessons from the teacher, it was assumed that nothing went on in the pupils' minds and the emphasis was placed upon activity interpreted as physical movement. One salutary result of this misinterpretation both of passive and of active learning, was a change in the character of the classroom furniture with movable chairs and desks taking the place of fixed desks and benches.

Since the emphasis was now placed on the individual as an entity, the size of classes began to be reduced. Discipline became less severe and its place was taken by the encouragement of self-control and self-discipline. Nor, indeed, could the old type of discipline be continued if the principle that education is life and not a preparation for life was accepted. For the principle means that pupils must be permitted to move about in an orderly fashion, to discuss their questions with the teacher and with others in the class, to consult books, and to study quietly for themselves as occasions permitted.

The influences from the psychology of education confirmed the theory of democratic education which emphasized the place of the individual as an independent and responsible personality and recognized his worth as a human being who would as an adult be called upon to play his part as a citizen, as a worker, and as a person. It is these functions which the individual is to perform as an adult that warn against a literal acceptance of the slogan that education is life and not a preparation for life. That all experiences affect the individual in some way is true, but to be educative those experiences must be selected in view of the life the individual is expected to lead. He cannot be nor is he educated in a vacuum. The individual lives and is educated in a social environment with "a heritage of knowledge and heroic examples — accepted values stamped with the seal of permanence," to quote Charles Beard.[3] The social heritage consists of keys to the understanding of the world. Its acquisition is more than "mere knowledge." Nor is knowledge of value only as it "functions;" it becomes valuable to the individual to the extent that in acquiring it he understands it, and as he masters its meanings. There is still another reason why the social heritage cannot be discarded, for it furnishes the basis for learning those subjects of social allegiance which give an individual a sense of belongingness in a community or nation. It is the methods by which such mastery is acquired that must be carefully considered; they must encourage thinking and critical ability rather than memorization without understanding.

The pendulum which swung to the extreme away from the tradition is gradually returning to a middle point. Activities and ex-

[3] *The Unique Function of Education in American Democracy* (Washington, D.C., 1937).

periences are not valuable in themselves; to flit from activity to
activity is to develop a "movie" habit of mind which cannot provide a foundation for depth or thoroughness. The value of activities and experiences lies in the extent to which they help in the
acquisition of knowledge with understanding and in the development of attitudes and ideals which contribute to the formation of
character. But the essential contributions of the middle position
are, first, the recognition of the child to be developed into a personality so that his abilities and interests must be taken as a
starting-point in the educative process; and, second, that an environment must be provided through which those abilities and
interests can be channeled into a socially desirable direction. Freedom and self-expression may be important ends, but freedom
must be under the control of a sense of responsibility for its use,
and self-realization may be more important than the cult of self-
expression before the self has anything to express. Care must be
taken to see that activities are also guided in desirable directions.
Just as the so-called "passive school" was assumed to provide no
opportunities to engage in intellectual activity, so in the "activity
school" there is no guarantee that the pupil engaged in visibly
"doing" things is acquiring something of intellectual value.

The shift of emphasis in teaching from the subject to the child
does not imply a child-centered school. The shift is in fact to the
teacher more than ever. He must have the goals of education,
both immediate and ultimate, always before him. He must select
from the broad environment of culture and experiences those aspects that are educative at a particular stage in the development
of the child. He must be a master of the subjects that he teaches
and of their relevance. He must encourage the active participation
of his pupils because they understand and appreciate the meaning
of what they are learning. Since the educative process is conducted
in a particular environment and with particular children, he must
be free, with the help of suggestions, to adapt his work to both.
Hence the teacher will not feel bound by one theory of education
rather than another. He will not discard merely because it is traditional what experience has shown to be valuable in it, any more
than he will accept without question the latest because it is new.

The outstanding change that has taken place and the direction in which education, when it is free from external control, is moving emphasize the importance of health and physical training, of intelligent participation through understanding by the pupils, of the relevance of what is taught to the pupils' lives and to community life, and of sound habits of recreation and the use of leisure. Education has the task that it has always had to promote the physical, aesthetic, and intellectual development, the cultivation of intellectual interests, and the bases of a well-balanced personality. But these ends today demand a more careful selection of what shall be taught and methods of instruction that stimulate the interested participation of the pupils.

## ENGLAND

### The New Organization

The adaptation of the English educational organization to the new principles of a democratic system has been provided for by the Education Act of 1944. Under the Act the statutory system of public education is to be organized in three stages of which the first is to be known as "primary education" for children between the ages of five and eleven or twelve. The next stage immediately following the primary is that of secondary education. Simple as this provision appears to be, it represents the abolition of the dual system of education, one for the masses and one for the privileged minority. It eliminates the traditional connotation of "elementary education" which, apart from its class connotation, ended at fourteen with little opportunity for full-time education beyond that. Elementary education paralleled or overlapped secondary education. Except for the continued existence of private schools, the Education Act establishes a common foundation of education articulated with some form of secondary education of at least four years since the age of compulsory school attendance has been raised to fifteen.

The primary stage itself is divided into several stages. If the preschool or nursery school is included, it forms the first but voluntary stage leading at the age of five, when compulsory school attendance begins, to the infant school till the age of seven. This

is followed by junior school up to eleven. The general practice
is to have these divisions in separate schools, except where nursery
classes are attached to infant schools and where the numbers, especially in rural areas, make it impossible to have separate infant
and junior schools. Kindergartens have always been private, fee-
paying schools without any aid from public funds. The modern
principles of kindergartens have, however, exercised an influence
on the practice of infant schools.

### Nursery Schools and Classes

Although children were permitted to attend infant schools between the ages of three and five, the provision for these "baby"
classes was unsatisfactory, physically and pedagogically, until experiments were undertaken after World War I to apply modern
principles to the care of the preschool children. The new spirit
was influenced largely by the work of Rachel and Margaret McMillan, who had established a nursery school in one of the slum
districts of London in 1908. The Education Act, 1918, gave local
authorities the power, but did not impose it as a duty, to provide
day nurseries and nursery schools out of local rates, half the cost
being borne by grants from the Board of Education. For economic
reasons progress in establishing public nursery schools and organizing nursery classes was very slow.

The social and national importance of the early care of infants
was impressed upon the public by the following statement in the
*Report of the School Medical Officer of the London County Coun-
cil* (1926): "The School Medical Service is a receiver of damaged
goods and spends most of its time and energies in patching them
up. What is now required is an intensification of social effort
directed to the care of the infant in arms and the toddler before
school age, so that children shall come to school in the beginning
with constitutions unimpaired and with bodies attuned to receive
the mental, moral and physical education which it is the primary
function of the school organization to impart." [4] The prevention
and remedial value of an early start in the nursery school or class
are considered to be as important as the educational. The early

---

[4] Quoted in *Report of the Consultative Committee on Infant and Nursery
Schools* (London, 1933), p. 104.

detection of physical weaknesses or disease through the watchful care of trained teachers and medical inspection can lay the foundation for a successful school career.

The recognition of the importance of the nursery schools or classes is emphasized by that fact that their provision is now imposed as a duty upon local education authorities. The Education Act of 1944, par. 8 (2b), requires among other things that: "In fulfilling their duties under this section a local education authority shall, in particular, have regard . . . to the need for securing that provision is made for pupils who have not attained the age of five years by the provision of nursery schools or, when the authority considers the provision of such schools to be inexpedient, by the provision of nursery classes in other schools."

The nursery schools or classes are expected to keep in close touch with the pupils' homes and to help mothers to a better understanding of what is needed to enable them to run the homes with a greater degree of comfort and to give them the opportunity to live a fuller life. Companionship and a variety of experiences are provided with play and activities in art and music, and periods of quiet, rest, and sleep. Food and medical supervision receive careful attention and more than other aspects of the schools serve as a link with the homes. The aim of the nursery schools is clearly described in the Ministry of Education's Pamphlet No. 1, *The Nation's Schools, Their Plan and Purpose:* [5] "The aim of the nursery school is threefold — to provide the medical care which such young children need; a training in good habits and right behaviour, and an environment in which they can learn the things appropriate to their age. Thus it provides a variety of play activities, manipulative, creative, and imaginative, and opportunities for the activity required for a child's bodily development. Opportunities, too, are provided to gain the experiences of the common property of things they see about them; to acquire skill and show enterprise in dealing with them, and to use language by talking to each other and to grown-up people."

Nursery schools and classes have thus advanced beyond their original purpose of serving as institutions for children whose home conditions are unsatisfactory or whose mothers are at work. They have an important physical, social, and educational function to

[5] (London, 1945), p. 6.

perform. For the reason that teachers should be specially qualified to take care of very young children the hope was expressed in the Government's White Paper on *Educational Reconstruction* "that new provision for children under 5 will be mainly in nursery schools, which, in addition to providing a more suitable environment for young children, are nearer to the homes than large infants schools and give less opportunity for the spread of infectious diseases" (p. 8).

The provision of nursery schools and classes by public education authorities has been slow, partly because of economic conditions since the war and partly because of shortage of teachers. Nevertheless there has been an appreciable increase from 114 in 1938 to 453 in 1953 with 22,672 pupils. In addition 141,737 children under five were enrolled in the same year in separate infant schools and in infant schools combined with junior schools, the majority probably in nursery classes.

The nursery school is a small school with an enrollment of about forty children, so that individual attention can be given to each and a homelike atmosphere be maintained. A definite framework of daily activities is maintained to avoid the disturbance of too many changes and to develop a sense of security and regularity of habits rather than leave the child too much to its own devices. The nursery school seeks to create the conditions of a good home in which healthy growth — physically, mentally, and emotionally — can be promoted. The ends to be attained are thus described in the Board of Education's last edition of the *Handbook of Suggestions for the Consideration of Teachers and Others Concerned in the Work of Public Elementary School* (1937): "Such a school will have achieved its aim, if the children who have been through it are found to be healthy and vigorous, active and even graceful in movement, deft with their hands, ready of speech, eager to learn, able to look after themselves, companionable and willing to respect the rights of others, and altogether well suited to begin the next stage of school life" (p. 77).

## Infant Schools

The next stage of school life is the infant school, in which a child begins his period of compulsory school attendance at the age of five. The infant school in Britain has a history of 140 years; Robert Owen opened such a school in New Lanark for the children of his workers in 1816. It soon departed from the original principle which Owen had in mind and in the school established by Samuel Wilderspin, who had a great deal of influence on the development of infant schools throughout the country, the emphasis began to be placed more on formal instruction than on play and educative activities. Later in the century Froebelian principles were introduced but the kindergarten occupations became formalized and ends in themselves. A fresh start was made when the Education Department, then the central authority for education, issued a Circular in 1893 for the guidance of infant school teachers. The leading principles advocated in the Circular were (1) the recognition and guidance of the child's spontaneous activity, and (2) the harmonious and complete development of the child's faculties. These principles were later incorporated in the first edition of the *Suggestions for the Consideration of Teachers*, published by the Board of Education in 1905.

Since the Board acted by suggestion and the advice of inspectors, the older established tradition of the infant school with large classes and a formal curriculum disappeared very slowly, although there were notable examples of the utilization of modern principles. One of the causes of the slow progress was the unsuitability of so many infant school buildings. The influences of child study, the work of Maria Montessori, and indirectly of John Dewey's philosophy of education, began to find a place in infant schools here and there. But the English teacher is more likely to work by intuition and interest in children and to be eclectic rather than bound by any one theory of education.

In 1931 the Board of Education's Consultative Committee under the chairmanship of Sir Henry Hadow undertook, according to its terms of reference, "To consider and report on the training and teaching of children attending nursery schools and infants departments of public elementary schools, and the further development of such educational provision for children up to the age of 7+." The Committee's report, *Infant and Nursery Schools* was published in 1933. The function of the infant school was to provide "for the healthy growth, physical, intellectual, spiritual, and moral" development of children between 5 and 7 plus. The same principle as had been recommended for primary schools in the Committee's *Report on the Primary School* was advocated for infant schools, that "the curriculum should be thought of in terms of activity and experience rather than of knowledge to be acquired and facts to be stored." These activities should include religious instruction, natural activities (physical training, open-air life, rest and play), expression training (speech, dancing, singing, handwork and drawing), and formal instruction in the three R's. Opportunities are provided for group and individual activities, and for class lessons.

An infant school, according to the *Handbook of Suggestions* (1937), "will be a place where life has all the freshness and vividness of early childhood, and where activities are pursued in a spirit of lively adventure. It will have provided the children with many new interests, and it will have given them in a measure suited to their age and maturity both the freedom and the discipline, through which their awakening of group membership may best be developed. Its product should be a child who, in comparison with the child of five, is self-possessed, responsible, independent, and capable of devoting himself to a straightforward task with a remarkable intensity of purpose and a high regard for the proper way of performing it" (p. 98).

There is a tendency to consider the preschool-nursery and infant school as a unit from the point of view of educational theory, even though it is considered more desirable to keep the children under five and between five and seven in separate schools. Here more perhaps than at any other stage in the educational careers of English children the major principle stated in the Government's White Paper on *Educational Reconstruction*, "to secure for children a happier childhood and a better start in life" — is put into practice. If there is a change when the child advances from the infant to the junior school — the next division of the primary stage — the fault is social rather than educational. In the early years there is closer cooperation between school and home than later when the mothers' interest is not as vivid as it was when their children needed them more.

In 1953 the enrollment in 5475 separate infant schools was 1,149,354 (591,682 boys and 538,272 girls), and in infant schools attached to junior schools the enrollment of children between five and seven was 476,649, most of whom were presumably in infant classes.

## Junior School

The junior school, the third of the divisions that make up the stage of primary education, receives pupils from the infant school at the age of seven plus and sends them on to some form of secondary education at eleven plus. Thus the primary school fulfills its mission as the common foundation school in a system of publicly maintained schools. This system was forecast in the Education Act, 1918, and recommended in the report of the Consultative Committee on the *Education of the Adolescent* in 1926. The reorganization proceeded slowly by the establishment of junior schools and senior schools, the latter for pupils who did not gain admission to a secondary (grammar) or central school. The reorganization is still proceeding slowly despite the provisions of the Education Act, 1944, the only advance that has so far been made is that the senior schools are now classified as secondary modern schools and are not conducted under the Elementary School Code. The distribution of schools is at present as follows: junior schools with infants 9,336 with 1,344,363 pupils (including 510,103 children under seven); junior schools without infants 3,950 with 1,172,341 pupils; and all-age schools 4,688 with 770,082 pupils. The retardation in the reconstruction of the system is due to shortage of buildings, the need of materials and workers for housing projects, and the unexpected postwar increase in the birth rate. The demand for secondary education for all has to some extent diverted attention from the needs of the junior schools and been given priority.

The junior school is intended to provide for the all-round development of the individual child and as a stage in his education rather than as directly preparatory to the next stage. Nevertheless, there has long been a feeling that the competition for special places in the secondary (grammar) school before the passing of the Education Act, 1944, and since its enactment by the desire of parents to get their children into the grammar school rather than the technical or modern secondary school has seriously affected the work of the last years of the junior school. The charge is made that in some schools pupils are coached for the test at eleven plus, on the basis of which they are allocated to one or other of these schools. The controversy about coaching is still going on and the general opinion seems to be that to familiarize pupils with such tests is justifiable, provided this is done for all.

The most striking characteristic of junior as of all other schools in England is that the Ministry of Education does not prescribe the curriculum and courses of study or methods of instruction. Nor is it likely that the Ministry would use the new powers granted to it under the Education Act, 1944, for such a purpose. The Board of Education, which was the central authority for education before the Ministry was created by the Education Act, 1944, published a *Handbook of Suggestions for Teachers and Others Concerned in the Work of Public Elementary Schools,* the last edition of which appeared in 1937. The development of the theory of primary education can be traced through the various editions of the *Suggestions,* the first of which appeared in 1905. The various editions incorporate in general ideas and practices garnered by the Government Inspectors (H.M.I.), who act as agents of cross-fertilization and advise the heads and teachers of schools. The Ministry has followed the practice established by the Board of instituting short courses on special subjects. The special reports of the Consultative Committee, which was abolished by the Education Act, 1944, and replaced by Central Advisory Councils, and reports of Departmental Committees have also made important contributions. The reports on the *Education of the Adolescent* (1926) and on *Infant and Nursery Schools* (1933) have already been mentioned. Between these two reports another on *The Primary School* was published in 1931 by the Consultative Committee. Local education authorities may also have their own inspectors and special subject supervisors, and may also publish their own suggestions.

The administration of each school is in the hands of the head teacher, who is responsible for the classification of the pupils, the general supervision of the teachers of the school, and the preparation, with or without the cooperation of his staff, of the curriculum and course of study or syllabus. Its flexible character is indicated by the fact that it is not in printed form. It is the head of a school who is its leader with the result that no two schools are alike, as they tend to be when the leadership is in the hands of the administrator of a local system or of the central authority of a national system. There may be a certain unevenness in the quality of the schools, but the flexibility and variety encourage those who have the ability to advance and point the way.

As in the development of the nursery and infant schools, radical changes have been taking place in the character of the primary school. Perhaps the most important has been the change that has proceeded slowly since World War I in the status of the primary school as an institution of democracy. The influences that have brought about this change are many, and psychology and the theory of education have played their part. But the evolution has been slow and the changes have not been as frequent as in American education. The traditional emphasis on the liquidation of illiteracy, on mental training, on the acquisition of a stock of knowledge have disappeared in favor of an all-round training of the individual. The newer point of view is stated in the *Handbook of Suggestions* (1937), as follows: "We realise more and more the importance of broadening the aims of education and of placing greater emphasis on the social development of children; we appreciate more thoroughly the value of space and of activity in securing and maintaining their health and vitality, and we feel more deeply the need of relating what is taught in the schools to what is happening in the world outside. We have discovered in recent years a great deal, too, about how we should teach the various subjects of instruction, but at the same time we are also beginning to find that we shall have to know still more about how the child himself learns, and what he should learn, if his subsequent development is to be as complete and healthy as possible. In other words, in consequence of the changes that are occurring there has been a shift of emphasis in teaching from the subject to the child" (p. 7).

Equally important is the change in defining the aim of the school. Instead of stressing the subjects to be taught, the function of the school is defined "as being (1) to provide the kind of environment which is best suited to individual and social development; (2) to stimulate and guide healthy growth in this environment; (3) to enable the children to acquire the habits, skills, knowledge, interests and attitudes of mind which they will need for living a full and useful life; and (4) to set standards of behavior, effort, and attainment by which they can measure their own conduct" (p. 15).

So far as the curriculum is concerned the principle stated in the report on *The Primary School* is generally accepted that "the curriculum of the primary school is to be thought of in terms of activity and experience rather than of knowledge to be acquired and facts to be stored" (p. 139). But activities and experiences must at some stage be organized as subjects and instruction in such subjects may well utilize activities and experiences. In the *Handbook of Suggestions*, which appeared six years later than this report, the important place of subjects is carefully defined as representing forms of skill and branches of knowledge found valuable in the experience of the race; "it is the function of the school to preserve and transmit the traditions, knowledge, and standards of conduct on which our civilization depends; and if the child at school is to assimilate the various highly systematised bodies of subject matter presented to him, due regard must be had to his natural interests and the way in which he acquires his everyday experience" (p. 37).

The evacuation and dislocation of schools and the use of camps for the care of children added a new note to education after World War II as after World War I. Since it fits in with current theory better today than previously it is likely to last longer. More insistent than ever before is the demand that education in the school should be related to the world outside the school. Accordingly the school has the duty of training childen to see and understand the world around them. Out of such activity may come the rudiments of nature study, geography, and local history.[6] Art in various forms, music, and handwork are given a place of importance along with language (speech and writing) and arithmetic. It must be remembered, however, as was pointed out earlier, that healthy physical development comes first. The principal aim of the primary school "must be to aid children, while they are children, to be healthy, and, so far as is possible, happy children, vigorous in body and

[6] This is analogous to the German *Heimatkunde* and the French *étude de milieu*.

lively in mind, in order that later, as with widening experience they grow towards maturity, the knowledge which life demands may more easily be mastered and the necessary accomplishments more readily acquired" (*The Primary Schools,* p. xvi). More recently the following statement of the aim of the junior school was made in view of the elimination of the competition to obtain a secondary education: "The junior school will be enabled to develop an education at once wider and less formal than it has commonly been hitherto. More stress will be laid on promoting the physical well-being of the children, on developing their own interest in, and knowledge of, their environment, and on learning to do things as well as learning from books" (*The Nation's Schools,* p. 10).

## FRANCE

### Reconstruction of the School System

The reconstruction of the school system in France is proceeding by instalments. Many of the proposals for reform that have been current since World War I have been adopted, but a general law for the reconstruction of education has not yet been enacted. Nor in view of the political and economic situation in France since the end of World War II could such legislation have been effected. Fundamental reforms cannot be successfully negotiated when Ministers change so quickly. Nor has there at any time since 1945 been a coalition government in power that would ensure a radical reconstruction of the school system against being rejected at some time in the future. The economic situation has also been unfavorable for a reform that would require large expenditures for new buildings and for salaries, if more pupils were to be brought within the range of secondary education. As in other countries there has been a shortage of building materials, while the birth rate has increased beyond expectation and led to oversized classes.

The consequence of all these practical difficulties is that the system of education is a mixture of the old and the new. The dual system still remains and the majority of pupils receive an education of the first level (*l'enseignement du premier degré*) in elementary schools up to fourteen and in junior secondary schools (*cours complémentaires*), while the normal schools for the preparation of teachers for elementary schools are still classed under the same division. On the side of reform, however, some types of schools which had previously been included in the elementary education division or in the division for technical education have been classified as secondary schools as part of *l'enseignement du second degré;* these include the higher elementary schools (*écoles primaires supérieures*) which have become *collèges modernes,* and both the *collèges techniques* and the technical sections in the *lycées* and *collèges.* The school system appears to be the most illogically arranged organization of institutions in a country which has prided itself on symmetry and orderliness. The blueprints for a common and well-articulated school system are available and bills have been drafted on the basis of the proposed reforms and the reconstruction can be legislated when the political and economic situation warrants it.

### Ecoles Maternelles

Schools for the care of young children have a long history in France. They were first established at Waldersbach in Alsace by Pastor Oberlin. In 1837 they were officially organized as *salles d'asile,* and in 1886 they were incorporated into the system of elementary education as *écoles maternelles* (maternal schools). These schools are open to children between the ages of two and six and attendance is voluntary. They may be established in communities with a population of over 2,000. In communities with a population below this number infant classes (*classes enfantines*) may be attached to the elementary school. The buildings for the *écoles maternelles* are provided by the localities, but their programs must be approved by a special commission in the Ministry of Education. The schools are separate from the primary schools and have their own principals (*directrices*) and teachers whose salaries are paid by the State. The principals are required to have had five years of successful experiences in a maternal school, while the teachers have the same qualifications as elementary school teachers and may teach in either the maternal or elementary schools. Special courses are offered in the normal schools and in educational conferences and institutes on the principles of educating the preschool child, and there is a special staff of inspectors who can advise the teachers. The staff of a maternal school includes, besides the teachers, a *femme de service* responsible for the physical care of the children, and a kitchen staff for the preparation and service of meals which are provided in many schools. Since the teachers are responsible for the children for three hours of each session in the morning and afternoon and since in industrial areas mothers may be employed the whole day, localities may employ women to care for the children (*gardiennes*) at hours when the teachers are off duty, so that children may be left in school from 8 a.m. to 6 p.m. Many schools include on their staffs a school hygienist to assist the school doctor during the visits which he is required to make each month and to keep records of physical development (height and weight) and of health; the hygienist also serves as a liaison between school and home on health matters.

Interest in the maternal schools is promoted by the *Comité français pour l'Education Préscolaire* (French Committee for Preschool Education), which has a division for international relations, locally there are *Sociétés des Amis de l'Ecole* (Societies of Friends of the School) which cooperate with parents in philanthropic activities (provision of clothing, for example) on behalf of needy children. In 1952–53 there were 3,929 *écoles maternelles* with 571,227 children enrolled. The number of children in the *classes enfantines* is not available for 1952–53 but in the previous year, 1951–52, it was 443,162. The regulations prescribe in detail the type of building and equipment required — a large playroom, rooms for activities, rest, and recreation, a playground, cloakrooms, washbowls, baths and showers, sanitary arrangements, and cots for the youngest group. A collection of toys and playthings of different kinds must be provided.

After many years the real function of maternal schools has been recognized as social and educational. They are no longer looked upon as philanthropic child-care institutions nor as schools to introduce the young children to the elements of a scholastic curriculum. Under the influence of Madame Pauline Kergomard (1838–1925), who for a long time was *inspectrice-générale* of maternal schools, a change has gradually been effected and modern principles have been applied to these schools. It is interesting, however, that apart from Montaigne and Rousseau, who are cited mainly to suggest a French tradition, the major contributions which are admitted are those of foreign psychologists and educators (the Swiss Piaget, Claparède and Ferrière; the Belgian Decroly; and the Italian Montessori).

A mixture of French tradition and foreign theory, the work of the maternal school combines the aims of good child care with initiation into the formal studies of the primary school. The teachers are free within the limits of a prescribed time-schedule to use whatever methods may be most useful at any given time. The primary aim is to create an atmosphere of joy and affection in which children can grow and develop interests. Rather than giving instruction, an environment is to be arranged in which the children may themselves discover the world around them. Special care is devoted to their physical development and sense training.

The general program for the thirty-hour week is defined by the regulations of the Ministry and include the following major divisions: (1) physical exercises, breathing, games, and graduated movements to the accompaniment of singing; (2) sensory and manual exercises, and drawing; (3) language exercises, recitations, and stories; (4) exercises in observation of common objects and creatures; (5) exercises designed to form the beginnings of moral habits; (6) exercises to initiate the pupils in reading, writing, and arithmetic. The last series is only for the highest section, the pupils being divided into three sections — two- to four-year olds, four to five, and five to six. Although the program is divided into periods of a time-schedule, teachers are free to introduce whatever modifications the local conditions warrant. The thirty hours per week are not as formidable as they would appear; five hours are devoted to physical care and recreation, two to rhythmic exercises, two to sensory exercises and observation lessons, two to recitations and stories, and ten to French language (speech, reading, and writing). Time is taken out for rest periods, and a room is normally set aside in which the youngest group may sleep.

The maternal schools, in which the first signs of the application of modern educational theories became apparent, will be found to hold an important place in the history of French education. Beyond their own social and educational contribution, they were the first educational institutions in which the teachers were given a certain amount of freedom to adjust the program to local circumstances. Certain schools were earlier permitted to adapt their work to local industrial or agricultural needs. But the freedom allowed in the maternal schools represents a break in the uniformity characteristic of French education. Beyond that it will also be found that the educational theory, based on a better understanding of children, has had some influence on the work of the elementary schools. While the influence of the maternal schools may work upwards, the experiments with the *classes nouvelles* in the secondary schools, which are described on page 283, will work downwards into the elementary schools. The scholastic pressure would be relieved and a middle way, combining the best in the French tradition with the best in the new methods, will be achieved. In the meantime the maternal schools, like the English nursery schools, have as their aim the healthy physical and mental development of preschool children in a serene and tranquil atmosphere which also makes for their healthy emotional development and feeling of security.

### Elementary Education

Compulsory school attendance in France begins at the age of six and under a law of 1936 continues to fourteen. Where the population of a locality exceeds 500, separate schools must be provided for boys and girls, unless special permission is obtained from the departmental council approved by the Ministry, to have a mixed school. The State bears the cost of teachers' salaries, and the locality the cost of buildings, equipment, and maintenance. The State may, but is not required to do so, grant subsidies toward the cost of building, enlarging, or repairing a school, while the alterations, provided by the law of 1951, may be used for the purchase of extra modern equipment or for the hygienic improvement of teaching conditions. Elementary education is free and lay, that is, religious instruction is not given in the school which is denominationally neutral; the schools are closed on Thursdays to enable pupils to receive religious instruction, if their parents so desire.

## Aim and Curriculum

The aims of elementary education are utilitarian and educational. The utilitarian aspect was defined in the *Instructions* of 1887, according to a formulation by Octave Gréard, that in the elementary schools pupils should "learn well in each of the branches that of which we cannot be permitted to be ignorant." On the educational side the function of the school is to cultivate the pupil as a human being. In the *Instructions* issued in 1923 the aim was defined as follows: "We have no intention of abandoning either one of these two aims (i.e., utilitarian and educational), which have been assigned to elementary education. We do not overlook the fact that most of our pupils, from the time they leave us will have to work for a living; and we desire to supply them with a fund of practical knowledge which tomorrow will serve them in their vocation. But we do not forget, furthermore, that we should be forming in them the man and the citizen that they are to become tomorrow. Concern with urgent realities will not cause us to neglect the cult of the ideal." [7]

Nevertheless, in practice the prescribed courses of study and the examination for the *certificat d'études primaires* (certificate of primary studies), taken at the age of twelve, tended to place more emphasis on the acquisition of facts and information than on general development. The schools were criticized for cultivating an elementary type of mind (*l'esprit primaire*) which amassed information without training in its use. The *Instructions* of 1938 attacked the system of drill and authoritarianism and advocated the cultivation of the mind and the development of personality. The school must prepare the young "for the tasks, the duties, the struggles, and the joys of the whole of life, develop their physical qualities, their gifts of heart and mind which make them workers, citizens, and real men."

A still later edition of the *Instructions* on the time-schedule and course of study introduced a new interpretation of the aims which now emphasized not only the acquisition of the fundamental tools

[7] I. L. Kandel, *French Elementary Schools, Official Courses of Study* (New York, 1920), p. 54.

but personal observation to give French youth "the grand bath of realism" that they need. The implication of this change is itself a criticism of the old approach as too bookish.

The chief criticism of the course of study, ever since the edition of 1887 appeared, has been that it was too overloaded with facts and information. The revision of 1887, which was published in 1923, retained the chief features of the earlier edition but sought to make "a definite statement of the proper use of the time allowed, of simplifying and graduating the programs, of vitalizing the methods, and coordinating the subjects." [8] Teachers were allowed some freedom, but the criticisms still continued.

In his concluding remarks on the edition of the *Instructions* in 1938, M. Jean Zay, then Minister of Education, wrote: "Each of the preceding pages reflects our desire to train children in the practice of precise and effective observation, to arouse and encourage the spontaneity of their reflections and their initiative, to inspire in them the taste for action, and lofty admiration of fine works, to develop in them the gifts of body, heart, and mind which will make them workers, citizens, and real men. Our method to this end is simple. It makes use of the qualities that we plan to strengthen, and restricts the course of study to questions and exercises which life in practice offers as examples or proves useful. The method is based at once on the theory of great educators, who are also great thinkers, and on pedagogical experience as old as the lay school itself and also as young. It is enough, with the devotion and ingenuity which the teachers exemplify every day, that the new arrangement of our education should fully respond to our hopes" (p. 94).

Finally, the *Instructions* of 1945, which are still in force, with modifications introduced in 1947 for the last years of the elementary school, seek to make the acquisition of the fundamental tools simpler and more effective, and to bring the work of the school closer to life to give that "bath of realism" that French youth needs. The methods by which the new aims are to be achieved are supported by groups that participate in the education courses established by academy and local inspectors, and by groups interested in the "new

[8] *Ibid*, p. 45.

education." They emphasize respect for the personality of the child and stimulate his activity; reading and writing are taught by the global method; statements are presented by pupils to their classmates; investigations are conducted by teams into the local environment, natural and human; and pupils study by themselves or in cooperative groups. These methods are far removed, if they can be put into practice, from the overemphasis on facts that used to prevail.

The "bath of realism" is extended by the use of audio-visual aids, for the purchase of which the Ministry bears half the cost and the assignment of a percentage of the allocations under the law of 1951 for this purpose. An increasing number of schools have projectorscopes, and for schools that have the necessary apparatus collections of moving pictures are available in the "regional office of the cinema educator" of which there is one in each academy, and in the central film depository in the *Centre National de Documentation Pédagogique* of the *Musée Pédagogique* in Paris. Short school excursions are encouraged, and the study of the environment (*étude du milieu*) brings the pupils into touch with world of nature and of man. Radio and television broadcasts are not yet employed for school purposes to any great extent. The introduction of guided activities (*activités dirigées*) is intended to have the same effect of giving reality to the work of the schools and to prevent it from being excessively bookish. The activities may be chosen and carried out by an individual or by a group and provide an opportunity for self-direction and the cultivation of hobbies. The teacher guides and suggests but does not impose activities to be taken up by the pupils.

The course of study (*programmes*) is organized not by years or classes but by courses as follows: *section préparatoire* for pupils six to seven years of age; *cours élémentaire* for pupils seven to nine; *cours moyen* (intermediate course) for pupils nine to eleven; *cours supérieur* (higher course), one year, for pupils eleven to twelve; and, since 1938, *section de fin d'études,* for pupils twelve to fourteen. The subjects of the curriculum are moral instruction, reading, writing, and arithmetic, French, history and geography, observation lessons, drawing and manual work, singing, guided activities, open air and physical education, recreation. In 1947 a new curriculum was issued for the *section de fin d'études* which included most of these subjects but made the following additions and changes: to moral instruction was added introduction to civic life; to arithmetic practical applications; music education replaced singing; and elements of applied science took the place of observation lessons. The time-schedule provides for thirty hours a week.

Teachers are permitted to modify the time-schedule with the approval of the local primary inspector, and may also adapt the courses to the local environment. The periods set aside for guided activities and recreation, which are generally placed at the end of the day, may be combined for walks in which features of the local environment can be observed and used in the study of history and geography. The most striking features in the evolution of elementary education are the freedom and flexibility that are encouraged. Whether the examination for admission to one of the secondary school types or even to the *cours complémentaires* which are still classed as of the elementary level, and the examination for the *certificat d'études primaires* which has been postponed to be taken at fourteen instead of at twelve years of age will reduce the pressure on teachers to cling to the older methods is uncertain. The more advanced preparation of teachers for elementary schools may give them greater professional confidence than they have had in the past.

There has been a departure since 1938 from the concentric plan of curricular organization, which was based on an unsound psychology, to a progressive organization. The courses of study no longer give the impression of a constant repetition of the subjects, more and more expanded in detail from one stage to another. The reforms in the latest edition of the course of study have been particularly addressed to history, geography, object lessons, and arithmetic in which an emphasis has been placed on imparting useful knowledge and developing good intellectual habits as a protection against the scourge of verbalism. Object lessons, for example, must not be taught from books but must utilize materials from everyday life. Ability to study a map must be one of the chief aims of geography instruction, working from the neighborhood beyond the terrain with which the pupils are familiar. The course in history discards the scholarly, abstract form that was followed and replaces it with an emphasis on local history as the starting point and on social and cultural rather than on political evolution, on realities through pictures and reproductions rather than on words. In arithmetic an important place must be devoted both to its practical applications and its integration with other aspects of the curriculum. Since a great deal of attention has always been devoted to teaching of the French language it has not been necessary to introduce any radical changes except that silent reading and the preparation of résumés of what has been read and the writing of practical documents such as letters, reports, interschool correspondence, minutes of a meeting, acknowledgement of letters, drafting of telegrams, and the like have been introduced into the language course of the terminal class. The course for environmental studies arranged for this class is a good example of what is intended by the new approach, "the bath of realism." It is a combination of general science and social and economic organization of the locality of the school, differing according to its urban-industrial or rural-agricultural character. The outline of the course in the regulations is given in two columns — the topic in one and practical exercises in the other. There is also a differentiation between the course for boys and that for girls which includes household management and child care. In English modern schools the course would be included in the curriculum of secondary modern schools, and in American high schools would correspond to a course in general science.

### Certificat d'Etudes Primaires

At the age of fourteen pupils may take the examination for the elementary school leaving certificate ( *certificat d'études primaires* ), for which the age limit was raised from twelve in 1947. The examination is conducted by a committee which includes the primary school inspector, teachers from normal and secondary schools, a representative of private schools, and some women teachers for the examination of girls. The subjects of the examination are based on the work of the terminal class and consist of: (1) a dictation and questions thereon; (2) two exercises in practical arithmetic; (3) an essay, which is also a test of writing (4) drawing or manual work for boys or sewing for girls; (5) questions on history, geography, and applied science; (6) oral examination in reading, mental arithmetic, and singing or a recitation. About 78 per cent of the pupils who take the examinations pass, but normally only 60 per cent of the pupils in the terminal class present themselves for the examination.

## Cours Complémentaires

The *cours complémentaires* are anomalous institutions which give a secondary or vocational training to a selected number of pupils but are still under the administration of the director of education at the first level (*l'enseignement du premier degré*). Their survival and the continuance of elementary education classes for pupils above the age of eleven or twelve point to the incompleteness of the reform of the French educational system.

The *cours complémentaires* originally offered a two-year course to pupils who desired a more advanced course than the elementary but who were unable to get into a secondary or a higher elementary school. They were advanced classes attached to an elementary school. Although the length of the course has been extended to four years, so that pupils may remain to the age of fifteen or sixteen, and although the course is like that of first four years of *collège moderne* (*le premier cycle* or the short course at the secondary level), the *cours complémentaires* are not classified as secondary. In addition to this course, vocational trade, commercial, and agricultural courses may be offered. Pupils are admitted on the basis of a qualifying examination (*examen probatoire*) up to the number of places available, but on an average about 80 per cent of the candidates succeed in being admitted. The teachers are mainly elementary school teachers with at least five years of experience, but there is a gradual increase in the number who have qualifications for secondary school teaching. In 1950 the general course was given in 87 per cent of the classes in the *cours complémentaires,* commercial courses in 8 per cent of the classes; 4 per cent of the classes gave trade training, and 1 per cent agricultural and household arts courses. For the vocational courses the authorities for technical education are responsible. The work of the *cours complémentaires* is thus diversified, but they perform an important service in smaller

localities where secondary schools are not available. The teachers
may, within the regulations of the curriculum issued in 1947, adapt
the course of study to the circumstances of the locality.

The curriculum of the general course consists of French, civics,
history and geography, a foreign language, mathematics and geo-
metrical drawing, physical and natural sciences, drawing, music,
and physical education. This course prepares for the *brevet
d'études du premier cycle du second degré* (B.E.P.C.), which entitles its holder to admission to the fifth year (*classe du second*) of a
secondary school or to a normal school. The vocational courses have
their own appropriate certificates — the *brevet d'enseignement industriel ou commercial* (certificate of industrial or commercial education), and the *certificat d'aptitude professionelle* (certificate of
vocational aptitude) in some special trade.

## Statistics of Elementary Education

In 1952–53 the total enrollment in 70,214 elementary schools was
3,900,686; this figure, however, includes pupils in *classes enfantines*
who probably numbered about half a million children below the
age of six. In 2,121 *cours complémentaires* which are included in
the 70,214 elementary schools there were enrolled 228,006 pupils.

## U.S.S.R.

In the education of the child in the U.S.S.R. the original plans of
the Revolution have had to be modified considerably. It was intended to eliminate family life and the housing plans were drawn
up in such a way as to implement this institution. Other traditional
bases of family life were also expected to be discarded. Women
were emancipated and given an equal place with men in the construction of the Communist state. Children were to be taken over
and brought up by the State at as early an age as possible. The
plans to destroy family life failed, but facilities were created to
enable the new emancipated woman to continue to work and leave
her children to be cared for by the State during working hours.
The purpose behind this scheme is not only social and economic;
educationally its purpose is to begin the conditioning of the younger

generation as early as possible. Undoubtedly the provisions for the care of the young child in the U.S.S.R. are analogous to those in the democracies, although the Communist pedagogues insist in this as in other matters that they owe nothing to foreign theory or practice. Froebel and Montessori are rejected because their ideas are artificial and formal. The fact that these ideas have been revised in the light of the contributions of psychology and child study, and that in other countries attention is devoted to health, play, physical development, and varieties of forms of expression is never mentioned; it would be a denial of the Soviet claim to originality. The use of the early years of childhood for purposes of nationalistic and ideological indoctrination is again not original with Communist educators; it was characteristic of childhood education in Nazi Germany and Fascist Italy.[9]

### Nurseries and Kindergartens

Mothers, whether they work or not, may leave their infants in crèches or nurseries, which are open for twenty-four hours a day to accommodate women working on night shifts. The staff of teachers, nurses, and domestic workers are on duty for six- or eight-hour shifts. The nurseries are provided by housing developments, cooperatives, factories, labor unions, farm collectives, or any organization in which women are employed in sufficient numbers. They are under the supervision of the health authorities, local and national. Parents cooperate closely with these institutions which serve as centers for training mothers in the care of children and for parent education. The infants, who may remain until they are three years of age, are fed and sleep in the nurseries and begin to receive training in group activities; toys, for example, are selected to encourage group or collective rather than individual action. Programs of play, games, music, and constructive work are organized on the same lines as in non-Communist nurseries elsewhere.

At the age of three the children may enter publicly maintained

[9] See I. L. Kandel, "The End of an Era," *Educational Yearbook, 1941,* of the International Institute of Teachers College, Columbia University (New York, 1941), pp. 192 ff.

kindergartens and remain until they are seven, when compulsory school attendance begins. The kindergarten program is similar to that for preschool children in other systems of education. Attention is paid to training the children in health and hygienic habits, in speech, in observation of the world of nature and of people. Time is devoted to story-telling, music, singing, drawing, modeling, and rhythmic movements. At the age of five preparation for the primary school is begun by initiation into the three R's. For the rest the difference of the Communist preschool from that in other countries may be gathered from the following description by Medinsky: "Children are taught to love their Soviet Motherland, their people and leaders; are brought up in a collective spirit; they are taught to acquire working and organizational habits," [10] and standards of conduct among themselves and to others. The kindergartens are in close cooperation with parents who appoint committees to work with the teachers and like the nurseries serve as centers to advise parents on the upbringing of their children.

### Primary Education

School attendance was made compulsory for seven years in the larger cities in 1930; in 1949 seven years of education became compulsory throughout the Union. Normally a four-year school has been available everywhere, and the extension of the seven-year incomplete middle school to rural areas has taken place only in the last five years.

Primary education may be given in the four-year primary school, and the first four years of the seven-year incomplete or ten-year complete middle school. Secondary school subjects are begun in the fifth year (see pp. 296 f.). The program of primary education is the same throughout all schools of the U.S.S.R., and the textbooks are the same, but, where necessary, translated into the national language. "The textbook contains the knowledge which pupils are obliged to master. Being the chief aid of the teacher, it must play an exceptionally important role as a weapon of communist education." The curriculum and course of study of the R.S.F.S.R. serve as a model for the rest of the U.S.S.R. "All teaching

10 Y. N. Medinsky, *Public Education in the U.S.S.R.* (Moscow, 1951), p. 45.

plans and programs, approved by the Ministry of Education, are obligatory state documents. Every teacher and school director is responsible for their execution. Arbitrary changes . . . are inadmissible. Compulsory uniformity of programs is one of the most valuable conditions for the improvement of schoolwork in our country." [11] Teachers may supplement the course of study but any additions must be in accord with Communist education and socialist reality. The school sections of the Party Central Committee of the U.S.S.R. and of the separate Republics are watchful to see that there are no deviations from the Party line or from approved methods and principles. The curriculum consists of Russian language and literature, arithmetic, physical training, drawing, and singing in the first three years; in the fourth year nature study, history, and geography are added. In non-Russian schools, where the native vernacular is used for instruction the Russian language is taught. "The principal methods of study," writes Medinsky,[12] "are the narrative with the teacher explaining things, talks, acquainting children with the textbook and other books, their written and graphic work." The work of the school is supplemented by nature study and geography excursions and visits to places of local interest. Pupils are promoted from one class to another on the basis of their annual progress until at the end of the fourth year they face an examination, oral and written, in the Russian language and arithmetic, and in their native language, if it is other than Russian. This examination is required for admission to the fifth year of school, when some secondary school subjects are begun.

Since 1945 a strong emphasis on inculcation of a spirit of nationalism and patriotism has been introduced into the schools. Yesipov and Goncharov, in their work on pedagogy, translated by Counts and Lodge,[13] write, "The cultivation of the spirit of Soviet patriotism in the younger generation is the most important task of moral education in our country. . . . To educate the young in the spirit of Soviet patriotism means also to plant in their consciousness the understanding that the interests of our people and the interests of the toiling masses of the entire world are indivisible."

[11] Counts and Lodge, *I Want To Be Like Stalin*, p. 19.
[12] *Op. cit.*, p. 49.
[13] *Op. cit.*, p. 36.

This instruction is part of the training in Communist morality which is described as "an education which in the light of the Communist ideal, shapes all the actions, all the habits, and the entire conduct of a person, determining his attitude toward people, toward his Motherland, toward labor, and toward public property." [14] This must be inculcated as a duty, for "In the life and conduct of pupils much is determined, not by personal needs and interests, but by a feeling and a consciousness of duty toward parents; toward the collective of comrades; toward the school, and toward the state. The Rules for School Children begin with the words "it is the *duty* of every school child." [15]

The atmosphere of Soviet education is pertinently summarized in the following passage with which Counts and Lodge close their translation of Yesipov and Goncharov's *Pedagogy,* published under the title *I Want To Be Like Stalin:* "In the resolutions of the Central Committee of the All-Union Communist Party the cultivation of conscious discipline in the school is powerfully emphasized. The school is under obligation to educate people to be organization-minded and disciplined. Without a system of organization and discipline it is not possible to master the foundations of science, it is not possible to prepare the younger to be a worthy successor of the older generation." [16]

What the school can or cannot accomplish for the indoctrination of children in Communist morality is supplemented or supplied by the organizations which provide for the training of future Communist citizens and members of the Communist Party. At the age of eight children may become members of the Octobrists and at the age of ten members of the Children's Organization of Young Pioneers. These organizations reenforce the ideological indoctrination of the schools, and foster interests in science, art, and crafts. They serve as another agency to guard the young against deviations and to keep them "in the right line." There is no break in gauge between school and society.

[14] *Ibid.,* p. 40.
[15] *Ibid.,* p. 77. The Rules for School Children, adopted by the Soviet of People's Commissars of the R.S.F.S.R. on August 12, 1943, are given on pp. 149 f.
[16] *Ibid.,* p. 148.

## UNITED STATES

### Organization of Elementary Education

The elementary schools constitute the first part of the broad educational highway which the American system was intended to be almost from its start in the early decades of the nineteenth century. With the elementary schools the kindergartens are generally included as a unit. Nursery schools have not yet acquired a recognized place in the public school system.

The length of elementary education varies from state to state and may vary even in one state. The most usual organization of the school system provides for elementary schools with eight grades; side by side with this organization there are also school systems with six grades for elementary education. The eight-grade elementary school is articulated with the four-year high school; the six-grade school with six years of high school, either continuous or divided equally into junior and senior high schools of three years each. In 1949–50 there were 60,000 one-teacher schools, which are being replaced by the consolidation of school systems and the transportation of pupils. Kindergartens are rarely found in school systems of local government areas with a population of less than 2,500.

The work of the full elementary school is organized in three divisions: kindergarten-primary (kindergarten and Grades I to III; intermediate (Grades IV to VI), and upper (Grades VII and VIII), which may offer the same course as the first two years of the junior high school.

### Nursery Schools and Kindergartens

Although day nurseries where young children of working mothers could be left for the whole or part of a day have long been in existence, the nursery school is a recent development which followed its establishment in England. The day nurseries are provided by voluntary agencies — philanthropic, religious, and welfare associations. Nursery schools are provided by private groups, by institutions for the study of education for observation, and by research groups. There are also private venture schools established to meet an obvious need. Nursery schools, established by cooperative groups or attached to institutions for the study of education are staffed by trained teachers and, as a general rule, are well equipped. Among the latter are the nursery schools of the University of Iowa; the University of California in Los Angeles; Teachers College, Columbia University; Iowa State College; the Merrill Palmer School of Home-Making in Detroit. A few high schools have nursery schools in connection with courses in home economics for girls. The number of nursery schools maintained as part of the public school systems of the country is very small. During World War II a large number of day nurseries and nursery schools were established and subsidized by the Federal Government, but they disappeared when the demand for women for war work declined.

The aims of the nursery schools are similar to those in England — to promote healthful living, cleanliness, hygienic habits, and a variety of activities through play, music, drawing and painting, and rhythm. In nursery schools attached to schools of education and teachers colleges careful records are kept of the physical, mental, and emotional development of the children. While in school, from 8:30 or 9 a.m. to 2:30 or 3:30 p.m., the children are fed and required to sleep or to rest quietly. Important as the trained care of children of nursery school age (two to five years) is recognized to be, nursery schools are still available chiefly to the children of the economically privileged groups able to pay the high tuition fees. The cost of maintaining nursery schools will probably prove a deterrent to their extensive provision in the public school systems.

For children from four years of age to the age of compulsory school attendance (normally six years, but later in some states) kindergartens may be maintained as part of the public school provision in cities of 2,500 population and over. Originally conducted on the principles laid down by Froebel (the first kindergarten was established in Watertown, Wisconsin, in 1855), the modern kindergarten was transformed early in this century as a result of what had been learned from the careful study of the physical and mental growth of young children. Froebelian principles were discarded as too formalistic; for the same reason the Montessori theory did not find a place in the American kindergarten. The chief emphasis in the reform was placed upon the development of good habits, training in cooperating with others, sound physical progress through a variety of activities adapted to their stage of growth, and mental progress through a variety of experiences — play, story-telling, music, rhythm, creative occupations in art and manual work. No attempt is made to begin instruction in the three R's, but the variety of activities and experiences that make up the program are intended to serve as a foundation for the later study of formal subjects.

The educational theory on which the kindergarten was based exercised a great deal of influence on the work of the early years of the elementary school. It directed attention to the needs and interests of children and, in helping to postpone the beginning of instruction in formal school subjects, rendered easier the transition from the kindergarten to the grades or, where the kindergarten was not provided, from the home to the grades. The pedagogy of the kindergarten fitted in with the changes that proceeded, more slowly perhaps, in the elementary school. One result of the recognition of these common aims was to regard the kindergarten's primary stage as a unit.

In 1949–50 of the total number of pupils enrolled in elementary schools (19,404,693) there were 1,034,203 children in public kindergartens.

### Elementary School

The public elementary school is the common school attended by more than 90 per cent of American children. When he thinks of education, the American always thinks of the public school, and is even likely to regard the private school as "divisive," a charge which could not be substantiated. Parents have the right to choose the kind of school that they desire for their children and any attempt to deprive them of that right would be unconstitutional, as it was declared to be in the decision in the Oregon Case in 1925 (see p. 196). The experiments in applying modern theories to education were first undertaken in private schools, which were un-denominational and were grouped together under the name of "Progressive" schools.

The elementary school has moved a long way from its original aim of educating for literacy to preparing alert and intelligent citizens of a democracy by promoting the fullest development of each individual and cultivating in him a sense of responsible citizenship. This aim is common throughout the country; the methods by which it is attempted to realize it vary from school system to school system, since the unit is normally a whole system rather than individual schools. It is impossible to generalize about American education at any level. Variations can be found in every aspect — the school building, the length of school attendance, the quality of leadership by the local board of education and its administrative officers, the qualifications and remuneration of teachers, and the amount of money available for education. The faith of the American public in education manifests itself more in the expenditure on buildings than in appreciation and remuneration of teachers. The work of the elementary schools may range from a limited curriculum and the use of the "recitation" methods, that is, the assignment of a number of pages in a textbook to be recited to the teacher or to be able to answer the teacher's questions on the following day, to an extensive curriculum. Except for a few subjects which may be retained, the so-called modern curriculum is organized in terms of activities or experiences or integrated subject matter, the problems to be studied being drawn from or relevant to the local environment.

It is characteristic of American education that theory precedes practice rather than grows out of it. Education, it is claimed, cannot remain traditional or static; it must be adapted to a changing environment. In the last four decades, at least, that environment has changed more rapidly than ever before in history — materially and culturally — and education must keep up with the changes. The public, accustomed to being told that the new is always better than the old, expects the schools to follow the same principle. The administrator, who realizes that his chief task is publicity for the maintenance of good public relations, is always ready to accommodate the public by pointing out and justifying innovations introduced in the schools. One result is that "many teachers are confused by the changes in theory and practice that appear to them to be advocated in rapid and bewildering sequence."[17] Since World War II the public in different parts of the country as far removed from each other as Scarsdale (New York) and Pasadena (California) have revolted against "the latest and best" but not entirely on educational grounds alone.

Modern theories of education have on the whole exercised a stronger influence on the early than the later years of schooling. Changes have come from the bottom upwards. The attack on formalism was hastened by the acceptance of the theory that children should not be taught the fundamentals of reading, writing and arithmetic until they show readiness for these subjects. The teacher's task is to provide experiences and activities which would develop that readiness. This was only one aspect of the revolt against what was described as the "lockstep" of tradition. The new approach meant that the work of the school must be based upon the needs and interests of the child. The shift of emphasis in teaching from the subject to the child, which was noted in England in 1937, had already taken place some fifteen years earlier in American schools. The "child-centered school," which embodied this principle, was the result of the psychological studies of the child and his development combined with the influence of John Dewey's emphasis on growth and his principle that education is life and not a preparation for life. But neither the purpose or goal of growth nor the fact that not all life activities and experiences are educative was considered.

While the two principles helped to get rid of much deadwood from the curriculum which served no other purpose than to train or discipline the mind because of its difficulty, the emphasis on the "use" or "function" of what was learned was also a misinterpretation of a principle attributed to Dewey. What Dewey wrote was that "Some goods are not good *for* anything; they are just goods. Any other notion leads to an absurdity. . . . The proof of a good

[17] N. C. Kearney, *Elementary School Objectives, A Report Prepared for The Mid-Century Committee on Outcomes in Elementary Education* (New York, The Russell Sage Foundation, 1953), p. 154. By permission of the publisher.

is found in the fact that the pupil responds; his response is use." [18]
In other words, the basic difference between the old and the new
is in the pupil's learning because he understands the *meaning* of
what he learns instead of memorizing without understanding. In
the same way activities, the activity curriculum, and activity
methods were exaggerated as a protest against "passive" learning
of the traditional school on the assumption that while the pupils
sat and listened nothing went on in their minds. Another form of
protest against the traditional practice was the revolt against
the subject organization of the curriculum; their logical organization, it was feared, was contrary to the psychological one which
took account of and built on the needs and interests of the pupils.
Dewey's criticism of this trend was the statement that "the educator
cannot start with knowledge already organized and proceed to
ladle it out in doses. But as an ideal the active process of organizing facts and ideas is an ever-present educational process." [19] Another critic, Professor Boyd H. Bode, attacked the tendency to
base education on the unselected needs and interests of the pupils
and to emphasize growth without a sense of direction. "The traditional subjects," he wrote, "stood for an educational value which
we neglect at our peril." [20]

There developed as a result of the opposition to an organized
curriculum a contempt for facts and information. Mere knowledge
was decreed as unimportant when compared with the cultivation
of scientific method, research ability, and critical attitudes. Opposition to the child-centered school, in addition to the criticisms of
educational philosophers from within the Progressive group, came
from two sources — the essentialists and the advocates of a community-centered school.

The point of view of the essentialists, of whom the late Professor
William C. Bagley was the outstanding leader, was that the primary
function of education is to transmit the cultural heritage of the
race. Subjects represent the intellectual capital for use in acquiring

[18] John Dewey, *Democracy and Education* (New York, The Macmillan Co.,
1916), pp. 281 ff.   By permission of the publishers.
[19] John Dewey, *Experience and Education* (New York, The Macmillan Co.,
1938), p. 102.   By permission of the publishers.
[20] Boyd H. Bode, *Progressive Education at the Crossroads* (New York,
Newson and Co., 1938), p. 96.

new knowledge and embody valuable experiences which have survived because they were found to work. The mastery of fundamental skills cannot be acquired incidentally as the need for them arises. The essentialists, often decried in derogatory terms as traditionalists, were concerned primarily with the content of education as establishing a sense of direction which would be more effective for social living than either the immediate needs and interests of the pupils or adaptation to rapid change. On methods of instruction they accepted the principle that the teacher must start with the interests of the pupils but must make those interests over to prepare the pupils for living in the community as free and independent but responsible citizens. The essentialist movement, on the whole, represented the middle way; it did not stand, as is often assumed, for a subject-centered school, and certainly was critical of the child-centered school. The principles for which essentialism stood was that as between subjects and the child, the shift of emphasis has been rather to a recognition of the importance of the teacher whose professional preparation must include a mastery of subjects and an understanding of the process of child development and the child's interests in order to be able to mediate successfully between the two.

The theory that appears to be dominant at the present time is that of the community-centered school. This theory is an attempt to meet the criticisms of the child-centered school as being too individualistic and failing to set up aims beyond meeting the needs and interests of the pupils. Like the child-centered school, the community-centered school is a reaction against the subject-matter emphasis of tradition. Its aim is through the utilization of activities and experiences in the community to develop both an understanding and appreciation of the environment and a sense of social and civic responsibility and loyalty to the democratic ideal. In teaching, the emphasis is on group learning and cooperation. The topics selected for study are those relevant to the local, national, and world community rather than subjects as such. The fundamental skills are learned as they are felt to be useful in working on the environmental issue that is being studied. Ability to recognize and to solve problems is the end aimed at and training this ability may take the form of participation in some immediate problem that is of local, national, or international importance. The school, it is claimed, must prepare pupils to face the problems of a world that is becoming more complex than it has ever been. For this reason controversial issues cannot be ignored, particularly since they train the pupil in seeing two sides of a question. The old curriculum may have been satisfactory in an era when the country's economy was predominantly agricultural. It will no longer be adequate in a world that is highly mechanized and about to see far greater changes when atomic energy begins to be utilized for industrial production. Already the means of transportation and communication — the jet plane, radio, and television — are changing the moral and cultural atmosphere in which pupils are being educated. These conditions, it is claimed, must be taken into consideration in planning the curriculum of schools.

In practice all the three types of curricular organization — essentialist, child-centered, and community-centered — can be found, while the recitation method also lingers in some schools. The aims that determine the work of the elementary schools are nevertheless similar, despite these differences of approach. The development of the pupil's personality, the promotion of good physical and mental health, and the cultivation of responsible citizens of a democracy are professed aims everywhere. To meet the criticisms of those who deplore the absence of religious instruction in the public schools, efforts have been made to inspire the work of the schools with moral and spiritual values. The schools also strive to develop standards of good taste and appreciation in literature, music, and the arts. Increasing attention is being given to the use of audio-visual aids, although the use of the radio and television has not yet been successfully exploited. The subjects normally associated with elementary education will be found under every type of organization, overtly in the subject-centered curriculum, incidentally or opportunistically in the child or community-centered curriculum. These subjects are reading, writing, and arithmetic, history, geography, science, music, art, industrial arts, home economics, and physical education.

These subjects may be taught separately, or they may be integrated, or they may be taught as their need arises in the solving of a problem. Thus social studies constitute an integration of history, geography, civics, and economics; the language arts include reading, spelling, grammar, literature, and speech; general science includes hygiene, nature study, and the science of everyday life.

The methods range from learning from textbooks to activity methods. The single textbook in any one subject is generally supplemented by books in the school or class library. The exclusive use of activity methods is giving way to the use of whatever method may be most appropriate in a particular situation. It has been found that there is a place for direct exposition by the teacher and for intelligent drill. There is, indeed, no warrant for the assumption that activity methods or activities always engage the intellectual powers of the pupil, while passive learning fails to do so. The important change has been not in differences of methods, each of which may have its use, but in the recognition that the pupil should understand what he is expected to learn.

Standards are maintained increasingly through the use of achievement tests. Class examinations of the old type have almost disappeared and external examinations have been discarded. The tests that are most widely used are for achievement in reading, arithmetic, and language usage. The achievement tests have several uses; they set up comparable standards of achievement in a subject for the whole nation; they help teachers to discover weaknesses in their methods of instruction and the difficulties encountered by their pupils. Many of these difficulties arise from the practice of promoting pupils, whether they are ready or not, in order to avoid discouragement from a sense of failure. Unfortunately the bad effects of promotion on this basis are cumulative and remedial classes in reading have to be established in high schools to correct deficiencies in reading ability.

There have in recent years been serious criticisms of the results of education. It has been said that the products of the schools are weak in the fundamentals of arithmetic, spelling, grammar, speech, and reading, and that there is a surprising amount of ignorance of history, including national, and of geography at a time when the United States is becoming a world power with interests — political and economic — all over the globe. The usual response of educators and schoolmen is that the tests show on the contrary that pupils today do better on the fundamental subjects than their prede-

cessors did. This may be true at the time when the tests are taken
in school, but the critics may also be correct in finding that a few
years after leaving school young persons have forgotten what they
may have known well at the time the tests were taken.

The public schools have been seriously attacked since the close
of World War II. The burden of the attacks was leveled mainly
against the elementary schools. Part of the attack stemmed from
the hysteria aroused by the fear of communism but the charges of
subversive activities could not be maintained. Unfortunately those
who made the attack on these grounds aligned other critics on
their side. The criticisms of the latter group were leveled against
new developments of curriculum and methods in which, on the
one hand, the fundamental subjects, always considered an integral
part of elementary education, were concealed and taught incidentally, and, on the other hand, efforts were made to stimulate the
pupils to think through the discussion of controversial issues. Certainly the character of the elementary schools had in more progressive centers changed radically since the critics were themselves
in school. The attacks have at any rate had the effect of promoting
a movement to combine the best in the traditional with the best
in the new educational theory without adherence to any particular
doctrine.

There has undoubtedly been a tendency to follow slogans and
labels. No attention was paid to Dewey's injunction at the end
of a book which was critical of "'Progressive" as it was of traditional
education. "What we want and need," wrote Dewey, "is education
pure and simple, and we shall make surer and faster progress when
we devote ourselves to finding out just what education is and what
conditions have to be satisfied in order that education may be a
reality and not a name or a label." [21] The chief source of the
changing fashions in American education has not been the desire
to adapt education to rapidly changing conditions. It is to be found
largely in the attempt to bring into education the methods of experimentation and research which have produced the rapid advances in science. It is forgotten that teaching is an art, that a
science of education may bring about changes but changes of no

[21] John Dewey, *Experience and Education* (New York, The Macmillan Co.,
1938), p. 116.

serious magnitude, and that the human being is not the same kind of material as that with which the scientist deals in laboratory. Further, there is a cultural heritage which is, as it were, a map to be explored and for the exploration of which each generation needs to be trained. Finally, the revolt of the public or parts of it is an answer to the question "To Whom Do Schools Belong?"

## REFERENCES

### England

Armfelt, R. *Our Changing Schools.* London, H.M.S.O., 1950.

Barnard, H. C. *Short History of English Education, 1760–1944.* London, University of London Press, 1947.

Birchenough, C. *History of Elementary Education in England.* London, University Tutorial Press, 1939.

Board of Education. *Handbook of Suggestions for Teachers.* London, H.M.S.O., 1937.

——— Consultative Committee. *The Primary School.* London, H.M.S.O., 1931.

——— Consultative Committee. *Infant and Nursery Schools.* London, H.M.S.O., 1937.

Curtis, S. J. *History of Education in Great Britain.* London, University Tutorial Press, 1948.

Dent, H. C. *Education in Transition.* London, Routledge and Kegan Paul Ltd., 1944.

——— *Growth in English Education.* London, Routledge and Kegan Paul Ltd., 1954.

Jay, Peggy. *Better Schools Now!* London, Turnstile Press, 1953.

Kandel, I. L. *Raising the School Leaving Age.* UNESCO Studies in Compulsory Education No. 1. Paris, 1951.

Lowndes, G. A. N. *The Silent Social Revolution.* London, Oxford University Press, 1937.

Ministry of Education. Pamphlet No. 1, *The Nation's Schools.* London, H.M.S.O., 1945.

——— Pamphlet No. 4, *A Guide to the Educational System of England and Wales.* London, H.M.S.O., 1945.

——— Pamphlet No. 14, *Story of a School. A Headmaster's Experiences with Children Aged Seven to Eleven.* London, H.M.S.O., 1949.

―――― Pamphlet No. 15, *Seven to Eleven, Your Children at School.*
London, H.M.S.O., 1949.

Niblett, W. R. *Essential Education.* London, University of London
Press, 1947.

Smith, W. O. Lester. *Compulsory Education in England.* UNESCO
Studies in Compulsory Education VI. Paris, 1951.

**France**

*Avenirs* 60–61. Paris, Feb.–March, 1954.

Cavalier, Marie-Louise. *L'Ecole Publique et ses Maîtres.* Paris, 1952.

Centre National de Documentation Française. *L'Organisation de l'Enseignement en France.* Paris, 1951.

Comité Français pour l'Education Préscolaire. *Activités Enfantines à
l'Ecole Maternelle Française.* Paris, n.d.

Debiesse, Jean. *Compulsory Education in France.* UNESCO Studies
in Compulsory Education. Paris, 1951.

Glatigny, M. F. *Histoire de l'Enseignement en France.* Paris, 1949.

Ministère de l'Education Nationale. Enseignement du Premier Degré.
*Instructions du 20 Septembre 1938.*

―――― Enseignement du Premier Degré. *Horaires et Programmes de
l'Enseignement du Premier Degré. Instructions du 7 Decembre 1945.*

Soleil, Joseph, *Le Livre des Instituteurs.* Paris, 1948.

**U.S.S.R.**

Counts, G. S. and Nucia P. Lodge. *I Want To Be Like Stalin.* New
York, The John Day Co., 1947.

King, Beatrice. *Changing Man — The Education System of the U.S.S.R.*
New York, Viking Press, 1937.

―――― *Russia Goes to School.* London, Heinemann Ltd., 1949.

Medinsky, Y. N. *Public Education in the U.S.S.R.* Moscow, 1951.

Moos, Elizabeth. *The Educational System of the Soviet Union.* New
York, National Council of American-Soviet Friendship, 1952.

**United States**

Association for Supervision and Curriculum Development. *Organizing
the Elementary School for Living and Learning.* Washington, D.C.,
1947.

―――― *Toward Better Teaching.* Washington, D.C., 1949.

Beck, R. H., W. W. Cook, and N. C. Kearney. *Curriculum in the Modern
School.* New York, Prentice-Hall, Inc., 1953.

Butterworth, J. E. and others. *The New Rural School.* New York,
McGraw-Hill Book Co., 1950.

Caswell, H. L. and W. Foshay. *Education in the Elementary School.* New York, American Book Co., 1950.

Cole, Luella. *The Elementary School Subjects.* New York, Rinehart Co., Inc., 1946.

Cremin, L. A. *The American Common School, An Historical Conception.* New York, Teachers College, 1951.

Department of Elementary School Principals, *Spiritual Values in the Elementary School.* Washington, D.C., 1947.

———— *The Elementary School Principal Today and Tomorrow.* Washington, D.C., 1949.

Educational Policies Commission. *Education for All American Children.* Washington, D.C., 1948.

Elsbree, W. S. and W. J. McNally. *Elementary School Administration and Supervision.* New York, American Book Co., 1951.

Forest, Ilse. *Early Years at School.* New York, McGraw-Hill Book Co., 1949.

Foster, Josephine C. and Neith E. Headley. *Education in the Kindergarten.* New York, American Book Co., 1948.

Gans, Roma, and others. *Teaching Young Children.* Yonkers, N.Y., World Book Co., 1952.

Johnson, L. H. *Books for the Elementary School Administrator.* Albuquerque, University of New Mexico, n.d.

Kcarney, N. C. *Elementary School Objectives.* New York, Russell Sage Foundation, 1953.

Kyte, George C. *The Principal at Work.* Boston, Ginn & Co., 1952.

Langdon, Grace and Irving W. Stout. *The Discipline of Well-Adjusted Children.* New York, The John Day Co., 1952.

Nehl, Marie, and others. *Teaching in the Elementary School.* New York, Ronald Press, 1950.

National Society for the Study of Education. *Early Childhood Education.* Chicago, 1947.

Otto, H. J. *Principles of Elementary Education.* New York, Rinehart & Co., Inc., 1949.

Reeder, E. R. *Supervision in the Elementary School.* Boston, Houghton Mifflin Co., 1953.

# 8

# The Education
## of the Adolescent

### INTRODUCTION

Of all the difficulties that have everywhere to be met in the movements for the reconstruction of the educational systems the most difficult is the provision of education for the adolescent. The problems of reorganizing the systems of education for the child in the nursery school, the kindergarten, and the primary school are difficult, but the solution does not encounter serious social or educational obstacles. Nursery schools and kindergartens are pre-schools which may or may not be established for young children below the compulsory age for attending school. The primary school, which, it is now generally agreed, continues up to about the age of twelve, requires the more general adoption of modern educational practices based on lessons learned from educational psychology; classes need to be smaller in size, and buildings and equipment need to be modernized. In general, however, the emphasis in the curriculum rather than the curriculum itself needs to be changed in accordance with the principle, now generally accepted, of a shift of emphasis from the subject to the child. This is essentially a teaching problem rather than a curricular problem. The task is to lay the foundations for further intellectual, emotional, and physical development.

The situation changes when the child enters upon the adolescent stage. Interests and abilities begin to be differentiated and the differentiation continues both in intelligence and in occupational plans and perspectives. Despite the differences, however, all the pupils must receive a common training for those tasks which they will be called upon to perform as intelligent citizens of their country in one of the most complex periods of the world's history. Beyond this the school has the task of giving all pupils some idea of the best that has been said and done or the rudiments at any rate of a liberal education to orient them in the world in which they live and to inspire living interests in various ways. This task presents the first of the serious problems to be solved in providing an education adapted to the different abilities of an increasing number of adolescents.

This difficulty stems from the traditional concept of the term "secondary education." For hundreds of years the term has been associated with the study of foreign languages and mathematics; the study of science was added later and modern foreign languages were included side by side with Latin and Greek. The recognition of these new subjects presented the major problem in the last half of the nineteenth century in Germany, France, and England (but not in the United States), at a time when an expanding economy required a better educated personnel for management, and increasing wealth made possible an increase in the enrollment in the secondary schools. The idea of providing equality of opportunity for all had not yet emerged, but the organization of new courses of an academic character and their recognition for certain privileges and for admission to the universities were achieved finally at the beginning of the present century. It must here be noted, however, that those responsible for the conduct of high schools in the United States continued to inveigh against the college entrance requirements well into the present century, and criticism of them has not altogether yet died out.[1]

The needs of business and industry were nevertheless not fully

[1] See I. L. Kandel, *History of Secondary Education* (Boston, Houghton Mifflin Co., 1930), Chs. VI — IX.

met by the modifications in the programs of secondary education.
For a long time in the nineteenth century it was felt that elementary
education did not provide an adequate training for workers in
business and industry. For the children of those who could not
afford the cost of sending them to a secondary school and of providing for their maintenance during a longer period of education,
new types of schools — *Mittelschulen* in Germany, *écoles primaires
supérieures* in France, higher elementary or higher grade schools
and later "central schools" in some localities in England — were
provided with more advanced and somewhat longer courses than
in the regular elementary schools. Technical schools, full-time or
part-time, sprang up. None of these schools, however, enjoyed the
status of the secondary schools in their respective countries nor did
they lead to the same privileges (*Berechtigungen* in Germany or
*sanctions* in France) as the secondary schools.

These privileges were accessible to a very small percentage of
the population, selected in each country because of the financial
ability of parents to pay the fees required or to a small number of
pupils who by their intellectual ability were able to win scholarships. When it was discovered that ability and talent were not
limited to a particular social group, and the movement for secondary education for all began, there was an expectation that the same
kind of education, hitherto enjoyed by the privileged groups,
would be made accessible to all. Any other kind of postprimary
education was regarded as an inferior substitute, an attitude which
has created serious difficulties when the question of "allocation"
or distribution of education according to ability has been raised.

The special status of secondary education, which was as much
social as it was economic, since it gave access to white-collar or
black-coat jobs, is the cause of another serious difficulty standing
in the way of providing varied types of post-primary courses in
schools for adolescents. In the popular mind, even the minds of
those who have not enjoyed its advantages, secondary education
has acquired a definite connotation in terms both of curriculum
and of social prestige. The consequence is that any departure from
the traditional academic courses in the effort to meet the demands
of individual differences of ability is regarded as an inferior in
prestige and quality. This is also true in the United States, where

a variety of courses is offered in the same comprehensive high school and the academic or college entrance course enjoys a far higher prestige than any other course that may be offered. In France it was noted in the thirties that, when enrollments in the *lycées* and *collèges* increased as a consequence of the abolition of fees, the pupils still chose the traditional classical course, although other modern or scientific options were available in the same schools. This problem causes no difficulty in Communist countries where virtually all education is of a technical or industrial nature, but elsewhere "education for status," which means a demand for the traditional type of secondary education, constitutes a serious obstacle to reform.

To these issues others of a political and technical character can be added. One of the major forces in promoting the ideal of equality of educational opportunity for all is the recognition that to implement it is an essential element in the ideal of democracy. There is unfortunately a tendency to confuse the political aspect of democracy with other aspects, such as the intellectual and the economic. Such equalitarianism would reduce equality of educational opportunity to identity of opportunity. When the existence of individual differences of ability is admitted, the creation of separate schools for different groups of pupils is objected to on the grounds that such separation of pupils according to ability would lead to social and class stratification. There is a failure to recognize that social and class differences reflect their existence outside the schools, as will be shown later in the section dealing with the American high school. There is also a further failure to realize that faith in democracy is not produced by juxtaposition of persons but by inner convictions reflected in conduct. The basic issue is whether "the right education for the right pupil under the right teacher" can be provided for all in one school better than in separate schools organized to meet individual differences of ability. The difficulties existing in the American high schools are constantly mounting as enrollments increase but the most serious of them is that charge that the gifted pupils are neglected and that the general atmosphere here in the high schools is one of colorless mediocrity. This does not mean, of course, that the standards of scholarship are permanently lowered but it does mean that the process of selection is both delayed and longer than else-where.

Those who are opposed to the distribution of pupils into separate schools according to ability put forward another argument. They claim that at the age of twelve the abilities and aptitudes of pupils cannot be determined and to attempt to do so at this early age may perhaps result in injustice to many pupils who develop late or who, through nervousness or other causes, do not give a satisfactory account of themselves on any examination or test yet devised. This claim is not borne out by the facts, nor in practice is the distribution of pupils based solely on a single test or examination. Other factors that play a part in the process are the opinions of the pupils' teachers and the cumulative records through the primary school period. In any case arrangements can be made for the transfer of pupils who have been assigned to the wrong course. In the last analysis the opposition based on fear of incorrect diagnosis of ability rests too often on the view that parents have the right to choose the kind of education that their children should have. In so far as there is any basis for the opposition it calls not for the abandonment of efforts to allocate or distribute pupils according to their ability, but for careful and more prolonged systems of guidance and closer relations between school and home.

On the administrative side those who advocate one comprehensive school for all argue that the difficulties in assigning pupils to the courses best adapted to their abilities would be simplified, an argument which, as will be shown later, is not borne out by American practices; nor does the argument that parity of esteem of different courses would be promoted by offering them all in the same school receive any support from the history of the American high schools in the past fifty years. The most pressing of all the arguments is that to educate all pupils in the same school would eliminate social class distinctions and promote social understanding and cooperation, something that has not been achieved by the American high school.

The problems to be met in reconstructing the educational provisions for the adolescent are further classified by a study of the traditional system of secondary education. It was based largely on the notion that certain subjects are good both for training the mind and for imparting a liberal education. So far as mental discipline, that is, the development through one subject of ability to deal with any other, is concerned it has now been established that it does not emerge spontaneously from learning subjects that are supposed to be difficult. Nor, again, is a liberal education necessarily imparted by the study of some subjects rather than others; its essence lies in teaching in a liberal spirit. Not infrequently so much time was spent on learning the fundamentals — the grammar and the syntax of a subject — that the structure of meanings and values was never understood.

This does not mean that the traditional curriculum, whether classified or modern, is not an excellent medium of instruction for those capable of profiting by it and of staying with it long enough to benefit from it. In practice, however, the majority of secondary school pupils leave at the age of sixteen, while a considerable number of the rest fail in the final test. Such studies of "elimination" and "mortality" in the American high schools at the beginning of the century stimulated the search for subjects of study and courses appropriate to abilities of those for whom the traditional academic curriculum was unsuited. It was recognized that a curriculum which attempted to impart a liberal education and at the same time to prepare for entrance to colleges and universities set a standard which only a minority could attain.

Unfortunately, the academic tradition from which the few can profit has either been sought by the less capable (*non-valeurs* as they were called in France) for reasons of status or has been generally attacked as "aristocratic." It is, of course, true that more can profit by this type of education than in the past, were the opportunities for education expanded, but it would be a waste of time and money to attempt to make it accessible to all adolescents under the illusion that equality of opportunity would thereby be provided. Nevertheless time has proved that this type of education has everywhere produced the leaders of thought and of action. The need of leaders — men and women who are well-educated and well trained and, today more than ever, socially understanding and enlightened — has never been greater than at present. There is a real danger that in the effort to provide educational opportunities for all in a spirit of equalitarianism the ends desired will not be attained. For equality of educational opportunity can only be interpreted to mean the adaptation of education to the abilities and aptitudes of the pupils. The criticism of the American comprehensive high schools seems to indicate the neglect of both the gifted and those below average. Efficiency in the organization to secure its successful operation, is as necessary in education as it is in any other large operation, perhaps it is more necessary because damage to human beings is more difficult to repair.

Whatever the difficulties in discovering the right course for the right pupils may be, whether in one school or in many, all are entitled to an education that will impart, by methods suited to the abilities of the pupils, common understanding, common ideas, common ideals, and common objects of social allegiance. All must be prepared to share in the tasks common to all. Beyond that, however, differentiation according to abilities, needs and aptitudes must be provided. The question that arises in this connection concerns the time when such differentiation should take place. Preparation for the common tasks as citizens and as human beings should come first, while the postponement of specialization or differentiation makes possible a better basis for guidance or choice of a career. Maturity facilitates more intensive preparation for most vocations. Besides general education the school has the opportunity of giving some form of generalized preparation for vocational adaptability rather than training for a special vocation. For many occupations special vocational schools will be needed, but the preparation can be more intensive, more practical, and more nearly approximating actual occupational conditions, if based on a longer course of general education.

The prolongation of education derives its justification from the fact that the problems of the citizens are more complex not only in local and national affairs but also in international relations. The whole world is in a state of transition; economic conditions are changing; under-industrialized nations are becoming industrialized. Not only are the problems faced by the individual as citizen becoming more complex, but the very conditions that produced this complexity have also brought about cultural changes. The changing cultural conditions demand from the individual as a human being an effort of understanding and acquiring standards of values and appreciation which was never demanded so urgently as today. For all these situations as well as for the position of the individual as a worker education must lay the foundations and stimulate living interests which will be pursued after school days are over, for education has come to be recognized as a lifelong process.

In the tradition of secondary education the emphasis has in the past been too much upon the subjects to be studied. In the education of the adolescent, that is, in the postprimary education of all young persons, the approach should be rather in terms of ends to be achieved. If this approach were made, the same subject could serve both the general end for which education is provided and the particular end which the subject itself is intended to serve. In other words a pupil may specialize in the study of the classics but both the value of the classics in themselves and their meaning in the present must be brought out by a teacher who looks beyond the immediate end. Only in this way can the narrowness for which specialization is criticized be avoided. In posing the following questions it is hoped that all types of education and courses planned for the adolescent can be guided by them as well as by the particular task of adapting instruction to the individual differences of ability among the pupils.

The following are some of the questions that those concerned with the education of the adolescent must bear in mind:

Are the schools developing young men and women who are informed and intelligent about the social, economic, and political tasks for which all have some responsibility?

Are the schools producing young men and women who have an appreciation of the form of government under which they live and its meaning in terms of their responsibilities?

Are the schools inculcating ideals and standards of cooperative living in a democracy?

Are the schools insisting upon any recognizable standards of achievement?

Are the schools seeking to cultivate and disseminate intellectual and other interests that will stimulate further education after school days are over?

Are the schools turning out citizens equipped with higher moral standards and intelligences trained to understand and meet the complexities of modern life?

Are the products of the schools not only more intelligent but healthier, happier, and better equipped than they would have been with traditional elementary education only?

It is assumed in general that, while technical education may constitute a distinct type of education for adolescents, specialized trade and industrial training requires a different type of organization from that of schools devoted to general education. Even technical education at the adolescent level not only can but should be general and liberal in character with a somewhat different emphasis from that in the academic or in what are coming to be called modern courses. Vocational education in the sense of direct training in skill requires a completely different type of approach from that in schools for general education. The claim that vocational education should also be liberal would defeat the ends for which it exists. Only in the sense that it provides a preparation for the vocation that lies ahead of all youth — membership in community and national life — can a liberal education be described as vocational. Many trades can be taught in from a few weeks to a few months in an economy based on technological developments. In view of the unionization of most trades it is probable that a modernized system of apprenticeship based on vocational adaptability developed in school would be preferable to prolonged vocational training in the schools.

There is, however, another difficult problem that has not yet been discussed. The prolongation of the period of compulsory education brings into the schools many pupils who become restive under the present curriculum provisions and create difficult disciplinary problems. Further thought must be given to devising courses that will hold the interest of pupils below the average so far as academic study is concerned. Methods of instruction may also have to be adapted to pupils of this type. Finally, some type of school or course which has never been tried may yet have to be explored. The statistics of the number of pupils who drop out of American high schools and the efforts to meet this situation are indicative of how difficult this problem is.

## ENGLAND

### Secondary Education for All

The most striking advance made in English education is the provision of the Education Act, 1944 to implement the ideal of secondary education for all. The provision is the final achievement of a movement which began during World War I and was foreshadowed in the Fisher Act of 1918. This Act, "with a view to the establishment of a national system of education available for all persons capable of profiting thereby," provided that "in schemes under this Act adequate provision shall be made in order to secure that children and young persons shall not be debarred from receiving the benefits of any form of education by which they are capable of profiting through inability to pay fees." The Act, however, made no provision for the reorganization of the whole system of administration. The Part III authorities, responsible for the management of elementary education only, continued to exist and did not have the power to provide schools beyond the elementary. This meant that young persons living outside the range of county and county borough education authorities were educationally virtually disfranchised.

In order to find a way out of the difficulty the Consultative Committee of the Board of Education, under the chairmanship of Sir Henry Hadow, was requested "to consider and report upon the organization, objective and curriculum of courses of study suitable for children who remain in full-time attendance at schools, other than secondary schools, up to the age of fifteen," and all matters relative to this. The Committee, in its report, *The Education of the Adolescent,* issued in 1926, recommended that on educational and on social grounds some form of postprimary education be made available for all normal children between the ages of eleven and fourteen, "and, as soon as possible, eleven and fifteen." The Committee advised that primary education continue to the age of eleven, that all normal children go forward to some form of postprimary education, and that "many more children pass to 'secondary' schools, in the current sense of the term." The system of postprimary education should consist of (1) the traditional secondary schools to be known as "grammar schools," (2) selective central schools giving a four-year course with a realistic or practical trend in the last two years, to be known as "modern schools," (3) non-selective central schools, adapted to the needs of children of different capacities and also known as "modern schools," and (4) "senior classes" within the public elementary schools for children who would not go to one of the other three types of schools. The Committee thought that it was desirable that these four types of schools should be known by the general name of "secondary education," following "primary education" at the age of eleven.

There were many obstacles to putting the recommendations into practice. Of these the two most important ones were that the age of compulsory attendance was still fourteen and that the "grammar schools" were administered under different regulations from the other types of postprimary schools, with more generous provisions as to staffing, size of classes, equipment and so on. Nevertheless, a reorganization did take place; in some areas separate schools were provided for pupils who did not proceed to "secondary schools," while in others senior classes with an enriched curriculum were organized in what have come to be termed as "all-age" schools, that is, in the ordinary elementary schools. In order to make a fuller reorganization possible an Act was passed in 1936 to raise the age of compulsory school attendance to fifteen. This provision was to have gone into effect in 1939 but the outbreak of World War II rendered this impossible.

In 1938 the Consultative Committee of the Board of Education, under the chairmanship of Mr. (later Sir) Will Spens, published its report on the terms of reference submitted to it in 1933 — "to consider and report upon the organization and interrelation of schools, other than those administered under the Elementary School Code, which provide education for pupils beyond the age of 11+; regard being had in particular to the framework and content of education of pupils who do not remain at school beyond the age of about 16." The tenor of the Report is suggested by the quotation from Rolland d'Erceville, *"Chacun doit être à portée de recevoir l'éducation qui lui est propre"* (1768). Although the title is *Report of the Con-*

*sultative Committee on Secondary Education with Special Reference to Grammar Schools and Technical High Schools,* the Committee also considered a third type which it called "Modern Schools." Parity of the three types of schools was recommended, so that the schools would "differ only in the kind of education they provide to meet the differing abilities and interests of the pupils." To secure parity the minimum leaving age should be raised to sixteen and fees be abolished in all publicly maintained schools. The three types of schools should be administered under a common code of regulations, thus eliminating the difficulties which stood in the way of the full realization of the Hadow Report on *The Education of the Adolescent.* The age of transfer from the primary to one of the secondary schools should be eleven plus and the selection of pupils for the school best adapted to their abilities should be by examination. The Committee believed that the selective examination at this age "is capable of selecting in a high proportion of cases (a) those pupils who quite certainly have so much intelligence and intelligence of such a character that without doubt they ought to receive a secondary education of grammar school type; and (b) those pupils who quite certainly would not benefit from such an education" (p. 379). The number of grammar schools should be increased and the provision of technical high schools with four year courses for pupils from eleven plus to fifteen plus should be increased. While the Committee believed that multilateral schools might be desirable under certain circumstances, with some reluctance it came to the conclusion that it "could not advocate the adoption of multilateralism as a general policy in England and Wales. . . . Each type of secondary school will have its appropriate place in the national system with its educational task clearly in view; and in the great body of schools maintained or aided by the Board of Education and the local authorities, educational considerations alone should determine the parents' choice, just as if the various schools were alternative sides of the same school" (p. 376).

### Equality of Opportunity

War broke out before any action could be taken on the Spens Report. In the proposals for the reconstruction of the educational system, which began to be put forward in the early years of the war, the promise of the years between the two wars was not forgotten. A new slant was given to the plans for reconstruction both by the causes for which the war was being fought and by the national needs envisioned in the postwar years. The fundamental principle on which all proposals were based was to realize more fully than ever before the meaning of democracy for education. This meant the abolition of any obstacles, social or financial, to the fullest education appropriate to the abilities of each individual. In the interests of the nation as a whole equality of educational opportunity was to be provided in order to discover and utilize to the best advantage such talents as had remained undiscovered under the traditional system of educational organization. Further, more and better educational facilities must be provided in the interests of greater efficiency in business and industry. Finally, in the interests of higher cultural standards more educational opportunities must be provided for the citizens of a democracy. This obligation was imposed by the demands made on the political intelligence of the individual for his own sake as a human being as much as for the welfare of society. Education was now considered to be a lifelong process from the cradle to the grave and it was an obligation of the nation to make it accessible to all under conditions that will enable them to profit by it. In the modern conditions of mechanized industry it became possible to prolong the period of compulsory education. With the vast accumulation of knowledge and the social and cultural changes produced by science and technology the great importance of education at the secondary level could not be ignored.

Hitherto the facilities for secondary education in publicly maintained schools were unevenly distributed because of the peculiarity of the system of administration under which only counties and county boroughs were permitted to provide education other than elementary. Further, the secondary education available was only of the academic type, with a relatively small number of senior technical schools to which the age of admission was thirteen. Finally, only those pupils from public elementary schools who ranked highest in a competitive examination could win "special places" which entitled them to free tuition. Except in a very small number of secondary schools where no fees at all were charged and there were 100 per cent special places, the number of special places averaged 40 per cent of the enrollment. The paradox was that pupils whose parents could afford to pay the fees were admitted on qualifying entrance examinations, while special places were awarded on results of a competitive examination. In addition to the publicly maintained schools there were available the direct grant schools and a wide range of independent schools, which will be discussed later.

In the White Paper on *Educational Reconstruction* put out by the Government in 1943 it was stated that principle on which the reform was based was the recognition that "education is a continuous process conducted in successive stages" and that "after 11 secondary education, of diversified types but of equal standing, will be provided for all children." The diversified types — grammar schools, technical high schools, and modern schools — would, according to the plan, be broadly equivalent. It was admitted, however, that the traditional secondary schools — the grammar schools — enjoyed a prestige which overshadowed all other types. As a result "too many of the nation's abler children are attracted into a type of education which prepares primarily for the university and for the administrative and clerical professions; too few find their way into schools from which the design and craftsmanship sides of industry are recruited. If education is to serve the interests both of the child and of the nation, some means must be found of correcting this bias and of directing ability into the field where it will find its best realization" (p. 9). A combination of different types of schools in one building or on one site was not excluded. The free interchange of pupils from one type of school to another was to be facilitated.

### Education Act, 1944

The Education Act, 1944, which was passed by a coalition government (Conservative, Labor, and Liberal), put on the statute books the plan outlined for purposes of public discussion in the White Paper on *Educational Reconstruction*. In Section 8 of the Act it was made a duty of local education authorities (L.E.A.'s) to provide sufficient schools for primary education and for secondary education, which is defined as "full-time education suitable to the requirements of senior pupils, other than such full-time education as may be provided for senior pupils in pursuance of a scheme under the provisions of this Act relating to further education." Senior pupils are boys and girls over the age of eleven. The secondary school must provide "such variety of instruction and training as may be desirable in view of their different ages, abilities, and aptitudes, and of the different periods for which they may be expected to remain at school including practical instruction and training appropriate to their respective needs."

The Act permits local education authorities to provide "boarding schools or otherwise, for pupils for whom education as boarders is considered by their parents and by the authority to be desirable." Such facilities may be provided in cases where distances to an appropriate school are too great and too much time must be spent in travel each day, or where home conditions are unsatisfactory. In a few areas the local authorities have entered into agreements with "Public Schools" to admit a few pupils each year, and in others the local authorities have established their own boarding schools. Parents may be required to pay for the cost of board and lodging in accordance with their financial ability and the Ministry of Education may reimburse the local authority for expenditures for fees, scholarships and other allowances.

## Three Types of Secondary Schools or a Comprehensive Type

It was generally understood that the three types of secondary schools (grammar, technical, and modern) recommended by the Spens Committee and, before the Education Act was passed in 1944, by the Report of Committee of the Secondary School Examinations Council on *Curriculum and Examinations in Secondary Schools* (known as the Norwood Committee Report) which was published in 1943, with combinations into multilateral schools would meet the criterion implied by the three A's (ages, abilities, and aptitudes). The Committee was seriously criticized for suggesting that the three types of schools corresponded to the division of pupils into three groups in terms of capacities. The Committee, however, put forward its suggestions as "rough groupings" only based on educational practice. The attack of the critics was concentrated mainly on the danger of premature determination of the educational careers and therefore the future occupations of children at the age of eleven plus. The recommendation of the Committee that a further allocation of pupils should be made at the age of thirteen, if it was discovered that the first assignment had been incorrect, and that pupils should then be transferred to the schools more appropriate to their abilities and aptitudes, was rejected on the ground that under existing conditions the three types of school did not enjoy the same prestige. It was also objected that the effect of the groupings would be to choose the pupils for the school rather than the school for the pupils.

The controversy affected the progress of reconstruction in two directions: The first was the expression of serious misgivings about the methods of selecting pupils at the age of eleven plus. Doubt was thrown on the use of intelligence tests for this purpose on the grounds that the I.Q. was not stable and that it could be raised by coaching, an advantage not enjoyed equally by all pupils. It was doubted, in fact, by the critics whether an accurate selection could be made at all at the age of eleven plus. The second consequence was the spread of the proposal to establish comprehensive high schools, a movement proposed by the Education Committee of the London County Council and adopted in 1947. The idea of the comprehensive high school replaced that of the multilateral school, the meaning of which was uncertain. To some it meant the provision of two or more types of courses in the same school under one principal; to others two or more types of schools on the same site each under its own principal. In neither case did it meet the criticisms levelled against the process of selecting pupils at the age of eleven plus, which would remain unchanged.

The advocacy of the comprehensive high school was unfortunately not based wholly on educational grounds; it was as much a political partisan proposal as it was educational. As a political proposal it was adopted by the Labour Party which, at its conference in Margate in 1950, passed a resolution calling upon the Government to implement the Party's policy of the comprehensive high school and to assist local educational authorities that might plan such schools. The National Executive Committee of the Party requested a sub-committee to prepare a report on secondary education. The report, *A Policy for Secondary Education* (1951) was a brief for the comprehensive high school. Objection was raised in the report against the tripartite system of separate schools (grammar, technical, and modern) for the reason that it would perpetuate the old practice of class segregation and would give children unable to proceed to the grammar school a feeling of inferiority. The possibility of predetermining at the age of eleven the future development of pupils was denied. It was admitted that the transfer of pupils at the age of thirteen was feasible, but it was stated that in practice it was almost impossible. The Education Act required that parents' wishes should be consulted, but with tripartite system they could not exercise their choice. The Committee favored the comprehensive school which "caters for all children through a system based on a central core of subjects common to all, from which branch classes in specialized subjects taken according to their desires, aptitudes and capacities of the children." The first two years would be diagnostic years and would be followed by courses adapted to the aptitudes and capacities of the pupils. The specialized courses would be chosen on the advice of tutors responsible for the guidance of pupils through their school career. The comprehensive school need not be very large (600 to 900 pupils) and could produce a sixth form to which great value has always been attached in English education. The principle of the comprehensive high school was adopted as part of the Labour Party's policy as defined in *Challenge to Britain: A Programme of Action for the Next Labour Government,* issued in December, 1953.

These arguments were supplemented by others from other advocates. The chief of these arguments was that the comprehensive school attended by children of all social classes would promote social unity and understanding, the bases of improved human relations in a community and in industry. No reference was made to the existence of individual differences of ability which could be gauged at the age of eleven plus. Nor was any reference made to the quality of education or the possible disfranchisement, educationally, of the gifted pupils. The problems of the American comprehensive high schools were either ignored or it was believed that the English tradition would prevent the rise of such problems. It was never clear which English tradition was referred to, particularly since a similar situation has never before arisen.

The Ministry of Education was prepared to view sympathetically the establishment of comprehensive high schools but only experimentally. When, however, the Education Committees of the London County Council and of Middlesex, proposed to establish such schools in large numbers and size (about 2,000 pupils), the Ministry became more cautious. The shortages in building materials proved to be a more serious obstacle than any governmental opposition. Nor were parents, on whom the advocates of the comprehensive school relied, any more enthusiastic, and considerable opposition was encountered from the governors and staffs of grammar schools which it was proposed to merge into the new ventures. Comprehensive schools are being established here and there, but on an experimental basis or in areas where it provides the only solution to making secondary education for all accessible.

The basic argument for the comprehensive high school, where it is not political is that methods of selection at the age of eleven plus are unsatisfactory or actually impossible. It is unfortunate that the word "selection" continues to be used instead of "distribution" or "allocation" of pupils to the type of school best suited to their abilities and aptitudes. "Selection" implies the superiority of one type of school over another, something which is not intended since secondary education is planned for all, fees have been abolished (1945), and parity of standards will be maintained so far as possible. The issue does, however, raise the question of the meaning of equality of educational opportunity which is today the basis of all proposed reforms. There is too much of a disposition today to confuse its meaning in the name of democracy and a certain egalitarianism, which in the long run may lead to a levelling down rather than to maintaining standards as high as possible in the interests of national well-being and individual happiness.

In 1953 according to the annual report of the Ministry of Education, *Education in 1953*, it was reported that "By the end of the year 17 comprehensive schools and instalments of such schools were under construction and plans were being prepared for another ten schools which had been included in approved building programmes. These 27 schools included 15 in London and six in Coventry." The Minister had stated in Parliament that "she was not against limited experiments, provided that extremely careful

thought was given to the practical educational problems that would
arise in the organization of such schools" (p. 7).

## Selection Methods

Methods of selection or allocation have been the objects of experimentation since the system of "free places" was introduced early
in this century and especially since 1944. In an account of methods
of selection the Ministry of Education in its report on *Education in
1951* found that the reports of the local education authorities show
"remarkable uniformity in administration and principle combined
with much variety in the techniques of assessment" (p. 11). The
chief cause of criticism arises from the desire of parents to have
their children admitted to the grammar school, the only type of
secondary school with which they are familiar, not because of the
education given there but for the status.

The methods of assessment show variety and flexibility. The
chief emphasis is placed on intelligence tests combined usually with
objective tests or other examinations in English and arithmetic.
To these are frequently added records from teachers of the pupils'
interests, aptitudes, and progress. In a few areas the tests are repeated at intervals in the last year in the primary school. Interviews are used in some areas. The chief difficulty arises in borderline cases where a margin of a few marks will separate those for
whom a particular type of education is considered appropriate and
those who just fail.

What makes it difficult to reach a decision in borderline cases is
the difficulty of determining the point at which some pupils are best
suited for one particular type of education and others for another.
This difficulty is intensified by the regional maldistribution of different types of schools, and by the fact that there seems to be a
policy to have about 15 per cent of the secondary school population in grammar schools, 15 per cent in technical schools, and the
remainder in modern schools. These figures almost correspond to
the distribution of pupils, within American comprehensive high
schools in academic, technical, and general courses.

Undoubtedly there are possible defects in the processes of allocation. The chief criticism of intelligence tests has been that they

are subject to coaching which may result in a rise in a pupil's I.Q. The remedy, of course, is to coach all pupils in the sense of making them all familiar with the general character of the tests. The importance of the problem, which is without doubt crucial, is indicated by the fact that it was one of the earliest research problems to which the National Foundation for Educational Research devoted its attention. The Examinations were found to be generally fair and accurate, but one weakness that is referred to is that different results may be produced by coaching in some schools and not in others.[2] Whether better results will be attained by postponing the allocation for two years as will be done in comprehensive high schools, it is at present difficult to say more than that the problem has not been solved in the American high school.

## Secondary Education Under the Education Act, 1944

### The Provision of Secondary Schools

Following the Education Act, 1944 and subsequent regulations, secondary education is provided in publicly maintained grammar, technical, and modern schools in direct grant schools, and in a large number of private or independent schools which include the "Public Schools." The publicly maintained schools are supported by rates (local taxes) and government grants distributed according to formula by the Ministry of Education. Pupils are allotted to each type of school according to their abilities and aptitudes as tested in an examination and on other information from their schools at the age of eleven plus. Although the grammar school enjoys a prestige in public opinion because of its long tradition, it is hoped that the public will in time come to appreciate the need and value of the new types of secondary schools (technical and modern) when parity of standards has been established in such matters as buildings, size of class, assembly halls, gymnasiums, libraries, rooms for art, craft, and other practical activities, and playgrounds and

[2] See P. A. Vernon, *Intelligence Testing* (London, *Times Educational Supplement,* Jan. 25 & Feb. 1, 1952); Institute of Education, University of Bristol, *Studies in Selection Techniques for Admission to Grammar Schools* (London, 1952); A. F. Watts, D. A. Pidgeon, and A. Yates, *The Allocation of Primary School Leavers to Courses of Secondary Education* (London, Newnes Educational Publishing Co., 1952).

playing fields. The size of classes has already been fixed at a maximum of thirty, a maximum which cannot for some time be enforced because of shortage of classrooms and teachers as well as the prospective bulge in enrollments on account of the postwar increase in the birth rate.

While each type of school will have a definite function to perform that distinguishes it from the other types, they will all have the same general aims in common. Of these the aim to which the greatest value and importance is attached is training of character. This is expected to be promoted by conceiving of the school as a community developing in the pupils a sense of responsibility and human relationships through participation in its corporate life and by the opportunity to cultivate interests through extracurricular activities in clubs and societies. Religious instruction and collective worship with which the schools are required to open each day are regarded as important influences on the cultivation of the spiritual side of character to which the inspirational teaching in the classroom is also expected to contribute.

The large majority of secondary schools are separate for boys and girls. There seems to be general agreement in favor of the separation of the sexes at the secondary level. There are, however, many "mixed" schools, most of which are temporary until the enrollment is large enough for separate schools. According to a statement in *The Nation's Schools,* a Ministry of Education publication (1945), "In the fields of primary and further education co-education is to be preferred. It is in the secondary field that the rival advantages of separation make themselves most apparent. At this stage boys and girls must be separated for physical training and major games and there are other respects, too, in which their needs and interests will run rather apart. . . . Where separate schools are provided, there will be clear advantages in placing them side by side or in close proximity so as to make possible joint activities and the pursuit of common interests" (pp. 2 f.).

### The Grammar School

While the three types of schools will have many aims and features in common and for the first two years will have, except for such subjects as foreign languages, a common curriculum adapted to the different abilities of the pupils, the schools will differ in the curriculum and methods of approach according to the variety of the aptitudes and abilities of the pupils and the probable length of their stay in school. Thus since the grammar school, according to an official statement of the Ministry of Education, "demands disciplined thought and the capacity to wrestle successfully with intellectual questions, they (the pupils) must have a high measure of general intelligence, they must be fond of books and readily drawn to abstract ideas, and they must be prepared to stay at school long enough to derive real benefits from the studies they will undertake." [3] The length of the grammar school course is seven years, from age eleven to eighteen. In practice a considerable number of pupils drop out soon after reaching the compulsory attendance limit. It is hoped that the introduction of a new examination system, to be taken normally at sixteen, will encourage pupils to stay on to that age. The majority of those who remain in school will begin to specialize, spend one to three years in a sixth form, the highest class, and then proceed to universities, technical colleges, or teacher training colleges.

The curriculum of the grammar school includes religious instruction, English language and literature, history, geography, mathematics, sciences, classical or modern languages, art, music, handicrafts, domestic subjects (for girls), and physical education. In the early years pupils begin the study of classical or modern languages, and when they reach the sixth form they may specialize to a standard not attained in American high schools in classics, Latin and modern languages, modern languages, sciences, and mathematics; in the larger schools opportunities are provided for specialization in history or geography. Other fields of specialization such as engineering subjects, commercial work, art and crafts, or domestic subjects are possible but not usual.

The sixth form is more than the final year of the school course. Its work is a measure of the scholarly standards of a school, and from the point of view of the school as a community and its corporate life a great deal of responsibility is, in the tradition of Arnold

[3] Ministry of Education Pamphlet No. 9, *The New Secondary Education* (London, 1947), pp. 25 f. By permission of Her Majesty's Stationery Office.

of Rugby, placed on the senior pupils as leaders in both the intellectual and the social activities of a school. The sixth form has been criticized for intensive specialization, but, while specialization can undoubtedly be narrowing, it can also mean, in the hands of a skillful teacher, intensive study of a subject and its ramifications. There is, however, some danger that the competition for scholarships, offered by the universities or the state or local authorities, may conduce to narrow specialization. Nevertheless, the sixth form has held an important place in English secondary education since the days of Arnold. One of the arguments against the comprehensive schools is that it may not be possible to organize sixth forms in them. The following statement in the Spens Committee's Report may be taken as accepted with approval by the majority of educators: "The sixth form is indeed the most characteristic and the most valuable feature of a grammar school in the training of character and a sense of responsibility, and on its existence depends all that is best in the grammar school tradition" (p. 166).

### Direct Grant Schools

The majority of the pupils attend publicly maintained schools, if they attend a secondary school of the grammar school type. To some extent opportunities for a grammar school education without the payment of tuition are available in "Direct Grant Schools." These are grammar schools, many with a long tradition, with their own governing bodies on which local authorities are represented, which charge fees and which receive state aid on condition that they are open to inspection by Her Majesty's Inspectors (H.M.I.'s) and offer 25 per cent free places to pupils who have attended a public primary school. In addition the local education authority may pay the fees for qualified pupils up to another 25 per cent. The remaining 50 per cent of the places are open to pupils who are likely to profit by a grammar school education and whose parents can pay fees; even in these cases the governors may remit the fees under certain conditions. The retention of direct grant schools in the system of secondary education has been criticized because they continue the practice of segregation and class privilege, since half of the pupils in them are fee-payers. In practice, because of competition, these pupils must pass a difficult entrance examination. Nor does the Education Act in any case prohibit parents from choosing the school they desire for their children; such a prohibition could not have been possible in view of the English tradition. The Minister of Education, Mr. R. A. Butler, who steered the Education Bill to its enactment in Parliament in 1944, said in this connection: "One of the fundamental principles on which this bill has been built is that there shall be a variety of types of schools. One of the varieties, which I think is quite legitimate is that there shall be schools in which it is possible for parents to contribute towards the education of their children." The Ministry, however, has the right to approve the amount of the fees.

### The Private or Independent Schools

The third type of schools giving a grammar school education consists of private or (as they are now more generally called) independent schools. These schools range from the "Public Schools" to small, obscure proprietary schools, day or boarding. In quality and standards this group has a range from the best to schools inferior in every way. The term "Public School" is no longer confined to the nine great Public Schools of English educational history, but includes schools which meet the conditions of eligibility of their headmasters to membership in the Headmasters Conference. These conditions are that the scheme of the school is satisfactory, that the governing body and the headmaster are independent from any external control and that a certain number of the pupils pass each year to the Universities of Oxford and Cambridge. Since they meet these conditions many direct grant schools belong to this group.

The majority of the schools, entitled to be called Public Schools, are boarding schools, whose fees range from £175 ($490) to £300 ($840) a year, sums which in view of individual incomes and taxes are considered to be quite high. The number of Public Schools listed in the Public Schools Yearbook is now close to 200. Independent schools may and increasing numbers do invite inspection by the Ministry of Education's inspectors, but, unless they conform, like the direct grant schools, to the regulations of the Ministry of Education, they do not receive any aid. If found to be satisfactory by the inspectors, independent schools may be recognized as efficient but not grant-earning.

The Education Act, 1944, as pointed out earlier, contains a provision under which private or independent schools will be required to be inspected and registered, if found to be satisfactory. The increase in the number of schools requesting inspection establishes a basis for registration when the clause in the Act is implemented.

In the movement for secondary education for all, the Public Schools have been attacked as the bastions of privilege. It was charged that those who attend the best of them constitute a clique which retains control of the country's affairs — political, social, and economic — in its hands, and that they represent the worst form of segregation and class stratification. In 1942 Mr. R. A. Butler, as President of the Board of Education, in response to these criticisms, appointed a committee, under the chairmanship of Lord Fleming, "To consider means whereby the association between the Public Schools and the general educational system of the country could be developed and extended; also to consider how far any measure recommended in the case of boys' Public Schools could be applied to comparable schools for girls." The Committee's, report, *The Public Schools and the General Educational System* (generally referred to as the Fleming Committee report) was published in 1944. The Committee recommended that opportunities for education in Public Schools and other schools that may be approved for the purpose should be made available to boys and girls capable of profiting thereby irrespective of the income of their parents. Two types of arrangements were suggested; in one the Board of Education was to provide bursaries to selected pupils and in the other local education authorities should have the right to reserve a number of places which they would fill. No regulations have been issued to implement the recommendations except that the practice mentioned earlier (p. 148) has been authorized under the Act. A Committee on Boarding Education was set up in the Ministry of Education to serve as a central body to pool the places offered by the Public Schools. This service was discontinued in 1951 when it was found that contact between the Public Schools and local education authorities had already been satisfactorily established. The

Committee then became a consultative committee on boarding problems.

## The General Certificate of Education

Except in the case of some publicly maintained schools where the local education authorities or governing bodies may from time to time interfere, the grammar schools enjoy complete freedom in the *interna*. The Minister of Education neither prescribes nor suggests the curriculum and methods of instruction. Indirectly there are suggestions in such reports as that of the Spens Committee, the Norwood Committee or the Board of Education's Educational Pamphlet No. 114, *The Organisation and Curriculum of Sixth Forms in Secondary Schools* (1938), or occasional pamphlets on the teaching of special subjects. Some control, however, is exercised by the eight examining bodies which were recognized in 1917 and whose work is coordinated by the Secondary School Examinations Council formerly in the Board and now in the Ministry of Education.[4]

Until 1951 these bodies administered two examinations — the School Certificate Examination, taken normally after four years of secondary education, and the Higher School Certificate Examination. In 1951 these were replaced by the General Certificate of Education which pupils could take when they had reached the age of sixteen. It was believed in general that too much importance had been attached to the School Certificate; it had come to be regarded as the equivalent of matriculation to the universities, which it was if obtained with high marks, and employers seemed to demand it for clerical positions. Another reason which prompted the change, particularly as to age, was to postpone premature specialization. Qualitative differences were also indicated; the standard of the General Certificate of Education was expected to be somewhere between those of the School Certificate and the Higher Certificate, and according to a Circular of the Ministry of Education, the new certificate "served to testify to a degree of mastery in the

[4] The examining bodies are the Joint Matriculation Board of the Northern Universities, the Universities of London, Bristol, and Durham, the Central Welsh Board, the Oxford Cambridge Schools Examination Board, the Oxford Delegacy for Local Examinations, and the Cambridge Local Examinations Syndicate. A ninth examining body is being added to this list (see p. 275).

particular subjects which should be secure and usable for the future."

The General Certificate of Education differed in another respect from the School Certificate since pupils may take examinations in any five subjects instead of required subjects in certain groups, as in the earlier examination. Papers can be taken at Ordinary, Advanced, or Scholarship levels. To gain exemption from a university entrance examination five subjects must be presented; a pass is required in English and two subjects must be passed at the Advanced level. The Scholarship level is intended for candidates for state or local education authorities.

The chief objection to the new examination, which had been recommended by the Secondary School Examinations Council in 1947 and went into effect in 1951, was the minimum age requirement of sixteen. It was thought that able pupils could take the examinations at an earlier age and then be free to proceed to their fields of specialization which would prepare them for the open scholarships at the universities. In 1952 the Council considered that greater flexibility was desirable to meet the needs of abler pupils, and accordingly recommended that, while the age limit should be retained, headmasters and headmistresses could enter a pupil earlier "if they certified (1) that it was educationally desirable that he should take the examination in the particular subject or subjects offered at the time proposed; and (2) that he had pursued a course of study with such a degree of competence as to make it very probable that he would pass in the subject or subjects offered." The recommendation was accepted by the Minister of Education.

## Scholarships

The scholarship system to which reference has been made is one of the striking methods of the English system for equalizing opportunities and recruiting able students for university study. The awards made by the state and local education authorities are in addition to the open scholarships offered by the universities and the leaving scholarships awarded by schools to students proceeding to universities. Under the state system of scholarships which were instituted at the end of World War I the number of scholarships awarded each year has risen from 200 to 2,000.

The total number of scholarships awarded for the first time for the academic year 1953–54 was 13,195, of which 3,267 in all were awarded by the state and 9,928 by local education authorities; the figures for state scholarships include sixteen to veterans, a number which has dropped from 8,690 for 1948–49. The total number of students entering universities in 1953–54 was 18,092 (including well over 1,000 overseas students not eligible for scholarships); accordingly some 75 per cent of the entering students received public subsidies. The amount of the scholarship grant is based on a means test and parents with incomes between £450 ($1,460) and £2,000 ($5,600) are required to make contributions to the expenses of the students.

### Technical Secondary Schools

Technical education at the postprimary level has been provided in junior technical schools, offering two or three year courses to boys and girls who were admitted from elementary schools at the age of thirteen. The schools were generally housed in technical colleges attended mainly in the evening by other students who work during the day. The courses included the study of mathematics and science appropriate to the particular industry for which they provided a preparation, and general subjects — English, history, geography, etc. They worked closely with the local industries concerned. In general they constituted a separate type in the educational system and operated under regulations different from those governing other types of schools.

The English backwardness in providing technical education of various levels as compared with other countries was frequently pointed out. What was provided did not constitute a system as such. Possibly the tradition of training through apprenticeship and promotion on the basis of experience in practice were retarding factors. The White Paper on *Educational Reconstruction* noted the absence of facilities for able pupils for whom some form of technical education at the secondary level would be more suitable than the academic grammar school. It was noted in the Paper (p. 9, section 28) that "An academic training is ill-suited for many of the pupils who find themselves moving along a narrow educational path bounded by the School Certificate and leading into a limited field of opportunity. Further, too many of the nation's abler children are attracted into a type of education which prepares primarily for the University and for administrative and clerical professions; too few find their way into schools from which the design and craftmanship sides of industry are recruited. If education is to serve the interests both of the child and the nation, some means must be found of correcting the bias and of directing ability into the field where it will find its best realization."

A few years earlier the Spens Committee expressed its conviction that "it is of great importance to establish a new type of higher school of technical character, wholly distinct from the traditional grammar (secondary) school, and as a first step in this end we recommend that a number of the existing junior technical schools which at present provide a curriculum based on the engineering industries (and among them we include the building industry), and any other which may develop training of such a character as (*a*) to provide a good intellectual discipline, altogether apart from its technical value, and (*b*) to have a technical value in relation not to one particular occupation but to a group of occupations, should be converted into technical high schools in the sense that they should be accorded in every respect, equality of status with the schools of the grammar school type" (p. 274).

The curriculum of the technical school, according to the Committee, "should be broadly of the same character as the curriculum in other types of secondary education of equal status." In other words, it was intended that the work should not be narrowly vocational but should offer a liberal education. Although the subject titles might be the same as those in the grammar school, "it is in the methods of approach and treatment that the interpretation of the curriculum of technical schools differs so materially from that of the grammar schools." The curriculum would include engineering drawing, practical crafts in the workshops, while science and its applications would serve "as the core of inspiration."

The progress of providing technical schools at the secondary level has been slow in terms of the number of schools and pupils. In 1953 there were 292 technical schools with 79,214 pupils (50,967 boys and 28,247 girls) as compared with 1,184 maintained grammar schools with 512,613 pupils (258,300 boys and 254,313 girls). The regulations for the General Certificate of Education are sufficiently flexible to permit pupils to take the examinations. In *Education in 1953*, the Ministry's annual report, it was announced that a ninth examining body was to be established on which organizations with experience of examining in the technical field would be strongly represented. It is expected that those who complete the course at sixteen will proceed to universities or technical colleges for full-time study or will enter some employment and engage in part-time study if they choose.

### Secondary Modern Schools

From the pedagogical point of view the secondary modern school, the third type of secondary education, promises to be the most interesting because it must be pioneering and experimental. Although it is not entirely novel in principle, its chief task is to win the confidence of parents and the public. In a small measure there is a precedent in the central schools established in London and a few other areas about 1910. They, too, were experimental so long as they did not try to emulate the grammar schools. It may also be claimed that the senior school for pupils in the last three years of the elementary schools had the same opportunity. There is an important and fundamental difference, however, because the secondary modern school for the same type of pupils will not be handicapped by the elementary school regulations. The modern school is a secondary school and operates under the Secondary School Regulations, which means that in time it will be housed in buildings appropriate to secondary education, the classes will have a maximum of thirty pupils, there will be ample equipment and facilities for physical education and recreation. It will probably take some time before there will be an adequate supply of teachers with a training appropriate to the new type of school.

The modern school will have the problem, which is educationally challenging, of educating pupils with an I.Q. range from about 80 to 110, a cross-section of the intellectual and social strata of society. The pupils at the upper end of the range might be borderline cases which just failed to qualify for entrance into a grammar or technical school. At the other end there might be pupils who

just missed being assigned to a school for the mentally handicapped. The large majority of the pupils, about 97 per cent, will
leave at the age of fifteen, and those who are able to profit by another type of secondary education can be transformed at the age
of thirteen. Some modern schools, which have been in existence
less than a decade, find it possible to bring a small number of
pupils up to the standard of the General Certificate of Education,
which offers a wide choice of subjects. But the great opportunity
lies in the fact that the modern school is not hampered by precedents nor is it likely to be directed by prescribed curricula or external examination requirements.

The statement in the Ministry's pamphlet on *The New Secondary
Education* (p. 29) is pertinent on this point: "The aim of the modern school is to provide a good all-round secondary education, not
focused primarily on the traditional subjects of the school curriculum, but developing out of the interests of the children. Through
its appeal to their interests it will stimulate their ability to learn and
will teach them to pursue quality in thought, expression and craftsmanship. It will interpret the modern world to them and give them
a preparation for life in the widest sense, including a full use of
leisure. It will aim at getting the most out of every pupil that he is
capable of, at making him adaptable, and at teaching him to do a
job properly and thoroughly and not to be satisfied with bad work-
manship, and to be exact in what he says and does. Freedom and
flexibility are of its essence and are indeed its great opportunity."

The function, then, of the modern school is to give the pupils a
broad general education, more closely related perhaps to the concrete environment in which they live and rising out of their interests. The curriculum will not be vocational but will provide a wide
range of activities as a preparation for life and leisure. Under
favorable conditions a foreign language may be added to the more
usual curriculum of Scripture, English, history and geography (or
social studies), mathematics, science, art, music, practical activities
(domestic arts, handicrafts and gardening), and physical education.
Since the teachers enjoy freedom from the control of external examinations, greater flexibility in instruction and content is possible.
The major problem, in fact, is not the question of the subjects that
should go into the curriculum, but of the methods of instruction

to adapt to the abilities of a widely heterogeneous group of pupils. Whatever methods are employed to enlist the interests of the pupils, they must have a sense of accomplishment and of purpose that links their studies with their future.

There has developed out of this principle a tendency to provide some vocational preparation in the last two years adapted to the occupations of the locality. In Southhampton there are courses leading to seamanship and shipbuilding; girls tend to be interested in office work or nursing or, as in Plymouth, in catering and art. The greatest variety of experiments and practices will be found in the modern secondary schools, not excluding an effort made in some schools to encourage certain pupils to stay beyond the normal four years and then to proceed to the sixth form of a grammar school until the time comes when the modern schools will be able to develop sixth forms of their own.

It is doubtful whether the modern school could successfully develop the kind of education adapted to the abilities and aptitudes of pupils in a comprehensive secondary school. Certainly the American high school has found it to be an extremely difficult problem to provide in the same school an education suited to the abilities of about 65 per cent of the pupils, who would correspond to the pupils for whom the modern school is intended. As Norman Fisher, formerly the chief education officer of Manchester, wrote in *Our Schools* [5]: "Against the third argument [in favor of comprehensive school] some people consider that unless it is separate the modern school curriculum will always be dominated by those of the Grammar or Technical Schools, and that it is the modern school above all others which should break new ground in devising a curriculum suitable to the great majority."

### School Life

One aspect that will be common to all schools will be the school life or extracurricular activities of the pupils. This is a tradition, first built up in the Public Schools, which has been accepted as of great value in all education for character formation by sharing in the corporate life of the schools. The prefect system has become

[5] London, 1949, p. 54.

a characteristic of English secondary schools. Athletics, games, sports loom large in the schools as they do in national life and there is more participation and less intense rivalry than in American high schools. Attempts by newspapers to exploit interschool athletics as public spectacles have always met with considerable opposition from school authorities. A great many activities that emerge from the interests of the pupils are found and include debating, literary, and scientific societies, clubs for natural history, photography, chess, stamp-collecting, and music, dramatic societies, glee clubs, school orchestras, boy and girl scout organizations, the school magazine, and many others. These activities are managed by the pupils with the benevolent interest of teachers but without authoritative control. Organizations like fraternities and sororities are unknown.

## FRANCE

### The French Tradition

Most educational issues in France are likely to have a political or religious repercussion. This is as true of secondary education as it is of elementary, where concern for the preservation of laicity is uppermost. In any proposals to reform secondary education there is sure to be added to the political and religious aspects the issue of *culture générale*, whose preservation is at the heart of the problem in the movement to provide secondary education for all. Politically it has been argued by advocates of reform that the responsibility for the defeat of France should be placed at the doors of leaders who had received the traditional type of education in the prewar *lycées* or *collèges*.[6] From the denominational point of view there is some alarm because 40 per cent of the pupils are in private secondary schools which are predominantly denominational. But more important than the political or religious aspects is the status of *culture générale*.

[6] Memories are short! In World War I it was claimed that the same kind of education that is now under criticism provided such a good intellectual training that civilians could quickly be trained to become good officers in the artillery branch.

The concern for *culture générale* is natural. It has a tradition of about 400 years. It has survived through a great variety of political regimes; despite attempts during the Revolution to suppress it as the basis of secondary education, it continued through the eras of the Napoleons and the Third Republic. It has been handed down by different religious congregations. It was considered the best means for training the élite for every kind of activity in politics, administration, and the intellectual field. It was regarded as the fundamental influence that accounts for the pre-eminence of French literature in the world. Finally, French influence in other countries (Eastern Europe, the Middle East, and South America) was undoubtedly spread through the medium of her culture.

It was for these reasons that proposals for reform of the curriculum of the secondary school (*lycées* and *collèges*) have always encountered great opposition. While it is true that at the end of the nineteenth century the equivalence of classical and modern humanities was recognized for purposes of university entrance, the majority of the pupils chose the classical course. Even when fees for secondary education began to be abolished in 1930 and pupils from a social stratum different from that of the traditional privileged classes began to enroll in larger numbers, the classical course continued to be the most popular. Nevertheless, the attempt made in 1926 by Léon Bérard, then Minister of Education, to return to a program of education in which Latin and Greek were made compulsory lasted only one year. It is perhaps significant that the only real progress that has been made in recent years has been in the area of vocational and technical education in which neither political nor denominational consideration can interfere.

### L'Ecole Unique

It is, however, generally recognized that a reform of French education is necessary from the points of view both of its organization and of its content and methods. So far as organization is concerned the recognition is, indeed, not new nor was it the outcome of considerations stimulated by World War II. The movement for the reorganization of the French system of education was begun during

World War I by a group of teachers at the front who called themselves *Les Compagnons de l'Université Nouvelle*.[7] Their program
called for a common school (*l'école unique*) with a common base
in the primary school and secondary education for all according
to ability and aptitudes. The first realization of the ideal, so far
as secondary education was concerned, was the gradual abolition
of tuition fees in *lycées* and *collèges* in 1930-33. The second came
when in 1937 M. Jean Zay, the Minister of National Education,
changed the nomenclature of divisions in the Ministry to *Direction
de l'Enseignement du Premier Degré* and *Direction de l'Enseignement du Second Degré,* thus indicating that the two divisions were
responsible for two stages of education, primary and secondary,
which are continuous with each other rather than for two types of
education. M. Zay was also responsible for the introduction on an
experimental basis of *classes d'orientation* or guidance classes in
the *lycées* and *collèges* which would advise pupils on the courses
best suited to their abilities on the basis of an accumulation of
observations by a group of teachers, parents, and physicians. This
measure was important because of the number of pupils who were
not competent (*non-valeurs*) in the courses they chose. It is to
be noted that considerable opposition was shown by parents against
attempts to compel them to accept the advice of the counselors.
A fuller implementation of the ideals of *Les Compagnons* still
awaits an Education Act to embody the reform plans which, following World War II, have incorporated these ideals.

### Changes in Educational Theory

Criticisms of the content and methods of secondary education
are more recent than the movement for secondary education for
all, although they are no doubt a result of the recognition that the
curriculum must be adapted to a far wider range of abilities and
aptitudes than in the past. Some of the criticisms are not entirely
new; chief among them is the charge that the work of the secondary school has been too bookish (*livresque*), that there was too

[7] It is to be noted that the word *université* may mean either the system of
education or university in the English sense of the term. The group's name
in English would be "Advocates of the New System of Education."

much memorization, and that there was too little relation to the contemporary world. These criticisms are corroborated indirectly by the frequent injunctions in the Ministry's instructions on secondary education against an apparent overemphasis on dictation as a method of instruction. The large number of candidates who failed in the two examinations for the *baccalauréat* taken at the end of the course attest to the severity of the standards or to the burden of content and the unsatisfactory methods of instruction. Nevertheless, for the best minds, secondary education with its aim of training in clear thinking, good speech, and good writing was unsurpassed.

The character of the criticisms has taken on a new note recently. There is a marked tendency to point out that the end of education is not to load the memory with a great amount of knowledge, but to train for the use of that knowledge in the practical affairs of man. The traditional type of secondary education was calculated to prepare for a static world, according to this line of criticism. This is not altogether true either for France, or any other country, for the aim was to preserve the cultural tradition and through instruction in it to train the mind. In addition to imparting *culture générale*, the aim also included *culture d'esprit* to which the English translation "intellectual training" does not do justice. The *Instructions* on secondary education of 1931 state definitely that the task of the schools is "without preparing for anything specific, to make the pupils apt for everything. It forges in the pupils . . . a vigorous and fine intellect, ready for all the beautiful adventures of the mind." It was the psychology rather than the content that was wrong and to that can be added the fact that little attention was paid to the professional preparation of the secondary school teachers in France.

The need of a new approach to secondary education was emphasized by M. André Marie, Minister of Education, in a foreword to a series of documents on secondary education,[8] in which he said: "Education at the second level, which more particularly has the responsibility for training our national élites, before they receive the specialized training in accordance with their several aptitudes and the needs of the country, is obliged at each instant to define

[8] *L'Enseignement du Second Degré* (Paris, *Musée Pédagogique,* 1954).

for itself its aims, its methods, and its needs in the interests of a
society which is evolving with extraordinary rapidity." This emphasis on a changing society and a changing culture is a note which
runs through all discussions of new plans. The training of the
mind is still regarded as an important function of education, but
it must be directed to problem-solving, to awakening a spirit of
research, to cultivating initiative, and to developing an open mind
free from prejudices. The educated man should have a critical
sense and as a member of society should be ready with the means
and methods to make adaptations to changing conditions.

In a circular of September 29, 1952, M. Charles Brunold, Di-
rector-general of education at the second level in the Ministry of
Education, defined the ends of this education (*Les Buts de l'Enseignement du Second Degré*). He emphasized the importance of
guiding the pupils to action as a necessary aspect of life. "What
more and more characterizes the élites of today, even those who
by the nature of their occupation are furthest removed from action, is their participation, deliberate or involuntary in this action;
it is the obligation that they have to discover, to create, to participate." The knowledge of the material universe and of human
societies is a heritage of culture that has no value except as it is
used in action to enable society to advance. The lesson must be
learned that ideas are not unchangeable and are valuable to the
degree that they can be adapted to the constantly expanding areas
of action and thought. "Every effort in education should have as
its aim to increase the capacity for adaptation, for enrichment, and
for creation." The statement seems to depart from the traditional
emphasis in French secondary education on *études désintéressés*
or studies for their own sake, for M. Brunold asks, "Does not the
quality of a culture or training depend more essentially on the
aptitude of a person to find the original and specific solution
whether in thought or in action?" The final note in this discussion
of the ends of education is a strong plea for a social point of view.
"Culture should not constitute an instrument of enjoyment in the
hands of one social class. The heritage which makes it up must
constantly be renewed and enriched by appeal to the new élites
of popular origin. Above everything that divides men, it should
ensure the humane effort to help to push back a little more each

day the frontiers of misunderstanding, suffering, and intolerance."

## Classes Nouvelles

The initiation in 1945 of an experiment in new methods of instruction pointed to the further departure from tradition. Under the inspiration of M. Gustave Monod, *Directeur-général de l'Enseignement du Second Degré,* and of Mme. Hatenguais, *Directrice du Centre International d'Etudes Pédagogiques* at Sèvres, the first *classes nouvelles* were started in a number of first classes (*sixièmes*) of secondary schools to try out new methods of instruction based on the latest knowledge of the psychology of the child. Teachers of these classes attended courses on the principles to be followed which were held at Sèvres and other places. The experiment was gradually extended to successive classes of the four years (*premier cycle*) of the secondary schools until some 700 classes were conducted under the new methods in 1952.

The essence of the experiment is a shift of emphasis from the subject to the child.[9] A beginning in this direction had already been made in the *classes d'orientation,* initiated by M. Jean Zay. The curriculum has remained the same as for all secondary schools, but certain changes were made in the time-schedule. The classes were limited to twenty-five pupils to provide opportunity for the study and observation of each of them. Not only is each individual given the opportunity to work at the level of his own abilities and interests as a check on the highly competitive spirit that was common, but work in teams (*travail par équipes*) is promoted in order to develop a sense of cooperation and community spirit. Better relations are maintained between teachers and pupils and among

[9] The experiment is interesting because of the belated appearance of the "New" or "Progressive" education in France, which until the establishment of *classes nouvelles* was not receptive to the innovations current in Germany after 1919, in the United States after 1915, here and there in England and other countries. In fact the only developments along new lines were the *Ecole des Roches,* which sought to combine the best features in English and French education, and in a school under the supervision of M. Roger Cousinet, which in a sense were extra-curricular. While France has had some distinguished psychologists (M. Henri Wallon, for example), their influence on education has been slight. In the new experiment the examples of Swiss and Belgian experimental schools have been carefully considered.

the pupils themselves. Theoretical lessons are followed immediately by practice in order to establish the relation of what is taught to life. The world of nature and of man is opened to the pupils by studying the environment (*étude de milieu, naturel et humain*). Special attention is devoted to a great variety of manual activities and to the integration of subjects to show the unity of knowledge. The aim on the whole is to give reality to the work of the school, to relate it to real experience, and to get rid of the incubus of bookish learning (*livresque*), on the principle of Decroly's *Par la vie pour la vie*. The pupils are all the time under observation by a council (*conseil*) of three teachers, of whom one is responsible for coordinating the work. The cooperation of parents is enlisted and a formidable cumulative record (*dossier*) is maintained.

The results, according to the principal of a school conducting the experiment, "were what might be expected; the pupils in the pilot classes succeed at least as well as their comrades and have enjoyed a happier childhood. They have acquired a taste for research, the spirit of cooperation, the qualities of balance and curiosity — indispensable qualities in the society now being shaped, in which the important problems will be those of a world becoming more closely knit, of a world subjected to constant and difficult choices promoted by technological changes and the availability of leisure." [10]

In 1952 M. Charles Brunold issued a circular (May 30, 1952) in which he announced that the *classes nouvelles* would be discontinued but twelve pilot classes (*classes pilotes*) would be established in each Academy under the direction of the Regional Pedagogical Centers (*Centres Pédagogiques Regionaux*) [11] located in the capitals of the Academies. The best that had been learned in the *classes nouvelles* would be extended to all schools in the classes of both the first and second cycles. The reasons for this measure were stated to be financial and a consequence of the rapidly increasing enrollment in the secondary schools. It was expected that the enrollment would be doubled in 1956 because of the post-

[10] P. H. Pol-Simon, *L'Evolution Pédagogique Actuel*, in *Avenirs*, 60–61 (Paris, 1954), p. 12.

[11] These centers were established in 1952 for educational study and research.

war birth rate, while the cost of equipment for the new classes was too great a drain on the budget. Even in the pilot classes the size of classes would be thirty pupils in order to cope with the numbers. As a summary of what experience with the *classes nouvelles* had taught M. Brunold wrote: "To the extent that the training given by our system of education progresses and approaches · its goal, the idea of man engaged in action, for whom every problem is in some way a new problem, should inspire our educative methods. These will not be satisfied with the acquisition of a certain stock of knowledge nor with a certain training of thought. They should try every instant to confront the man whom we wish to train with problems to study as if they were new. . . . To develop in the pupil the spirit of research, to give him a sound method needed for each discipline, to arouse his initiative, to show him the need of perseverance and above all of the most perfect intellectual integrity, to teach him that the grand lesson of the development of modern scientific theory is to rise above all prepossession; that, if this is necessary, to maintain a keen critical sense and to prepare oneself constantly to perfect, to enrich or to modify the instruments of one's thinking and action; in a word, to give to the pupil a feeling for open questions; such seem to be the ends to achieve in a training which seeks to provide our society with men fertile in adaptations, means, and a tested method."

### Plans for Reform

The plans for reform and the bills based on these plans which have been drafted have received a great deal of attention and aroused widespread discussion, but no radical reconstruction of French education has yet been enacted. Such changes as have taken place have been piecemeal. The reforms that are proposed must be considered in the light of the background presented in this section. The underlying principle is that the richest opportunities must be opened to the individual to obtain the education best suited to his abilities and aptitudes. This means that greater attention than in the past must be paid to the individual and that instruction must be made more flexible so that the methods appropriate to the abilities and aptitudes of each individual can be discovered and used. At the same time in view of the many divisive forces — political, economic, social, and religious — there must be developed a sense of cooperation and responsibility to promote social solidarity. The overemphasis on intellectual education must be abolished and replaced by a proper balance of the concrete and the abstract, of practice and theory. This is all the more necessary because of the rapidity with which social and cultural changes are taking place as a result of the scientific and technological changes. These changes, as was pointed out earlier (pp. 74 f.), constituted the basis of the arguments for the Langevin plan of reform. Finally, it is recognized that the economic needs of the country must be met by promoting technical education of various levels to provide the skilled artisans, foremen, managers, and leaders.

## Organization of Education at the Second Level

For the present education in France continues to be organized on three levels — primary, secondary, and higher, with "popular" or part-time education under the division in the Ministry charged with supervision of primary education. The Langevin Commission recommended three stages or cycles following the *école maternelle* (nursery school) for children from three to seven years of age: (1) For pupils from seven to eleven; (2) For pupils from eleven to fifteen (*cycle d'orientation* or guidance cycle); and (3) for pupils from fifteen to eighteen (*cycle de détermination* or cycle for specialization in practical, vocational, or theoretical courses). The three divisions or cycles would constitute *l'Enseignement du 1er Degré,* for pupils fifteen to eighteen; and would be followed by *l'Enseignement 2e le Degré* with two stages: (1) *propédeutique* or preuniversity, and (2) university courses. This has created a confusion in terminology.

The *Projet* or bill proposed by Yvon Delbos in 1949 suggested five stages or *étapes:* (1) elementary stage for pupils from six to eleven; (2) secondary stage with a guidance section (eleven to thirteen; (3) third stage or secondary education (thirteen to eighteen); (4) fourth stage or period of guidance or initiation to higher education (eighteen to twenty); and (5) higher education stage.

Secondary education would follow the same lines as the Langevin Commission's report. No action was taken on this *Projet,* which was followed by another in November, 1953, prepared under André Marie, then Minister of Education. This bill proposed an extension of compulsory education to 18 and an organization in four cycles: (1) primary, (six to eleven); (2) secondary (eleven to eighteen) with classical, modern, or technical courses following two years of guidance; (3) higher technical education or period of initiation into higher education; (4) higher education cycle. The traditional *baccalauréat* would cease to be a university degree and would not entitle the holders to be admitted to the university. The requirement for entrance would be a new *baccalauréat* obtained by examination after the propedeutic period.

## The Present Situation

The disturbed political situation and straitened financial conditions have delayed legislative action to organize the whole system of French education on a national and unified basis, but progress in the direction of the suggestions contained in the Langevin Commission's report and bills cited above is actually being made by decree. The movement had in fact already begun in 1941 when the *écoles primaires supérieures* (higher elementary schools), which within the division of elementary education gave an education in advance of the elementary, were brought within the provision of *l'enseignement du second degré* and renamed *collèges modernes* for pupils aged 11 to 15, but are still part of the division of elementary education. So too, the *collèges techniques* are included with other types of industrial and commercial training in the division of technical education (*Direction de l'Enseignement Technique*) in the Ministry, while in the *lycées* and *collèges* there is a section in the last three years which offers a major in technical subjects.

Secondary education in the traditional, academic sense is thus given in the *lycées* and *collèges* and in the *collèges modernes.* The course in the two former institutions is seven years in length for boys and girls from eleven to eighteen; the majority of the *collèges modernes,* which in smaller localities may have *collèges techniques* combined with them, offer a four-year course (*le premier cycle*), more practical than the courses in the *lycées* and *collèges*, and they may be adapted to the needs of their locality. Here too the no- menclature may be confusing, since the *lycées* and *collèges* (the *collèges classiques*) offer a modern option, while an increasing number of *collèges modernes* are beginning to offer the classical option of the other secondary school.

The difference between the *lycées* and *collèges* lies in the fact that the former are established and wholly maintained by the State, while the latter are established and maintained as to the fabric by the municipalities. There is also a difference with respect to the teachers; candidates who have passed the *agrégation*, a competitive examination of very high scholarly standards, are entitled to ap- pointments in the *lycées;* they are, however, accepting appoint- ments in the *collèges*. The majority of teachers must have the certif- icate of aptitude to teach in a secondary school (*le certificat d'apti- tude au professorat du 2e degré*). These are the only differences; salaries, courses and curricula, and examinations are the same for *lycées* and *collèges*. Fees have been abolished since 1933 except for pupils in boarding schools (*internats*) where a charge is made for board and lodging.

The principal of a *lycée* is known as *Proviseur*, of a *collège* as *Principal*, and of a secondary school for girls, *Directrice*. Each is assisted by a bursar (*Intendant* or *Econome*), and in *lycées* by a *Censeur* or in *collèges* by a *Surveillant général*, responsible for su- pervision of discipline and studies. In the boarding schools the supervision of the pupils is entrusted to the *Maîtres* or *Maîtresses d'Internat* and in day schools to *Surveillants d'Externat*, who are assistants generally preparing for further study.

Entrance to the secondary schools is by examination at the age of about eleven. The first two years of the course (*classe de sixième* and *classe de cinquième*) are the same for all except those pupils who wish to start Latin. In the *classe de quatrième*, the third-year pupils may choose between Greek or a second modern language. The first four years are devoted to general education for all ex- cept for the choices of language indicated. The distinction in this respect is that in the third year the course with Latin and Greek is denominated as *cours A;* that with Latin and a modern language as *cours B;* and that with two modern languages as *cours moderne.* Promotion from one class to another depends upon maintaining a certain average through the year, otherwise an examination must be taken.

The subjects of the first four years are: French, Latin, Greek, two modern languages, civics and moral instruction, history, geography, mathematics, observation lessons, physics, natural sciences, physical education, manual work, drawing, music, and environmental study (introduced in 1952).

The first four years of the secondary school constitute the first cycle (*le premier cycle*) at the end of which the *Brevet d'Etudes du Premier Cycle du 2e Degré* (B.E.P.C.) is obtained by examination. The four year course of the *collèges modernes* is known as *l'enseignement court,* the short course, as distinguished from the long course (*l'enseignement long*) of seven years in the *lycées* and *collèges classiques.*

The second cycle consists of *classe de seconde, class de premier,* and *classe terminale.* This is the cycle of specialization (*détermination*). At this stage great flexibility and variety are allowed in the combination of subjects. The number of sections was increased as follows: A, classical; $A^1$, classical-scientific; B, modern; C, modern with Latin and two modern languages; $C^1$, modern with Latin and one modern language; M, mathematics with two modern languages; $M^1$, mathematics with one modern language and another optional, and natural sciences; B, technical, with two modern languages, introductory economics, products, with optional stenography and typewriting. Every course includes history, geography, physics, physical education, and drawing, with music and manual work optional. At the close of the two years the examination for the first part of the *baccalauréat* is taken. The status of the *baccalauréat* has not yet been changed; it is still necessary as a requirement for entrance to the university, but at least an additional year of preparation and the passing of an examination beyond the second part of the *baccalauréat* is required, as will be shown later.

In the final class several new forms of specialization have been added to the traditional philosophy and mathematics sections. It is now possible to specialize in (1) philosophy — letters; (2) experimental sciences or philosophy-sciences; (3) mathematics; (4)

technical and economic sciences. The fourth specialty was introduced in 1949. In all sections philosophy holds a special place of
importance as a synthesis of all the instruction that the students
have had in the previous years of secondary education. All the
subjects are continued but the time allotted to each varies with
the specialty. The final examination, that is, the second part of the
*baccalauréat,* consists of written or oral tests. In all sections candidates are examined in philosophy both in writing and orally as
well as in their special fields and general subjects such as history,
geography, and literature.

Before World War II the successful completion of the two parts
of the examination for the *baccalauréat* entitled students to be
admitted to the universities without further requirements. Since
1926, however, there had been a movement to introduce a propedeutic or preparatory year for *bacheliers* or holders of the *baccalauréat* before taking up their university studies. The reason then
put forward by M. Lapie, *Recteur* of the Sorbornne, was that secondary education did not provide an adequate preparation for
university study and that a general synthesis of the secondary
school studies or *culture générale* was desirable. The introduction
in 1948 of the propedeutic or preparatory year (*année propédeutique* or *année préparatoire*) was to serve this purpose as much as
to provide another hurdle in the form of another examination to
keep down the number of students flocking to the Universities and
ultimately leading to an overproduction and consequent unemployment of intellectuals.

In the larger *lycées* or *collèges classiques* additional courses are
offered in advanced letters or special mathematics, and advanced
rhetoric or advanced mathematics in preparation for the competitive examinations (*concours*) for admission to *les Grandes Ecoles.*
These institutions are advanced centers outside the universities
for the preparation of secondary school professors, teachers of
special subjects, higher civil servants, engineers, technologists, and
other higher ranks of government, industrial, and commercial officials, as well as officers in the defense forces. Because of the cost
of the additional one or two years of preparation required for the
competitive examinations the *Grandes Ecoles* have been regarded
as institutions for the privileged classes, and proposals have been
made to incorporate them in the university system.

The total enrollment in 1952–53 in public secondary schools, including pupils in the primary classes attached to *lycées* and *collèges* was 483,052 (254,753 boys and 228,299 girls). Of this total 32,141 were in the final classes, and 12,869 in classes preparatory to *Grandes Ecoles.* In the private schools (*enseignement privé* or *libre*) the total enrollment, including pupils in primary classes and in classes preparatory to the *Grandes Ecoles* was 359,316 (167,988 boys and 191,328 girls).

### Technical Secondary Schools

Of the total number of boys and girls between eleven and eighteen years of age some 14 per cent are enrolled in all secondary schools. In addition 4 per cent attend *cours complémentaires* (see pp. 227 f.), and 4 per cent are in technical schools. The technical schools which parallel the secondary schools are the *collèges techniques*, which, with other vocational and technical education, lower and higher, are supervised by the *Direction de l'Enseignement Technique* in the Ministry. The *collèges techniques*, not only train for intermediate positions in industry and commerce, but also prepare students for a recently created *baccalauréat technique* and for competitive examinations for admission to more advanced technical schools. Pupils are admitted at about the age of fourteen after completing two years of a secondary school course or its equivalent and successfully passing a competitive examination. The course is four years in length and includes general and technical subjects as well as practical work. The time schedule is heavy and may run to as many as forty hours per week. The subjects of the curriculum are French, history and geography, civics and moral instruction, mathematics, physics and chemistry, mechanics, electricity, biology and hygiene, introductory economics, technical drawing, construction technique, technology, industrial organization, practical work, graphic arts, and physical education. The time is divided about equally between general and technical education, and the hours spent in the workshop, *atelier,* or office range from twelve in the first year to nineteen in the last year of the course. The practical work is as a rule adapted to the local industry. In technical schools for girls it consists generally of fashion design and dressmaking. Students who complete the regu-

lar course and are not candidates for the *baccalauréat* or *concours*
receive the *brevet d'enseignement industriel, commerciel, hotelier,*
or *social.*

There are in addition to the *collèges techniques* many schools
for adolescents of ability, but they are more highly specialized for
a particular industrial or commercial career. Such are the *écoles de
métiers* and the *écoles professionnelles* (national and local), which
lead to their respective certificates of aptitude and with further
practical experience and study to a more advanced diploma, the
*brevet d'enseignement professionnel.* The total enrollment in the
*collèges techniques* in 1951–52 was 94,532, including also pupils
in the *sections techniques* (*section B*) of the *lycées* and *collèges.*

## Guidance

The modern trend that indicates the shift of emphasis from the
subject to the child is shown by the increased attention that is paid
to guidance (*orientation*). The importance of guidance was recognized by M. Jean Zay who as Minister of Education introduced
an experiment with *classes d'orientation* in 1937. Special emphasis
was given to guidance in the *classes nouvelles* in which the teachers
as a team or council (*conseils*) met at frequent intervals to exchange information about the pupils, especially in the first two
years, based on observation and records and the reaction of parents.
The idea of *conseil d'enseignement* has been retained to coordinate
the work of different teachers in the different subjects and to keep
records of the pupils in order to assist them when the time comes
to choose their lines of specialization. The *conseil* takes the place
of the "form master" in English secondary schools or "the home
room teacher" in American high schools.

To facilitate the work of guidance the records for each pupil
are kept in a *dossier scolaire* as described in a Circular issued by
M. Charles Brunold on October 25, 1952. "Education," he wrote,
"to achieve the maximum efficiency must be adapted to all the
needs imposed on it and especially to the character, often very
variable, of the pupils. The effort at individualization is one of the
striking features of all recent experiments in education. . . . The
pupil record (*dossier scolaire*) through which the collaboration of

parents and teachers is expressed thus becomes a symbol of our common action and our intimate association in this action." A model *dossier* accompanied the Circular, but it could be adapted to the needs of each school. The *dossier* calls for information on the home conditions, health, and conduct of the pupil, his previous school record, his general and special aptitudes, his conduct and character in school, any other points that call for mention, and the advice given to parents. The circular directs attention to the fact that teachers must remember that no judgment about a pupil can be permanent, since his development is at no time completed. "The task is to prepare each pupil in the best way for his destiny as a man."

In 1938 a decree was passed requiring the establishment of a public or private vocational guidance center (*centre d'orientation professionnelle*) in the largest city of each department and providing that no young person under the age of seventeen be employed in an industrial concern without a statement from such a center. The guidance centers are consulted by parents for advice on the training of their children. Advice is given on the basis of a medical examination, an examination of the school records, a psycho-technical examination, various tests, questioning, and observation. The whole service of guidance is stimulated by the *Bureau Universitaire de Statistique et de Documentation Scolaire et Professionnelle* (B.U.S.) in the *Musée Pédagogique* in Paris. The B.U.S. has regional centres and teacher delegates in the secondary schools to whom the latest results of research conducted by the organization are transmitted. The change in the attitude to guidance was well stated by M. Gustave Monod, then *Directeur-Générale de l'Enseignement du Second Degré,* in an address in 1947 before a workshop of the B.U.S. "I recall the objection raised not so long ago to every attempt at guidance and somehow as a protection against a control or statism which it was far from our intention to establish. I note with satisfaction that at the present time the attitudes are no longer the same and that in the homes one no longer turns a deaf ear, rather the contrary. One must undoubtedly recognize in this the result of the efforts of the regional centres of the B.U.S., efforts justly appreciated. One must also see in this that the difficulties which at present render the problem of the choice of studies and occupations still more distressing point to the still greater need of more complete and accurate documentation. With the aim of allowing each individual to be sure of the complete development of his abilities as much as in the interest of society well understood, the reform of education must insist on the importance and the continuity of the effort to be put forward for documentation and guidance." [12] The statement is a good summary of the problems that France has still to face. But the chief problem in France at the present time is to coordinate the various types of schools into a national system.

## U.S.S.R.

### The Unified School

The many problems that cause concern to educators in many parts of the world have been met very simply in the U.S.S.R. by elimination. The system provides a common school divided into three stages — primary, the incomplete middle school or equivalent of the junior secondary school, and the complete middle school or equivalent of the senior secondary school. Four years are devoted to primary education, and three years to each of the other types. Transfer from one to the other is by examination, and only those who pass with high marks may continue to the last three years' course. The primary school of four years is the one most commonly found, especially in the rural areas; the seven-year or incomplete secondary school (four years primary and three years junior secondary) is found in the larger centers; and the ten-year school, offering all the three stages in the same school, is found in the larger cities. Until 1943 the secondary school was coeducational. It had been coeducational since 1918 designedly to promote the full equality of the sexes. Coeducation was abolished in the larger cities in 1943 when the country could afford to provide separate schools and when it was discovered that the needs of boys and girls differed because they differed psychologically in the tempo of their growth and in intellectual and occupational interests.

[12] *Avenirs* 60-61 (Paris, 1954), pp. 124 f. The documentation referred to in the text is the publication of information on educational institutions and careers.

It was argued that thirty-five years after the Revolution the idea of sex equality had been firmly established. These may have been the reasons for the abandonment of coeducation, but since the measure was adopted other reasons are suspected.

It is also interesting that in 1940 fees were introduced in the upper secondary schools and in higher institutions in spite of the guarantee of free education in the Constitution, a provision which was not changed until 1947. It was argued that the workers were now so well off economically that they could afford to pay fees for the education of their children. Exemptions from fees are granted under certain conditions, mainly in recognition of distinguished war service of parents. It is perhaps significant that on the same day in 1940 young persons between fourteen and seventeen began to be drafted into the Labor Reserves to keep them out of the school, and to train and utilize them in such trades as needed manpower.

The problem of diversity of courses has also been met by elimination; the only choice that is open is in the foreign language to be studied in the last years of the course. The basic aim of the school is to impart a general education in the same subjects as are found in the secondary schools of other countries. There is, however, an important difference; every subject is used as a hammer blow against western ideas as capitalistic and exploitive and to contribute to the aim that dominates all Soviet education, and expressed in the following quotations:

"The Soviet school cannot be satisfied to rear merely educated persons. Basing itself on the facts and deductions of progressive science, it should instill the ideology of Communism in the minds of the younger generation, shape a Marxist-Leninist world outlook and inculcate the spirit of Soviet patriotism and Bolshevik ideas in them." *Kultura: Zhizn* (Culture and Life), August 31, 1947.

"It is important that pupils should clearly realize the doom of the capitalistic world, its inevitable downfall, that they should see on the other hand the great prospects of our socialist system, and actively get prepared when they leave school to be ready to take their place in life, in the struggle for a new world, for Communism." Teachers' Gazette, September 13, 1947.[13]

According to Professor Y. N. Medinsky, the aim is stated as fol-

[13] Both quotations are from *The Kremlin Speaks*, Department of State Publication 4264 (Washington, D.C., 1951), pp. 25 f.

lows: "Great attention is paid to educational work in the school. The lesson — the process of study — is the principle form of instruction. The education of conscious builders of Communist society, the instruction of children in the high qualities of the new man is carried out by the teacher at the daily lesson." [14]

Secondary school subjects are begun in the fifth year of school and continued for six years. They are Russian language and literature (and the native language and literature where Russian is not the native language), mathematics, natural science, physics, chemistry and astronomy, history, geography, foreign languages, drawing, singing, and physical training. Except in foreign languages there are no options. But the names of the subjects do not convey any idea of their purpose. In literature in the higher classes Medinsky writes, "The pupils learn about the importance of literature in the life of Russian society; about the national traits and patriotism of Russian literature, the big role it played in the liberation and revolutionary struggle of all peoples. They learn to understand the ideological essence of a literary work, its composition, plot, characters and language; they acquaint themselves with the main periods in the development of literature and principal literary trends. The course in literature introduces the pupil to the outstanding works of world literature, and shows the leading role of Russian and Soviet classics in the development of world literature." [15]

The teaching of history is slanted in the same direction — the cult of patriotism and Soviet pre-eminence as a world force: "The course in history in the 8–10 classes gives the pupil a most profound understanding of the Marxist-Leninist teaching about the productive forces and their role in the historical processes, about the relations of production, the class struggle, the socialist revolution and the dictatorship of the proletariat, about the leading role of the great Russian people in the history of the peoples of the U.S.S.R." [16] In the teaching of geography the aim is to give "a scientific materialistic world outlook," love for the motherland and understanding of economic progress of the country under the five-year plans which utilized the enormous resources of the country.

[14] Medinsky, *Public Education in the U.S.S.R.* (Moscow, 1951), p. 68.
[15] *Ibid.*, pp. 64 f.
[16] *Ibid.*, pp. 65 f.

In mathematics and the sciences the practical applications are emphasized. Astronomy is taught in the highest class, and "like natural science, physics and chemistry, this subject is of great importance in developing materialist views among the youths." [17]

Pupils are promoted on passing examinations at the end of each year. The graduation examination at the end of the complete middle school covers the last three years of work. Written and oral examinations must be passed in Russian language and literature, written and oral examinations in algebra, geometry, and trigonometry, and oral examinations in history of U.S.S.R., a foreign language, physics, and chemistry. Gold medals are awarded to pupils who obtain a grade of 5 (the highest mark) in all subjects, and silver medals to those who obtain a grade of 4 in not more than three subjects of which the native language and literature may not be one, and 5 in all others. Medal winners are admitted to institutions of higher education without an entrance examination and are granted stipends but not free tuition.

The return to the rigorous system of examinations and discipline, characteristic of Tsarist days, represented a reaction against the experiments in freedom in the first fifteen years of the Soviet regime. The methods of discipline are, according to Medinsky, "persuasion, explanation, encouragement and reprimand"; corporal punishment ("which, incidentally, is still practised in some bourgeois states") is resolutely rejected.[18] In 1943 the Soviet of People's Commissars of the R.S.F.S.R. adopted a code of "Rules for School Children" which prescribe the duty of every school child. Obedience, conformity, and respect for teachers, directors, and parents are the principle duties, but specifically the following are the most interesting: "1. To strive with tenacity and perseverance to master knowledge, in order to become an educated and cultured citizen and to serve most fully the Soviet Motherland. . . . 11. To make accurate notes of the teacher's assignment for the next lesson, to show these notes to the parents, and to do all homework without assistance." [19]

[17] *Ibid.,* p. 67.
[18] *Ibid.,* p. 69.
[19] The complete list of 20 rules, translated from *Sovietskaia Pedagogika,* October, 1943, p. 1, is given in G. S. Counts and Nucia P. Lodge, *I Want to be Like Stalin* (New York, The John Day Co., 1947), pp. 149 f. By permission of the publisher.

The encouragement of activities that might develop initiative and independence among the pupils is an obvious need if one examines the time-schedule and the "Rules for School Children." From the fifth to the tenth school year of the middle school an average of thirty-two hours per week are spent in the classroom. Information is not available about the amount of time required for homework. Rule 8 gives some hint as to methods of instruction which point to dictation by the teacher. It runs as follows: "To sit erect during the lesson period, not leaning on the elbows or slouching in the seat; to attend closely to the explanations of the teacher and the responses of the pupils, not talking or engaging in mischief." It will be recalled that the textbook was described by Yesipov and Gonchaiov in their book *Pedagogy,* as "the chief aid of the teacher," and that "Compulsory uniformity of programs is one of the most valuable conditions for the improvement of schoolwork in our country." [20] Uniformity is also a wise measure to overcome the shortage of well-prepared teachers of which there are frequent complaints.

In a comparison of the Soviet ten years of school and twelve years in the United States, Medinsky finds that pupils in the former have 330 school days or 1,650 school hours more than pupils in the latter. "The course in physics, chemistry, literature, natural science, history and geography," he writes, "is a more profound one in the Soviet school and gives the pupil a much broader and systematic knowledge than do the schools of the United States." These, he claims, offer a total of nearly 500 subjects and up to twenty-five or more subjects in each school, from which the pupils choose those they prefer.

The "polytechnization" of education in the schools described up to this point seems to have disappeared. According to the educational theory of Karl Marx, polytechnization is designed to impart "the general principles of all processes of production and simultaneously to initiate the child and young person in the practical use and handling of the elementary instruments of trades," in addition to intellectual, aesthetic, moral, and physical training. Only to the extent that the applications to practical purposes are brought out in the teaching of the several subjects; the aim is to give reality

[20] See Counts and Lodge, *op. cit.,* p. 19.

to the meaning of the subjects taught. The dominant aim in these schools is not to give any vocational training as such but is still to train "builders and defenders of a socialist society."

To the same aim an important contribution is made by the great variety of extra-curricular activities which include a certain amount of pupil self-government and clubs to cultivate cultural interests, dramatics, choruses, fine arts, as well as sports and physical culture. "All these circles," says Medinsky, "which help to broaden the outlook of the pupil, train him to work independently and develop his aesthetic tastes, are guided in their work by teachers." [21] But even more important than these activities are the Young Pioneer and Young Communist Leagues which not only supplement the Communist training of the schools but serve as a coercive force over the children and youth of the land and as educational agencies to propagate "the spirit of Soviet Patriotism" and "boundless devotion to the cause of Lenin-Stalin."

### Vocational Education

The various five-year plans and the expansion of Soviet economy required a supply of specialists and trained man power. The specialists who require a university training are selected in the main by examinations at the close of the full ten-year general course; others come through the specialized *technikums* of various kinds. Trade training for youth outside of the *technikums* is given in the Labor Reserves into which boys and girls between the ages of fourteen to seventeen are drafted to be employed as needed and to receive direct training in some skills for trades, railways or factories. Organized in 1940, the Labor Reserves were in 1946 placed under a Ministry of Labor Reserves of the U.S.S.R. For the skilled trades there are schools giving two-year courses, and for the semi-skilled occupations six months' training in factory-plant schools is provided. All who go through these training courses are required to serve for four years at jobs in locations assigned by the Ministry of Labor Reserves. The right to work, established by the Constitution, must not be interpreted to mean "the right to choose their own place of employment in disregard of the interests and needs of

[21] Medinsky, *op. cit.*, p. 68.

the state." (*Pravda*, January 22, 1941).[22] The trainees receive board, lodging, tuition, and textbooks free of charge and, since the schools are production schools, the trainees receive a certain proportion of the standard wage for any work performed.

For middle-level specialists courses are provided to graduates of the seven-year incomplete middle school in *technikums*, which offer courses varying in length according to the specialty taught. The number of specialties is great and varied: they include training for industry, transport and agriculture; there are medical schools for the training of midwives and doctors' assistants, and training schools for elementary school teachers; training is also provided for the theatrical, musical, and fine arts professions. The most unusual length of course is three years for seven-year school graduates who must pass an entrance examination in Russian language and literature, mathematics, and the Soviet Constitution. *Technikums* that train for dentistry, junior legal assistants, and the drama require for entrance the completion of the ten-year complete middle schools for all students, in others only for students who pass the school as well as the examinations. Stipends are available in some entrance examinations with a mark of 4 or 5. Graduates must spend the three years after completing their courses in the practice of their speciality. A few of the graduates, if they are in the top 5 per cent of their year, may be admitted to a university without entrance examination or the three years of practice. The *technikums* also offer evening and correspondence courses for students of all ages, if employed at a job closely related to the specialty for which the training is provided.

The *technikums* are under the supervision of the U.S.S.R. Ministry of Culture, which has a responsibility for the academic part of the course, but are administered and financed by the ministry responsible for the specialty provided by the particular *technikum*, such as the Ministers of the Coal Industry, of the Electrical Industry, of Justice, etc.

Whether the schools for adolescents are successful in their particular objectives, there can be no doubt that in the dominant objective of turning out acquiescent patriots who accept the Communist

[22] *The Current Status of Soviet Education*, p. 12. Intelligence Report No. 6314, U.S. Department of State, July 28, 1953.

ideology without question or hesitancy complete success is attained. There is no reason why this should not be so, for a generation is growing up that knows nothing about the world outside the area of communism which might serve as a challenge to thought. Such information as may come about the outside world is presented through the eyes of Communist interpreters. Further, there is no break in gauge between school and society. The same controls that subject the adults to the domination of the Party are carried over to the schools and utilized by the Young Pioneers and Young Communists.

## UNITED STATES

### Secondary Education and Cultural Changes

From the point of view of organization the United States has settled, if not solved, the problem of the education of the adolescent by creating a single system of education from the nursery school or kindergarten to the university, with a break either at the end of the sixth or of the eighth grades. In fact the grades are counted from the first to the twelfth, and, where a recent organization has been adopted, to the fourteenth. The United States, before any other country became conscious of the problem, began to implement the ideal of equality of educational opportunity for all without distinction of race, social status, and residence. The enrollment of boys and girls in the high schools doubled every decade since 1890. In 1952–53 the enrollment was over 7,300,000, and by 1960 it is expected that, as a consequence of the increased birth rate during and after World War II, the enrollment will reach 8,000,000. The percent of young persons, fourteen to seventeen, in the high schools in 1890 was 7 per cent; the figure at present is 77 per cent.

Of 1,000 children enrolled in 1942–43 in the fifth grade, 505 were graduated from high school in 1949–50. Of 1,000 pupils in the first year of high school in 1946–47, 625 graduated in 1950. The number of pupils who leave high school without completing the course varies from 40 to 50 per cent, according to a report of the U.S. Office of Education on the *Holding Power and Size of High Schools.* There is no significant difference in the holding power of large and small high schools. In most states pupils are required by the attendance law to remain in school until they are sixteen, though they may leave a year earlier if they secure employment. The reasons for dropping out of school vary: some leave because they wish to become wage-earners; some because they dislike school work or their teachers; others for financial reasons of the home are unable to continue their education. The scholarship systems of England and France are unknown although scholarships may be available here and there through the interest of service groups (labor unions or Rotary, Kiwanis, and Lions organizations). While tuition is free, there are charges for extra-curricular activities which, though not large in themselves, are a burden for some pupils. On the other hand, many pupils engage in paid activities while still in school, whether they are in need or not. The practice is regarded as a valuable and educative experience and does not in any way affect the status of those who engage in it.

The increasing enrollment in the high schools is due to a number of factors, the majority of which are economic. Boys and girls have been compelled under the school attendance laws of most states to remain in school up to sixteen or seventeen, and of some to eighteen. The raising of the age of compulsory attendance is due to a change in the character of the nation's economy, of technological development, and of the increasing per capita wealth. From an agricultural economy there has been a shift to an industrial economy, which has been made possible both in agriculture and in industry by the multiplication of mechanical appliances and the use of electric power. The result has been mass production and the virtual disappearance of handwork and craftsmanship. The consequence of the technological development has been to shift the emphasis to the training for managerial and directive functions and to reduce the amount of training needed for most operations to a few weeks or months. At the same time the disappearance of craftsmanship has rendered unnecessary, for most trades, a long period of apprenticeship. Most vocations were able to dispense with the labor of young persons.

These forces rendered the task of keeping youth in school much easier; the rest was done by propaganda urging youth to remain in school and pointing out the value of continuing in school in terms of increased earnings. It is interesting that such propaganda was thought to be most needed at times when there was a shortage of manpower and when there were more opportunities for youth in the labor market. Such occasions occurred during World War I to some extent but more particularly during World War II. It is interesting to note that the success of high school graduates in attaining officer rank in World War I exercised a profound influence in directing youth to the value of staying in school as long as possible. In World War II the educational standard for officer material had advanced beyond the high school.

The age of compulsory school attendance began to be raised after the enrollment in the high schools had already begun to increase. The forces that brought about the change in the nation's economy also changed the distribution of the population from rural to urban areas. Urbanization in turn made it possible to establish high schools which in many cities served to attract more people assured of facilities for the education of their children beyond the primary or elementary school. In the rural areas the provision of high schools increased as roads were improved, transportation by bus became easier, and consolidated schools could provide the same opportunities as urban high schools.

### Articulation with Primary Schools

The issue in organization was how to articulate primary and high school education. About forty years ago it was recognized that even though the grades might be numbered serially from one to twelve, the transition from the eighth elementary grade to the four-year high school, the only form then available, was too abrupt in every way. The junior high school was then adopted for two reasons — to begin postprimary education in the seventh instead of the ninth grade and to provide three years of exploration or orientation before entering the three-year senior high school for specialization.[23] There was thus developed a 6–3–3 plan (six years

[23] Historically a reorganization of the school system had been suggested much earlier. President Charles W. Eliot of Harvard University had recommended its desirability, and the Committee of Ten of the National Education Association in 1893 and the Committee on College Entrance Requirements in 1899 recommended a redivision of the system into two six-year periods. The establishment of the first junior high schools followed the endorsement of the idea by the Committee of Five of the National Education Association in 1905, 1908, and 1909.

of primary, three years junior high and three years senior high school), or a 6–6 plan (six years primary and six years high school). More recently another organization has been tried in which the junior college is added to the common school with a 6–4–4 plan (six years primary, four junior high with a year of senior high school, and four years senior high and junior college combined). In 1952, of the total number of public high schools (23,746), 42.8 per cent were organized on the 8–4 plan; of the remainder, 13.6 per cent were junior high schools, 7.4 per cent were senior high schools, and 36.2 per cent were junior-senior high schools. The reorganized system is most commonly found in cities of 10,000 or more population. Advantages are claimed for both systems, but for the junior high school the strongest argument is that flexibility is more possible and that the transition from instruction in the same class by one teacher to departmentalized teaching by several subject-matter specialists can be facilitated. Better opportunities are offered in the junior high school, it is claimed, for guidance of pupils and for the organization of extra-curricular activities. Originally one of the major functions of the junior high school was to provide exploratory courses to discover the abilities and interests of pupils. This feature is no longer stressed as it used to be, but provision is made in the programs of junior high schools for both general and unspecialized vocational education.

## The Comprehensive High School

Whatever the form of organization, the high schools are in the great majority "comprehensive" and coeducational. The comprehensive high school is open without tuition fees to all pupils and offers general and vocational education in the same institution. It performs the functions which in other countries are assigned to differentiated types of special schools — trade and industrial, commercial, household arts, fine arts, and so on. In a number of larger cities specialized high schools are being provided, like the High School of Music and Art, the High School of Science, and the High School of Commerce as well as several technical high schools in New York City, the Technical High School in Brooklyn, the Central High School in Philadelphia, the Latin Grammar School in Boston, the Lane Technical High School in Chicago. Separate high schools for boys and girls are found but mainly in the East.

The comprehensive high school which is attended by all the children of all the people is the response to the American ideal of education in a democracy. It is not only considered educationally more efficient than separate schools but is regarded as essential for developing a sense of social unity and solidarity. Neither argument has been proved sound in practice. The problem of sorting out the pupils for different courses according to their aptitudes and abilities is transferred from the period before to the period after they enter the high school; that this is not wholly satisfactory is shown by the number of pupils who drop out of school before graduation. As will be pointed out later in this section, the high school course is satisfactory for 20 per cent of the pupils with academic ability and 20 per cent who plan to enter a skilled vocation, but it is unsatisfactory for 60 per cent of the pupils who derive no profit from their attendance at school. Tests are available for the selection of the academically able pupils. In a report on the *Education of the Gifted* issued by the Educational Policies Commission, there appears the following statement: "Several tests have been developed for indicating special aptitude for such fields as language, medicine, science, and teaching. Such tests, when used to supplement the data obtained from tests of general intelligence, can be useful in guidance on the high-school and college level" (p. 19). Nevertheless, the comprehensive high school attended by pupils of all levels of intelligence tends to cater to the average. "The tendency," according to the Harvard Report on *General Education in a Free Society*, "is always to strike a somewhat colorless mean, too fast for the slow, too slow for the fast." The neglected pupils in the comprehensive high school are not only the 60 per cent referred to above, but, as will appear later, the gifted pupils as well. That the comprehensive high school organization has not settled the problems of the education of the adolescent was indicated in the Educational Policies Commission's report, *Education for All American Youth, A Further Look* [24] in the following state-

[24] Washington, D.C., 1952. This was a revised edition of the report, *Education for All American Youth*, issued in 1944. By permission of the Secretary of the Commission.

ment: "What most needs to be done can be indicated by an enu-
meration of present deficiencies: (1) Many American youth who
should be attending secondary school are not doing so. (2) Ap-
proximately half of American youth are either not in secondary
school or are dropping out before completing the twelfth year.
(3) A very large number of youth in secondary school are not
getting an education fully suited to their abilities, interests, and
needs. (4) Many youth who could advantageously use more education than they are receiving are not getting it because cost-free
schools of an appropriate type are not available to them" (pp. 8 f).

Nor is the second claim, that the comprehensive high school
develops a sense of social unity and understanding, proved in
practice. It was shown conclusively in *Who Shall Be Educated?*
by W. Lloyd Warner, R. H. Havighurst, and M. B. Loeb, that the
social class distinctions that prevail outside the school are brought
into the school and affect every form of activity — both the choice
of course and extra-curricular activities; only in athletics does a boy
at the lower end of the social scale have an opportunity to rise to
the top. In *Social Class in America* (1949), W. Lloyd Warner,
Maria Mocker, and Kenneth Wells write that "Every major area
of American life is directly or indirectly influenced by our class
order," and this includes the schools. Warner and P. Lunt in
*The Social Life of a Modern Community* (1945) and A. B.
Hollinshead in *Elmtown's Youth* (1949) noted the existence of a
hierarchy of courses. Hollinshead writes: "If you take a college
preparatory course, you're better than those who take a general
course. Those who take a general course are neither here nor
there." He found in the city investigated by him that the college
preparatory course was taken by pupils who in the majority belonged to the lower upper social class. The upper social class sent
its children to private schools. Indirectly it has been recognized
that the high school had failed as a unifying social force, since it
has been found necessary to encourage what has been called "in-
tercultural education" to promote better understanding among
pupils of different national origins, races, colors, and religion. The
assumption underlying the idea of the comprehensive high school
that social understanding and elimination of social class differences
would result from the mingling of all pupils in the same school
has not been proved to be valid.

## Aims of High Schools

As contrasted with the administration of education in most countries there does not exist in the United States any official body with authority to define the aims of education or to prescribe the curricula of schools. Nor, in spite of the charge that postprimary education is dominated by college entrance requirements, is any traditional aim or curriculum so strongly entrenched that it cannot be overridden. The problem is further complicated by the fact that the high schools must be adjusted to the needs and abilities of pupils with a range of I.Q. from about 80 to 140 or above. According to Professor Lewis M. Terman, an I.Q. of 110 is requisite for success in the academic work of a high school. The definition of the function of the high school has consequently occupied the attention of a succession of committees and commissions representing the national organizations of teachers, the U.S. Office of Education, and subject matter associations, since the last decade of the nineteenth century.[25]

Perhaps the most influential statement of aims has been that of the Commission on the Reorganization of Secondary Education appointed by the National Education Association. The Commission's report, published under the title "Cardinal Principles of Secondary Education," has been quoted more frequently than any other statement since it defined the aims of education in 1918. The Cardinal Principles, seven in number, are founded on a consideration of the meaning of democracy and the function of education in a democracy. The first of these considerations leads to the conclusion that "The purpose of democracy is so to organize society that each member may develop his personality through activities designed for the well-being of his fellow-members and of society as a whole." To achieve these ends is the task of education. "Consequently, education in a democracy, both within and without the school, should develop in each individual the knowledge, interests, ideals, habits, and powers whereby he will find his place and use that place to shape himself and society to ever nobler ends." The nobler ends were nowhere defined.

[25] See I. L. Kandel, *History of Secondary Education*, Ch. IX. (Boston, Houghton Mifflin Co., 1930).

The main objectives of education are derived accordingly from a consideration of the individual as a person and of his place in society. To achieve these objectives secondary education must promote the following ends: health, command of fundamental processes, worthy home membership, vocational efficiency, civic participation, worthy use of leisure time, and ethical character. Since this report appeared in 1918 there has been a succession of statements of aims, but in general they have merely rung the changes on the Cardinal Principles. The Educational Policies Commission of the National Education Association in the 1952 edition of its original 1944 report on *Education for All American Youth* sought to define the objectives of the high school in the light of the increased enrollment since 1918 and the consequent variety of needs, interests, and abilities of the pupils. According to the report every youth in the United States "should experience a broad and balanced education which will (a) equip him to enter an occupation suited to his abilities and offering reasonable opportunity for personal growth and social usefulness; (b) prepare him to assume the full responsibilities of American citizenship; (c) give him a fair chance to exercise his right to the pursuit of happiness through the attainment of mental and physical health; (d) stimulate intellectual curiosity, engender satisfaction in intellectual achievement, and cultivate the ability to think rationally; and (e) help him to develop an appreciation of ethical value which should undergird all life in a democratic society." [26]

In *Planning for American Youth,* a pamphlet issued by the National Association of Secondary School Principals in 1944, the aims of the high school are stated in terms of the common needs of all youth as follows: "1. All youth need to develop salable skills. 2. All youth need to develop and maintain good health and physical fitness. 3. All youth need to understand the rights and duties of the citizen of a democratic society. 4. All youth need to understand the significance of the family for the individual and society. 5. All youth need to know how to purchase and use goods and services intelligently. 6. All youth need to understand the influence of science on human life. 7. All youth need an appreciation of literature,

[26] Educational Policies Commission, *Education for All American Youth, A Further Look* (Washington, D.C., 1952), p. 32.

art, music, and nature. 8. All youth need to be able to use their leisure time well and to budget it wisely. 9. All youth need to develop respect for other persons. 10. All youth need to grow in their ability to think rationally."

While these statements of aims were being elaborated, an approach was being made from another angle — the suitability of the present organization of the high schools to pupils in terms of their probable future after leaving school. At a conference held in 1945 to discuss the future of vocational education it was stated that vocational education was suited to 20 per cent of the pupils of secondary school age who would enter upon desirable skilled occupations; that another 20 per cent could profit from an academic course as a preparation for entrance to college; but that the remaining 60 per cent would not receive "the life adjustment training they need and to which they are entitled as American citizens — unless and until the administrators of public education with the assistance of the vocational educational leaders formulate a comparable program for this group." [27]

### Education of the Gifted

The influx of pupils into the high schools has raised still another problem, that of providing an education suited to the needs of talented or gifted pupils or pupils of superior ability. In considering the statements of aims of the high school it will be noted that no reference is made to this group of pupils. In fact the idea of an élite is rejected in American educational thought. The pupil of superior ability may serve as a guinea pig in psychological investigations and the road for talent may be open to him, but until recently his existence was ignored. Separate schools for pupils of different abilities and needs are ruled out entirely by the idea that a democratic system of education cannot tolerate segregation which might lead to stratification, social or intellectual. Equality of op-

[27] Office of Education, Federal Security Agency, Bulletin 1951, No. 3, *Vitalizing Secondary Education* (Washington, D.C.), p. 29. It is interesting to note that the distribution of the pupils corresponds somewhat to the proposed distribution in English secondary education — 15 per cent in grammar schools, 15 per cent in technical secondary schools, and 70 per cent in secondary modern schools.

portunity has too frequently been thought to mean identity of opportunity. Nevertheless the waste of talent has been recognized as dangerous and efforts of different kinds — acceleration or enrichment of programs — have been made. The grouping of pupils according to ability is regarded as socially unsound, but such groups are found in high schools throughout the country, and experiments have been made to provide for talented youth in a school within a school as in New York City.

The Educational Policies Commission, in a report on the *Education of the Gifted,* [28] has directed attention to the problem. "The democratic ideal," says the report, "can be most fully attained when every individual has opportunity for educational experiences commensurate with his abilities and for vocational opportunities commensurate with his qualifications" (p. 4). And again, "The implications for the education of potential leaders in the sciences and their application are clear; their study of mathematics and the basic sciences must be extensive; and it must start early, for they will need their later college and post-college years for professional training and other kinds of specialized work" (p. 8). This need of an early start in modern humanities is also recognized. And, finally, the report states that "to the extent that the American people fail to face reality by recognizing that the superior abilities of gifted individuals do in fact exist, they tend to impair the full development and fruition of those abilities, thus denying to themselves a measure of the potential benefits" (p. 11). The report closes with a plea to the American people to appreciate the need for able leaders and to teachers and educational leaders to develop "a sharpened awareness of the problem and exert determined efforts to make American schools and colleges more effective agencies for the conservation and development of human talent." But no change in the structure of high schools is suggested.

### Curriculum

The problem in most countries of Europe is how to preserve the academic tradition of a liberal education against the new demands that are being made on the school by the cultural changes that

[28] Educational Policies Commission of the National Education Association, *Education of the Gifted* (Washington, D.C., 1950).

have been under way in recent decades. The problem in the United States is how to avoid the charge of being static by showing any serious regard for a tradition whether in education or any other aspect of culture. The schools must be dynamic lest the cultural lag becomes too marked. Education must be adapted to the increasing number and rapidity of the changes that are going on; at the same time education must give full consideration to the needs, interest, and abilities of each individual as a person. Hence the curriculum and methods of instruction must be so organized as to promote the fullest development of the personality of each individual and at the same time cultivate in him a sense of responsibility as a member of society in its many-sided forms of expression — as citizen, as the member of a family, as a worker, and as a human being.

The academic tradition is criticized not only because it is no longer suited to the needs and abilities of the greatly increased number of pupils in the high schools, but also because the claims on which it was defended are no longer valid. The psychological basis on which that tradition rested, that it trained the mind and the mind so trained could successfully deal with other subjects and problems outside the areas studied — the doctrine of formal discipline and transfer — has been proved unsound. Even if the reservations under which transfer could be effected were accepted, the subjects associated with the tradition are, it is claimed, of no great value in any case for understanding the world of today. Further, the tradition was for the minority that studied it a vocational preparation and at the same time a mark of class distinction. The traditional curriculum cannot be entirely discarded and should be retained for the few who have the ability to profit by it. But even this minority should have an opportunity to pursue courses that will prepare them to recognize and meet the problems of life in modern society.

The problem of what to teach must according to current American theory be approached from an entirely different angle in terms not of subjects but of the needs of the individual and of the society of which he is a member. This point of view has been expressed as follows: "In behalf of this group [the middle group of 60 per cent referred to earlier] of American youth we must come to grips with the educational goals of our modern society. If not a college education, then what? How are these young people to be encouraged to remain in school beyond the legal age limit? How are they to be helped best to utilize the time they do spend in school in preparation to face the problems of life?

"For these young Americans secondary education must have objectives designed to meet their particular needs. Young people vary greatly in their abilities and in their capacities to learn. All of them, however, are capable of development as valuable members of society. A narrow academic education, far from helping all youth to mature properly, often causes social maladjustment, thwarts the desire to learn, and creates attitudes of failure and resignation detrimental to youth and to society as a whole. The large number of youth who leave high school before graduation is an indication that for them we have failed to establish a suitable education." [29]

### Life Adjustment Education

The task of suggesting a revised curriculum was undertaken by the Commission on Life Adjustment Education for Youth, a nationwide representative organization which has held conferences since 1947 and stimulated the organization of state commissions. In 1951 the Commission issued a report on *Vitalizing Secondary Education*. [30] "Life adjustment education," according to the report, "is designed to equip all American youth to live democratically with satisfaction to themselves and profit to society as home members, workers, and citizens. It is concerned especially with a sizable proportion of youth of high-school age (both in school and out) whose objectives are less well served by our schools than the objectives of preparation for either a skilled occupation or higher education" (p. 1). Although the Commission had its origin in the realization that 60 per cent of the boys and girls in high schools derived no benefit from it and was expected to suggest a curriculum better adapted to their needs and interests, it was in the end felt that a life adjustment education should be for all, since it deals with areas of living — home, work, citizenship — of importance to all.

[29] Office of Education, Federal Security Agency, *Annual Report 1952* (Washington, D.C., 1952), p. 15.
[30] Office of Education, Federal Security Agency, *Vitalizing Secondary Education* (Washington, D.C., 1951).

The sponsors of a life adjustment education do not propose a particular curriculum, but rather seek to stimulate the adoption of a new point of view, new methods of instruction and pupil-teacher relationships, the utilization of the direct experiences and problems of the pupils in and out of school, and training in problem-solving. The basic aim is to get away from "verbal and abstract learning" and "undue emphasis on specialized courses useful to a relatively small number of pupils" (p. 1). The emphasis must be placed on action rather than learning figures and facts, rules and regulations. "Modern high schools do not believe that the development of social attitudes and values can be ignored or left to chance. Civic competence, effective home and family living, relationships between employer and employee, occupational efficiency — all these have more and more come to be recognized as significant fields for constructive educational planning and development" (p. 9). The provision of "work experience," especially for the 60 per cent not adequately adjusted, offers an excellent opportunity for using their experiences and relating instruction to it.

The following paragraph from the report may serve as a summary of the curriculum trend that seems to be at present in the ascendant in the theory of high school education: "In life adjustment education programs the common, personal, political, social, and economic problems of individuals, along with those of the local community, state, region, and nation, are made the basis of special concern and study. The emphasis is upon direct pupil-teacher planning, sharing, and participation in real-life experiences while seeking solutions to individual, social, and civic problems. Such an approach requires the abandonment of the concept of 'extra-curricular activities' and makes excursions, travel, community surveys, schoolwork programs, study and hobby clubs, and any other form of direct experience for pupils integral parts of the educational program" (p. 38).

## Core Curriculum

Paralleling or supplementing the life adjustment education movement was the "Core Curriculum Development." This movement is variously defined: " 'To provide all youth a common body of experience organized around personal and social problems;' 'to give boys and girls successful experiences in solving the problems which are real to them here and now, thus preparing them to meet future problems;' 'to give youth experiences which will lead them to become better citizens in a community;' 'to increase the holding power of the secondary school by providing a program that has meaning for all' — these are some of the reasons for a core curriculum." [31]

The core curriculum is a course in "common learnings" to provide learning experiences for all youth to prepare for "effective living." The movement represents another effort to depart from both the subject-centered curriculum and the formal organization of the time-schedule. It does not represent any one subject but usually combines two or more that are drawn upon as needed by the problem under discussion or investigation or that are unified into a core studied for a longer period than the usual forty- to fifty-minute period. The usual subjects that are combined into the core curriculum are the basic subjects like English and social studies, science and mathematics, art and music. The essential characteristic of the core curriculum is that it is pupil-centered and the method is through problem-solving and activities.

## The High School Curriculum in Practice

It will be noted that in the trends that have been described there is no mention of subjects as such, but rather experiences, problems, activities, and interests. Paradoxically the Biennial Survey of Education in the United States, 1948–50, devotes a chapter to *Offerings and Enrollments in High-School Subjects, 1948–49*. The report [32] lists 274 special subject-titles. This does not mean necessarily separate subjects but separate courses in the same subject are included; Ninth-grade English and Tenth-grade English, for example,

[31] Office of Education, Federal Security Agency, Bulletin 1952, No. 3, *Core Curriculum Development: Problems and Practices* (Washington, D.C., 1952), p. v. By permission of the Acting Chief, Reports and Technical Services.

[32] Office of Education, Federal Security Service, Biennial Survey of Education in the United States, 1948–50. *Offerings and Enrollments in High School Subjects* (Washington, D.C., 1951), Chapter 5. By permission of the Acting Chief, Reports and Technical Services.

are counted as two courses. The report shows a decline in the percentage since 1934 of pupils studying mathematics and foreign languages, while the largest enrollments were in subjects generally required by most states — English, physical education, health, and safety. The greatest increase between 1934 and 1949 took place in home economics and industrial arts (vocational and nonvocational). Enrollments in general courses have grown at the expense of specialized courses — in biology at the expense of zoology and botany, in general mathematics at the expense of algebra and geometry, and in general science in place of specific subjects in science. There was a decrease in the percentage of pupils studying Latin and French, and more pupils were studying Spanish than Latin, which was second in the list of foreign languages studied. In addition to subjects that are expected to be found in a secondary school list there are new additions such as conservation, consumer buying, safety education, driver education, home management, remedial English, radio speaking and broadcasting, vocational radio, and cooperative store and office training.

Except for those who plan to enter college it is impossible to say what a high school curriculum is. All that can be inferred is that a pupil has had courses in English and social studies (including United States history) and for the rest has made up his program himself or with the help of a counselor in subjects he felt he needed or was interested in. The function of the counselor in view of the wide range of abilities among the pupils and the number of courses is one of increasing importance. In the larger school systems there are special guidance officers who cooperate with the home-room teachers and are concerned not only with the intellectual ability and vocational aptitude of the pupils but also with their physical and emotional condition. Tests and interviews as well as school records are at the disposal of the guidance officer. In smaller schools a teacher may be assigned to the duty of guidance, since there are so few required subjects which a pupil must study and since he is not required to study any subject longer than he chooses, the need of guidance becomes all the more important. A program for a year's work is usually "tailor made" or drawn up for each pupil on the basis of all that is known about him. In order to graduate at the end of the four- or six-year course a pupil must successfully complete fifteen units of studies, a unit representing a year's study of a subject for four or five periods a week. Only in the case of pupils who plan to enter college is there a requirement of about eleven units of prescribed studies, the remaining units being elective. Those who complete fifteen units of any group of subjects, generally including English and social studies, receive a "general certificate" which attests to high school graduation but is not accepted for college entrance.

The usual method of admission to colleges in the past was by examination. While this method survives, particularly in a large number of non-tax-supported colleges, examinations conducted by individual colleges disappeared when the College Entrance Examination Board was established in 1899. The Board conducts examinations (scholastic aptitude, achievement, and aptitude tests) throughout the country. Another substitute for the examinations was the system of accreditation, first adopted by the University of Michigan in 1870 and later adopted by a number of state universities. Subsequently regional associations, like the North Central Association (1894), Northwest Association (1918), Middle States Association (1921), and the Southern Association (1921), was formed. The function of the accrediting organizations is to set standards (library and laboratory equipment, and qualifications of teachers) and inspect high schools and to publish lists of accredited high schools whose graduates will be admitted to college on certification by their schools. Individual states may have their own system of inspection and standardization but their lists of schools do not always correspond with the lists of accrediting associations and the graduates of state-recognized high schools are admitted to colleges within the state only. In New York State the Regents conduct annual examinations and the candidates successful in the final examination are eligible for admission to college. Nevertheless, taking the country as a whole there is a great variation in standards, the results of which are seen in the large number of students who drop out of college in the early years of the course mainly because of inability to meet the standards. The weakness of the accrediting system lies not in the absence of external examinations, but in the fact that teachers set and mark their own examinations and there is a great range of variety in the quality of the teachers.

The nature of their preparation and qualifications will be discussed in the next chapter.

Whether the system of admission to college is by certificate of a recognized examining board or from an accredited school, candidates are generally expected to have included the following units of subjects in their high school course: English, three units; mathematics (algebra and geometry), two units; social studies, two units; science, two units; and a foreign language, two units. The standards reached are not as high as the standards reached in the academic secondary schools of other countries. It has in the past been the practice to recognize a leaving certificate from such a foreign school as equivalent to the completion of the first two years of the American college. Certain advantages of general social maturity are claimed for the graduate from a high school which the more scholarly product of a foreign secondary school does not possess. It must be remembered, however, that the high school is not selective as is the academic secondary school abroad; the selective process in the United States is longer and is continued through college and graduate school. In the end, however, the contributions to scholarship by Americans are recognized and appreciated abroad not only in the traditional fields of research, but in advancement into new fields. The American educator would, as has already been pointed out, reject the idea that the selection of an élite should begin as early as it does in foreign school systems. It is only recently that the education of the gifted student has been recognized as a responsibility that democracies must assume, and this in a nation that has come to be considered as the leader in the preservation of free institutions in the world.

### Extracurricular Activities

Extracurricular or out-of-school activities emerged spontaneously as pupils wished to express interests which were not met in the classroom. Today they form an important part of school life since they are regarded as important media for the development of character and the stimulation of interests for leisure time. They take a great variety of forms — pupil government and student councils, debating, hobbies, extension of interests arising out of classroom work (language clubs, dramatics, band, orchestra), junior Red Cross, boy and girl scouts, and the school journal and yearbook. Athletic activities may be extracurricular in so far as they are not part of a physical education program, but they may also be limited to small groups which represent the school in swimming, baseball, and basketball with their own professional coach or under the direction of the physical education instructor. The athletic activities, particularly basketball in which interschool tournaments take place, plan an important part in the development of school spirit.

Extracurricular activities are generally managed by the pupils themselves and provide opportunities for the emergence to leadership of boys and girls whose ability in that direction would not be recognized. Supervision by teachers as advisers is generally required. For some activities "credits" or "points" are allowed toward graduation. The extracurricular activities have acquired a place of such importance that they are in some places called co-curricular to indicate the recognition of their educative value. One criticism, however, is that the poorer pupils often cannot participate because certain charges are involved ranging from $75 to $150 a year, enough to debar some from the advantages they offer. These charges in addition to the cost of books, where they are not provided by the school system, supplies for school work, and so on, constitute "hidden charges" which defeat the aim of providing complete equality of opportunity. Only the athlete is well taken care of, so far as expenses are concerned, irrespective of social or financial status of his family. For the athletic activities serve as spectacles which bring school and community together, as much at the high school as at the college level.

## REFERENCES

### General
Kandel, I. L. *History of Secondary Education.* Boston, Houghton Mifflin Co., 1930.

### England
Alexander, W. P. *Education in England.* London, Newnes Educational Publishing Co., 1954.

Board of Education: Consultative Committee: *Secondary Education with Special Reference to Grammar Schools and Technical High Schools* (Spens Report). London, H.M.S.O., 1938.

———— Education Pamphlet, No. 114. *The Organisation and Curriculum of Sixth Forms of Secondary Schools.* London, H.M.S.O., 1938.

———— Report of the Committee on Secondary School Examinations Council. *Curriculum and Examinations in Secondary Schools* (Norwood Committee Report). London, H.M.S.O., 1943.

———— Report of the Committee on Public Schools, *Public Schools and the General Educational System* (Fleming Committee Report). London, H.M.S.O., 1951.

Dent, H. C. *Growth in English Education, 1946–1952.* London, Routledge and Kegan Paul Ltd., 1954.

English New Education Fellowship. *The Comprehensive School.* London, n.d.

Fisher, N. *Our Schools.* London, 1949.

James, Eric. *An Essay on the Content of Education.* London, George G. Harrap & Co. Ltd., 1949.

———— *Education and Leadership.* London, 1951.

Leicester Education Committee. *Secondary Modern Schools.* Leicester, 1948.

London County Council. *Replanning London Schools.* London, 1947.

Ministry of Education. *The Nation's Schools: Their Plan and Purpose.* London, H.M.S.O., 1945.

———— *A Guide to the Educational System of England and Wales.* London, H.M.S.O., 1945.

———— *The New Secondary Education.* London, H.M.S.O., 1947.

National Union of Teachers. *Transfer from Primary to Secondary Schools.* London, 1949.

———— *The Curriculum of the Secondary School.* London, 1952.

Smith, W. O. Lester. *Education in Great Britain.* Oxford, University Press, 1949.

*The First Five Years.* An Account of the Operation of the Education Act of 1944 in the East Riding of Yorkshire from 1945 to 1950.

West Riding Education. *Ten Years of Change.*

### France

Centre National de Documentation Pédagogique. *L'Organisation de l'Enseignement en France.* Paris, 1952.

Gal, Roger. *La Réforme de l'Enseignement et les Classes Nouvelles.* Paris, n.d.

Glatigny, M. *Histoire de l'Enseignement en France.* Paris, 1949.

Ministère de l'Education Nationale, *Principes de l'Organisation de l'Education Nationale*. Paris, 1950.

―――― *La Réforme de l'Enseignement*. Projet soumis à M. le Ministre de l'Education National par la Commission Ministérielle d'Etude Langevin Plan.

―――― *Les Classes d'Orientation*. Paris, 1937.

Musée Pédagogiques. *Abrégé de l'Organisation Scolaire Française*. Paris, n.d.

―――― *L'Enseignement du Second Degré*. Paris, n.d.

*Nouveaux Horaires et Programmes de l'Enseignement du Second Degré*. Seizième Edition. Paris, n.d.

*Programme des Examens du Baccalauréat de l'Enseignement Secondaire*. Paris, n.d.


**U.S.S.R.**

Counts, G. S. and Lodge, Nucia P. *I Want To Be Like Stalin*. New York, The John Day Co., 1947.

Florinsky, M. T. *Towards an Understanding of the U.S.S.R.* New York, The Macmillan Co., 1951.

King, Beatrice. *Russia Goes to School*. London, 1948.

Lamont, Corliss. *Soviet Civilization*. New York, Philosophical Library, 1952.

Medinsky, Y. N. *Public Education in the U.S.S.R.* (In English) Moscow, 1951.

Moos, Elizabeth. *The Educational System of the Soviet Union*. New York, National Council for American-Soviet Friendship, 1950.

United States, Department of State, European and British Commonwealth Series, No. 25. *The Kremlin Speaks*. Washington, D.C., 1951.

―――― Office of Intelligence Research, Intelligence Report, No. 6314. *The Current Status of Soviet Education*. Washington, D.C., 1953.


**United States**

Alberty, H. B. *Reorganizing the High School Curriculum*. New York, The Macmillan Co., 1953.

Bent, R. K. and H. H. Kronenberg. *Principles of Secondary Education*. New York, McGraw-Hill Book Co., 1949.

Briggs, T. H., J. Paul Leonard, and J. Justman. *Secondary Education*. New York, The Macmillan Co., 1950.

Douglass, H. R. *Secondary Education*. New York, Ronald Press, 1952.

Douglass, H. R., *et al. Education for Life Adjustment*. New York, Ronald Press, 1952.

Jacobson, P. B., W. C. Reaves, and J. H. Longdon. *Duties of School Principals.* New York, Prentice-Hall Co., 1950.

Kandel, I. L. *Impact of the War upon Education in the United States.* Chapel Hill, N.C., University of North Carolina Press, 1948.

Rivlin, H. *Teaching Adolescents in Secondary Schools.* New York, Appleton-Century-Crofts, Inc., 1948.

# 9

# The Preparation
# of Teachers

## INTRODUCTION

### Cultural and Educational Changes and Teacher Preparation

The changes in the culture patterns which have been proceeding with increased rapidity since the beginning of the century have inevitably resulted in changes in the theory and practice of education. There has undoubtedly been a lag between the recognition of these changes and the recognition of the need for reconstructing the educational system; the tempo varies from nation to nation. The changes in the educational system may be made more quickly in a country in which the administration is decentralized than in a country where control is in the hands of a central authority. Revolutionary governments, which claim to know no compromises, make a clean sweep with older patterns and adapt the educational system to conform to their ideology.

The preparation of teachers has been affected by the changes which, as discussed in other chapters, have already resulted in the educational reconstruction described earlier. There have, however, been additional causes for the changes that are at present being introduced in the preparation of teachers. Since the beginning of the century the influence of organizations of teachers has grown and has made itself felt not only in the demand for improved material conditions but also in proposals for higher standards of preparation.

They have insisted that the aims of education and the character of instruction have advanced from the days when the aim of education was to promote literacy and when the function of instruction was to impart a certain limited quantum of knowledge to large classes of pupils without giving any attention to individual differences. Further, the teacher was not expected to exercise any initiative but was required to follow a prescribed curriculum and course of study and standardized methods of instruction. Successful teaching was measured by examination results and the strictness of the discipline. A good teacher was a skilled craftsman, successfully using the most approved tricks of the trade.

Preparation was accordingly simple and followed the lines of apprenticeship training. For elementary school teachers that preparation was a little more advanced in content than the curriculum for the elementary schools. Secondary school teachers were in general expected to have a mastery of the subjects that they planned to teach. As a rule they were not required to have professional preparation except in Germany. Teachers in secondary schools were supposed to teach subjects in contrast to elementary school teachers who were supposed to teach children. The difference in the ages of pupils in elementary and secondary schools presumably accounted for this distinction. In neither case was teaching in elementary or secondary schools considered to be a profession, but was rated on the level of minor white-collar jobs. The reasons for this denial of professional status were the low salaries and the notion that "anybody can teach," if he knows a little more than the pupils. There was, of course, a distinction between the teachers at the two levels; the secondary school teachers were normally university graduates, while the elementary school teachers had a narrower and shorter period of training in institutions which they entered with little more than an elementary education. The distinction was further exaggerated by the fact that secondary education was open only to a select and privileged minority.

## The Beginnings of Reform: Teaching a Profession

The picture began to change, first in England and the United States, when future elementary school teachers began to go to

secondary schools before they entered institutions for the training
of teachers. The length of training still continued to be only two
years and the emphasis in the course was more on professional subjects and methods than on content. A change in the direction of
more advanced standards came, partly as a consequence of the demand of teachers' associations for a type of preparation more nearly
corresponding to that for other professions, and partly because of
the changing character of education, at first at the elementary level
only. The traditional type of training was no longer adequate when
the theory of education began to place particular stress on the pupil
as an individual to be developed intellectually, physically, aestheti-
cally, morally, and emotionally. That development must take place,
further, in a particular environment with a particular culture. The
teacher's preparation must, therefore, include a broad general or
liberal education, training in ability to understand the place of the
cultural assets that he finds in the environment, and acquisition of
skill in understanding his pupils as growing individuals. He must
accordingly have a grasp of the meaning of education in the past
and in the present, of its relation to social progress, and of the contribution of psychology to the learning process.

Teaching, therefore, has become more than a matter of the relation of the mature to the immature learner. It involves not only
imparting a mastery of knowledge of a limited number of subjects, but sympathetic understanding of the place of knowledge in
the growth of each pupil and of its value to society. The general
trend means that teaching is gradually becoming a profession, since,
with the acceptance of the new theory of education, the teacher can
no longer look upon his job as one of imparting doses of a curriculum and courses of study prescribed by a central authority,
whether local or national. He must rely not only upon his own cultural background and upon principles that will guide him in helping each pupil to realize his potentialities to the fullest. His work
is in a sense more delicate than that of the physician; like the physician he must diagnose and determine what principles to apply not
to one individual alone but to a whole classroom of individuals for
whose all-round development he is responsible. Since that responsibility is shared by a number of other agencies of the community
where the school is located, he may at times discover influences

which he must take into consideration in his work. It will be found on examination that the shift of emphasis from the subject to the child has, in fact, been a shift of emphasis to the teacher who must understand both the child and the meaning of the subject or what he teaches in a particular cultural environment.

This is what is meant by the change needed in the character of preparation from an apprenticeship to one suited to a profession. For apart from its social connotation, the most distinctive character of a profession is that its practitioners must have a prolonged and specialized preparation leading to a mastery of certain principles and techniques which are themselves based upon a specialized body of knowledge. Professions emerge as soon as there is developed a body of knowledge on which principles and techniques are based. Medicine, law, engineering, and architecture have emerged in this way. A number of occupations are today passing through the stage of semi-professions to become professions in time. Teaching has thus become a profession. This development coincides with the principle that the purpose of sound administration is to release the teacher for his proper work under the best possible conditions, in which regimentation and uniformity can have no place.

Increasingly teachers are being called upon to participate in administration and to contribute from their experience to the formulation of policies in the conduct of education. They exercise an important function in linking the school with the home through parent-teacher organizations. It is unfortunate that, except for outstanding personalities, who are not as rare as is sometimes implied, teachers as a body are the heirs of a bad tradition which has set them aside as "a race apart," to cite a phrase used in the McNair Report on *Teachers and Youth Leaders*. The popular enthusiasm for education is not always a measure of the esteem for the teachers who are responsible for it.

### Recruitment Standards

One obstacle to the development of a profession of teaching has been removed by requiring candidates for admission to institutions for the preparation of elementary school teachers to have had a secondary education or its equivalent. The most serious difficulty, however, is to decide which candidates are likely to become good teachers. The only criteria available at present are scholastic ability and character. Beyond that, despite numerous attempts to develop prognostic tests of teaching ability, particularly in the United States, none have been found to be of real value. But before the selection of candidates for admission has to be considered there is the problem of recruitment. There was a time when to become an elementary school teacher was regarded as an advance in social status. This is no longer true, particularly since World War II. Teaching in elementary and secondary schools is in serious competition with other activities — civil service, industry, and business — for manpower. Salaries have been improved, retirement allowances are provided, conditions of teaching are, or will become, better in terms of class size, and there is security of tenure, except in parts of the United States; even in the U.S.S.R. a teacher is safe in his position provided he does not deviate from the ideology of the moment.

The problem of recruitment has been and will remain serious owing to the war, in which so many teachers were killed, and owing to the higher birth rate. It is particularly serious in elementary education generally and in secondary education in certain fields, such as science and mathematics, since experts in these fields can readily find more remunerative employment in other occupations. A variety of methods has been used in England and the United States to bring to the attention of pupils in secondary schools the features of teaching as a career, and a slow increase in the number of candidates has recently been noted everywhere.

### Organization of Teacher Preparation

The organization of a system for preparing teachers is surrounded with many difficulties. In the case of the future elementary school teachers the length of the course is in many countries too short, while in the United States, where it has been lengthened to three and four years, it is charged that too much time is devoted to the study of professional subjects. The real difficulty lies in the fact that the subjects that the teacher must study for his general or liberal education constitute at the same time the content of the curriculum that he must use for purposes of instruction. This raises the question whether studies in the preparation of teachers should be purely academic or whether they should be professionalized, that is, studied from the point of view of their social meaning and purpose and their educative value to the pupils at different levels of their development. Since the general methods course has been found to be of little value, at some time the future teacher must learn how to use his subjects for instruction purposes.

When to general or liberal education there must be added the study of professional subjects and observation and practice teaching, it becomes clear that in a two-year course following secondary education there is not enough time. This gives rise to two additional questions: (1) What is the relation between the academic studies and the professional studies such as history and principles (or theory or philosophy) of education and educational psychology either general or for different school levels? and (2) What is the relation between theory and practice through observation and actual instruction?

The issues are somewhat different in the preparation of secondary school teachers who usually receive their general education in a university, although in the United States they may be trained in independent teachers colleges or in schools of education of a university. In most other countries general education is followed by a year of professional study which includes professional subjects and induction into practice. The time is all too short and there is no reason why such subjects as the history and philosophy of education should not be included as parts of courses in general history and philosophy.

### In-service Training

The completion of a course of preparation does not produce a finished teacher any more than does the course in medicine or law, both of which are followed by one or two years of internship. One or two years of probation have been introduced for teachers, but they are years in which, unless he is particularly fortunate in receiving guidance and advice from his principal and colleagues, the young teacher is apt to learn by his own mistakes or fall into routine ways. The period of probation, like the period of medical internship, should be looked upon as a period of further preparation under supervision and guidance. Since conditions in actual school practice are not the same as those of student teaching, and since conditions of environment and of interest of principals, colleagues, and inspectors vary from school to school, it is important that beginning teachers should, during their period of probation, receive special care and advice from a group specially assigned to this work.

One of the manifestations of the changing character of education is the development of courses for teachers in service. So long as instruction was a matter of routine following of prescribed courses of study and methods, the notion that the initial training could serve for a life time might be valid. When, however, the basic knowledge, both academic and professional, which contributes to the science and art of education, is being constantly enriched, the teacher who does not continue his studies is likely to stagnate and drop into routine ways. It is for these reasons that education authorities, schools of education, research organizations, professional associations and other agencies have in the last quarter of a century begun to offer courses which are expected to keep teachers abreast of the times. Additional remuneration may serve as an inducement to teachers to add to their qualifications, but on the whole it is a genuine interest in their work as members of a profession that serves as a stimulus to engage in further study, often at a sacrifice of the "free" time that the public believes the teachers enjoy.

### Preparation of Secondary School Teachers

The preparation of secondary school teachers has developed more slowly than that of teachers in elementary schools. As already pointed out, the idea that he who knows can teach was and is still prevalent. Many of the problems with which elementary school teachers had to deal did not arise in the secondary school before the recent reconstruction of educational systems was adopted. The pupils belonged to a select group; they were in the secondary school because their parents could pay the fees or because of their own superior ability; the special privileges that could be obtained on completing a part or the whole of the course kept them up to the mark; and in any case pupils who failed to keep up to that mark could be asked to leave or would leave voluntarily.

This situation has changed and for two reasons — the raising of the school leaving age and the provision of secondary education for all. One result is that the old line of demarcation between the academically and the professionally prepared teachers — that is, between the secondary and elementary school teachers — is being obliterated at least in the newer types of secondary schools in England and France and in the earlier years of secondary education in the United States and the U.S.S.R. The common school may result ultimately in the general recognition of the unity of the profession, within which there will be room for the specialists as in the medical profession. Since the trend is also in the direction of lengthening the course of preparation for intending elementary school teachers, the distinction between those who teach in secondary schools and those who teach in elementary schools may disappear. The length and general character of the preparation for both groups may become the same. Already the unity of the profession is indicated in the adoption in some systems of a single basic salary scale for all teachers with additions for additional qualifications.

## Changing Status of Teachers

The changes that are still proceeding to raise the qualifications of teachers, the higher educational standards of recruitment, and the longer preparation will undoubtedly have an effect on the status of the profession. The gradual increase in salaries, which, in view of the rising cost of living everywhere, is at present illusory, may also contribute to raise popular esteem for the teacher. The widespread recognition of the importance of education for national security and economic advancement through the improvement of a nation's human resources is not matched as yet by public recognition that the ultimate success of an educational system depends upon the teachers in it. In no country is the esteem in which teachers are held commensurate with the appreciation of and faith in education. Nevertheless, the improved position that teachers are beginning to hold in relation to administration must be a source of professional self-satisfaction. The teacher is ceasing to be a cog in a large administrative machine. Allowing for differences, the teacher is becoming more and more a practitioner in a profession and more or less independent in so far as he recognizes his professional responsibilities to the pupils, the public, and his colleagues.

## ENGLAND

### Proposals for Reform

The preparation of teachers in England was reorganized in 1945 following a line of development which was first proposed in 1919. Immediately after World War I the Council of Principals of Training Colleges adopted a resolution that "Any scheme for the improvement of general and professional education of teachers should secure that the work of the training colleges should be brought into close touch with that of the universities and should provide for a course of study extending over not less than three years." The training colleges, or institutions for the preparation of elementary school teachers, were brought into closer relations with the universities following the report of a Departmental Committee of the Board of Education on *The Training of Teachers for Elementary Schools* in 1925. Up to that time the Board of Education had conducted examinations for the teaching certificates. Following the recommendations of the report the Board undertook to leave the arrangements for and the conduct of the examinations to joint boards representing the training colleges, universities, and local education authorities. The Board retained the right to inspect the training colleges and the practical work of the candidates for certificates.

The new system based on these principles went into effect in 1930, when nine regional joint boards were organized with a Central Advisory Board to supervise the standards that might be adopted by the regional boards. While the new system brought the training colleges closer to the universities, the universities were not directly responsible as such for the education of teachers. The training colleges were still left more or less in isolation. The situation was not considered to be satisfactory, and the changes that were going in the character of the work of the schools strengthened the realization that further improvement in the preparation of teachers was needed.

In 1938 the Joint Standing Committee of the Training College Association and the Council of Principals issued a report on *The Training of Teachers* which was followed in 1939 by a report on *The Training of Teachers and Grants for Intending Teachers,* prepared by a Committee of Investigation of the National Union of Teachers (N.U.T.). The first report stressed the quality of the teachers on which the success of the schools depend. The idea that training colleges produce ready-made teachers trained mainly in classroom management and methods had been demolished by the experiment and development in education in recent years based on the principle that "the more liberally the teacher's function is conceived, the more complex and delicate is his task, and the more difficult it is to prepare him for it." More time than the normal two years was needed to meet the new aim, which is "to encourage the student's individual work and the development of his powers of constructive thought rather than to provide him with pre-digested information and ready-made opinions in the shape of formal lectures."

The N.U.T. Committee recommended a three-year course to leave more time to the students for reflective thought and leisure. It suggested that "in the interests of a unified educational system and a unified profession" there should be a certain degree of equivalence between the qualifications of teachers whether obtained in a training college or in a university. To make this possible every training college should "eventually become an integral part of the university in whose area it is situated," and the teaching qualifications should be university awards.

The Joint Committee, while favoring a three-year course leading to a degree, recommended that "the course for such degrees should include pedagogical studies, while the treatment of academic subjects would not be the same as in existing degrees. At the same time the course would have at least as large an intellectual content as existing degree courses. Those who advocate this proposal maintain that teachers, like engineers or medical men, lose nothing and may gain much by following at college a course, which without being narrowly vocational, is yet directed towards a particular profession." The N.U.T. Committee in suggesting that training colleges should eventually become integral parts of universities expected then to acquire a status analogous to that enjoyed by faculties or schools of medicine, engineering, domestic science, architecture, and agriculture. The requirements for degrees should, however, be adapted to the needs of intending teachers.

### The McNair Report

In 1942, the President of the Board of Education, R. A. Butler, appointed a Committee with Sir Arnold McNair, Vice-chancellor of the University of Liverpool, as chairman, "to investigate the present system of supply and the methods of recruitment and training of teachers and youth leaders and to report what principles should guide the Board in these matters in the future." The Committee in its Report, *Teachers and Youth Leaders,* issued in 1944, recommended the appointment by the President of the Board of Education of a Central Training Council for England and Wales "charged with the duty of advising the Board of Education about bringing into being that form of area training service recommended in this Report which the Board may decide to adopt."

The reason for this recommendation was that the Committee was unable to agree on the form of a national integrated organization for the preparation of teachers. Both sections of the equally divided Committee agreed on the creation of "area training authorities." One group proposed that each university establish a school of education which "should consist of an organic federation of approved training institutions working in cooperation with other approved educational institutions," and that the university schools of education "should be responsible for the training and assessment of the work of all students who are seeking to be recognized by the Board of Education as qualified teachers." The other group recommended the continuation of the joint board system in closer relation with the university represented on it, the constituent members "preserving their identity and being in direct relation with the Board of Education and the Central Training Council."

Both schemes, known as A type and C type, had these points in common: that the area training authority was given responsibility for the approval of curricula and syllabuses for all types of students in training; that the Board of Education would accept the recommendation as to the eligibility of students for recognition as qualified teachers on the basis of the final assessment of the student's work by the area training authority; and that the Board of Education retain the right to inspect every aspect of the work of an area training authority. Among other important recommendations were these proposals: that students should not be required to sign a declaration which morally committed them to teach in return for grants to enable them to prepare for teaching; that the length of course be extended to three years; and that there should be a basic salary scale for qualified teachers in primary and secondary schools with additions for special qualifications or experience.

The recommendations are of great significance in many ways, but perhaps the most significant feature is that they represent an important step forward in advancing the recognition of teaching at the primary and secondary levels [1] as a unified profession with a basic salary scale and with all teachers being denominated as qualified teachers provided they have gone through a period of professional preparation. In terms of English tradition the proposals promote the self-determination of teaching as a profession, somewhat analogous to other professions like medicine and law. The analogy is not complete since teachers are engaged in a public and national service and are remunerated by public authorities local and central. For this reason the Ministry retained the award of certificates of recognition as qualified teachers in its hands, but examinations and assessment of the work of students which form the basis of their eligibility are conducted by the professional organizations immediately concerned — the area training organizations (A.T.O.'s).

## The Present System: Area Training Organizations

Seventeen area training organizations were formed in association with the Universities of Birmingham, Bristol, Cambridge, Dur-

---

[1] Primary and Secondary School Regulations appeared as one set of regulations in 1945 for the first time.

ham, Leeds, Liverpool, London, Manchester, Nottingham, Oxford, Reading, Sheffield, Southampton, and Wales, and the University Colleges of Exeter, Hull, and Leicester. Of these fifteen chose the A type and two (Cambridge and Reading) the C type of organization. The majority of the organizations are called Institutes of Education; others are Schools of Education. Financially the difference between the two types lies in the fact that the A type are aided by grants made to the relevant university by the University Grants Committee, while the C type is aided directly by the Ministry of Education and the university "does not take full administrative and financial responsibility for them, but shares in their government with the local education authorities and training colleges of the area."

The administrative authority of each institute of education or area training organization is the council, which consists of representatives of the university concerned, the training colleges, local education authorities, and teachers in service. The Ministry is represented on each council by an administrative officer and an inspector, who are not voting members, and on the academic board of the council by two inspectors. The A.T.O.'s under C type are in direct relation with the Ministry; the A type act through the government of the university with which they are associated.

The functions of the A.T.O.'s are thus described in *Education in 1953*, the annual report of the Ministry: "These include supervising courses in member colleges and recommending to the Minister for the status of qualified teacher students who have completed their training satisfactorily. They are also concerned with planning the development of training facilities in their areas, providing educational centres for the use of students and serving teachers and organizing facilities for further study of qualified teachers in the schools" (p. 35). They have full responsibility for the examination and assessment of students in training as a basis for recommendations to be made to the Minister for the status of qualified teacher. Although experimentation is going on and is encouraged in the training colleges, standards are maintained for the area as a whole by the Council and its two boards — the academic and the professional — on which the universities are represented and by inviting external examiners from outside the area concerned.

The institutes or A.T.O.'s vary in size. The number of colleges in the University of London Institute [2] is thirty-eight with nearly 7,000 students; the University of Birmingham Institute has fourteen colleges with 2,000 students; six institutes have ten or eleven colleges each with between 1,400 and 2,000 students; and three institutes have six or seven colleges each, and four have only two or three colleges each in their organization.[3]

## National Advisory Bodies

Following the recommendation of the McNair Committee a National Advisory Council on the Training and Supply of Teachers (N.A.C.) was set up in 1949 by the Minister of Education. Its membership represents the area training organizations, local education authorities, and national associations of teachers. Its function is "to keep under review national policy on the training and conditions of qualification of teachers, and on the recruitment and distribution of teachers in ways best calculated to meet the needs of the schools or other educational establishments." [4] The Council deals with general questions of policy and has two Standing Committees, of which one deals with training and the other with recruitment and supply.

The area training organizations have a Standing Conference of Representatives of Area Training Organizations which was also set up in 1949 "to help in considering matters on which a common policy is desirable," such as facilities for teaching practice, assessment and examination methods, and the form and content of certificates and diplomas to be awarded on the successful completion of course. Officials and inspectors attend conference meetings, and secretarial services are provided by the Minister. In general the Conference exists primarily to exchange ideas and experience.

## Institutions for the Preparation of Teachers

The area training organizations of both A and C types include the university department of education and training colleges. In 1953–54 there were 23 university or university college departments

[2] This is distinct from the Institute of Education of the University of London.

[3] See *Education in 1953*, p. 35.

[4] *Education in 1949*, p. 45.

of education, 114 training colleges, of which one was provided by a university, 64 by local education authorities, 25 were Church of England, 13 Roman Catholic, 2 Methodist, and 9 undenominational. In addition there were 16 art schools, 14 training colleges for domestic subjects, 7 training colleges for physical education, and 3 technical training colleges. The total number of university departments of education and training colleges was 177. The university departments of education, art schools, and technical training colleges are mixed; the training colleges for domestic subjects and physical education are for women only; of the training colleges 14 are mixed, 18 for men only, and 82 for women only.

The two-year training colleges are devoted in the main to the preparation of teachers for infant and primary schools, and for the time being for secondary modern schools. They may offer one-year courses for graduates who plan to teach in secondary schools, and may extend the two-year courses for an additional year for students who wish to obtain additional qualifications. The specialist colleges usually offer a three-year course.

The new organization of these institutions into institutes or area training organizations breaks down the isolation of the training colleges, and brings the colleges into close association with universities of their area, and makes possible the adoption of common policies not only in each area, but throughout the country through the Standing Conference mentioned earlier. The institutions, however, retain their independence and autonomy under their own governing bodies and staffs, since flexibility and experimentation are essential characteristics of the new organization. The recent development carries a stage further the relaxation of the Ministry's control, which began when joint boards were established in 1926, and the adoption of higher standards is advanced by bringing the training colleges more closely under the aegis of the universities.

The university departments of education are supported financially out of grants paid to the universities by the University Grants Committee. The training colleges, if voluntary or denominational, are maintained as to buildings and fabric by their respective denominations; in 1945 the Ministry gave grants up to 50 per cent of approved expenditure on the improvement, extension or replacement of their accommodation. Since 1946 the voluntary or denominational colleges have been permitted to raise their tuition and boarding fees the cost of maintenance, with the Ministry's approval; the fees for recognized students are paid by the Ministry, fees for resident students were paid by the Ministry and day maintenance grants were paid to day students; in both cases the students were required to make contributions according to their parents' means. Local education authorities were allowed to receive applications for help toward the cost of books, travel, clothing, and incidental expenses.

Local education authorities which provide training colleges receive 100 per cent grant on all net recognizable expenditure, capital and maintenance. Since students are not required to teach or may not teach in the schools of the local education authority in whose training college they are educated, all local education authorities are required to contribute between them an amount equal to the total grants from the Ministry; such contributions rank for the Ministry's grant for education, amounting to 60 per cent of the authority's total expenditure. In the publicly provided training colleges the students do not pay tuition fees but are assessed on an approved scale for boarding fees for which they receive grants like the students in the voluntary training colleges.

Students are admitted to the training college on the basis of the General Certificate of Education (G.C.E.) which was introduced in 1951 for the examination of pupils in secondary schools (see pp. 271 f.). They are required to present a certificate showing five passes at the ordinary level or a combination of passes at the advanced and the ordinary levels. The colleges may admit students who are considered to be suitable but who do not possess the prescribed qualifications.

### Training College Courses

The courses are two years in length and include academic and professional studies and practice teaching. Each college enjoys freedom and autonomy in working out the courses which must, however, be approved by the board of studies of the institute of which the college is a member. There is a general framework within the institute which serves as a guide for the colleges in it.

Students are expected to receive a sound general education and may select one subject from a list usually found in the curricula of schools to carry to an advanced level — a second subject may also be added, but is optional.

The professional studies include principles and practice of teaching, health education, history of education, and educational psychology. Special method is taught in connection with instruction in the relevant subject. As part of their professional preparation students are trained in environmental studies of life and nature of the locality to accustom them to give a more concrete emphasis to their instruction in the classroom. These studies are taught as integrated or combined subjects. Such a course would prepare them to guide their pupils later on projects that deal with local studies.

The experiment with the emergency training scheme which provided a one-year course for selected students and necessitated considerable thought in the formulation of a suitable curriculum contributed new ideas when the time came to formulate the curriculum and syllabuses in the regular two-year courses. Provision is made for specialization in two directions — the teaching of young children, that is, in infant schools, and teaching in the junior schools attended by pupils from the age of seven to eleven.

Arrangements for practice teaching vary. Provision is made for observation visits connected with courses in child study and psychology. Normally students are expected to have a total of twelve weeks of practice teaching under the supervision of all the members of the faculty, both academic and professional, instead of by those responsible for method courses. Increasingly the local schools are encouraged to cooperate with the training colleges in the arrangements for practice teaching. A few colleges have schools adjacent to them, but the general opinion favors practice in the regular schools of a locality.

The training colleges also provide a course of one year's duration for uncertificated teachers to obtain the status of qualified teacher. The uncertificated class of teachers consisted of men and women who had passed an examination conducted by the Board of Education but who had not had a course of training. In 1946 the Ministry began to provide special one-year courses for uncertificated teachers with not less than five years or more than twenty years of experience, who wished to become qualified teachers. The scheme was continued only to 1952 but institutes were requested by the Ministry to give special consideration to the application of uncertificated teachers with more than five years experience who wished to take a one-year course in a training college.

## Preparation of Secondary School Teachers

Secondary school teachers normally receive their academic preparation in a university and on graduating take a one-year course of professional preparation in a university department of education or training college. Until 1951 intending teachers, as a condition of the grant paid to them for four years, were required to sign a declaration "which morally committed them to teaching as a career." In 1951 the pledge was abolished because it was considered undesirable to ask young persons to make such a commitment before they had an opportunity to consider other possibilities. In place of the grant which earmarked students for the teaching career, the system of scholarships offered by national and local authorities was considerably expanded. At the end of the academic course students who wish to take a postgraduate course of professional training then sign a declaration and receive a grant for one year. The course of professional training is similar to that offered in the training colleges and includes history and principles of education, educational psychology, and methods of teaching special subjects. At the end of the course on recommendation of their institute they obtain the status of qualified teacher (Q.T.).

## Assessment for Certification

The recommendation for students who have followed a course of preparation in a university department of education or a training college are based on a combination of a written final examination and assessment of the student's work during the course. The latter method began to be tried out experimentally before World War II and was used almost entirely during the war. At present both methods are used in combination, but a great deal of diversity prevails among and within the A.T.O.'s on the weight to be given to each, but the assessment always plays an important part in the final judgment of a student. It is to be noted that the area training organization as a whole and not the individual institution is responsible for the final assessment and recommendation. This is in accordance with recommendations of the McNair Committee (Par. 304).

Finally, a step in the direction of a unified profession has been made in denominating all teachers who have passed a course of training successfully as qualified teachers.

### Salaries and Pensions

A further contribution to the same end has been made in the adoption of a common basic salary scale with additions for qualifications above the minimum required and for positions of responsibility. The settlement has not been altogether satisfactory because of the current competition for manpower at the level of experts. New opportunities have been opened for specialists in mathematics and science in general and for the first-class graduates in other fields. Salaries are determined by a committee generally referred to as the Burnham Committee, originally set up in 1919 with Lord Burnham as chairman. The name has been continued although there have been several chairmen since Lord Burnham's death. The Committee includes representatives of teachers' organizations, local education authorities, and the Ministry. The latest scale is for both primary and secondary school teachers. The scale agreed upon by the Committee must be paid by the employing authorities.

A pension system was established for teachers in 1925 and revised in 1946. It is based on contributions by teachers and their employers. Normally a teacher becomes eligible to a retirement allowance at the age of sixty and after thirty years of pensionable service. Disability allowances and gratuities on death are also paid under the scheme.

### In-service Training of Teachers

The establishment of area training organizations has increased the opportunities for the training of teachers in service and for study for more advanced professional awards. In this work the A.T.O.'s work in cooperation with local education authorities, especially for the release of teachers who wish to take a full-time course. A further important contribution of the new organization is the opportunity provided for research in the field of education, which has been greatly expanded since World War II. A great deal of research is being conducted locally by education authorities and institutes of education, and nationally by the National Foundation for Educational Research.

In addition short refresher courses are offered by the Ministry of Education, both nationally and regionally, without any charge for tuition. The Ministry is here following a practice initiated many years ago by the Board of Education. Today there is a greater demand than ever for such courses, a demand which may be attributed not only to the changing character of the school but also to a heightened professional consciousness. The first of these two reasons is amplified in the following statement in *Education in 1953*: "The teacher can no longer hope or expect to prepare himself by learning specifically at college all he will need to know for the education of the children he will teach. The emphasis is therefore on the teacher as an educated person with interests, ideals, and ideas, who has had the chance of reaching at least in one field of study the highest standard of which he is capable and of acquiring in others some experience of the ways in which children learn and grow. Firsthand knowledge of actual children has become the prerequisite for textbook study, and though the students may not acquire a coherent and systematic knowledge of psychology and logic, most of them have, at least, developed the habit of observing children carefully, and of basing their teaching on what they observe to be the real needs of children both as individuals and as members of a community" (p. 84).

Much of the advance in the status of teachers is due to the activity of the major teachers' association, the National Union of Teachers (N.U.T.), whose members teach in primary and secondary schools. Although denominated a "union," the organization does not operate as a union and has resisted proposals to become affiliated with trade unions. It not only seeks to advance the welfare of teachers but is also one of the most active promoters of the advancement of education in general. With the other leading organizations, representing secondary education — the Headmasters

Conference, the Assistant Masters Association, and the Assistant
Mistresses Association — the N.U.T. is always consulted by the
Ministry of Education when important issues are being considered.

## FRANCE

### The Tradition

The suppression of the normal schools by the Vichy Government provided the opportunity after the Liberation to reorganize
the system of preparing teachers for practically all forms of education. The reactionary Vichy Government suppressed the normal
schools, which had been established in 1879, through legislation
introduced by Jules Ferry and Ferdinand Buisson on the grounds
that they were the bulwarks of radicalism and laicity. The reorganization of the preparation of teachers for elementary schools, which
was undertaken in 1945, was based on the principle that the standards which had prevailed with slight modifications in 1905 and
1920, should be raised and that the future elementary school
teacher, besides being well prepared professionally, should be a
well-educated person.

The weakness of the old system was that the intending teacher
remained within the sphere of elementary education throughout the
whole period of his education. He passed from the elementary to
the higher elementary school and thence, if successful in the competitive entrance examination, into the normal school; there he was
under the influence of instructors who, though able and the products of experience and advanced training, were of the same social
origin and had had the same educational career. The resulting
*esprit primaire,* or elementary school mind, was a derogatory term
for the products of this system. Paul Lapie, a distinguished educator, sought in 1920 to raise the level, but in general the revision of
the curriculum was effected without a change in the system.

For a long time the leaders of the elementary school teachers
had demanded a radical change which would rest on a completed
secondary education leading to professional preparation for teaching in the same way as it served as a basis for other liberal professions. It was not only a desire to raise the level of elementary
school teaching and the elementary schools that prompted this

movement, but the fact that the elementary school teacher was frequently the only person in a community who had had more than an elementary education and could become a force for raising the cultural standards of a locality. Of 38,000 municipal organizations or *communes*, 23,643 had less than 500 inhabitants, and 7,818 from 500 to 1,000 inhabitants. The rural population, living in *communes* of less than 2,000 inhabitants, constituted 46.8 per cent of the country's population.[5]

The elementary school teacher in such communities is expected to serve as secretary to the mayor. He is responsible for local records, and the transmission of information on new legislation and regulations of the government. He is expected to promote adult education or post-elementary education and to look after the library located in the school. He promotes an interest in cultural activities of various kinds in general, and sports and other recreational interests among the youth in particular. He may be called upon to serve as secretary-treasurer of an agricultural mutual association or a farmer's cooperative. All these activities, which the teacher may be called upon to perform, require a person with social insight and understanding as well as broad educational background.

The preparation of teachers for secondary schools, while of high academic standard, included little or no professional courses. This neglect was frequently the object of criticism, but nothing was done to remove it. It was based on the traditional application of that summation attributed to Sir John Adams that the whole philosophy of education is contained in the phrase that the function of education is "to teach John X." Elementary school teachers were expected to know all about John in order to educate him. The secondary school teacher, if he has a good mastery of X, the subject matter, need not worry about John. The general overhaul of French education since 1945 has included the reorganization of the preparation of all teachers.

## Proposal for Reform

The Langevin Commission recommended a reform of the system of preparing teachers along the following lines: (1) compulsory

[5] *La Rôle Sociale de l'Instituteur* in *L'Ecole Publique et ses Maîtres* (Paris, n.d.), pp. 63 ff.

education to eighteen; (2) pre-university education; (3) university education; (4) professional preparation. The traditional distinction between elementary and secondary school teachers should be abolished, the only distinction should be between teachers of common subjects (pupils aged six to eleven in general and eleven to fifteen in part) and teachers of special subjects (pupils eleven to fifteen in part and fifteen to eighteen generally). All intending teachers must obtain the *baccalauréat*. The pre-university course should be taken in the normal schools with observation and practice in the attached schools and preparation for academic specialization in the universities. The two years in the normal schools would provide an opportunity for guidance. Here the distinction could be made between those who are wholly interested in children and their psychology and in educational problems, and those whose bent is more in the direction of literacy and scientific studies. Following this period would come university education for two years leading to a *licence,* a degree entitling the holders to an appointment in schools according to their bent, aptitude, and studies. After one year as probationers (*stagiaires*) and a practical examination teachers would obtain their permanent appointment as *titulaires.* The road would still remain open for those who wish to study in the universities and higher normal schools for an *agrégation* entitling successful candidates to teach in the higher classes of a secondary school or in pre-university cycle. The reform proposed in which one old distinction (teaching John and teaching X) seems to survive, has been adopted in part.

### The Present System

In 1945 the normal schools were re-opened despite the fact that owing to the war most of the buildings were in poor condition, and their equipment and libraries destroyed or looted by the invader. In the reorganization the traditional administrative character of the system was retained. Each department is required to provide two normal schools, one for men and one for women. The provision and maintenance of the buildings and of their boarding facilities are the responsibility of the departments. All the normal schools are boarding institutions (*internats*), but provision is made for partial boarders and for day students. The Ministry of National Education pays the salaries of the faculty, and prescribes the courses of study and time-schedules in general terms, and supervises the conduct of examinations. The governing body of each normal school, which includes besides the *Recteur* of the academy and the inspector in charge of education in the department, two elected members of the departmental council, and four members, including the principal of the normal school, appointed by the *Recteur*, is responsible only for the administration of the *externa* of the school, but has no voice in the *interna* (faculty, curricula, time-schedules, etc.).

The faculty consists of a principal (*directeur* or *directrice*), a bursar (*économe*), and professors. The principal and professors must hold a certificate of aptitude to teach in normal schools or colleges (*certificat d'aptitude au professorat des écoles normales ou des collèges*) or a *licence d'enseignement;* the principal must be at least thirty-five years of age, and hold a certificate of aptitude for a primary inspectorship or principalship of normal schools (*certificat d'aptitude à l'inspection primaire et à la direction des écoles normales*) in addition, and two years of experience as a deputy principal. The size of normal schools varies; some have as few as thirty students, others from sixty to ninety. Specialist teachers of modern languages, music and art may teach in several schools in the same locality. Since the standards of normal schools have been raised since 1946, professors with qualifications to teach in secondary schools will be eligible for appointment in normal schools; those qualifications include the *agrégation* in addition to the *licence d'enseignement* already mentioned.

### Admission Requirements

Admission to normal schools is by a competitive examination (*concours*) and not by a qualifying examination (*examen*). Each year the *Recteur* and the departmental council determine the number of teachers that will be needed in the department four years from that time to fill vacancies created by death or retirement, or, at present, by the expected phenomenal increase in the primary school enrollments. The numbers so calculated are submitted to the Ministry who decides on the number to be allotted by sex to each normal school in the department and filled by the candidates successful in the *concours*. The prospective cost on the national budget must also be taken into consideration, since the Ministry of Education carries the burden of the grants to students for tuition, board, and lodging for three years and the salaries of students in their fourth year.

Three classes of students are admitted to the normal schools each year as follows: (1) the majority, consisting of candidates who have not completed a course of secondary education and who will take the four-year course in the normal schools; (2) students who have obtained the *baccalauréat*, that is, have successfully completed their secondary education and will take two years of professional studies in the normal school; and (3) substitute teachers or replacements who replace regular teachers who are ill or on leave and who have the minimum requirement to work on a temporary basis; for these a one-year course of professional preparation was authorized. For permission to take the competitive examination for admission as regular students candidates must be French; must be between the ages of fifteen and seventeen; must hold the certificate showing the successful completion of four years of secondary education (*brevet d'études du premier cycle de l'enseignement du second degré* (B.E.P.C.); must present a medical certificate after examination by a board of three physicians, one of whom must be a specialist in pulmonary diseases; and must submit a notarized pledge to serve as a teacher for ten years (*engagement décennal*) or reimburse the Government for its expenditure. In addition enquiries are made about the candidate's character and record. About one candidate in three is admitted each year, the total being 4,000, divided almost equally between men and women.

The competitive examination, which is in two parts, written and oral or practical, consists of: (1) a dictation, which serves as a test in spelling and writing, and as the basis for questions on vocabulary, expression, and grammar; (2) comments on a French text; (3) mathematics (problems in geometry and arithmetic or algebra; (4) modern languages (translation into French). The oral or practical examination, to which those successful in the written tests are admitted, includes: (1) reading of a French text and questions on its meaning; (2) questions on mathematics; (3) written report on a literary or scientific subject presented to the students from history or geography or physical and natural science; (4) freehand drawing; (5) music (exercises in sol-fa and singing); (6) handicraft for boys or needlework for girls; and (7) physical education. A mark of zero, confirmed by the board of examiners, is eliminatory. The names of candidates are submitted in order of merit to the *Recteur* together with a list of alternates.

Normal school students are educated at the cost of the Government and receive (1) free tuition, board, lodging and laundry, and (2) a sum for clothing and equipment for dormitory and sports needs, and books. The cost of (1) is included in the amounts paid by the Ministry to each normal school, and of (2) is paid to the students' families. These costs are met for each student for the first three years; in the fourth year, which is an innovation, the students are regarded as probationary teachers (*stagiaires*) and receive salaries out of which they pay for tuition, board, lodging, standard supplies, and a contribution to the general expenses of the normal school; the students are given 4,000 francs each for pocket money; a balance is retained by the bursar as a provident fund, which is given to the students when they leave to help them as they start their careers.

### The Course

The student's day is regulated (five hours a day for personal hygiene, meals, recreation, games, domestic duties, and physical exercise; five hours for personal work, reading, homework, and practice teaching; eight hours a day for sleep, and four hours a day for class work, not including singing, drawing, handicraft, and physical training). Nevertheless, the practice of encouraging greater independence and initiative, begun by Paul Lapie in 1920, has been extended. The only prohibition is that they must not join or form political or denominational associations or receive propaganda publications. They may, however, join professional and trade union organizations and receive the publications of such organizations.

The most important changes that have taken place in the postwar reorganization of the normal school by the *Arreté* of August 28, 1946, were the extension of the course to four years and the devotion of the three (ultimately two) years of the course to general education leading to the *baccalauréat*. The B.E.P.C. *(brevet d'études du premier cycle),* which is required as a condition of candidacy, is obtained after four years of secondary education, generally in the *cours complémentaires* (see pp. 227 f.). Students, therefore, enter the *classe de seconde*[6] and spend the next two years in preparing for the first part of the *baccalauréat* and, if successful, a third year in preparation for the second part. Since most of the students are expected to teach in elementary schools they normally follow the modern-scientific course of secondary education (see pp. 289 f.) for the first two years and the experimental-scientific course for the last year. The program departs somewhat from that prescribed for secondary schools in that drawing, music, handicraft and horticulture, and in the second and third years practical exercises and psychology in the attached school are included as compulsory instead of optional subjects. The experimental-science section is preferred for future elementary school teachers, but students who show ability may specialize in preparation for the philosophy-humanities section or the mathematics section, and, if successful, take the competitive examination for entrance into the higher normal schools of St. Cloud (men) and Fontenay-aux-Roses (women).

The first two years of general education include the following subjects: French, one modern language, history, geography, mathematics, physics, natural sciences, physical training, and the additional subjects mentioned in the preceding paragraph. The third year for students who have passed the first part of the examination for the *baccalauréat* and are preparing to take the second part in experimental sciences follows the same curriculum with the addition of philosophy and humanities, but without French.

The fourth year is devoted to professional courses, theoretical and practical. The courses in theory include child and educational psychology, sociology, principles of education, principles of elementary education, history of education and educational theories, professional ethics and school law, and review of elementary school sub-

[6] Classes in secondary schools start with *sixième,* so that the completion of four years of secondary education means completion of *troisième.*

jects. In addition a course is offered in preparation for extracurricular and post-school activities which introduces the students to an understanding of such activities in a community as mutual and friendly societies and cooperatives, youth hostels, cultural centers, workers' education, and holiday camps. Within the normal schools students are encouraged to organize their own associations — cooperatives, athletic associations, glee clubs, and so on. The course also includes instruction in the use of audio-visual aids, and organization of dramatics, orchestras and choirs, dancing, libraries, and adult education in general including lectures on the psychology of peasants and workers.

The work of the normal schools is closely associated with schools attached to them *(écoles annexes)* for observation and demonstration purposes and for experimentation. Classes in other schools selected by the academy inspector and taught by specially selected teachers are also used for the purpose of demonstration. The students are required to do practice teaching for a month in each term, or twelve weeks in all. The teachers and principals of the classes and schools in which they do the practice teaching are required to grade the students.

### Certification

At the end of the course a final examination is conducted by a board of examiners consisting of the academy inspector, principal and professors of the normal school, one or more primary school inspectors, and elementary school teachers including two principals. The written examination consists of two essays on principles of education and of elementary education; the oral examination is on professional ethics, school laws, or history of education, on child psychology; and on personal activities in the four years as students. The certificate obtained by successfully passing the examination *(certificat de fin d'études normales)* entitles the students to appointments as probationary teachers *(stagiaires)* in schools in the department in which the normal school is located. The probationary period lasts three months, at the end of which there is a practical examination conducted by a primary school inspector, a school principal, and an experienced teacher. The examination consists of instruction of a class for three hours in elementary school subjects including physical training and singing, followed by questions on school management. Successful candidates receive the *certificat d'aptitude pédagogique* which entitles them to appointment as permanent teachers *(titulaires)*.

## Other Students

The second class of students, those who already possess the *baccalauréat,* must meet the same conditions as the first class except that of age. They must be between seventeen and twenty years of age to take the two-year professional course or between eighteen and twenty-one to take a one-year professional course in a normal school. The competitive examination is almost identical with that for the first group. Between 200 and 300 students of this class are admitted to the normal schools each year.

The third class of students consists of substitute teachers *(suppléants* or *interimaires)* who are recommended for admission without examination by a committee made up of the academy inspector, primary and nursery school inspectors, the principals of the two departmental normal schools, and classroom teachers. The recommendation must be approved by the *Recteur* of the academy. Candidates must be under twenty-five years of age, must have at least two years of experience as teachers, and must hold the *baccalauréat.* Substitute or temporary teachers who had completed their secondary education were appointed without training at a time of teacher shortage and taught under the guidance of the principal of the school to which they were assigned. They are admitted to the third year of the course and take the professional studies for a year; in the second year they are employed under the direction of maternal and primary school inspectors as replacements and follow courses given by the normal school faculty.

Once appointed the teacher is assured of tenure and opportunities for advancement. The social status of teachers in the rural areas has already been indicated. Since the war the status has been generally improved by increasing the scale of salaries, the value of which cannot be understood abroad because of differences in the cost of living. The salaries do not, however, represent the total remuneration of the elementary school teachers, since they are entitled to a residence or rent indemnity, which varies in amount according to the zones in which they live, and maternity and family allowances according to the number of children. Allowances are paid for additional duties or service in a demonstration school. On retirement teachers receive a retiring allowance to which they contribute 6 per cent of their annual salaries; they may retire at the age of fifty-five after twenty-five years of service; the age limit may be lowered for mothers of children and for veterans. Retirement is compulsory at the age of sixty. The allowances range from 60 to 75 per cent of final salary.

### Higher Normal Schools

Primary school inspectors and principals of normal schools receive their preparation in the higher normal schools at St. Cloud (men) and Fontenay-aux-Roses (women), established for this purpose in the same period as the normal schools. These schools were transformed into institutions for the preparation of teachers for *collèges,* but in 1944 the original purpose was restored for the preparation of teachers with experience admitted on a competitive examination. The main function of the two institutions is at present to prepare teachers for secondary schools.

### In-service Training

The in-service training of teachers is provided by educational conferences arranged in each *canton* by the primary inspector. The topic of the conference is selected by the Minister several months in advance of the meeting at which it is discussed; teachers may themselves suggest topics to be discussed at subsequent conferences. Young teachers may be advised by their inspector to visit and observe more experienced teachers or they may attend demonstration lessons in groups. There are also courses offered by organizations founded to promote new methods, and opportunities for further study and research are provided by the *Centre National de Documentation Pédagogique,* an information center in Paris on a variety of educational topics, the postwar *Centres Pédagogiques*

*Régionaux,* the *Bureau Universitaire de Statistique et de Documentation Scolaire et Professionnelle* (Paris) with branches, and a rich variety of professional organizations and publications both official and private.

## Preparation for Secondary School Teachers

Candidates for appointment in secondary schools may prepare in a variety of ways — in universities or in higher normal schools. Teachers in *lycées* are selected by way of the *agrégation,* a competitive examination of the highest standard in the special subjects that the candidates wish to teach. The preparation for the *agrégation* is by way of the *licence d'enseignement* obtained after three years of study beyond the secondary school, and the *diplôme d'études supérieures,* also a university degree granted on presentation of a thesis. The *licence d'enseignement* differs from the ordinary *licence* of the university in that specific combinations of subjects taught in the secondary schools must be studied. The high standards of selection and the strenuousness of the competition are illustrated by the following statistics for the 1953 competition: *Men,* humanities 1,081 applications, 885 sat for the examination, and 100 were "admitted"; in modern languages the corresponding figures were 433, 346, and 66; in sciences and mathematics 321, 280, and 86. *Women:* in humanities 773, 628, 54; in modern languages 364, 299, and 43; in sciences and mathematics 198, 169, and 60. The figures for "admitted" are not indication of quality but rather of the actual number of vacancies to be filled. The status of *agrégé* is highly sought after because of the small number of teaching hours to be given (fourteen to sixteen hours a week), leaving ample time for research, which may lead to appointments in the universities.

The more normal route to the *agrégation* is through the higher normal schools *(l'Ecole Normale Supérieure de la Rue d'Ulm* for men, and *l'Ecole Normale Supérieure des Jeunes Filles* for women, generally known as *l'Ecole de Sèvres* although no longer located in Sèvres. The history of *l'Ecole Normale Supérieure* is woven into the cultural history of France. Both schools are entered through a difficult competitive examination for which preparation is given in post-*baccalauréat* classes in the larger *lycées.* The students receive grants for all expenses for the three-year course. Since 1903 the higher normal schools have been part of the Sorbonne and students may take courses in both institutions. Since the end of the war two new higher normal schools have been added; they are the institutions already mentioned at St. Cloud and Fontenay-aux-Roses.

A recent development has been the introduction of a new certificate of aptitude for the professorship in a secondary school (*certificat d'aptitude au professorat de l'enseignement public du second degré*, or C.A.P.E.S.) which is also a competitive examination for candidates who hold the *licence d'enseignement* or of the *diplôme d'études supérieures*. The examination is in two parts, written and oral, on the special subjects that the candidates wish to teach. Successful candidates are then assigned to a regional education center (*Centre Pédagogique Regional*) for a year, during which they receive a salary for professional and practical training, unless they are students in one of the higher normal schools. On completing this one-year course a practical examination is held as a test of the practical teaching ability of the candidates. Only the number needed to fill prospective vacancies in secondary schools are passed for admission to the regional pedagogical centers. The numbers in 1953 were as follows: *Men*, 1580 applied and 294 were admitted, although there were 401 vacancies to be filled. *Women:* 2,704 applications and 286 admitted (number of vacancies 320).

The introduction of professional requirements for teachers in secondary schools reflects the new status of secondary education and the increasing enrollments which will bring to the schools a new type of pupil.

### U.S.S.R.

### Status of Teachers

The importance attached to education in the U.S.S.R. as an essential weapon of the revolution has already been mentioned. Accordingly considerable attention has been devoted to the preparation of teachers. Lenin declared that "We must raise our teacher to a height such as he has not attained and never will be able to attain in a bourgeois society." This status has not yet been reached, perhaps because so many teachers have been needed to meet the rapid increase in the number of schools and pupils. Lenin's injunction may some day be carried out, but for the present the teacher is a cog in a vast machine, while in "bourgeois" countries the tendency is for teaching at all levels to move toward greater professional freedom. The scale of salaries does not yet indicate a superiority of status, and the allowances in addition to salaries can be matched in other countries. The political activity of Soviet teachers simply means that they are good conformists, not that they are more politically conscious than the teachers of other countries. In the latter teachers may belong to any party and seek to represent any party in elected local or national assemblies. The fact that able teachers may be given the title of Honored Teacher by the Presidium of the Supreme Soviet of the U.S.S.R. is no greater distinction than the award of national distinctions conferred on teachers in other countries.

## The Present System

The institutions for the preparation of teachers are organized on three levels corresponding to the primary school (grades 1–4), intermediate (grades 5–7), and upper (grades 8–10). The normal schools ("teaching schools" or pedagogical schools) give a four-year course to students who have completed seven years of education and intend to teach in preschools or primary schools; pedagogical institutes prepare students to teach grades 5 to 7 in a two-year course based on a completed ten-year school. The higher pedagogical institutes give a preparation of four years to graduates of the ten-year school who plan to teach the three highest grades, 8 to 10; the last group of teachers are also recruited from students who have a five-year course, including professional studies, in a university. The first two types of institutions for the preparation of teachers are under the control of Minister of Education of each Soviet Republic; the last is under the supervision of the Minister of Higher Education of the U.S.S.R.

A basic requirement of teachers at all levels of education is the study of the science of society from the Marxist-Leninist point of view. According to Stalin: "There is one branch of science whose knowledge must be compulsory for all Bolsheviks of all branches of science — that is the Marxist-Leninist science of society, of the laws of development of society, of the laws of development of the proletarian revolutions, of the victory of communism. For it is impossible to consider him a genuine Leninist, who calls himself a Leninist, but who is cloistered, let us say, in mathematics, botany or chemistry, and who sees nothing beyond his specialty." To this the statement of the authors of *Pedagogy*, B. P. Yesipov and N. K. Goncharov, may be added: "Culture, literacy, political orientation, sound knowledge of science, technique, and loyalty to the work of socialist construction — these are the principal traits of a Soviet specialist." [7] The teacher is a specialist and his socio-political indoctrination is provided not only through courses but also through participation in cultural activities of a community and visits to representative Soviet institutions like collective farms.

The "teaching schools" prepare students for the primary schools in a four-year course which includes instruction in all the subjects of the first four grades — Russian language and literature, mathematics, sciences, history, geography, writing, drawing, singing, and physical education. The professional studies include hygiene, psychology, principles of education, history of education, methodology, and practice teaching. Manual work and practical agriculture are also included in the course, since the majority of the graduates will teach in rural schools.

The two-year course of the pedagogical institutes does not devote as much attention to academic subjects as the "teaching schools," because their students have reached a more advanced stage of secondary education. The subjects covered in the professional program are thus described by Mikhail Malyshev, secretary of the Academy of Educational Sciences: "Soviet teaching, teaching methods as a science, historical and class character of education and teaching as a science, the aims and tasks of Soviet education, peculiarities of the different ages of the growing generation, system of public education, fundamentals of Soviet didactics, the substance of education and training, the lesson in the Soviet school, methods of education, methods of controlling and appraising the knowledge of the pupils, principles of moral education, methods of moral edu-

[7] Quoted in Counts and Lodge, *I Want To Be Like Stalin*, p. 12.

cation, manual training, training of conscious discipline, aesthetic education, physical education, children's organizations in the school, extra-curricular activities, the teacher in the Soviet school, the up-bringing of the child in the family, school management." [8] Provision is made for teaching practice.

Specialist subject-matter teachers are prepared in the four-year course of the pedagogical institutes, of which there are two types, one of which provides for specialization in Russian language and literature, physics and mathematics, chemistry, history and geography, and the other for specialization in foreign languages. Irrespective of the field of specialization, all students take the course in social and economic science. The professional subjects include psychology, history of education, school hygiene, physical education, and methods of teaching the special subject. Practice teaching is carried on for twelve weeks. The five-year course in the university for prospective teachers in the highest classes of the ten-year school follows the same pattern.

Teachers in service have a variety of opportunities for further study — in institutes for the advanced training of teachers which are regional, special district courses, conferences on problems of the teacher, and correspondence courses from the pedagogical institutes. Educational literature, general and special, is issued by the Ministry of Education and the Academy of Educational Sciences, while contributions are made by the educational workers' union which not only promote the professional and material improvement of teachers but also provide opportunities for contact with and work in the activities of other labor unions. The educational workers' union is associated with the All-Union Central Council of Labor Unions.

Teachers are paid a basic salary in accordance with their preparation. The number of teaching hours are four hours per day in the primary school and three hours per day in grades 5–10, with extra pay for additional hours for marking written work, for practical work on an experimental plot, and for supervising science laboratories. Salary increases are provided every five years and pensions,

[8] In Robert King Hall, N. Hans, J. A. Lauwerys, *The Year Book of Education, 1953*, London, and Yonkers-on-the-Hudson, N.Y., 1953, p. 408. By permission of the publisher.

amounting to 40 per cent of salary, are available after twenty-five years of service. The salaries of urban teachers are higher than those of rural teachers, but flats with heat and light and plots of land are provided for the latter.

## UNITED STATES

### Current Issues

The problem of the preparation of teachers for elementary and secondary schools has been solved in the United States as far as the basic foundation in secondary education and the length of preparation thereafter are concerned. But the solution is still an ideal that has not been attained in all parts of the country. It is in fact not possible to generalize about educational conditions in the United States except about the widespread faith in education. Concern about the recruitment, preparation, and status of teachers began to be widely expressed about 1910 when elementary education was entering upon a new stage of development and the enrollments in high schools began to increase. Although a number of important investigations of the whole problem have been made, particularly in the thirties, and general agreement on desirable requirements has been reached, the greatest variety of standards for preparation and certification of teachers still prevails. The only real advance that has taken place throughout the country is that all intending teachers must have completed a course of secondary education. Beyond that future teachers in elementary schools may receive anywhere from one to four years of preparation, and high school teachers four or five years of preparation.

The problem is further complicated at the present time by a number of various causes. Since the end of World War II the schools have been under serious attacks which have served as a deterrent to young people who may have thought of taking up teaching as a career. With the attacks on the schools, teachers more than any other public employees have been singled out and required in many places to take loyalty oaths and sign statements that they were not members of subversive organizations. A greater obstacle to the recruitment for the profession is the prevailing competition for man-

power and the opportunities for employment in other careers, where
remuneration is higher. While salaries have been raised almost
everywhere and the average salary is a good deal higher than it has
ever been, they have not risen as fast as the cost of living.

The situation is further complicated by the increasing enrollments in schools since the end of the war. The combination of increased enrollments and opportunities for employment in other
occupations has resulted in a serious shortage of teachers. A further
consequence of this shortage has been the employment of teachers
on emergency certificates granted on sub-standard preparation of
a few weeks. The most serious aspect of this situation is that the
dilution of the standards which have been proposed may seriously
affect the quality of education generally and the status of the profession in particular.

This is especially serious as one looks forward to the development of education in the next decade. In 1949–50 there were 28,-
628,547 boys and girls enrolled in elementary and secondary schools.
There has been an increase of 58 per cent in the number of live
births in the country in 1951 as compared with the number in 1940.
In ten years it is expected that the enrollments in the schools will
be ten million pupils more than in 1949–50. These statistics pose a
grave problem for those responsible for planning the organization
of education ahead of time. More school buildings and classrooms
are already needed, and there has been a shortage of teachers for
at least ten years.

The problem has to be solved locally so far as finances are concerned and by state authorities for education so far as standards of
preparation and certification of teachers are involved. The Federal
Government assists only in areas that have been affected by the
influx of workers to newly created defense plants, and that assistance may not be continued much longer. The employment of
teachers is wholly a local matter, and there are about 80,000 local
education authorities varying in size from those which may employ
one teacher to a large city, like New York, which employs over
36,000 teachers. The standards for preparation and certification of
teachers are defined and controlled by state departments of education under laws which define the minimum standards, leaving local
areas to fix their own standards above the minimum. It is for this

reason that it is not possible to present more than a superficial general picture of the system of teacher preparation and certification. There are no standards universally accepted throughout the country, nor do all the forty-eight states accept each other's certificates unless reciprocity agreements have been adopted.

Although the Federal Government takes no active part in the recruitment, preparation, and certification of teachers, the informational publications on the subject are of considerable assistance. In 1935 the U.S. Office of Education published the *National Survey of Education of Teachers* which was the result of an investigation conducted for three years. In 1946 the American Council on Education published a volume on *The Improvement of Teacher Education* by its Commission on Teacher Education. One of the strongest influences for the raising of standards has been the National Commission on Teacher Education and Professional Standards of the National Education Association (N.E.A.), which has published *The Education of Teachers as Viewed by the Profession* (1948) and *The Teaching Profession Grows in Service* (1949). The Commission on Standards of the American Association of Colleges for Teacher Education (A.A.C.T.E.) publishes annual reports on the progress of the theory and practice of teacher preparation. This Association was the result of the merger of an older organization, the American Association of Teachers Colleges, also a department of the N.E.A. and two other professional associations to define the standards for accrediting institutions for the preparation of teachers.

### Institutions for the Preparation of Teachers

Institutions for the preparation of teachers fall into two groups according to the nature of their control, public or private. The institutions under public control numbered 432 in 1952 and were provided by states (315), counties or townships (27), municipalities (61), and school districts (29). The 661 private institutions were either secular (169) or denominational (472). The total of 1,093 institutions fall into another classification according as they are normal schools, teachers colleges, liberal arts colleges with education departments, or schools or colleges of education in universities. The normal schools usually offer two-year courses to prepare teachers for elementary schools; the other institutions offer four-year courses or a fifth year where demanded by certification require-ments for the preparation of teachers for both elementary and sec-ondary schools. The only feature that they all have in common is that students must have graduated from a high school in order to be admitted, and not infrequently the grade that they must have on graduation is specified.

There are no national requirements or standards for certification. Nor is there any consensus on the curriculum appropriate for stu-dents in preparation. In 1939 the American Council on Education appointed a National Committee on Teachers Examinations to assist the administrative officials of local education authorities in one phase of the process of selecting teachers. This phase was de-fined as "that of providing comparable examinations of intelligence, general cultural background, awareness of current social problems, professional educational information, and mastery of academic sub-jects that the candidate aspires to teach." The examination was not intended to interfere with the right of local education authorities to establish whatever standards they desired in selecting teachers for their area, nor was it expected to become compulsory except as local authorities might decide. The fundamental purpose of the examina-tion was to establish a national currency in the matter of teacher qualifications.

National standards valid throughout the country have not yet been accepted, but it is recognized as a desirable goal that four years of preparation be required for elementary school teachers and five years for high school teachers. Until these standards are accepted the greatest diversity prevails and requirements range from one to four years of preparation for the elementary school teachers' cer-tificate, and from two to five years of preparation for the high school teachers' certificate — either general, permitting the holder to teach any subject, or special, defining the subjects that the holder might teach.

## Academic or Professional Subjects?

Not only is there diversity in the length of preparation, but for many decades a controversy has existed on the nature of that prep-aration, which arises on where to put the emphasis on the phrase mentioned earlier, "To teach John X." The controversy was inherited from the character of the old two-year normal schools, which before the high school became generally accessible, devoted themselves to reviews of the subjects of the elementary school curriculum and the methods and practice of teaching them. The whole emphasis was on imparting skills in teaching rather than turning out men and women with a broad education and intelligences trained to apply principles rather than to rely on routine methods of teaching a prescribed course of study with the help of a textbook.

The problem which is faced today is to find a proper balance between academic and professional education. The remarkable increase and proliferation of courses in professional subjects in the last three decades has complicated the problem because sufficient attention has not been given to drawing a line of demarcation between the number of professional courses to be given in the early preparation of teachers and the courses suitable for in-service training and research. The result, it is often charged, is that there is at times a considerable amount of repetition in the courses offered for professional preparation.

On the other hand, it is stated by critics that teachers should be broadly educated persons and thoroughly conversant with the subjects that they teach, and that the time spent on professional studies encroaches too much on the time that should be devoted to general cultural education.

The reply to these criticisms is that they may have been true at a time when the length of preparation was only two years and the students had not had an opportunity to receive a secondary education. With the gradual extension of the period of preparation to three and four years for elementary school teachers and to four or five years for secondary school teachers, the time devoted to professional studies and practice teaching is only about one-eighth or one-sixth of the total course. Further, the time to be given to professional courses is in the main prescribed by the state authorities in the requirements for certification.

## Normal Schools to Teachers Colleges

The normal schools assumed the title of teachers colleges for at least two reasons. The first was to secure better recognition of the importance of the preparation of teachers by placing the institutions on the same level as liberal arts colleges. Secondly, they were then in a position to extend the period of preparation and to offer degrees to those who completed a four-year course. They were thus able to undertake the preparation of teachers for secondary as well as for elementary schools, their primary purpose. The extension of the period of preparation made it possible to provide, more than heretofore, a general liberal education and at the same time to compete with the liberal arts colleges. After the war, when under the G.I. Bill of Rights veterans were given opportunities to continue their education, the teachers colleges sought to attract the veterans by offering a greater variety of courses to meet the needs of the large number who did not intend to enter the teaching profession.

## Administration of Institutions for Preparation of Teachers

The control of public normal schools and teachers colleges is in the hands of state boards of laymen. The practice varies from state to state; in some there is a board for each institution; in others one board for all teacher-preparation institutions; and in others again one board for all forms of higher education institutions, including teachers colleges. The board of control is concerned primarily with general problems of education and personnel. The internal affairs of an institution are in the hands of the president and his staff who are concerned primarily with curricular matters and with the students. The amount of faculty participation depends upon the president and is not prescribed in any regulations.

The faculty consists of deans of men or deans of women, subject-matter specialists, teachers of professional subjects, a director of training or teaching practices and critic teachers or teachers in the "campus" practice or laboratory school who look after students during their periods of practice training. The teachers of subject-matter and of professional subjects are usually expected to have a Ph.D. or Ed.D. degree. Increasingly the former are expected to give instruction on methods of teaching the subjects that they profess and to supervise students in the practice schools.

Students are admitted on graduation from high schools. They pay for board and lodging but not for tuition. An increasing number of teacher-preparation institutions are providing dormitories for their students. No pledge to teach for a number of years after completing the course of preparation is exacted from the students. The practice of self-support during the course is as common in teachers colleges as in other American educational institutions.

## Curriculum

The curriculum in teacher-preparation institutions has been strongly influenced by the changing aims of elementary and secondary education, by the movement against excessive specialization by the provision of "general education," and by the increasing knowledge of the growth and development of children and adolescents, of the meaning of interest, and of the learning process. Through professional organizations as well as a result of the public recognition of the importance of education the status of the teacher is changing from one of dependence on routine skills, prescribed courses of study, and textbooks to one of utilization and application of principles. To this the improved relations between administrative officials and teachers has contributed, so that teachers are increasingly called upon to participate in curriculum-making and in determining educational policy. The status of teaching is changing from that of a trade to that of a profession.

The character of the change of emphasis which has taken place in the preparation of teachers is indicated by the importance attached to their general education in a report of the American Association of Colleges for Teacher Education: "A broad education program to equip the student with a wide range of competencies is needed for him both as a person and as a professional worker. Many aspects of such general education are also part of the teacher's professional equipment. Students must be helped to see the interrelatedness between this general education and professional education." [9]

A new importance is also attached to the place of the teacher as a force in his or her community. While teachers are not expected

[9] American Association of Colleges for Teacher Education, *School and Laboratory Experiences in Teacher Education* (Washington, D.C., 1948), p. 61. By permission of the Secretary of the Association.

to take an active part in politics, local or national, they are expected to be politically and socially alert on the problems of the day. Increasingly the profession supports the theory that one of the functions of the school is to teach controversial subjects in order to train pupils to recognize and discuss controversial problems [10] when they meet them in after-school days. In contrast with the nineteenth-century function of the teacher may be cited the following statement of the teacher's task: "The task of today's teacher in the classroom with children is more complex than ever in the past. Work in the classroom is only part of the responsibility of a good teacher. He participates in many school activities, he shares in the formulation of administrative policies, he contributes to improvement of the curriculum, and he is an active member of his community. He is also a wholesome, well-adjusted personality. The extension of professional laboratory experiences from the typical student teaching period to varied direct experience during the entire pre-service programme, calls for additional use of facilities and their extension. The laboratory or practice school nevertheless remains a very important facility in the teacher education programme. But no single school can meet all the needs of a group of students. Not only are many schools needed but other types of facilities should be available, e.g., various community service agencies, camps, playgrounds, libraries, co-operatives." [11]

The curriculum of the four-year teachers college accordingly consists of general education, specialization in one or more allied subjects, professional studies, and practice teaching. The time on the average seems to be divided as follows — three-eighths for general education, half for specialization, and one-eighth for professional studies and practice teaching. The students who attend a liberal arts college and who are in the main to become secondary school teachers follow the usual requirements for a degree and may include enough professional studies to satisfy certification requirements or take their professional studies and special methods of teaching their subjects in a postgraduate course.

"General education" is not too clearly defined; in some cases it

[10] This, as the recent attacks on public schools have shown, is not yet accepted by the public.

[11] *The Education of Teachers in England, France and U.S.A.* (Paris, UNESCO, and New York, Columbia University Press, 1953), p. 285. Quoted by permission of UNESCO.

consists of orientation courses in humanities, social studies, and sciences; in others it may consist of a collection of introductory courses in the separate subjects that make up these groupings. The Committee on Teacher Education of the American Council of Education, after stressing its importance for both the cultural and the professional education of the teacher, thus defined general education: "The aim of general education should be to enable young men and women to meet effectively the most important and widespread problems of personal and social existence; in the case of prospective teachers such education should seek to further the development of knowledge, skills, attitudes and interests that are fundamentally related to the needs and responsibilities shared with contemporaries destined for other vocations." [12]

The trend is in the direction of balance and integration of subjects, especially those subjects that are integrated in the school — social studies, general science, and so on. The general education program may be followed in the first two years or distributed over the four years of the course.

The professional studies, which may be started in the early years of the course, are generally taught in the last two years. They include the history and principles (or philosophy) of education, educational psychology, classroom (or school) management, general and special methods of teaching, and practice teaching. Under each of the basic courses there may be separate subdivisions, like history of education in the particular state where the college is located, principles of elementary or secondary education, or child psychology and psychology of the adolescent, and tests and measurements. In some cases a general course, "social foundations," may be given, including history and principles, and educational sociology. Practice teaching, which includes observation and participation as well as actual classroom practice, is done in the "campus" or laboratory school and in public schools of the locality. From observation and participation the student advances to practice increasingly on his own responsibility but under supervision and guidance of appropriate members of the faculty and of the critic teachers.

On completing the course successfully and meeting the state re-

[12] In *The Improvement of Teacher Education* (Washington, D.C., 1946), p. 86.

quirements students are certified by the state. Generally the certificate entitles teachers to appointment anywhere within the state which granted it. But in the larger cities additional requirements may be imposed or selective examinations conducted, as, for example, in New York City and Chicago.

### In-service Training

It is no longer considered that the institutions for the preparation of teachers can, even in the longer period of four years, turn out a finished teacher any more than medical or law schools expect to turn out full-fledged practitioners. Many of the larger areas require a period of probation before a teacher receives a permanent appointment. This is satisfactory if the probationer is helped and guided, something that does not always happen. But for all teachers an extensive system of courses is either provided or required as a condition of salary increases. Such courses may be taken after school hours or in summer and lead to further qualifications, or they may be offered by the employing authorities in the form of institutes, conferences, discussion groups, workshops, and the like.

### Appointment and Status

Although in most discussions and writings about the teacher the masculine gender is used, the fact is that some 80 per cent of the teachers are women, and of the men the majority teach in high schools or hold administrative positions. The prohibitions against the employment of married women in the education service have disappeared not only because of the shortage of teachers but also because of the trend toward equal status for men and women. Appointments are made for one year at a time in the rural and smaller areas, but increasingly teachers have been guaranteed tenure rights after a few years (usually three) of service.

The economic situation of teachers is slowly improving, but in the years after the two world wars the cost of living rose more rapidly than salaries. Between 1939 and 1952 it is estimated that prices rose 90 per cent but average salaries only 27 per cent. Average salaries are, however, an unsatisfactory measure, since they include salaries in such wealthy states as New York and California and salaries of administrative officers, on the one hand, and salaries paid by the poorer states of the South on the other. The teacher shortage and the difficulty in the past ten years of recruiting an adequate supply of candidates are better indications that teaching from the financial point of view is at present not regarded as an attractive career. The security offered under tenure laws and the provision of pension allowances in many states are not enough to attract the more ambitious young men and women who wish to take chances in the open market.

Nevertheless, when the status of teachers forty years ago is compared with that at the present time there has undoubtedly been a great improvement, due not to better economic conditions, but to changes in administration which give teachers a greater chance to contribute from their experience and insight, and to the advances in their preparation toward a recognized professional status. Nor can the part played by the professional organizations, local and national, be omitted from a list of factors that have contributed, materially and professionally, to that advancement. The National Education Association, whose history goes back to 1857, with its twenty-nine departments touches every branch of education and has a greater influence on the progress of education than many national government ministries of education in other countries. The American teacher is on the way to achieving a status commensurate with the great task which the American public has set for itself — to provide educational opportunities for all the children of all the people as an essential basis of democracy.

## REFERENCES

**General**

Hall, Robert King, N. Hans, and J. A. Lauwerys, eds. *The Year Book of Education, 1953: Status and Position of Teachers.* London, Evans Brothers, and Yonkers, N.Y., World Book Co., 1953.

Kandel, I. L., *Comparative Education.* Boston, Houghton Mifflin Co., 1933.

Richardson, C. A., Helene Brule, and Harold E. Snyder. *The Education of Teachers in England, France, and U.S.A.* Paris, UNESCO, 1953.

### England

Board of Education, Committee to Consider the Supply, Recruitment, and Training of Teachers and Youth Leaders, *Teachers and Youth Leaders* (McNair Report). London, H.M.S.O., 1944.

———— *Report of the Departmental Committee on the Training of Teachers in Elementary Schools.* London, H.M.S.O., 1925.

———— *Report of the Committee on Universities and Training Colleges.* London, H.M.S.O., 1928.

Ministry of Education, *Challenge and Response: An Account of the Emergency Scheme for the Training of Teachers.* London, H.M.S.O., 1950.

———— *Education 1900–1950.* London, H.M.S.O., 1951.

National Union of Teachers, Committee of Investigation. *The Training of Teachers and Grants for Intending Teachers.* London, University Press, 1939.

Rich, R. W. *The Teacher in a Planned Society.* London, University of London Press, 1950.

Training College Association and Council of Principals, Joint Standing Committee, *The Training of Teachers.* London, 1939.

### France

*Avenirs,* 60–61. *Fevrier-Mars,* 1954. *Les Carrières de l'Enseignement.* Paris.

Cavalier, Marie-Louise, *L'Ecole Publique et ses Maîtres.* Paris, 1953.

Centre National de Documentation Pédagogique. *L'Organisation de l'Enseignement en France.* (Paris, 1951.)

Debiesse, Jean. *Compulsory Education in France.* Paris, UNESCO, *l'Enseignement en France.* Paris, 1951.

Glatigny, M. *Histoire de l'Enseignement en France.* Paris, 1949.

Soleil, J. *Le Livre des Instituteurs.* Paris, 1948.

### U.S.S.R.

King, Beatrice. *Russia Goes to School.* London, Heinemann Ltd., 1948.

Medinsky, J. N. *Public Education in the U.S.S.R.* Moscow, 1951.

Moos, Elizabeth. *The Educational System of the Soviet Union.* New York, National Council for American-Soviet Friendship, 1950.

### United States

American Council on Education. Commission on Teacher Education. *The Improvement of Teacher Education.* Washington, D.C., 1946.

Elshree, W. S. *The American Teacher.* New York, American Book Co., 1939.

National Education Association. National Commission on Teacher Education and Professional Standards. The Education of Teachers. Washington, D.C., 1949.

United States Office of Education. *National Survey of the Education of Teachers.* Six vols. Washington, D.C., 1933–35.

# 10

# Problems and Outlook

The four educational systems discussed in this book illustrate most of the problems that are being encountered by most industrialized countries or countries on the way to becoming industrialized. The problems of education in underdeveloped countries in which there is an awakening nationalism and a realization that considerations of food, clothing, shelter and health are paramount fall into an entirely different category. They have not been dealt with in this book, but their solution constitutes an important part of the work of UNESCO, which under the rubric of "Fundamental Education" has made valuable contributions already and given much-needed guidance. In the light of the discussion in Chapter 3 of "Forces that Determine the Character of Educational Systems," it is clear that an urgent aspect of the problem in these areas is how to relate education to the existing cultures and avoid the effects of a sudden impact upon it of another civilization.

The countries with whose educational systems the present volume has been concerned represent, of course, the contrast between the concept of democracy that prevails in three of them — England, France, and the United States — and the meaning of Communist totalitarianism in the U.S.S.R., which is offered to the world as a genuine form of democracy. With this contrast in mind the countries of the world can be ranged on one side or the other of the Iron Curtain. Those that are already or are striving to become democracies, as the western world understands the term, are occupied with the same problems of educational reform or reconstruction as those that have been illustrated in the systems of England, France, and the United States; those that have been brought under the aegis of Communist ideology are gradually being compelled to adopt the practice and theory of education already developed in the U.S.S.R. In the one case the character of the state is determined by the intelligent decision of the individuals who are its citizens; in the other the state molds the individuals who are its subjects in accordance with its ideology. In the one case education is for enlightenment; in the other education and propaganda are indistinguishable. This becomes especially obvious as one examines the trends in secondary education. In the countries behind the Iron Curtain the nature of secondary education is determined by the needs of the particular five-year or other plan adopted by the state and is becoming increasingly technical and vocational with an emphasis on mathematics and natural sciences. In democracies the aim of secondary education is to produce citizens and workers with broad interests as human beings.

Now, while it is axiomatic that the character of every educational system is determined by the ethos or culture pattern of the nation that it is designed to serve, an examination of the accounts of the educational reforms planned or already under way in the three democracies — England, France, and the United States — discussed in this volume will show that many of the problems which have been dealt with are common to them all. This does not mean that the solutions can be the same or that a universal theory of education can be formulated to cover all cases. The idea is, indeed, not new. In 1888 the German philosopher, Wilhelm Dilthey, discussed the question whether a universally valid educational science is possible.[1] He denied such a possibility and maintained that "The educational ideal of a period and of a people in the richness and reality of its content is historically conditioned and formed." In 1902 Emile Durkheim, in an inaugural address at the Sorbonne on

[1] Wilhelm Dilthey, *Über die Möglichkeit einer allgemeingültigen pädagogischen Wissenschaft.* See also Ch. 1 of the present volume.

*Pédagogie et Sociologie,*[2] stated that there cannot be a universal aim in education since it is always adapted to the culture pattern of a community. Sir Michael Sadler's emphasis on the idea that an educational system is rooted in a nation's culture has already been cited.

An analysis of the descriptions of the educational systems of the countries of Western Europe,[3] of New Zealand, Australia, and Japan cannot fail to impress the student with the similarity of the problems with which they are coping in education and the obstacles to their solution. The problems are the same as those which have already been discussed in the preceding chapters. An analysis of these problems points to the possibility not of concerted action or solutions to fit all situations but to an exchange of ideas through international conferences devoted to the discussions of particular issues. Such conferences UNESCO has already promoted along some lines; there are many others that still remain to be arranged.

Although many of the problems that are now being considered have been in the making for some time, particularly since World War I, there is one which is likely to create administrative, organizational, and financial difficulties for some time to come. This problem could not have been anticipated. The general trend before World War II was in the direction of a falling birth rate. Following World War II there has been a phenomenal increase in the birth rate in all countries, which would under normal circumstances have created serious difficulties for education authorities — local and national. But the times have not been normal since the outbreak of World War II. School buildings were destroyed, materials were in short supply for new constructions and repair of school buildings, and there has everywhere been a shortage of teachers. Consequently, where the reconstruction of the educational system has already been legislated, progress is piecemeal, while in other countries long-range plans for reform (Norway and Sweden, for example) are being implemented by easy stages or being postponed until the situation becomes more stable than it is at present.

---

[2] Reprinted in *Education et Sociologie* in 1922.

[3] Erich Hylla and W. C. Wrinkle, eds., *Die Schulen in Westeuropa* (Bad Nauheim, 1953). The countries included are Norway, Sweden, Italy, England, Belgium, German Federal Republic, Holland, Switzerland, France, and Denmark.

In a country like Germany, of course, the day for reform must wait until the country is again independent, in whole or in part, and is free to determine the shape of the educational systems in each *Land* without the restraint, direct or indirect, of external circumstances. The same may also be true of Japan, where the postwar reconstruction of the whole system of education has taken place in a pattern designed by the leading occupying power. The transition from the prewar to the postwar educational system of Japan has on the whole been too rapid and adjustments may some time have to be made.

The outlook for education on the democratic side of the Iron Curtain presents at least three outstanding aspects. The first of these is a movement to raise the school-leaving age. For this there are a number of reasons, not the least important of which is the recognition that the nineteenth-century elementary education for the large majority of citizens is no longer adequate. The political and economic situation is too complex to be understood with that type of limited education, however thorough it may have been. The challenge of ideologies alien to democracy must be met in the best way possible and, outside of economic improvement, that way is through education. The changing economic situation — from an agricultural to an industrial economy — also demands a longer and richer education. For the present the sights are set for advancing the age of compulsory school attendance to fifteen full-time and eighteen part-time. Where these aims have already been achieved, the possibility of a further extension to sixteen for full-time schooling is contemplated.

Difficult as it is to extend the period of compulsory education following a more generous provision of preschool opportunities, the difficulty is material — the provision of classrooms and an adequate supply of teachers — and is simple in comparison with changing the traditions of about a century and a half, and replacing elementary with primary education to be followed by some form of education. It is recognized in most countries that primary education should be continued to ages eleven or twelve, so that all boys and girls will have an opportunity for pursuing a form of postprimary education at least for three or four years.

Here, however, another and perhaps a more serious set of difficulties presents itself — first, to determine the various types of postprimary education to provide to meet differences in ability and interests, and second, to convince the public that equality of opportunity means differentiation according to individual capacity. A third is to determine the age for differentiation and to discover acceptable methods for the allocation of pupils. The term "postprimary" is here used deliberately because, as already pointed out, the term "secondary education" has inherited a definite connotation and a curriculum associated with it which is no longer suited to the majority of boys and girls who will now have the opportunity to continue their education beyond the primary stage. Variety and flexibility are needed in postprimary education, which, according to reforms proposed, is to include the traditional academic courses leading to the universities, new types of general courses, and courses in vocational education at different levels (technical, commercial, trade, agricultural, and household arts).

Two obstacles in the way of an appropriate organization of postprimary education that are frequently cited are the second and third of the difficulties mentioned. Through the ages secondary education of a particular type — the academic — has been available to the children of the privileged classes or to children of sufficient ability to win free tuition and scholarships in secondary schools in a competitive examination. In either case it came to be regarded not only as the privilege of a minority, but also as a method of selecting the élite for the more important and more remunerative careers — public and private — in society. Accordingly the academic secondary education gained a prestige that cannot be shaken, even among those members of the public who had never enjoyed it. At the same time the oldest of the academic courses, the classical, is gradually losing its place of superiority in favor of the mathematical-scientific course or to some degree to the modern language course which also includes Latin. At the same time the notion has been built up that a liberal education is impossible without the study of foreign languages, ancient or modern. Both traditions — the prestige status of secondary education and the concept of a liberal education — stand in the way of developing new types of postprimary schools and courses on a large scale.

The lack of confidence in objective methods of allocating pupils — intelligence and other tests — to the type of course best suited to them has given rise to objections in many countries to differentiation at the age of eleven or twelve. It is claimed that this is too early an age to discover the abilities and aptitudes of pupils and to determine their future development and careers. Accordingly proposals have been made to extend the period when pupils are taught in the same school, to introduce specialization slowly, and then to allow pupils to transfer to special courses. In other words, the idea of the comprehensive school is proposed up to a point corresponding to the completion of the American junior high school, and a special self-contained course thereafter. Such a system, it is argued, not only keeps pupils together for a longer period and postpones differentiation, but provides an opportunity for the more mature development of interests and abilities under the guidance of teachers or sometimes of special counselors. A considerable amount of experimentation can be foreseen in the rest of the century, both on the types of courses to be provided to ensure variety and flexibility, and on methods of allocating pupils, whether at the end of primary education or later.

Another important movement which is as marked everywhere as it was shown to be in England, France, and the United States, is the trend to a new method both of curriculum-making and of instruction. The two main criticisms of inherited practices are: (1) that the curriculum was sterile and inert in the sense that the content had little meaning for the pupil and was unrelated to the life and times in which he lived, and (2) that the method of instruction, combined with the influence of and importance attached to examinations, encouraged memorization rather than intelligent and active participation by the pupils. Another criticism which is only another aspect of those mentioned is that too much emphasis has been placed on intellectual training and too little on character formation and training of the emotions.

These criticisms, which are the stock in trade of the new or Progressive educators, have this much foundation — that in many schools the pupils memorize without understanding the meaning of what they learn and that much is included in the curriculum content that has little or no value either for intellectual training or for present living. But the remedy is not to allow the pendulum to swing too far in the opposite direction. The problem is a teaching

problem and no solution can be suggested in universal terms. It is
for the well-educated and well-prepared teacher to determine,
within the limits of suggestions or guides, what in a particular environment is meaningful and what methods to use. There is no
guarantee that pupils' interests furnish a safe guide to follow or
that activity methods are always likely to be superior to any others.
Undoubtedly a serious problem presents itself both at the primary
stage and at the postprimary level when an effort is to be made to
continue the education of large numbers for whom elementary
education had in the past been thought to be enough.

Educational statesmanship cannot disregard traditions. It is generally expected by the older generation that the younger generation will receive somewhat the same kind of education that it had.
Even in the United States where the people are habituated to
change, the innovations preceding World War II came under suspicion in the postwar years. Undoubtedly teachers are apt, like
other professionals, to fall into routine ways and to perpetuate practices without any other justification than that they have used them
for a long time. Thus, in addition to the public's resistance to both
the reorganization of school systems and to innovations in the classroom, the opposition of teachers to new curricula and methods
must be taken into account. The professional resistance of teachers
is likely to continue as long as the profession remains segregated
into groups who teach pupils at different levels — preschool, primary, and postprimary (academic and vocational). The teachers
themselves have in the past come from different social origins and
have had different types and amounts of general and professional
preparation. The issue, therefore, resolves itself into one of the
unification of the teaching profession in terms of general education,
professional preparation, and basic remuneration. In the light of
the tradition of the teaching career at different levels, the idea of
unification may seem utopian, but it is no more fantastic than unification of other professions. But it has taken a long time for the
acceptance of the idea of organizing educational systems on the principle of providing equality of opportunity. It should take less time
for the idea to be generally accepted that equality of opportunity
also implies instruction by men and women who have had the same
basic preparation and who specialize in teaching at different levels

because of their own interest. The idea of requiring the same basic preparation from all members of a profession and specialization according to interest and ability beyond that is already exemplified in many liberal professions. The difference, however, deplorable as it may seem, is that the teaching profession can never expect to enjoy the same financial rewards as are available to members of other professions. Nevertheless, a new stage is being reached by the teaching profession and some day it may enjoy a status commensurate with the high esteem in which the public and politicians in most countries profess to hold education.

# Index

Ability, determination of, 250

Academic tradition, and equality of opportunity, 251

Accrediting, of American high schools, 316, 317

Achievement tests, in American elementary schools, 241

Activity, increased importance in elementary education, 202–204

Administration, of education, 115–195; determinants of, 119, 120; purpose and function, 120–122; England, 129–153; France, 153–165; U.S.S.R., 165–174; United States, 174–195; teachers and, 325

Administrators, danger of power, 128

Adolescent, education of, 246–318; major questions, 253, 254; England, 255–278; France, 278–294; U.S.S.R., 294–301; United States, 301–318

Agricultural economy, and elementary education, 96

Aided schools, England, 142

Appointment, of American teachers, 366, 367

Area Training Organizations, preparation of teachers in England, 333–335

Aristotle, on education, 21; on authority, 33

Art, under Communism, 30, 31

Articulation, of American secondary and primary schools, 303, 304

Association, freedom of, 26

Australia, educational reform in, 69, 79

Authority, rejection of, 4; freedom and, 32–34

Autonomy, of education, 38

Average, secondary school catering to, 113

Baccalauréat, standards of, 73; current status, 289

Bagley, William C., essentialism, 238, 239

Baldwin, Stanley, on British government, 31; on elementary education, 202

Balfour, Sir Graham, on educational opportunity, 92; *Educational Administration*, 121

Bauer, Raymond A., *The New Man in Soviet Psychology*, 36

Beard, Charles, on social heritage, 205

Bérard, Léon, compulsory classics, 279

Bernal, J. D., on national character, 6, 7; *The Social Function of Science*, 7

Beveridge, Sir William, on freedoms, 43, 44

Birth rate, rise in relation to education, 372

Boarding schools, at public expense in England, 149

Boards of education, characteristics and functions, 190, 191

Bode, Boyd H., *Progressive Education at the Crossroads*, 238

Bouglé, M., on general culture, 154

Brown, Edward J., *The Proletarian Episode in Russian Literature, 1928–1932*, 30

Brunold, Charles, *Les Buts de L'Enseignement du Second Degré*, 282; on *les classes nouvelles*, 285

Brunschvicg, Léon, on educational organization, 202

379

Bureaucratic control, resistance to, 65; disappearance of, United States, 191

Burnham Committee, England, teacher salaries, 340

Burns, C. Delisle, on liberty and order, 33; *Political Ideals*, 33

Business, compared with education, 118

Butler, R. A., on direct grant schools, 269

Butler, Samuel, on extremes, 27

Canada, educational policy in, 80

Capitant, René, reforms in French education, 73

Central Advisory Councils (England), 138

Central authority, in France, 158, 159

Centralization, of administration, 117–119; merits of, 124, 125; in France, 153; through Communist Party in U.S.S.R., 171, 172

*Certificat d'Etudes Primaires*, 226

Certificate. *See* General certificate

Certification of teachers, England, 339; France, 349, 350; United States, 359, 365, 366

Chief education officer, in England, 149, 150

Chief state school officer, functions of, 188

Child, education of, 198–243; England, 207–217; France, 217–228; U.S.S.R., 228–233; United States, 233–243

Child, emancipation of, 50, 51

Children's Bureau, functions of, 182, 183

Cities, and school administration, in United States, 190

Clarke, Fred, on critical understanding of democracy, 35; *Education and Social Change*, 35

Class, size, 101

Class distinction, and educational reform, 48, 49; and concept of primary education, 102

*Classes Nouvelles*, aim and nature of, 283–285

Clothing, English schools, 145

Coeducation, in U.S.S.R., 294, 295

Cold war, effect on education, 3; and totalitarian methods, 20

College admission, in United States, 316, 317

College Entrance Examination Board, 186

Commissioner of Education, United States, 182

*Commission pour la Réforme de L'Enseignement*, 74

Common school, in France, 68, 69; (*l'école unique*), in France, 279, 280; in U.S.S.R., 294–299; in United States, 301

Communication, as an aim of education, 22

Communist Party, position in Russian state, 29–31; dominance of, 168; and primary education, 231

Community centered school, 239, 240

*Compagnons de l'Université Nouvelle*, 280

Comparative education, content and method of, 3–17; primary concerns of, 45; scope and meaning of, 6–8

Compensation, to parents, 94

Complexes, popularity of, 19

Comprehensive schools, secondary, 54; in America, 82; arguments for, 111; England, 261–264; secondary, in United States, 304–306

Compulsory education, prolongation of, 55, 56; in England, 68, 151; in France, 68, 69, 163, 164; in U.S.S.R., 173

Conant, James B., *Education in a Divided World*, 113

Conditioning, education as, 36–38

Conformity, to serve nationalism, 61, 62

*Conseil Départemental*, France, 160

Consent, authority by, 26

Constitution, in a democracy, 27

Consultative Committee, of British Board of Education, 67, 68; *The Education of the Adolescent*, 134, 255

Controlled schools, England, 142

Controversy, educative value of, 127

Core curriculum, in United States, 313, 314

Cost. *See* Finance

Council of Principals of Training Colleges (England), on reform, 330

Counts, George S., and Lodge, Nucia, *The Country of the Blind*, 30; *I Want to Be Like Stalin*, 166, 231

County, as administrative unit, 190

County colleges, England, 144

County schools, England, 142

*Cours Complémentaires*, 227

Cubberley, Elwood P., *Public Education in the United States*, 177
Culture, in Communist Russia, 30, 31
Culture changes, and teacher preparation, 322, 323
*Culture générale*, concern for, 278, 279
Culture pattern, education influenced by, 45; of free societies, 47; as criterion of nationalism, 61
Current problems, teacher preparation in United States, 357–359
Curriculum, changes in elementary, 204; of American elementary schools, 240, 241; French secondary schools, 288–290; in U.S.S.R., 296–299; in United States secondary schools, 310–312; of teachers colleges, England, 337–339; in American teacher training institutions, 363–366

Decentralization, effect on educational system, 45
Delbos, Yvon, projected educational organization, 286
Democracy, and war, 4; study of, 14; totalitarian use of terminology of, 25; as a way of life, 27; concept of freedom in, 31, 32
Democratic state, 25–27; freedom of association in, 26
Denominational schools, 58–60
Denominational schools (England). *See* Voluntary schools
Department of State, *The Kremlin Speaks*, 295
d'Erceville, Rolland, on educational opportunity, 89
Description, comparative education as, 9
Development, English provisions for, 143
Deviation, in the totalitarian state, 24
Dewey, John, on authority and freedom, 33; on the use of learning, 237; *Democracy and Education*, 238; *Experience and Education*, 238
Dilthey, Wilhelm, on universally valid education, 12, 371
Direct grant schools, England, 268, 269
Discipline, in elementary education, 204, 205; under compulsory education, 254, 255; in U.S.S.R., 297, 298
District school, obsolescence of, 189, 190

Diversity, of administration, 122–124
Draft Covenants on Human Rights, provisions on education, 86
Dual system, traditional education under, 53; in England, 129, 130
Durkheim, Emile, *Education et Sociologie*, 12, 372

*Ecoles maternelles*, building, staff, function of, 218–221
*Ecole unique*, 68, 69, 280
Ede, Chuter, on prescribed teaching, 132, 133
Education, purposes of, 22; for understanding democracy, 34–36; as sociopolitical process, 38–40
Education Act, 1918, England, 67, 133
Education Act of 1944, England, 59; central and local administration, 135–142; articulated system, 207; education of adolescent, 259, 260
Educational Councils, France, 159
Educational finance, in England, 146–148
Educational Policies Commission, of N.E.A., on educating for democracy, 36; *Education and the Defense of American Democracy*, 36; *Education of the Gifted*, 305, 310; *Education for All American Youth*, 305, 306
Educational reconstruction, 259; and democratic ideals, 53–55; new pattern of, 65–87; problems of, 84, 85
Educational system, and the state, 18–44; forces that influence, 45–63
Educational Testing Service, 186
Educational theory, changes in France, 280–283
Elementary education, tradition and development of, 201–203; modern problems of, 198–207; in England, 207–217; France, 217–228; U.S.S.R., 228–233; United States, 233–243
Elementary school, France, 221–226; aim and curriculum, 222–226; criticism of traditional, 223; modernization, 223, 224; course of study, 224, 225
Elementary school, United States, 235–243; variation in, 236; modern theory, 237–241; criticism of, 241–243
Elementary schools, establishment of higher, 248

Elementary school teachers, France, responsibilities, 342, 343

Employment, and education, 106

England, educational reform in, 67, 68; reform of primary and secondary school in, 68; administration and organization of education, 129–153; theory of administration, 131–134; inter-war years, 134; Education Act, 1944, 135–138; local administration, 138–142; voluntary schools and religious instruction, 142–144; auxiliary services, 144–146; finance, 146–148; private schools, 148, 149; education of the child, 207–217; nursery schools, 208–210; infant schools, 210–213; education of the adolescent, 255–278; secondary education for all, 255–257; equality of opportunity, 257–259; education act of 1944, 259, 260; comprehensive or three types of secondary schools, 260–264; selection methods, 264, 265; types of schools, 265–271; general certificate of education, 271, 272; scholarships, 272; technical schools, 273–275; modern schools, 275–277; school life, 277, 278; preparation of teachers in, 330–342; teachers union, 341

Essentialists, criticism of progressive education, 238, 239

Equality of educational opportunity, concept of, 44; problems of, 88–114; historical development, 89–92; implications, 92–94; primary education, 94–102; and individual difference, 107; the academic tradition, 251; post-war England, 257–259; in American secondary education, 301

*Ethics*, Aristotle's educational theory in, 21

Examinations, international problems of, 7

Experiment, national educational systems as, 8

Extracurricular activities, in United States, 317, 318

Family, change in character of, 50

Family Allowance Act, England, 151

Federal aid, fear of, 184

Federal government, and American education, 181–185; United States, teacher preparation, 359

Fees, for education in U.S.S.R., 169, 295

Finance, educational, 126–129; of education in U.S.S.R., 172; of education in United States, 189

Fish, Carl Russell, *The Rise of the Common Man*, 175

Fisher Act. *See* Education Act, 1918

Fisher, Norman, *Our Schools*, 277

Fitch, Sir Joshua, on experiment in American education 181

Fleming Committee, *The Public Schools and the General Educational System*, 270

Florinsky, Michael T., *Towards an Understanding of the U.S.S.R.*, 29, 168

Fontainerie, F. de la, *French Liberalism and Education in the Eighteenth Century*, 89

Fontenay-aux-Roses, higher normal school, 351

France, educational reform in, 42; educational reconstruction in, 68, 69; Langevin reforms, 74, 75; administration and organization of education in, 153–165; tradition of administration, 153–158; regional administration, 159–162; educational finance, 162; the educational career, 162–164; private schools, 164; education of the child in, 217–228; reconstruction of school system, 217, 218; *écoles maternelles*, 218–221; elementary education, 221–226; *certificat d'études primaires*, 226, 227; *cours complémentaires*, 227, 228; education of the adolescent, 278–294; tradition, 278, 279; *l'école unique*, 279, 280; changes in educational theory, 280–283; *classes nouvelles*, 283–285; secondary education, plans for reform, 285, 286; organization at the second level, 286, 287; preparation of teachers, 342–353; tradition, 342; present system, 344, 345; admission to normal schools, 345–347; training courses, 347–349; certification, 349; in-service training, 351; preparation for secondary school teachers, 352, 353

Frederick the Great, on control of education, 21, 23

Freedom, restriction of, 18; democratic interpretation of, 31, 32; under English administration, 131–134

Frontier, influence on American education, 174, 175

Fundamental Law, of U.S.S.R., 167

General Certificate of Education, England, 271, 272

General education, nature of, 364, 365

Germany, indoctrination in, 6; national education in, 11; educational reform in, 42; independence and educational reform, 373

G.I. Bill of Rights, and education, 195

Gide, André, on enslavement, 19; on Russian conformity, 29; *Return from the U.S.S.R.*, 29

Gifted pupils, neglect of, 249; education of, 309, 310

Goebbels, Paul Joseph, on conformity, 28

Grammar school, England, curriculum, aims and organization, 267, 268

Grammar schools, England, 256. *See also* Secondary education

*Grandes Ecoles*, 290

Gréard, Octave, on elementary education, 154; aim of elementary education, 222

Growth, education for, 22

Guidance, and secondary education, 105; organization of, in France, 292–294

Hadow, Sir Henry, and adolescent education, 67, 68

Handbook of Suggestions, nursery school, 210; infant school, 211; junior school, 214; new pedagogy, 215

Hansen, A. O., *Liberalism and American Education*, 89

Headmasters Conference, England, 269

Health, in English schools, 144, 145; and the new pedagogy, 206, 207

Hegel, G. W. F., on the state, 24

Herriot, Edouard, on need of an élite, 112

Higher Council of National Education, France, 159

High schools, aims in United States, 306

Hocking, W. E., on the two purposes of education, 22

Hollinshead, A. de B., *Elmtown's Youth*, 306

Home, changes in, 50; effect on educational system, 57

Homework, in secondary schools, 70

Hungary, Communist control of culture in, 31

Ideas, the war of, 13, 14

Illiteracy, in United States, 183, 184

Individual, relation to the state of, 20–22

Individualism, and modern thought, 4; in postwar period, 18, 19

Indoctrination, through education, 6; and education, 13; in democracy, 35, 36; in Soviet primary schools, 232

Industrialization, and primary education, 96

Infant schools (England), 210–213

Inkeles, Alex, *Public Opinion in Soviet Russia*, 172

In-service training, of teachers, 327, 328; England, 340–342; France, 351, 352; United States, 366

Inspection, modern, 126; of English schools, 148, 149; in France, 158

Instruction, size of classes, 101

Intangible forces, in education, 8–12

Intelligence tests, objection to, 264, 265

*International Conference on Public Instruction*, recommendations of, 85, 86

Internationalism, and nationalism, 62

Japan, postwar education in, 11; thought control in, 29; occupation and education, 313

Jefferson, Thomas, on enlightened popular government, 66

Juhasz, William, *Blueprint for a Red Generation*, 31

Junior high school, establishment in United States, 303, 304

Junior schools, in England, 213–217

Justice, in educational opportunity, 83

Kalamazoo Case, legality of free secondary education, 177

Kandel, I. L., 67, 222, 247, 307

Kearney, N. C., *Elementary School Objectives*, 237

Kellogg Foundation, 191

Kergomard, Pauline, modernization of *Ecoles maternelles*, 219

Key, Ellen, *The Century of the Child*, 198

Kindergartens, United States, 234, 235

Komsomols, in U.S.S.R., 173

Kotschnig, W. M., on national character of universities, 7, 8

Labor reserves, in U.S.S.R., 299

Lamont, Corliss, *Soviet Civilization*, 30

Langevin Commission, recommended organization of secondary education, 74 f., 155, 286, 287

Language, as criterion of nationalism, 60

Larsen, Roy, National Citizens Committee, 192

Laski, Harold on differing cultures, 47

Laugier, Henri, on class-consciousness, 48

*Laws*, Plato's educational theory in, 21

Leadership, in American education, 180, 181

Leisure, education for, 55

Liberal education, 108–110; essence of, 251

Liberalism, and modern thought, 4

Life adjustment, education for, 312, 313

Lindsay, Kenneth, *Social Progress and Educational Waste*, 91

Literacy, and political ends, 6; as aim of education, 98

Livingstone, Sir Richard, *The Future of Education*, 99

Local administration, in England, 138–141; in United States, 189–192

Local authority, in English education, 131–134; nature of, in France, 160, 161

Lowndes, G. A. N., *The Silent Social Revolution*, 67

Lunt, P., and Warner, *The Social Life of a Modern Community*, 306

*Lycée*, present situation in, 287–291

Lynd, Robert S. and Helen M., *Middletown*, 91

Malyshev, Mikhail, curriculum for prospective teachers in U.S.S.R., 355, 356

Marie, André, *L'Enseignement du Second Degré*, 281; projected organization of education, 287

Marx, Karl, on the state, 24

Massiglio of Padua, on popular government, 26, 27

Mass media, effect on individualism, 19

Materialism, increase of, 19

Maud, Sir John, on power of administrators, 128

McMillan, Rachel and Margaret, nursery school, 208

McNair Report (England), *Teachers and Youth Leaders*, 325, 332; supply and recruitment of teachers, 332, 333; area training organizations, national advisory bodies, grants, General Certificate, 333–337

Meals, in English schools, 145

Medinsky, Y. N., *Public Education in the U.S.S.R.*, 168, 230, 296

Mill, John Stuart, on the individual, 28; on fear of state control, 66, 67; *On Liberty*, 126

Milton, John, on freedom of religious discussion, 37

Ministry of Education (England), functions, 135–138

Ministry of National Education, France, 158, 159

Modern schools, England, 256; secondary, 275. *See also* Secondary education

Montesquieu, on freedom of opinion, 26

Moos, Elizabeth, *The Educational System of the Soviet Union*, 170

Morrill Act, 182

Napoleon, on control of education, 21

Nation, meaning of, 60–62

National advisory bodies, England, teacher preparation, 335

National character, and the sciences, 6, 7; and professional educators, 7, 8; observed by Bertrand Russell, 8; Sadler's views on, 9, 10

National Citizens Committee, 192

National economy, and education, 95–97

National Education Association, Educational Policies Commission, 36; *Moral and Spiritual Values in Public Schools*, 59; *Education for All American Youth*, 308; and status of American teacher, 367

National School Lunch Act, 183

National system, lack in England, 130, 131

National Union of Teachers (England), 341, 342; report on teacher-training, 331

National welfare, education an instrument of, 14, 15

Nationalism, education an instrument of, 15; resulting from war, 18; and education, 60–63

New Zealand, educational reform in, 69; aims of education in, 79

Normal schools (France), suppression in Vichy France, 342; present French system, 344, 345; admission requirements, 345–347; in U.S.S.R., 354–357; in United States, 359, 360, 361, 362

Nursery schools, growth of, 51, 101; emergence of, 199–201; in England, 208–210, in U.S.S.R., 229, 230; in United States, 233, 234

Office of Education, United States, 182; *Vitalizing Secondary Education*, 312

Opportunity, equal educational, 15. *See also* Equality of educational opportunity

Order, basic to democracy, 32–34

Organization, of education, 115–195; England, 129–153; France, 153–165; U.S.S.R., 165–174; United States, 174–195

Outlook, for education, 370–377

Owen, Robert, infant school, 211

Parochial schools, aid for, 193

Part III authorities, in England, 139, 140

Patriotism, intensification of, 18

Pensions, England, teachers, 340

Percy, Lord Eustace, on teaching patriotism, 131, 132

Philosophy of education, comparative education and, 11 ff.

Physical Training and Recreation Act, 1937, England, 145

Plato, on education, 21; on liberty and coercion, 33

Playgrounds, in England, 145

Police power, increase of, 20

*Politics*, Aristotle's educational theory in, 21

Politics, education related to, 39

Pol-Simon, P. H., *L'Evolution Pédagogique Actuel*, 284

Population, shift of, 56, 57

Postprimary schools. *See* Secondary schools

Practice teaching, England, 338; in United States, 365

*Pravda*, and thought control, 29

Preparation of teachers, England, 330–342; France, 342–353; U.S.S.R., 353–357; United States, 357–377. *See also* Teachers

Preschool education, development of, 199 ff.

Pressure groups, educative influence, 66

Price, Richard, on self-government, 66

Primary education, traditional purpose of, 98; change in concept of, 99, 100

Primary school, residual functions of, 52; in England, curriculum, 216

Private schools, England, 148 f.; France, 164; United States, 192, 193.

Privilege, and concept of secondary schools, 103

Problems, of modern education, 370–377

Profession, teaching as a, 323–325

Professional freedom, 125, 126

Professional training of teachers, balance with academic, 360, 361

Prolongation, of school attendance, 15

Propaganda, in Russian schools, 296. *See also* Indoctrination

Public, participation in American education, 178–180

Public schools, in England, 130, 269–271

Publications, English educational reform, 71

Race, as criterion for nationalism, 60

Ramsbotham, H., on decentralization, 132

Rationalism, decline of, 19

Reading, decline of, 56

Reconstruction, in postwar education, 5, 6; obstacles in England, 153. *See also* Administration, England, France, Organization, and Reform

Recruiting, of teachers, 325, 326

*Recteur*, of French academy, 159

Reform, educational, 41–44; under democracy and dictatorship, 42, 43; plans in France, 285, 286; (England), teacher training, 330, 332.

Regents examinations, 186

Regional administration, France, 159–162

Religion, decline of, 58, 59

Religious instruction, in England and United States, 59; in public schools, 193, 194

*Republic, The,* educational theory in, 21

Responsibility, in democracy, 28

Roosevelt, Franklin D., on republican government, 32; on education, 176

Rural education, changes in, 57

Russell, Bertrand, on national character, 8

Russia, and literacy, 6; concept of state in, 29–31; educational experiment in, 42. *See also* U.S.S.R.

Sadler, M. E., basis of educational system, 9; *How Far Can We Learn Anything of Practical Value from the Study of Foreign Systems of Education?,* 10; on outside influences on schools, 56

Salaries, England, teachers', 340

Santayana, George, on democracy, 27

Scholarships, needed under compulsory education, 55; in England, 272, 273; in United States, 302

School Health Service, in France, 161

Schools, secondary, types of, 102–104

Schools, types of English, 72

Science, effect on society of, 4

Secondary education, equalizing opportunities of, 102–114

Secondary education, types of schools, 102, 103; certificates and privilege, 103; comprehensive schools, 104; allocation of pupils, 104; guidance, 105; curriculum, 106, 107; and employment, 106; traditional concept of, 247–255; social prestige, 248; in England, 255–278. *See also* Adolescent, England, France, United States, U.S.S.R.

Secondary schools, traditional view of, 54; dissatisfaction with, 70, 71; three types, 81; England, teacher training for, 339. *See also* Adolescent, England, France, United States, U.S.S.R.

Secondary school teachers, England, 339; France, preparation, 352, 353; U.S.S.R., 356; United States, 357 ff. *See also* Preparation of teachers

Selection methods, English secondary schools, 264, 265

Shortage of teachers, in United States, 357–359

Sixth form, nature of, 267, 268

Smith, W. Lester, *To Whom Do Schools Belong?,* 121

Smith-Hughes Act, 182

Smith-Lever Act, 183

Smuts, Jan Christiaan, on government and freedom, 34; *Africa and Some World Problems,* 34

Social background, and education, 93

Social prestige, and secondary education, 248

Social services, and the school, 100

Social status, and educational opportunity, 48, 49

Social unity, and education, 107, 108

Society, school and, 63

Soviet. *See* Russia and U.S.S.R.

Special Agreement Schools, England, 142

Special places, in English secondary schools, 258

Spens Report, on secondary education, 68, 256, 257

Standards, maintenance of, 185, 186

State, increased functions of, 18; and education, 18–44; relation of individual to, 20–22; necessity for understanding, 22; and values, 40–41

State boards of education, functions and organization, 187, 188

States (United States), and education, 186–189

Status, of American teachers, 366, 367

St. Cloud, higher normal school, 351

Superintendent, of state education, 188; under county administration, 190; city administration, 191

Taft, Robert A., legislation for federal aid for education, 185

Taxes, on land and buildings, 192

Taxpayer, concern with education, 127

Teachers, preparation of, 322–367; Germany, 323; England and United States, 324; organization of, 326–330; in-service training, 327–328; secondary, 328, 329; reform in England, 330–332; Area Training Organizations, 333–335; secondary school, England, 339;

France, 342–353; U.S.S.R., 353–357; United States, 357–377

Teachers, shortage of, 16, 185, 357–359; concept of, 98; primary importance of, 128; changing status of, 329, 330; England, salaries and pensions, 340; status in U.S.S.R., 353, 354

Teachers colleges, England, 335–337; curriculum, 337–339; United States, 361–366

Technical schools, in England, 273–275; French secondary, 291

Technikums, in U.S.S.R., 299, 300

Technology, and compulsory education, 55; and changes in education, 56, 57

Tests and measurements, relation to philosophy, 12

Theory, criticism of French educational, 280–283

Theory. *See* Educational theory

Thurber, C. H., on comparative education, 11, 12; *The Principles of School Organization*, 12

Thurston, Lee M., on local control, 76

Totalitarianism, and democratic ideals, 4, 5; emergence of, 20; culture pattern of conformity, 46

Totalitarian state, idealistic nature of, 23; criticism in, 24; compared with democracy, 25

Tradition, of elementary education, 98; importance in France, 278, 279

Training, of teachers. *See* Preparation and Teachers

UNESCO, purpose of, 62, 63; educational policy of, 87; and fundamental education, 98; *The Education of Teachers in England, France and U.S.A.*, 364

Uniformity, under democratic administration, 119

Unions, of teachers, England, 341

United States, administration and organization of education, 174–195; the American tradition, 174, 175; education a public concern, 175, 176; founding the system of public education, 176–178; participation of the public, 178–180; leadership in American education, 170, 181; federal government, 181–185; maintenance of standards,

185, 186; the states and education, 186–189; local administration, 189–192; religious instruction, 193, 194; the educational career, 194, 195; organization of elementary education, 233; nursery schools and kindergartens, 233–235; elementary school, 235–243; education of the adolescent, 301–318; increase of secondary education, 301–303; articulation with primary schools, 303, 304; the comprehensive high school, 304–307; aims of high schools, 307–309; education of the gifted, 309, 310; curriculum of secondary schools, 310–312; life adjustment, 312, 313; core curriculum, 313, 314; secondary curriculum in practice, 314–317; extracurricular activities, 317, 318; preparation of teachers, 357–367; training institutions, 359, 360; curriculum in teacher training schools, 363–366; in-service training, 366; appointment and status of teachers, 366, 367

University Council, France, 160

University Grants Committee, England, 336

University of Bristol, *Studies in Selection Techniques for Admission to Grammar Schools*, 265

Urban education, changes in, 57

Urbanization, and growth of nursery schools, 201

U.S.S.R., administration and organization of education, 165–174; background, 165–170; fees, 169; administration, 170–172; the educational career, 172–174; education of the child in, 228–233; nurseries and kindergartens, 229, 230; primary education, 230–232; education of the adolescent, 294–301; the unified school, 294–299; vocational education, 299–301; preparation of teachers, 353–357. *See also* Russia

Vernon, P. A., *Intelligence Testing*, 265

Vocational education, in U.S.S.R., 299–301

Vocational training, purpose of, 254

Voluntary schools, England, 142

War, and educational reconstruction in England, 134. *See also* Reconstruction

Warner, W. L., Havighurst and Loeb, *Who Shall Be Educated?*, 306

Warner, W. L., Mocker, and Wells, *Social Class in America*, 306

Washington, George, on public opinion, 66

Watts, A. F., Pidgeon and Yates, *The Allocation of Primary School Leavers to Courses of Secondary Education*, 265

Welfare, state provision for, 19

Wilderspin, Samuel, infant school, 211

Workers Education Association, in England, 152

World War II, reform plans during, 71; effect on education, 216; effect on American high school attendance, 303 *See also* Reconstruction

Yesipov, B. P., and Goncharov, N. K., *Pedagogy*, 172

Young Pioneers, in U.S.S.R., 173

Youth leaders (England), training of, 146

Youth Service, in England, 145, 146

Zay, Jean, on guidance, 92